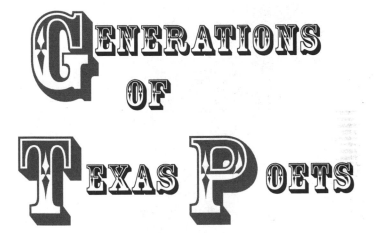

GENERATIONS OF TEXAS POETS

Selected Works by Dave Oliphant:

Poetry

Brands
Taking Stock
Lines & Mounds
Austin
Maria's Poems
Memories of Texas Towns & Cities
Backtracking
KD: a Jazz Biography
The Cowtown Circle

Memoir

Harbingers of Books to Come: A Texan's Literary Life

Criticism & History

On a High Horse: Views Mostly of Latin American & Texan Poetry
Texan Jazz
The Early Swing Era, 1930 to 1941
Jazz Mavericks of the Lone Star State

Edited

Contemporary Chilean Poetry
The New Breed: An Anthology of Texas Poets
Washing the Cow's Skull / Lavando la calavera de vaca
Roundup: An Anthology of Texas Poets

Translated

Figures of Speech, by Enrique Lihn
Love Hound, by Oliver Welden
After-Dinner Declarations, by Nicanor Parra

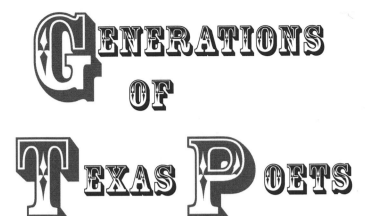

Generations of Texas Poets

Dave Oliphant

WingsPress

San Antonio, Texas
2015

Generations of Texas Poets
© 2015 by Dave Oliphant

Cover art, "Pencil Cactus" by Larry McEntire, used by permission of artist.

First Wings Press Edition

Printed edition ISBN: 978-1-60940-481-9
Ebooks:
ePub ISBN: 978-1-60940-482-6
Kindle/mobipocket ISBN: 978-1-60940-483-3
Library PDF ISBN: 978-1-60940-484-0

Wings Press
627 E. Guenther
San Antonio, Texas 78210
Phone/fax: (210) 271-7805
On-line catalogue and ordering:www.wingspress.com
All Wings Press titles are distributed to the trade by
Independent Publishers Group
www.ipgbook.com

Library of Congress Cataloging-in-Publication Data

Oliphant, Dave.
    Generations of Texas poets / Dave Oliphant. -- First Wings Press edition.
        pages cm
    ISBN 978-1-60940-481-9 (pbk. : alk. paper) -- ISBN 978-1-60940-482-6 (e-pub
ebook) -- ISBN 978-1-60940-483-3 (mobipocket/kindle ebook) -- ISBN 978-1-
60940-484-0 (library pdf)
    1. American poetry--Texas--History and criticism. 2. American poetry--20th
century--History and criticism. 3. American poetry--19th century--History and
criticism. 4. Poets, American--20th century--Biography. 5. Texas--In literature. I.
Title.
    PS266.T4O45 2015
    810.9'9764--dc23
                                        2015021322

Contents

III. Before & After *Roundup*

for María,
as always

Preface

In 1973, I self-published under my own imprint, Prickly Pear Press, an anthology of Texas poets entitled *The New Breed*. In my Introduction to that book, I initiated something of a program in support of native and longtime resident poets of the State, even though a few of the poets had only lived in Texas briefly and had already left for other parts by the time the anthology appeared. At the time, I could hardly have foreseen that I would continue to promote Texas poetry for the next forty years, from the date of that Introduction up to the last piece here, published in Fall 2013.

A decade after publishing *The New Breed*, I would self-publish another book: my collection of essays and book reviews entitled *On a High Horse: Views Mostly of Latin American & Texan Poetry* (1983). In *Choice* magazine for April 1984, an unsigned reviewer commented that *On a High Horse* was "not likely to be superseded anytime soon; and Academia, not enthusiasm, will produce its successor." In about 1995, I added—to the section on Texas poetry in *On a High Horse*—a number of articles and reviews written during the previous decade and entitled the manuscript "Generations of Texas Poets," which I submitted to three university presses in the State. Outside readers for two of the presses rejected the manuscript; the third press never responded. One outside reader suggested that I start over and, instead of a collection of articles and reviews, that I put together a real history of Texas poetry, with the assistance of another writer. Being contrary and largely a loner, I set the manuscript aside, but continued from year to year to contribute to various publications my articles on, and reviews of, books by Texas poets.

After almost two more decades without a history of Texas poetry having appeared in print, I decided that it was high time that I added to the "Generations of Texas Poets" manuscript twenty-four of my articles and reviews written during the eighteen years from 1995 to 2013. Even when I submitted the earlier "Generations" manuscript, I had believed that my compilation of essays represented something of a history of poetry in my native state. At the same time that such articles and reviews traced the publishing careers of the state's most prolific poets, they also represented a record of my readings and charted the consistencies or changes in my responses to the poets' writings. In a sense, each piece owed something to the moment in which it was written and my own particular perspective at the time, but overall I felt that the various essays and reviews surveyed rather broadly the extensive field of Texas poetry and developed fairly in-depth analyses of poems by prominent figures and of those by a number of fine poets with less of a name recognition. With the addition of the two-dozen more-recent articles and reviews, the present collection, it now seems to me, has only strengthened my original thesis that Texas poets have produced a substantial and vital body of work. Even so, I know that my more subjective approach will certainly be supplanted by an objective evaluation of the type that Texas poetry requires and merits. Nonetheless, I offer in the meantime these admittedly partisan views with the simple hope that they will in one way or another lead or return readers to the consideration of poems worthy of their time and attention.

I have been and remain indebted to the editors of the Texas periodicals in which many of the review-essays in this volume were first published, in particular *The Pawn Review, Southwestern American Literature, Texas Books in Review,* and *The Texas Observer,* and I am deeply grateful to Bryce Milligan of Wings Press for his continuing encouragement of Texas writers like myself.

Dave Oliphant
Cedar Park, Texas
March 2015

I.

HISTORY

IN THE

TEXAS POEM

Readings in Early Texas Verse

In 1925, when the French government invited President Calvin Coolidge to send modern American paintings to Paris for exhibition, Coolidge replied that this would be impossible since there were no painters in the United States.[1 & 2] Of course, Coolidge could have exported the work of such active figures as Charles Demuth, Marsden Hartley, Edward Hopper, George Bellows, and Grant Wood, to name but a few. Even from Texas the President could have sent paintings by Julian Onderdonk (who had died only three years earlier), Olin Travis, Frank Reaugh, and Otis Dozier as representative artists active in the state during the 1920s. Although the Texans are less well-known nationally, an Onderdonk with his bluebonnet scenes is still familiar today to the state's general museum goer. As for Texas poets of the Coolidge period, the names of John Lang Sinclair, Ed Blount, Hans Hertzberg, and Leonard Doughty are even less recognizable to most readers of poetry than those Texas painters' names are to art lovers, even though Sinclair was the author of "The Eyes of Texas"; Hertzberg's "would-be" epic poem on his law school class of 1891 at the University of Texas has much to recommend it; and Doughty not only wrote poetry but translated some 80 poems by the German poet Heinrich Heine. It is perhaps indicative of a rather persistent need to look for art beyond the state's borders that Doughty translated Heine instead of German-Texas poet Fritz Goldbeck (1831-1899), the author of two volumes of poems in German based on life in the early German-Texas settlements.

The work of early Texas poets like Goldbeck was probably unknown or even ignored by most readers in the 1920s, as it still is today. Neglect of a poet like Goldbeck is owing largely to the fact that the Calvin Coolidge syndrome is still very much in evidence today,

---

1. Originally published under the title "Fritz Goldbeck and the German-Texas Poets" in *Southwestern American Literature*, 22, no. 1 (Fall 1996): 7-18.
2. David A. Shannon, *Between the Wars: America, 1919-1941* (Boston, MA: Houghton Mifflin Co., 1965, p. 99; quoted in *Public Policy for the Humanities in Texas* (Austin, TX: LBJ School of Public Affairs, 1986), Report No. 74, p. 4.

essentially because the very phrase "Texas poetry" is considered by many to be a contradiction in terms. It is thought that to attempt the study of Texas poetry would be impossible since, for the general public, it does not even exist. As for those who might be inclined to read early Texas poetry, a number of obstacles immediately present themselves. First, there is the problem of finding it in print. One important poet from the nineteenth century, Heinrich Ochs (1820-1897), reportedly wrote some 260 poems that remain in manuscript, but where they are located I have been unable to determine, since the article in which they are mentioned—Selma Metzenthin-Raunick's "German Verse in Texas"—fails to identify their whereabouts.[3] Ochs's manuscripts are not, for example, in the Center for American History in Austin, and even were they deposited there, it would be impossible for most readers to study them because they were written in German and by hand. Even in the case of Fritz Goldbeck's verse, which was published and survives among the holdings of the Center, there is the troublesome matter of having to read the gothic typeface in which his books were printed. And even these difficulties do not represent the most insurmountable challenge to a reader of early Texas verse.

Because Texas has been occupied in its brief history by nations flying six different flags, the state's poetry record consequently involves a number of languages other than German and English. The earliest inhabitants, who were not among the emigrating flag-wavers, had no written languages, but they did leave a type of poetry on the walls of caves. To "read" these "poems" we can consult W.W. Newcomb's book, *The Rock Art of Texas Indians*, and find copies of primitive drawings reproduced in the 1930s by Forrest Kirkland.[4] Had this modern draftsman not copied the rock art drawings at Missionary Shelter near the Rio Grande, they would now be inaccessible, for in 1954 the most massive flood in the 10,000-year history of the Pecos River eradicated the site completely. According to anthropologist Solveig Turpin, the central figure displayed in the Missionary Shelter scene presents:

---

3. Selma Metzenthin-Raunick, "German Verse in Texas," *Southwest Review* 18, no. 1(Autumn 1932): 45.
4. W.W. Newcomb, *The Rock Art of Texas Indians: Paintings by Forrest Kirkland* (Austin, TX: University of Texas Press, 1967).

a symbolic duality not often seen in Lower Pecos pictographs. This character is either a mission made human by the addition of a head and arms or a priest whose body is a church building, complete with towers and crosses. A long lance penetrating his body prompted Newcomb to comment that this "figure visualizes what Lipans and Mescaleros often wanted to do and occasionally did do to missionaries" and that the painting commemorated an actual event. Kirkland included this panel among those he thought verged on true pictographic writing, a design that told a story. The graceful horse is painted in the Plains Indian tradition, causing Jackson to attribute it to Kiowa or Comanche artists. The handprints above the frontal posture, and the protruding ears of the missionary are characteristic of a late-prehistoric art form called the Red Monochrome style. A possible import from the Plains late in prehistory, it suggests that the pictograph is the expression of new experiences within the framework of an established tradition.[5]

This description of Indian pictographs contains many elements in common with the kinds of experiences recorded within the tradition of poetry. Like the Indians, European immigrants to the state documented their lives and times, telling their stories in poems in such languages as German, Spanish, French, Swedish, and English. Often, however, the poems these peoples must have written may not survive, just as the Texas Indian rock art "writings" have frequently been obliterated by the ravages of time, natural events, and vandalism.

Poetry in Spanish was first written in the Southwest by Gaspar de Villagrá, who accompanied Juan de Oñate's conquest of New Mexico in 1598. Other figures may have composed verses at the various missions in Texas, and newspapers from the nineteenth century reveal that verse in Spanish was written and published throughout the period. Today Spanish is the only language other than English that has continued to serve as a medium for the practice of poetry in Texas. But beginning in the 1840s with the arrival of German immigrants under the leadership of Prince Solms-Braunfels,

5. Solveig A. Turpin, "The Vanishing Rock Art of Texas Indians," *Heritage* 5, no. 1 (Spring 1982): 36-39.

a number of German poets would be active during the second half of the century, and the Prince himself wrote what was perhaps the first poem in German composed in and about Texas. Prince Solms's untitled poem is divided into three nine-line stanzas, rhyming in the original German according to the pattern *ababccdde*. Since no English version exists, I offer my own crude rendering of the Prince's verses:

> Separated from the Fatherland
> By the ocean's waves,
> On emigrating far from homes
> And our many bonds of love,
> We cross on spirited horses
> These hot Texas plains.
> And we shorten the way with song,
> Which rings aloud with the sound of:
> Cheer, Deutschland! Deutschland cheer!
>
> Around the bright fire,
> We think from afar
> Of our loved ones dear;
> And as glasses of rare wine mirror
> The flames reflected here,
> We drink with song,
> Which rings with joyful sound:
> Cheer, Deutschland! Deutschland cheer!
>
> If then to battle we go
> With Indians wild and fierce,
> In the dense powder smoke
> Out we sing in German!
> And who encounters death here,
> Died yet for the Fatherland;
> And fought and fell with song,
> Which rings with vigorous sound:
> Cheer, Deutschland! Deutschland cheer![6]

---

6. For the original German, see Metzenthin-Raunick, p. 38. I am indebted to Professor Winfred Lehmann for explanations and suggestions in regard to my translation.

In commenting on this poem, historians of the Germans in Texas have dismissed it as lacking in any poetic value. When I first showed the piece to a German-Texas language teacher, she too found it a laughable, amateurish work. Only after I pointed out my reasons for reading it closely did she agree that there was more to it than she had realized. Readers who are looking for great art will not find it in early Texas verse. But even minor efforts can provide insights into history, as well as offer touches of artistry that are like gems in the rough.

What Prince Solms achieves in his poem is the recreation of a vivid scene from the 1840s, charged with the emotions involved in separation from one's homeland and a continuing attachment to one's national heritage. Essentially, the poet captures several German qualities that have been transferred to Texas: they shorten their journey across the endless prairie by singing loudly; at night they drink to their far-off loved ones with their remaining wine ("seltene" in the original German meaning scarce as well as rare) from the bottles brought with them from home; their glasses, also brought over from their homeland, reflect the leaping flames of the campfire; and in their meeting with "inhuman" Indians, the Germans seek, after the thick gun smoke has settled, consolation for those who died protecting the "Fatherland." At the same time that German writers like Prince Solms maintain their Germanness (and this has been a distinctive characteristic of their settlements in Texas) by upholding customs (music and wine drinking) and values (patriotism and civilization vs. the barbarism they considered to be the state of the aborigines), they also exhibit their keen observation of their new surroundings and incorporate into their poems the sights and trials of their new Texas life. Many of the German immigrants were highly educated, and this certainly shows in their poems. That they chose to express themselves early on in verse is itself a sign of their cultured way of life.

One of the earliest German poets to combine both Old and New World views was Fritz Goldbeck, who came to Texas, probably in 1845, and who Metzenthin-Raunick asserts "undertook the task of historian."[7] Like his better-known descendant, the Texas photographer

---

7. Metzenthin-Raunick, p. 41.

E.O. Goldbeck of panoramic fame, Fritz Goldbeck documented the people and places in Texas that he personally witnessed, in particular the German settlements of New Braunfels, Fredericksburg, Sophienburg, Boerne, and Comfort. Having arrived when he was fourteen, Fritz and his brother Theodor were in Comfort by 1854. Some forty years later, in 1895 and 1896, Fritz Goldbeck published in San Antonio two thin volumes of verse, entitled *Seit fünfzig Jahren*, parts I and II. Translated, the title reads something like "After Fifty Years" and refers to the poet's half century in Texas.[8] This collection bears the subtitle "prose in verse," an indication that the poet made no claims to artistic merit for his modest production. Nonetheless, as Metzenthin-Raunick observes, "not one of the other [German-Texas] writers of verse, except perhaps Heinrich Ochs, approaches Goldbeck in the vivid portrayal of early Texas types."[9]

Even though Metzenthin-Raunick avers that Goldbeck occasionally "rises to the genuine poetic expression," she does not rate him so high as she does Ochs or Johannes Romberg (1808-1891), the latter, according to the critic, "undoubtedly the most important of the early German poets in Texas."[10] Nevertheless, while Goldbeck does not offer the kind of speculative philosophy that Mezenthin-Raunick finds and discusses in Romberg's poetry, Goldbeck was a Texas poet who concerned himself with depicting the history of his times, and in doing so he not only recorded an era but created in the process a clear, lively style that brings his subjects vividly to life. The following stanzas from Goldbeck's "The Source of Song"—the final six out of thirteen—suggest something about his attraction to the Texas landscape as well as to the life of neighboring Mexico, which he visited and wrote about in several of his verses:

> I found the stuff of song
> In nature's kingdom,
> In the valleys, on the mountains,
> In the woods and on the plain.

8. Fritz Goldbeck, *Seit fünfzig Jahren: Prosa en versen*, 2 vols. in 1 (San Antonio, TX: J. Schott, 1895-6).

9. Metzenthin-Raunick, p. 42.

10. Ibid.

In the rage and in the roar,
In the wild waterfalls,
In the high rugged crags,
In the repeated echoes.

In the far desert land
Where the sun shines hot,
And near the giant cactus
Where blooms the yucca plant.

Where over the empty prairie
The savage speeds on horseback,
His foes in hot pursuit,
Menaced by the bullet.

In the land of Montezuma
Where the agave flowers,
Man in the mountains' lap
Toils for the sake of silver.

At the quiet, secret graves,
The dead's own resting-place,
The life of those now gone
Lent me words for song.

Another piece by Goldbeck, "About San Pedro Years Ago," sketches
some of the highlights of Mexican life, which seemed both to appeal
to the poet and to elicit from him a certain moral indignation:

In little Chihuahua,
In the old quarter,
There is today a fandango
Can fill with delight.

There the violins sound
And the sweetest of harps,
While one eats frijoles
And peppers so hot.

Dark-eyed maidens
Are sprightly and willing,
As they dance like elves,
So nimble and light.

People play at monte
For the highest of stakes
Have lured so many
Straight to the abyss.

There was a fellow in Bexar
Who had he not been witness
To this pleasure here
Had lived to resist.[11]

These quatrains—on a stereotypical scene on the Texas-Mexican border or in the Mexican section of most Texas towns—present a German viewpoint toward eating, drinking, and gambling. Certainly the German could appreciate good music and good food, but there is something of an implied criticism in the tale of the card playing that was apparently the ruin of a good San Antonio citizen. The dancing, gambling, and perhaps prostitution represent an attraction to idle pleasures that can only lead away from the German devotion to hard work and responsible conduct. The clash of two cultures is portrayed here through a verse in German that not only evokes a recognizable aspect of Mexican life but incorporates such Mexican terms as "fandango" and "frijoles" (present in the original German verse), the Texas and Mexican place names of San Pedro, Chihuahua, and Bexar, and reference even to Germany's folklore tradition in the verse's comparison of the dancing maidens to elves. In many ways, then, this piece brings together two opposing cultural traditions, both of which have been instrumental in

---

11. This and other poems by Fritz Goldbeck have been translated by Gabriel Blashy; see *Since Fifty Years: The First German Immigrants to Texas, 1844-1846, Prose in Verse by Fritz Goldbeck* (Hubbard, TX: Elinor Goldbeck Wilkes, Publisher, 1982). I have chosen to print my own version for purposes of analysis, even though mine does not rhyme completely as Blashy's does.

making Texas what it is.[12]

Goldbeck could also write of Mexican life in more glowing terms, as he does in a poem in rhyming couplets entitled "Twenty-Four Hours in Monterey, 1858." Here he notes the vendors selling their wares (some yelling "hot tortillas"), comments on the refreshing night with its star-filled skies, extols the midday custom of a siesta, the graceful ladies on the balconies, and the free and open life of the plaza, and then attends the theatre for a reenactment from Spanish history. On first entering the city behind pack animals and wagons filled with silver ore and lead from local mines, the poet reports:

> My wagon carries yearning; it's a stubborn load.
> After noon, no one willingly goes without a siesta,
> Not maids or servants, not the ladies or gentlemen.
> I close the window shutters, latches creaking sorely,
> The streets like all other spaces deserted and empty.
> I'm feeling quite lonesome; everyone's asleep in the house.
> So I open the shutters to look out upon the street.
> As if life were extinct, no sign of it is stirring anywhere,
> A donkey laden with kindling stands napping at the door.
> Annoyed, I once more have closed the shutters,
> And finally put my own bored body to rest.
> The sun sinks deeper, exhausted in her own red heat.
> Then a new spirit rises in every creature.
> Many a slender, proud rider bedecked in native dress
> Draws attention to himself on his lively steed.
> The women too take a stroll, something unseen by day;
> The fresh coolness pulls them out of their homes.
> Gradually it turns dark; the shops all are open;
> There the women go and spend their gold.
> By lamplight they choose a new wardrobe,
> Come daylight it won't suit them, they won't put it on.
> The night is cool and refreshing, the sky star-bright.

---

12. This incorporation of words from other languages in the Southwest was practiced as well by novelist Pater Hörmann, whose *Life on the Prairies* from 1866 "illustrates one characteristic of the [German] language in Texas, the adoption of new words for the new scenes." See Winfred Lehmann, "Lone Star German," *Rice University Studies* 63, no. 3 (1977): 73-81.

The plaza, already lit, quickly fills with a crowd,
A colorful crush wandering back and forth.
This time easy to while away is greatly loved in the South.
The señoritas passing by whisper quietly,
With silken rebozos they shyly wrap themselves.
Rancheros, caballeros proudly strut up and down
In their smart outfits decorated with silver trim.
Here one can see something of the heart's desires.
For a few small coins, exchanges are made.
Orange pyramids and grapes, dark brown,
And figs and peronas are lovingly displayed.
With frijoles and tamales the men come by,
"Tortillas calientes" their often-heard cry.
Now in the middle of the plaza, brass music sounds
And from the high mountains in echo resounds.
From balconies many a charming lady looks down
On those below going about their merry rounds.
Many a bell-light laugh is heard from above;
Not one disturbs the plaza's unfettered life.
The aroma of orange blossoms pervades the mild air.
Crests of the Sierras gleam in the light of the moon.
Now it's time for theatre, folk already streaming there.
The plaza lies desolate, the people's mood is light.
The curtain rises, I'm in luck tonight,
"Boabdil el Chico" will prove a delightful play.
The Moorish city of Granada with its Alhambra castle,
The last Moorish king with his colorful court.
Here I see old Spaniards, many a brave proud knight,
The Crusades' banners of Christ waving on high.
The spirit of Castilians from an earlier time,
Many a noble lady and gentleman in native attire,
As stately on the boards as in Spain they were,
In speech and gestures so skilled and polite.
Now the brown dancers dance their finale.
All head homeward, the evening soon at an end.
On the next corner sits a watchman slumbering,
His lance shining sinister by the lantern's beams.

The old one will grow quite lively, my guiding star.
He's happy to accompany me with lance and lantern.
Soon he knocks at the gate, we're in the right place,
A silver piece instead of words, Adiós!, and he's gone.[13]

The care with which the poet etches this scene is exemplary and is matched by his insights into the cultural habits and attitudes of the people he portrays. Although Goldbeck rather infrequently creates a metaphor as striking as the one that begins this excerpt from his poem, the indirect allusion to his own yearning adds greatly to the entire presentation and prepares for his later expression of loneliness and his desire to escape the boredom for which he obviously found release through the experience of another culture.

One other scene versified by Goldbeck from the same year is also a romantic sketch of a Mexican city and its environs. Through its rhyming quatrains, "In Saltillo, 1858" lends both a human and a sacred touch to the poet's description of a fountain and its natural source:

A street corner in Saltillo
Pours forth silver-bright waters,
An offering through a dolphin's mouth
Made by the mountain's spring.

Many a slim brown maiden
Fills her jug with a fresh, chilly draught,
Chatting here with her lover
At the twilight hour.

Here too the old, blind beggar
Lingers on within his sweet rest,
Listening refreshed by
Its splashing jet.

From up on the mountaintop,
One sees so far away,

---

13. I am indebted to Gloria Traylor for assistance in translating from this Goldbeck poem.

Looks down on a little church
Of the sanctified Virgin.

Beneath the decorated altar
Breaks a darker spring,
And there at the sturdy gate lock
A gray-headed man is keeping watch.

That spring brings rich blessing
To the great old city,
Feeds still its many fountains,
Field and garden will have enough.

Out of the womb of the god woman,
The lap of our mother Nature,
Who nourishes all her offspring,
Only from her comes this blessing.

Other verses by Goldbeck take as their subjects his landing in Galveston and the founding of the various German settlements in Texas. "Hurrah, hurrah, the Prairieland!" begins the first line of a poem on the thrill of arrival. References to the settlements abound in Goldbeck's verses, as he characterizes life on the frontier: music concerts, observance of the Fourth of July, a jury trial, farming, dancing, beer drinking. In his poem entitled "On the Springs of the Comal," one stanza depicts the German-Texan hospitality that was praised by Frederick Law Olmstead in his *Journey Through Texas* (1857):

The farmer with his modest mind
Not only wants his own to feed.
His house is open any time,
He always gives to those in need.[14]

A humorous anecdote-poem by Goldbeck, entitled "A Bear Hunt Fifty Years Ago. On the Way to Fredericksburg," recounts the shooting at night of a mule by an overeager member of the hunting party.

---

14. From Gabriel Blashy's translation, in Fritz Goldbeck, *Since Fifty Years*, p. 49a.

The poet comments:

> At times the love for hunting did
> Bring disagreeable side effects:
> Everywhere by the way you must
> Discover deer increase the lust.[15]

This narrative poem recalls a similar episode in James Fenimore Cooper's *The Prairie*, where the satirized naturalist, Dr. Obed Battius (blind as a bat), mistakes his ass for an unknown American species he names Vespertilio horribilis. Although Cooper's and Goldbeck's points are quite different and the former's episode ends without Dr. Battius doing any harm to his beast of burden, the two tales share a similar view of man's tendency to jump to conclusions, either to prove himself intellectually or to satisfy his appetite for bloodshed.

Fritz Goldbeck would also write on the Texas war of independence. In a patriotic but poignant piece on the massacre at Goliad (in which the poet uses the word "gringos"), he laments the fact that at the time no monument marked the site, no "word" of the "heroism" and sacrifice, only the murmur of the San Antonio River flowing past. His poem entitled "The Sufferings of the Immigrants" contains a reference to the Alamo and predates "Texas," a twentieth-century sonnet by the Argentine poet, Jorge Luis Borges, who compares the Texan stand to the Greek battle of Thermopylae. For his part, Goldbeck writes:

> The small number of Texans
> With true heroic courage
> Fought like the Spartans once,
> Till the last man lay in blood.[16]

Even though Goldbeck clearly identified himself with and wrote patriotically about his new home in Texas, he never thought of himself as a Texan but as a German through and through. Indeed, he asserts in his poem entitled "A German Am I":

---

15. Goldbeck/Blashy, p. 90a.
16. Ibid., p. 45a.

The country where on mother's breast
I once unconsciously found rest,
Is and remains my fatherland,
Though I have built another nest.[17]

Nevertheless, Goldbeck's depiction of his Texas and Mexican subjects makes him a poet who in many respects is truer to the time and place of his writing than most English-language versifiers of the same period and even many of those from the first half of the 20th century. Much can be learned from this German's approach to his adopted land and its subjects and from his penchant for dealing with the realities around him. While his writing may not rise to the level of high art, it certainly appears to take as its point of departure the "noteworthy stuff" that gives "some flavor of an actual peculiarity," as William Carlos Williams advocated by incorporating historical documents into his own *In the American Grain* (1925).

Another German-born poet to write of historical events and scenes in Texas was Marie Anna Weisselberg (1835-1911). This poet's opposition to slavery—another German trait also noted by Olmstead in his *Journey Through Texas*—and her strong Northern sympathies led to a poem on the rescue of the stars and stripes from Rebel hands, in which she dramatizes her fears that the flag would no longer adorn the halls of the state capitol. The poet also wrote on the Fall of the Alamo and on women's rights, but perhaps her most moving piece, "Of a Mad Young Girl," resulted from her life at the insane asylum in Austin, where her husband was the superintendent. In this piece, Weisselberg closely observes the effects of madness on a female patient:

What wrong, poor creature, have you committed,
That your wild, cold eye stares into space?
Was a damning curse cast upon you,
You withered flower the storm has nipped?

What does the monotone, soft singing mean,
That night surrounds you with delusion and death?

---

17   Ibid., p. 50a.

Do you recognize the black wings of madness
That have beaten about you, you tender lovely maid?

Do you know how madness has robbed you
Of shining eyes, smiling lips, and rosy cheeks,
Can you identify your saucy suitor?
Who for death, his friend, whirls about to woo you![18]

To suggest the psychological disturbance afflicting the young girl, Weisselberg employs in her poem a pattern of three images of movement: the storm, the beating wings, and the whirling suitor. The description of insanity's curse is also presented in three related descriptive terms, one for each stanza: the patient's staring eye, her monotone song (reminiscent perhaps of Ophelia in *Hamlet*), and her loss of a pleasing color and expression. As in the verses by Prince Solms and Fritz Goldbeck, this piece combines the reality of an historical circumstance with the use of traditional literary techniques to achieve immediacy and a timeless emotive response in the reader.

John Sjolander (1851-1939) was a Swedish-Texas poet who shared with the German-Texans a concern for focusing on the immediate surroundings and conditions of a Texas life and employed for the purpose an appropriately vital diction and imagery. When such poets concentrated on the realities of their existence, they on occasion created work that can be compared favorably with some of the masterpieces of American literature. Sjolander's "Drought" looks forward to the powerful description of the Oklahoma Dust Bowl in John Steinbeck's *The Grapes of Wrath* (1939):

Like an army left in a desert world,
Stand the ranks of corn, with their banners furled;
And their plumes droop low on that side and this,
While their rusty blades swing curved and curled,
Like writhing serpents that touch and hiss.
. . .

---

18. For the German original of my translation, see Mary Jo Vines, "A Pioneer Poet of Texas," *The American-German Review* (June 1948): 28-30.

And the dust lies deep, everywhere, everywhere,
On the doorstep wide, on the winding stair,
And as far beside as the eye can scan;
And it seems, from the hush of both song and prayer,
That it lies as deep on the heart of man.

And under the sun that molten clings
In the haze-hid sky, like an omen swings—
A speck as large as a human hand—
A voiceless vulture on tainted wings,
The only shadow to cool the land.[19]

Undeniable as it is that Sjolander resorts to poeticisms and unnatural inversions that offend our contemporary ears, he manages nonetheless to capture both the visual and visceral nature of this Depression-era event. The irony in the end—of the vulture's shadow providing the only means of cooling for a heat-parched land—conveys through a traditional figure of speech the harsh reality of an experience common to so many of our forebears and one to which any reader can respond empathetically. John Sjolander's combination of carefully made rhymed stanzas, realistic description, and telling analogies—the dust lying deep both physically and psychologically—is deserving, like the work of Goldberg and Weisselberg, of closer scrutiny by a Texas readership that can take pride in such early writers who recorded their responses to their environment in artful and affective verses.

---

19. Barbro Persson McCree, *John Sjolander: Poet of Cedar Bayou* (Austin, TX: Eakin Press, 1987), pp. 90-99.

A Beginning with William Barney

For readers trained in world literature and in the major writers of the United States, familiarity with any poetry outside the mainstreams of classroom consideration tends to come only, if at all, early or late in one's reading career.* The more's the pity, since not always at those times are we so able to judge properly or to accept so readily the value of regional writing. Perhaps the first poets or poems sighted on our narrow horizon are those of the region where we are born or reared, but with our education either lacking or quickly taken in hand by those aware of more far-reaching contemporary currents, the regionalist pales in importance as a lower mountain does before the higher, more imposing peaks that rise beyond. Indeed, we often reach those distant heights by the foothills of the regionalist's work, yet little thanks he has for his efforts, much less for the worth of his own unassuming prospects. After years of studying "foreign" giants, often in search of what has all along been cultivated in our own backyards, it is only out of curiosity that we return to consider the long-since adjudged "minor" figures of a native landscape. With a shock of recognition we may well see in these local artists not only poets worthy of critical acclaim on their own account but poems of a tradition other than the one we have fallen into feeling exclusive, as well as of a thought and technique quite deserving of our notice and equal in some ways to those of more famous figures.

Just such a case is that of William Barney, the accumulation of whose work as a Texas poet has taken place quietly until today it forms a body of poems unique to Southwest letters and in certain respects original even beyond any regional tag. Born in 1916 in Tulsa, Oklahoma, William Barney has, since 1928, made his home in Fort Worth, Texas. Author of two volumes published in the 1950s, *Kneel From the Stone* (1952) and *Permitted Proof* (1955), both from Kaleidograph Press of Dallas, Barney is a retired postal worker,

---

* Introduction to *The Killdeer Crying: Selected Poems of William Barney* (Fort Worth, TX: Prickly Pear Press, 1977), pp. 11-19. A second, expanded edition of this work appeared from Prickly Pear in 1983.

though still a very active poet, as poems from the '60s, '70s, and '80s brought together here in *The Killdeer Crying* so amply and remarkably demonstrate.

While it is perhaps his more recent work which merits special attention, in order to understand from whence he has come and to appreciate better where his previous work has carried him, *The Killdeer Crying* is a selected poems that gathers representative pieces from Barney's earlier collections characterized essentially by their use of traditional techniques, which the poet would continue to employ even more effectively in his later work. The question of whether a poet's predilection for standard meters, rhyme, and conventional stanza patterns may act as a hindrance to his fullest expression is one which must be treated in any consideration of such a "traditional" poet as Barney, since it is a central point in regard to his achievement, for in spite of his at-times old-fashioned sound and sense, his use of traditional forms often proves the source of his very decided triumphs. Even as a self-confessed admirer of Robert Frost, Barney has managed to create a poetry of his own, peculiar to his own region and to his own inexhaustible yet meticulous use of vocabularies drawn from fields as remote as mathematics and ornithology. In general, Barney's poetry does not call attention to the poet, does not bring judgments against any group or type, nor does it complain or disparage. Even though it is largely impersonal, it leaves the reader with the impression of a man behind the poems of great humility, one who is high-minded (in the best sense of this phrase), imaginative, thoughtful, reflective, and ever sensitive to language and to the world about him. Above all, William Barney's poetry is one of praise.

Despite the strength of his mind and the delicate music of its expression, Barney and his work have for the most part gone unknown or ignored by Texas readers. To suggest that his poetry has not been noticed at all, however, would be to overstate the case, for both of Barney's collections from the 1950s won Texas Institute of Letters Awards and the title poem of his selected poems won the Robert Frost Award of the Poetry Society of America, which was presented to Barney in 1961 by Frost himself. Barney's work also has been taken into account by such critics and anthologists as Frederick Eckman, Martin L. Shockley, and Betsy Colquitt. While *The Killdeer Crying* is to date the fullest gathering of the poet's work, it was the commentaries and selections made by earlier critics and editors that encouraged the making of this third collection of William Barney's warm and engaging poems.

In *Poetry* (Chicago, volume 89), Frederick Eckman reviewed Barney's *Permitted Proof* along with works by Robert Creeley, Robert Duncan, Paul Blackburn, and Lawrence Ferlinghetti, all the latter, as Eckman points out, writing under the influence of William Carlos Williams. While Eckman sees Barney's book as less daring than, say, Creeley's, he does state that the Texan is not conservative, though formal in expression, and that more than the other writers reviewed, Barney has "in his work a good deal more of affirmation, of an ultimate (if hard-won) faith in the human condition." The critic admires especially Barney's handling of animal poems, his Bach-like lines in "Bach as a Propagation of Cells," and his strong narrative bent. Although Eckman believes that Barney's poetry "deserves a wider audience," he does not feel that the poet is so highly successful when it comes to his treatment of local western themes, as in his "Canticle for a Cutting Horse."

Martin Shockley, in his edition of a *Southwest Writers Anthology* (Steck, 1967), takes quite the opposite view from Eckman, with respect to that very same canticle, and remarks on the poet's deftness in following its poetic form. Shockley explains how praise for the mount develops, first, from pleasure in her sheer movement, then to delight in the relation between animal and spirit, next to a rejoicing in the glory of the subject itself, on then to treating of the animal as a symbol for the mind, and finally to simple celebration of the cutting horse as "her image, nothing shall rightly encompass." Within the poem's five stanzas, the phrases, word combinations, and concepts are worked out wonderfully. The pointed phrase, "A blend of desire and dissent," presents the canticle's central paradox: the horse's urge to perform well but at the same time to be free of the force that demands a performance. Instead of a poet's own subjective response to the creature, weakening the poem by that very fact, Barney's canticle provides an objective portrait on a more universal level—thus denying any local limitations his subject matter might otherwise suggest. The whole poem is, however, rich in suggestiveness, as the uncommon analogies and the natural allusions combine to form a right relationship between the real and the imaginative:

> Like a spider she weaves the kinetic web of enclosure,
> she throws her great breast as a shuttle.
> ... A talisman in her tawniness
> for any who praise the pursuit
> of the quick metaphor, the well-cinched word. . . .
>
> Leave her to the high mesas,
> to the open llano, her proper stage: let her dance
> her tango of intricate measures. . . .

In addition to the notice of Barney's work taken by critics Eckman and Shockley, Betsy Colquitt, anthologist and editor of *descant* magazine, included the poet in her fine collection, *A Part of Space: Ten Texas Writers* (T.C.U. Press, 1969). The selection of a dozen poems from work done during the '50s and '60s served as an important introduction to this little-known Texas poet. Among Colquitt's choices are two poems from Barney's 1955 volume, *Permitted Proof,* and this earlier work occupies a significant place in the poet's development during a span of more than thirty years.

Beginning with *Kneel From the Stone* (1952), Barney exhibited many of the linguistic and thematic preoccupations which mark the entire range of his work, although, as in most first books, there are single poems that point to a learning process which will only later result in a surer touch. The influence of Frost is quite evident, even though this is not derivative in a dependent way. Perhaps an even more important influence has been Audubon; indeed, Barney has even written an unpublished verse play on the life of the naturalist. "On a Detail from Audubon" contains a stanza that illustrates concisely the poet's awareness of the need for both manliness and control in the best of writing:

> A soft stroke lames
> the line, depraves.
> The fierce detail
> enhances, saves.

It is another instance of the success accorded poets of the contemporary persuasion who make use of a historical figure like Audubon that simply because they versify from letters, journals, or government documents it is thought they have created "modern poetry," especially when they adapt an Audubon to their own special views of history or art. I am thinking specifically of William Heyen's use of Audubon in *Noise in the Trees* (1974). Although I much admire this poet's work, I tend to agree with one critic who commented that "the advantage of setting the facts in verse isn't always apparent." Working much earlier within a strict rhyme scheme and meter, William Barney reveals the firm and exact art of Audubon, and as in the best of Yeats's rhymed poems, Barney's meaning is strengthened by his crafted stanzas. Unlike Heyen's account of Audubon's career, which simply states the facts in a prosy, journalistic fashion, Barney's poem is stark, wastes no words with self-consciousness, nor with cutesy introductions to the poet's own philosophical plight:

> The hand that snared
> the cobalt wing,
> that froze the blue
> thief plundering
>
> caught also look
> the vine's hard claw
> of tendril writhing
> at the bird's craw.

The directness, the clarity of color and interaction, and the shrewd observation of the artist's design are all done with the greatest respect for the object in view; its reality is presented and the poet receives, or should receive, our total attention for this reason alone and not for any "poetic" rendering of another's notes or correspondence. The writing here is Barney's, and the subject is fortunate in having it so.

Even more to the point of objectivity is "Bracero," the last poem in the 1952 collection, which is a first-rate narrative and recalls R.G. Vliet's better-known "Clem Maverick" in its presentation of a Texas subject matter. The style is somewhat dated, but the viewpoint is convincing. Told partly in the words of the bracero himself, the story is moving at the level of its portrayal of the love of a man for his wife and children, for whom in his lowly position he is incapable of doing much of anything. The tragedy is not of the kingly sort, but it is gripping in its presentation of the bracero's attempt to give his wife a false satisfaction. Throughout the poem Barney's language sustains the irony. The drama derives from the father's desire to keep certain facts from his wife: that the son is dead and that the daughter has prostituted herself, both owing largely to the father's having crossed his family over the border in search of a better life. But again, it is Barney's craft that makes of what is unfortunately a typical tale a memorable piece of writing:

> The lies came quickly to his lips; he fashioned them with ease.
> Yet his soul was not in his voice, and Suerta would not listen.
> She would have but truth, she would press his heart like the
> yellow grapefruit
> and drain the last bitter drop.

There are many poems full of power and pleasure in Barney's two collections from the 1950s, but it is in the poems from the '60s to be found in Colquitt's *A Part of Space* that one observes how the poet has come into his own as a master of language and its objective use. Of the poems from the 1960s included in the Colquitt collection, all are worthy of comment, but four pieces are particularly representative of Barney as a model Texas poet: "The Calculus," "A Matter of Nerve," "The Day They Moved the Post Office," and "On Greer Island a Copperhead Lies Slain."

An indication of how Barney has slowly developed certain consistent themes may be seen by comparing "The Calculus" with a 1975 poem, "A Stone for Stumbling," where the poet writes of "The Man from Split City" that

> He'd a solid-geometry mind, he supposed;
> liked to see things fleshed out in space
> (otherwise they'd be figments, skinny abstractions,
> and you couldn't tell shape from shadow).

As earlier "The Calculus" had suggested, Barney finds mathematics a fascinating subject, perhaps because it reveals our need to live with "mid-fact, half-lie." The poet notes in calculus that "what is given never is defined," as if to say that we always posit the unreal. In doing so Barney seems to feel that we should not "dissolve / the fabric of what's real, or rip the seam, / unhinge the valve." The poem teases us with its playful treatment of a serious theme: trying to tell "shape from shadow." In what is probably a pre-Borges vein, the Texas poet ponders the relationship between subject and object in any calculus problem:

> In dry despair I sit and think how I
> should think, or not;
> yet do I think, or am I by and by
> but something thought?

This stanza illustrates the metrics and rhyme scheme of the entire poem, but from first to last the reader can hardly hear the poet at work. Just as the language is natural, so is the thought, even while it turns upon itself, inside out, and leaves us every way but loose.

"A Matter of Nerve" is a similar poem, in which the poet once again plays with the problem of who is doing what to whom. Here the subject is a western one, with the use of a barbed-wire fence as antagonist (or protagonist). The situation is this: the "he" of the poem is caught between gate post and wire:

> And so he stood in equipoise:
> there wasn't any slack
> to let away the post, and none
> to slip the held hand back.

After several stanzas of trying to figure out a "mathematical" solution, the narrator affirms:

> It came down to a matter of nerve:
> whether something could assert
> the necessary injury
> it took to quit the hurt.

Barney assumes, rightly I think, that there is no easy way out, and of course the metaphor and paradox loom larger than the mere western image the poet employs.

In much of Barney's work, despite a certain serious intent, there is almost always a touch of humor very tender and human. An example is "The Day They Moved the Post Office," in which we find the objections registered to the move by a town drunk. The poem recreates the speech of the character but more movingly suggests the way it is with his life:

> "There's a boon knot between me and this place.
> Didn't I stand for counting?" . . .

> We thought for certain now he'd make it clear
> how it could make a difference to a sot
> where the post office was, where it was not,
> and who'd have written.

Although many of Barney's ideas for poems come from his long association with the postal service and from his bird-watching activities, there is nothing limited in his scope, for these two subjects alone have supplied the poet with a far-ranging variety of observations and insights. This is the result principally of the poet's ability to settle into his surroundings. As a poem from the 1970s has it,

> The only need is to adapt your roots
> to where you are, gather up what feeds
> your kind (once you know it) and let bloom.

The final poem from the Colquitt collection is the beautifully-structured piece on the death of a copperhead snake. Barney's diction here is exquisite in its realization of the aesthetic qualities of the creature, as well as in its recreation of the observer's reaction to the living reptile. The reference to Ichabod is to Whittier's poem of that title and to I Samuel IV:21, "The glory has departed."

> This jack of diamonds dull and smooth,
> this copper-coopered smoldering band,

thicket can never again soothe
him sleeping in sleek ampersand.
> The spice of peril shall be gone
> from fallen log, from flaggy stone.

What easy thing now shall we say
for sentiment, a small rebate
to salve with pardon? Rather pray
for your enemy in his strait.
> This Ichabod has left us poorer.
> Where will we turn for simple terror?

While these highly developed poems date from the early 1960s, Barney fortunately did not let up, his production continuing, his eye as observant as ever. Among his work from the 1970s in *The Killdeer Crying* is the marvelous "Episode with Tomato." The ease of the language (almost a Chaucerian simplicity, yet modern), the naturalness of the rhyming, the down-to-earth subject matter, and the conclusion that makes us pause in sadness but assent that the worlds of quail and man "touch only an instant / and even to glimpse is to intrude"—all of this is characteristic of the best poetry of William Barney. And it is much, not only in a state almost entirely unknown for poetry but in a nation where poetic fads come and go as quickly as the frivolous fashions, where yet the authentic poet, to quote a popular western song, "seldom is heard."

What makes of William Barney a Texas poet of whom we may be especially proud is the penetrating manner in which he has come to depict the state's flora and fauna, as well as her people—in poems on Mr. Bloomer and his boat-tailed grackles, on the town drunk (with that most telling and complex aside: "and who'd have written"), on the negro with a new car, on the bracero, and on the women who learn to live with their men and the weather. In observing natural and human lives, Barney has a special awareness of the knot and the flaw ("A Crooked Feast" and "Thaw"), an ability to see in these the beauties passed over by the impatient and undiscriminating eye. Arthur Sampley, in writing of his friend and fellow poet, touched on these same qualities he personally felt were most striking in Barney's work. In a letter dated 21 June 1975, Sampley wrote that William Barney "has his own way of seeing things and his own taut, figurative way of recording what he sees. His nature poems catch the fleeting, unexpected glimpse, the surprise beauty in the commonplace or in the grotesque." To experience Barney's poems on both the tangible and technical levels is to appreciate, then, their fullest range and import, for it is through an integration of these two worlds that the poet has achieved a body of work truly rich in sympathy and earthly intelligence.

Texas Poetry and the Hi-Tech Race

In Aesop's tale of the tortoise and the hare, the slower, steadier creature catches and passes his faster but more easily distracted fellow.* In reading lately of the technological race, I find that there are a number of "turtle" countries in the Third World which are about to beat the United States to the gold carrot of commercial enterprise. This turn of events could well affect our literature adversely, since nations healthy economically tend to enjoy the leisure necessary to create and support the arts. If this financial situation is crucial to artistic creativity, it may be that Texas, despite the rest of the nation's economic decline, could well achieve greater stability and as a result perhaps could reach to higher levels of creative quality, for it is clear that the state is on the verge of becoming a giant in more than size. Yet literature is no respecter of riches and can thrive in such poor countries as Chile, Paraguay, or modern Greece. And when it comes to great art, Milton, Bach, and Brahms were actually behind their times yet have outdistanced the field of those running for an ageless appeal.

While much of modern art has rushed to originality, only to find it a diverting patch of greenery along the tedious path to true artistry, the most patient and dedicated artists have tended to appear old-fashioned or preoccupied with following a tradition which over the short haul provides neither a simple thrill nor another record-breaking print-run. But once the decades have been clocked, it is often seen that it was the turtles who crept across the line to claim the trophies of admiration along with a continuing and growing audience. And even though this has yet to happen for the turtles of Texas poetry, I foresee that the case may well be just as I have

---

* A talk delivered at Cooke County College in Gainesville, Texas, on Awards Day, spring 1978. Quoted passages are found in the following publications: *Chicago Review* (Winter 1975/76): 34, for the translation of Yannos Ritsos' "Harvest of Space"; William Burford's *A Beginning* (Norton, 1966); William Barney's *The Killdeer Crying: Selected Poems* (Prickly Pear Press, 1977); and Joseph Colin Murphey's *A Return to the Landscape* (Prickly Pear Press, 1979).

described it for some of the poems of William Burford, William Barney, and Joseph Colin Murphey—three among an even larger number of Texans writing significant work during the past thirty years.

For such turtle-poets as Burford, Barney, and Murphey to receive their well-deserved recognition, however, it is still necessary that their poems be read with a clear sense of the unique contribution they have made to Texas letters at a time when more trivial writing has captured the attention of a college-educated readership. The attraction of the distant and fashionable blinds us to the near and familiar which are too often precisely from what we so wish to escape. In choosing to flee the familiar, however, we abandon our best means of understanding ourselves, as well as our basis for comparison and contrast with other cultures, attitudes, and literary practices. As a result, we lack both a point of departure and, as Joe Murphey has phrased it, a landscape for return. Just as these three Texas poets have learned to take pride in where they are, their readers need to do the same. Not a false pride that one place is bigger or better than another, but a realization that any place, and especially where we are, is the surest source of meaningful experience and the most significant provider of a fund of words and scenes able to contain and express our deepest discoveries. And unlike oil wells or technological advances, it is doubtful that a place will ever be drained dry or become obsolete in terms of literary inspiration.

A prime example of such longevity is the modern renaissance of Greek literature in the hands of such poets as George Seferis and Yannos Ritsos, the latter especially basing his work on contemporary scenes from Greek streets to achieve a timeless moment in a timeworn nation. Consider, for example, Ritsos's "Harvest of Space":

> Tall plane-trees, muscular torsos of coolness.
> The shade is not intended to hide anything.
> Brave light, brave shade—
> Useless—daring to counter what?—
> simplicity breathes in the air.
>
> People sit beneath the trees,
> they dine on small wooden tables, they talk,

they do not suspect the magnitude covering them, the
    magnitude
that regulates their innocent gestures. Toward evening
someone sang (drunk perhaps). The plane-trees
moved in a silent procession toward the horizon.
The area emptied. The waiter, with his white apron,
appeared for a moment at a distance, in the crimson dusk,
holding in priestly fashion the tray with the empty glasses.

Here the everyday is the source for a renascence of the religious nature
of a simple scene faithfully and feelingly rendered. And should one
think that description of an outdoor cafe scene is a limited subject,
this poem by Ritsos seems proof against such an assertion. On the
other hand, if such scenes cannot produce in every poet or for every
generation a new theme and technique, Evolution continues to furnish
new plants, animals, and man-made objects set against an essentially
unchanging backdrop. As William Barney points out—ornithologist-
poet that he is—the cattle egret in recent times has made its way to
Texas from Africa and now provides him and other "naturalist" writers with yet another exotic image in their own backyards. Or like the
geologist who retraces the rich layers of fluvial deposits to discover the
force that keeps wheels on the road and wings in the air, the poet can
search through the arts of antiquity, its flora and fauna, for a deep store
of poetic inspiration and power. Just as technology finds new uses
for the past, so the poet can turn to his advantage the ageless images
forgotten yet still intact and awaiting him to touch them back to life
with the magic of his imaginative art.

    One positive fact about Texas poetry is that, unlike that of the
Greeks, it does not need to attempt merely to recapture the glories of
a past tradition but is confronted rather with the challenge of creating for the first time a body of poetry worthy the name. So that in
a sense the problem of reworking materials on which Homer and
Plato stamped their unmistakable genius does not face the Texas poet.
Certainly he or she must contend with an overworked western image,
but this has little to do with a tradition in poetry. No form aside from
the ballad is strongly associated with the western mode, so we are free
to seek new forms or to find in tried and true ones a proper vessel for

our own homegrown philosophy or vision. Also, little in poetry has come of the western theme or landscape, especially as it relates to the cowboy convention, so that here too we have a fertile field for interpretation, reinterpretation, or even, if we choose, to let it lie fallow.

For the most part Burford, Barney, and Murphey have only incidentally been attracted to the typically western motif of range life. If a cowboy appears in one of their poems, he bears little resemblance to those of movie or folklore fame, versions so familiar to all the world. More common in their poems are small-town or city people, figures who inhabit the populous regions of the state and have almost nothing to do with ranching as a way of life. William Burford, who is the youngest of the three (though ironically he taught Joseph Colin Murphey, his teacher's elder by a dozen years), has perhaps most fully ignored the Texas images as we know them—those of the rough-and-ready past and of the now jet-age blend of country-western guitar and NASA sophisticated hardware or Texas Instruments software. He has, however, written on those fearless western types who handle rattlesnakes, on the American Indian, and on the ubiquitous hunter drawing a bead on an endangered species. And in fact two of Burford's finest pieces—"South, Southwest" and "Going to School"—do use metaphors deriving from the cattle industry, as well as from physics. Nonetheless, Burford principally has taken as his province the mind as such, in Texas, in England, in France, in legend. By tracing back to its beginnings the mind's desire for happiness, the poet calls for "the new heroes" to "bring this [happiness] in their hands." The idea that man must make his life himself, and essentially in the mind, eliminates in one way a concern for place. In "The Days of Love," a poem for and of his wife, the poet observes how far we remain from what or whom we love, even when that thing or person should lie near or even beside us. Burford would have us realize that each mind is inevitably separate, sadly but perhaps rightly so. Speaking of the physical man, he writes:

> In this same mortal place
> That stones can break—
> How thin is the division
> Which holds the one life here,
> And the other, there beyond touch.
> . . .

Each thing must teach us
That we are elsewhere,
Not to be held.

When Burford does come to reproduce a familiar Texas scene, as in "South, Southwest," which depicts the Capitol in Austin, he finds it an image of our lost past and our even greater loss of any present satisfaction with lives that are marked by the "savage clasp" in love and the "snatch" of "shiny rings that make [our] eyes wide." As he puts it bluntly, "We are animals." Despite his despairing tone here, Burford generally concludes, as he does in "South, Southwest," with a hopeful image, in this case of the Capitol by night when the lighted building appears

> . . . like white salt we come to eat;
> Take into our eyes, our thin or thick hides,
> Let our spirits lick. This was cattle country,
> And now we have come to sit at the dome,
> To wait. At midnight the sprays are turned on
> That keep the grass green—which touching us
> Feel suddenly sweet. . . .

Even when Burford does turn to such a familiar Texas scene, he renews it through a powerful symbolism tied to his deep concern for contemporary man's loss of significant attachments and experiences, as well as to his (the poet's) need to discover a simple image that will limn for the mind a type of replacement for the meaningfulness that we are missing.

Another example of Burford's urge to suggest a lasting source of mental nourishment, along the lines of his salt-lick image, is found in section III of his subtly rhymed poem entitled "Twenty-year-old Poet":

> From far down the street
> Shone a light like a star,
> But the rays were cold
> And did not reach
> To warm the heart.

In all the world
The only thing heard
Was our own echoing feet

Approaching the place
Where the paving stone
Broke off in empty space—
The Museum loomed up
In whose cavernous rooms
Christ's body lies
For the dissecting knives.
And the stumps of the trees

Confronted us,
Monstrous teeth
Breaking through from beneath.
We reached the canal
Where the black water ran
And the barge at the bank
Lay huge and still
As the funeral bier.

"Here we must part, and not fear.
"Clasp hands. Pledge eyes."
And he gave me manly blessing.
Then he turned. But I
Stood and watched on that bank
The living coal of his pipe
Glow through the engulfing night.

Burford's poems range widely from subjects in Greece ("Cypris, Athene" or "A Reply") and Spain ("Barcelona") to those in Africa ("Famine in Africa"), and include as well a consideration of such seemingly disparate literary figures as T.E. Lawrence ("Lawrence / Ross / Shaw") and Goethe ("Chapters for My Faust"). But when Burford does write of the near-at-hand, as in "Local God," "The Oaks," and "The Spell," he seems always to focus on a simple image that conveys an "intellectual and emotional complex," as Pound advocated. In "Local God" the poet describes the man who "can grasp the rattlers behind the head / And snap them like a whip," observing also how he "Milks the venom out of their mouths." In "The Oaks" Burford describes a risen white moon "Through the black oaks— // Luminous, like bread before it is touched." But in "The Spell," especially, the poet finds in the images of a bullet-rosebud "splintered / Into flower," of Oswald's ax "Cutting a path for himself / In the midst of America," and of President Kennedy's "invincible thick hair," the essential elements of an historic drama. The idea that JFK's hair could keep his head from being "horribly shattered" and stop the "blind dark," from spreading and overwhelming him and us, illustrates Burford's concern to bring to bear on "local" events the larger issues confronting man and nation.

Although William Barney has not gone so far afield as Burford in order to find likely images for his own highly-wrought stanzas, neither has Barney depended on what is most typical about the Texas landscape or what at least has been taken as characteristic of its western image. Instead, Barney has looked closely at the knots and scars of the familiar, discovering in them a cosmos of meanings beyond their common Texas associations. Beginning with a scene on a popular pier, the poet notices how the weathering process has created nebulae in the wood, and simply by observing these "unspectacular" gnarls and grains in the planking he opens up the reader to a new sense of time, space, and, as he puts it, "patterns not meant to be understood" but which we joy in through his discriminating eye and his careful way with words and formal poetic design. Here is the entire poem, entitled "A Crooked Feast":

> Out on that narrow fishing pier
> he'd walk gingerly on the planks,
> not because of some dizzying fear,
> rather because wherever he stepped
> nebulae spread in amazing ranks.
>
> Weathering did it. A two-by-six
> paled into shining strand, sunswept,

except for a giant cicatrix
here and there in the vacant grain
(in the nothingness gnarls of pain).

He knew a flaw only marked the place
where a branch or knuckled burl
had interrupted the wooden space:
cut cross-wise, it showed a swirl.
So would the earth, if you cut it right.

He sensed it came of over-sight,
from paying heed to things awry,
patterns not meant to be understood.
It was some crookedness in his eye
feasting on knots instead of wood.

When Barney has chosen western subjects, such as the cutting horse and a barbed wire fence, he has used them as a means for exploring, in these cases, the nature of symbol, the process and end of writing, and the realization that freedom only comes through an acceptance of pain. The poet's ability to involve a wide range of topics and images within the western context is the mark of his truly creative imagination and his understanding of the function of poetry as a form of meditation upon the deeper meanings of even the most commonplace scenes or objects. In "Canticle for a Cutting Horse," Barney not only employs a sophisticated stanza pattern based on the canticle form but moves through some half-dozen stages of thought, much as he does in "Danse McClobber," a poem based on the calling of a square dance. In "The Cranes at Muleshoe," Barney describes an annual scene in the Panhandle and turns it into an apocalyptic allegory:

With no more skill than men
can they arrange a right society,
resolve their noisy dithering in space.
A simple symmetry eludes them:
too many compasses must be divined,
and the vague, skittish auspice will not form,
the pattern riddles, escapes the tribal mind.

Like Brahms waiting until he was forty-four to write his first symphony, taking his time to learn his trade, Barney has slowly but surely developed a theme and technique which will endure beyond what Chaucer, in his critique of those who "can not love ful half yeer in a place," terms a constant need for "newefangelnesse."

Joseph Colin Murphey belongs in any discussion of the poetry of Burford and Barney not merely because he is of their same generation, but also because his own poetry represents a slow development toward formal and thematic achievements vital to the creation of a lasting Texas literature. In fact, Murphey's development has been longer and perhaps fuller than that of his fellow poets, in that he has moved from a traditional line, as in "Ode to the Statue That Found a Trade" or "Requiem for a Long Dying," to the contemporary prose-like rhythms of his portrait poems, such as "Beauty Is Kin Deep" or "The Short Happy Bloom of Lurline Scruggs." And even though in this sense as well as formally the three poets are ultimately quite dissimilar, they all share an intense and accurate perception of the contemporary world, especially those manifestations of it in Texas which have been overlooked or misunderstood.

In a poem like "Crop Duster Disaster," Murphey has caught for all time the sad glory of the cowboy image modernized yet still as untrue as it has ever been, as any such romanticized self-image will be, even as it mesmerizes those who worship its "hard core death defying" look. What Murphey has done in a number of such poems is to reinterpret the heritage we have all lived with uncomfortably but with a certain awe. And though his reinterpretation reveals the reality behind the mask, it is done with such sympathy that even as we acknowledge its essential unreality we are moved by the scene he depicts.

In "A Meeting of Saints," Murphey has revisited the revivals to which his own generation and many later ones have owed their religious upbringings and their grudging sense of a spiritual world. If many of us feel we have left behind such "superstition," Murphey reminds us of an undeniable emptiness to which his "dumpy, red-faced" aunt's revivalism still speaks volumes. For despite the down-to-earth world his aunt returns to after the service is over, during it

she would rise arms extended
and on small tippy toes
dance all around the pulpit
like a toy bear on wheels.

At the same time, while
she shouted and sang, "Hallelujah!"
a tall, long-faced man
in a gray-hung scarecrow suit
would jump flat-footed: Boing!

boing! silently over benches
in great inverted U's lightly;
and an old lost Jewish rabbi
with a long beard would stand
translated, "speaking other tongues."

How my aunt bloomed then
beneath her bonnet like a ripe peach!
Was this the woman who made such
miraculous pies and whose kiss
was apple-sweet?

All the next week I watched
how serious and slow she hoed
her patch of corn, how heavy
the dancing feet went down
the long, hot rows of her days.

In the poet's remembered world of aunts, dare-devil fliers, and men who drink coffee at the Texas Cafe (in "Yippee Yi O Ti Yay"), there is a renewal of spirit much like that of the revival era, when the disbeliever is suddenly lifted unwillingly into a realm of regeneration and greater sympathy, even with those he had laughed at or rejected as cracked or touched in the head, those he held below himself.

Like William Burford and William Barney, Joe Murphey returns us to what is seemingly insignificant but fulfillingly vital in our regional experience. And all three have done so by focusing on where they are, whether at the Capitol grounds in Burford's case, walking a fishing pier in Barney's, or observing in Murphey's a pilot having his coffee at Duffers Cafe the morning after the crash of his crop duster. The result has been a penetration through to the real, a tapping of the poetic reservoir with its allowance of associations never to be depleted in our own generation nor in those to come. When every form of fuel has burned itself out, like the cocksure hare running himself headlong to lesser attractions off the familiar path, these Texas turtles will still be crossing the finish line with their carefully thought-out regional but universal poems that celebrate, reinterpret, and advance the cause of Texas letters. I thank them every time I read their work, as should those truly interested in the real thing: the tortoise poet who will lumber past the technological rabbit that has lost track of where he started for, of why the getting there requires patience and dedication along the way, and of all that it means to stick with the little one receives from any time or place.

Texas Poet as Olympic Medalist

Without a doubt, the publication by Southern Methodist University Press of Vassar Miller's *Collected Poems* is a major event in the short history of Texas letters—if for no other reason than the fact that this represents the first collected poems by a Texas poet.* Although to have her poems collected is an achievement in itself, it is more so when one considers the level of thought and artistry attained by Miller over the span of some forty years of writing. Bringing together all the poetry from eight individual volumes (from 1956 to 1984), as well as work included in her *Selected and New Poems* (1981) and a group of previously uncollected poems, *If I Had Wheels or Love: Collected Poems of Vassar Miller* demonstrates the variety, range, and power of the poet's writing, acclaimed at the time of its first appearances in book form as the most important contemporary religious poetry in America. Ten years ago, in the October 23, 1981, issue of *The Texas Observer*, Larry McMurtry bestowed the laurel on this Houston poet above all other Texas authors. Though born with cerebral palsy and afflicted with a speech impediment, Miller has created some of the most eloquent lines in modern English verse. In an essay entitled "Vassar Miller and Her Peers: A Causerie," collected in *Heart's Invention: On the Poetry of Vassar Miller* (1988), Thomas Whitbread—University of Texas professor and a noted poet in his own right—has proclaimed Miller's "Age of Aquarius, Age of Assassins," a work inspired by the shooting of then presidential candidate George Wallace, "one of the great poems of this century."

My own reading of Vassar Miller's poetry dates from a discovery of her work as anthologized in the 1957 *New Poets of England and America*. Her *Collected Poems* reinforces my impression then and now that indeed her principal subject was and is religious in nature—though not limited to nor by this preoccupation. Much of Miller's early work recalls such seventeenth-century poets as John Donne in England and Edward Taylor in America, and in "The Ghostly Beast"

---

* *The Texas Observer* (October 4, 1991): 18-20.

from her 1963 volume, *My Bones Being Wiser*, she depends heavily on paradox, the metaphysical poet's hallmark:

> Your weight withdrawn weighs burdensome
> Upon my flesh till I become
> The interval between two breaths,
> A life lived out in little deaths.

Characteristic of her finest work, this poem is composed of stanzas with, in her own words, "rhymes like catapulted stones," and is an instance of her tendency to begin a poem with a line ("My broken bones cry out for love") that by the end turns upon itself and inverts the meaning ("My love cries out for broken bones"), a circular effect that evinces her attraction to such forms as the sonnet, the villanelle, and the sestina. Unlike her public poem on George Wallace, "The Ghostly Beast" is representative of her more private writing, although both poems are enhanced, as Whitbread points out in the case of the assassins poem, through the use of strict form, a "rip tide rigorously held in check by the brilliant rhyme scheme." More significantly, "The Ghostly Beast" alludes to—if it does not actually concern— a consistent theme in Miller's poetry: the absence of father, God, and/or lover.

Deprived at her father's death of her chief human support (he it was who first encouraged her writing of poetry), unable to communicate with a silent God except through prayer, and frustrated physically from not being able to experience sexual union, Vassar Miller writes passionately of all three. A concomitant theme is found in a poem like "Letters to a Young Girl Considering a Religious Vocation," where the poet acknowledges that her days have been spent learning "how well we do / to get through our lives alive!" In a similar letter-poem, "Bread-and-Butter Letter Not Sent," she refers to her two primary means of enduring her especially difficult existence without father, God, or lover—that is, through sleep and poetry:

> Dear friend, in the swing of sunlight
> let me hold the knowledge of my pain
> far away, like the sea in a shell[,]
> and wash my wounds for awhile in sleep.

I am sorry to sing you
no more melodious song, yet only
the taste of its notes biting my tongue reminds me,
sometimes, that I am alive.

In "Another Sleep Poem," the poet recalls Donne's great sonnet, "Death Be Not Proud," when she writes that "far more than death sleep soothes me." Instead of a lover, the poet takes to bed only sleep (as she says in "The Final Hunger"), on which evanescent state she has written some of her most vivid poems, as in "Rescue," which describes her return

... from the tides of sleep
The body slackened and aching,
Swaying from tug and sweep
Of the kelp that, glued around it
Like tentacles, have bound it
And dragged it deep to deep.

Once the poet has been "marooned upon the coasts of morning," as she writes in "Bout with Burning," it is her courageous effort to deal with her losses—with living in her imperfect flesh—that leads her to share with an Edward Taylor that Puritan's view that because God can take a special interest in man, corrupt though he may be, it moves him to sing his creator's praises the more, even to glorying in his pigsty of a body. This consolation can be found in such a poem as Miller's "A Duller Moses":

I tremble, dreaming between sleep and sleep
That He, both radiance and incendiary,
In my heart lies as on the cross He lay
(Which bed is fouler?), making my bone-heap—
Oh, monstrous miracle!—God's sanctuary.

The ugliness of her body is a persistent motif in Miller's writing, but she consistently attempts to accept her condition, as in "Casual," where she declares that the grief that "wears" her she "will wear yet /

cut to a pattern with pain's shears, / sown with a fine seam of sorrow, / stitched with tears." She moves on to compare, a la Herrick, her "grief turned into my skin" to the body of a beautiful woman who, she says, will never

> go more proudly
> in silk or satin, velvet or furs . . .
> or with the flounce and flaunt of that body of hers
> proclaim
> more loudly
> or with more shine
> "Mine!"

Miller's poem concludes with the speaker casting aside her grief/skin, and dancing for the Lord in her "crazy bones."

An equally obsessive motif in Miller's poetry, as indicated by the title of her collected poems, is the search for love. In a sonnet entitled "The Quarry"—reminiscent of Shakespeare's sonnet 73— Miller defines love as the "magic creature none can ever snare . . . the air itself, the breath ashake / Among the leaves—the bird no longer there." Similarly, in "Love's Eschatology," the poet discovers that absence paradoxically produces the fullest knowledge of an object of love: "Never has your body / before so budded to my senses / as to my empty fingers." Or in "Thorn in the Flesh," Miller declares "My days are full / but sometimes / only of your absence." Love for Miller is not, however, simply Platonic, for in spite of what she describes metaphorically in "Offering: For All My Loves" as her vessel "shaped to misshapenness / In a hunk of corroded tin," she longs for a physical, even lustful consummation. In place of such, the poet finds, from time to time, a way of being "a stranger in my own skin," as she puts it in "Encounter." In this and other poems she refers or alludes to herself as a stranger, an exile, a refugee, but ultimately, as in "Encounter," she awakens at the word of an unnamed person

> astonished in the streets
> of my identity,

and there you left me, but not before
your flesh, breathed in a muted sentence,
instructed me in mine.

On occasion, as in "Spastics" and "Nuptial Benediction," Miller acknowledges the agony faced by the physically unbeautiful, who "rarely marry, expected to make it with Jesus," "disrobe, so some might guess, / For crosses, not for marriage sheets." Despite a feeling of worthlessness that is expressed or implied because of her inability to know physical love, the poet repeatedly finds that she, like the figure in "For a Senile Woman," is "ransomed from life's discard table," and fortunate we are that Vassar Miller has managed for all these years, as the title of her second book puts it, to "wage war on silence," overcoming not only handicap but self-pity, as well as a body that is, as she says in "Epitaph for a Cripple," a "wry reproach / To athlete mind." For Miller's mind is indeed as agile and muscular as the toned and trained body of any Olympic gold medalist.

While much of Miller's poetry is preoccupied with her private struggles (in the words of her 1984 volume, "to swim on concrete"), there is also the public voice to be heard in the poem on George Wallace and in the many elegies, memorials, and tributes to friends, relatives, her dog Buffy, cats, the singer Sophie Tucker, Billy Carter (brother to the former president), her maid Rosa Sells, Thomas Merton, and even the wife of Lot. Miller's ability to write heart-felt and insightful observations on others' lives is owing, it would seem, to her own deeply pondered life. And while it has perhaps been more difficult for her to find humor in her own condition, in the more public poems there is at times a touching bit of comic relief at work, as in "Elegy for a Good Ole Boy" and " A Rage for Order for Rosa." The former remembers how "Thay taken [Billy Carter's] beers," and it "made my heart melt / 'cause I knowed what he felt." The poet recalls how she herself behaved as Billy did when "'I done things I shouldn't / 'n I caught the blame, / done things I should (Wouldn't / you know?), caught the same'." The poet ends her poem with this appeal: "Lord, give him the cheer / of many a beer. / There [in heaven] it won't hurt his liver / 'n nobody don't ever / have no hangover." Like the elegy for Billy, "A Rage for Order," one of two poems for Rosa Sells, employs humorous dialect for treatment of the charge that God is a poor housekeeper. "You wouldn't want Him in your house," the poet exclaims in Rosa's voice:

> No Lordy! Like them mens, no good at sweeping,
> And look, just will you, all those leaves let loose!
> That great big broom God makes those old fall winds with
> Like He ain't thought about nobody's yard.

Miller's poem entitled "Mrs. Lot" also contains a number of humorous touches, in this case in connection with an issue in need of reconsideration: the reason women are "apt to cling to their homes

>   not having
> in those days much else to cling to—and
> what if they clung—like Lot's poor wife whose
> name we don't even know to recall, she
> having to pull up stakes and get out
> just because some men liked other men, that
> being none of her affair, besides which
> she'd never liked Uncle Abraham's loose
> foot she swore he was born with, and so
> she has long gazed back on her past which she
> couldn't put back any more than a pulled
> tooth. . . .

In another essay in *Heart's Invention: On the Poetry of Vassar Miller*, Texas A & M professor Paul Christensen has attempted to define the Texas side of Miller's poetry, looking at it as an expression of a frontier vision, in particular in terms of its religious concerns. (He does not, however, cite nor discuss in this regard her poem "Revival" as an instance of what Thomas Whitbread sees as Miller's use of a religious setting for a grand poetic effect.) While Christensen makes an interesting point, comparing Miller's vision and situation to those of Emily Dickinson during the frontier period in New England, he does not establish as convincing a case for Miller as critic Charlotte McClure does for Dickinson in the former's "Expanding the Canon of American Renaissance Frontier Writers: Emily Dickinson's 'Glimmering Frontier'," printed in *The Frontier Experience and the American Dream* (Texas A & M University Press, 1989). Nonetheless, Christensen does identify the most thoroughly Texas piece in Miller's work—"Whitewash of Houston," which first appeared in the 1984 volume *Struggling to Swim on Concrete*. Christensen is correct in thinking that this is the kind of Texas poem that attracts me. But it is not simply because this is an identifiably Texas poem; it is also because it is one of the truly unique pieces in Miller's *Collected Poems*: stylistically; in its focus on her hometown's history; and in its subtle blending of the lives of poet and place.

In this two-part poem that depicts various characteristics of Houston, Miller employs a series of two-word phrases that appear, in part I, at intervals of 14 or 15 lines (almost sonnet-like): "mother small"; "mother sleek"; "mother gunning." In part II the phrases are closer (separated by 11, 7, and 10 lines): "mother mad"; "mother fed"; "mother light." In each group of lines Houston is seen from a feminine perspective, and in both parts of the poem some of the descriptive passages seem to parallel Miller's own self-portraits found elsewhere in the *Collected Poems*:

> she stuffs her mouth
> with garbage drooled onto her front until
> she drops dead in her tracks to bed hot for
> that prick and prong of sleep's sweet long and hard
> . . .
> gunning
> down eerie corridors of her dark self
> dented and bent
> . . .
> the hollow of her womb
> more hollow than the opening leading to it
> to gobble down her shacks and spires till time
> has hulled them all like winter's dried pecans.

I may be reading the private dimension into the poem, but there is no doubt that Miller identifies deeply with what has happened to

Houston during her own lifetime. (The passage on the destruction of shacks in the city's Black neighborhoods will remind readers of the May 17, 1991, article in *The Texas Observer* entitled "Razing History: Black Houstonians Fight For a Piece of Their Heritage.") Each passage begins with a line that ends with one of the "mother" phrases and each is a single unpunctuated sentence that runs on with an essentially unrhymed but absolutely majestic sound. The poem's title is paradoxical in that it suggests the idea of covering up Houston's cruel record by recounting it as a tribute to this mother figure of a city:

> Who would have thought of her as mother fed
> and fudged till fattened on her lentil vigils
> as open as her covert cesspools ripe
> with the rich grain of avarice and April's
> froth of green and dogwood's lace hung over
> the land and greening all her lawns until
> she lies down with her apron smelling of summer?

There is nothing quite like this piece either among Miller's own poems about Texas or among those by other Texans. The rhetorical control and the weaving of a place's particulars into a fabric with an historical point of view both private and public—these are some of the many exceptional features of this masterful performance. For me this work stands as Vassar Miller's finest effort, and even though I admit to a personal program in my own reading of Texas poets, I firmly believe that "Whitewash of Houston" encompasses and even goes beyond all the best of Miller's most accomplished qualities. Naturally other readers will find their own favorites among her 385 poems, but then there are enough masterpieces in the *Collected Poems* to satisfy everyone—Texan, the religiously inclined, the student of confessional, deep image, or feminist poetry, or just the lover of the well-made, athletic poem.

Toward a Texas Renaissance

With the passing of the big three in Texas letters—Dobie, Bedichek, and Webb (a sort of literary equivalent to the King, Goodnight, and XIT ranches, and identifiable in many respects with that rural way of life)—not much has been heard from the Lone Star State.* A few novelists like Larry McMurtry and William Humphrey have staked out their claims and been made into movies, but for a concerted effort aimed at reviving the serious achievements of DB&W, little has been undertaken in that direction. McMurtry has clearly made the most significant contribution toward an understanding of the modern Texas writer's relation to his region's history, at the same time that he has attempted to record and comment upon the contemporary situation in which such a writer finds himself. But neither the novel nor the essay is the genre to look to for an authentic link with the past or a penetrating account of the present. It is from the poet that we must ultimately seek the meaning of where we have been, the problems with how we are, and a prophecy as to what the future can hold, once we have learned from his/her songs our true inheritance and from his/her recitals of our backsliding ways the challenge of the here and now.

Unfortunately, there is still today the stigma of any such regional tag as "Texas poet." We would be universal, not down-home. This despite the fact that most all of our celebrated poetry has grown from a clearly definable region, that of Williams, Sandburg, Lowell, Olson, or Jeffers. Frost himself said he would first be an individual, then a native of a given ground, and only last a universal poet. For many in our own day the difficulty is not so much learning to know a specific region or to identify with it; rather, it is a matter of retaining a regional feel or developing it once we have been uprooted. So many poets today earn their livings as teachers—which may or may not be a handicap, depending on the individual—that it is common to find

---

* Introduction to *The New Breed: An Anthology of Texas Poets* (Malta, IL: Prickly Pear Press, 1973), pp. 10-17.

these recorders of a region's heartbeat transplanted where they never quite belong, and unable, once their profession calls, to carry on as poets of any one place. Forced by the academic system to leave the state where they had put down their roots and received their education, their fundamental memories, and their basic inspiration, they often either dry up or adopt themes and manners untrue to their poetic nature. Thus far I have been speaking mainly about my own predicament, although a few other poets gathered in *The New Breed* may share my experience and point of view. But since only about a fourth of the poets in this anthology are in "exile," the concerns of most are not necessarily my own. Even to the rest, however, being a Texas poet is, as Carolyn Maisel has written, "a matter of survival in the most difficult sense." And yet this same poet is "convinced that for reasons we all know but find hard to explain . . . Texas is one of the most fertile artistic environments in America," if only because of this necessity to survive in alien surroundings. For those who find none of this reason enough for a collection of Texas poetry, it may appear that I simply have wanted to make an anthology, which is true—one entitled after a phrase in Walt Whitman's 1855 Preface to *Leaves of Grass*. For it has long been a dream of mine to awaken in Texas poets a sense of the heritage they share and to encourage in the state's publishers and their audiences a greater receptivity to a new variety of regional writing.

One result of having lived in another section of the nation has been the advantage of gaining a certain objectivity with regard to the question of regional literature. For many poets, rejected by those readers for whom their poems were originally intended, there is a warm reception awaiting their work outside their native states. This, though a comforting fact, does not excuse a region's disregard for the writings of her native sons and daughters who render such a vital service. It is the age-old "no man's a prophet in his own land." To some, even being granted asylum elsewhere is no bargain, for, as John Steinbeck observes in *Travels With Charley*, "A Texan outside of Texas is a foreigner." Nevertheless, I for one have found that Midwest audiences do not look upon me as a curiosity but listen with the same enthusiasm with which they hear their own region's poets. This is the consequence, I believe, of a respect on the part of such listeners for the regional poet and all that he/she represents. It may just be the nature of a Texas poet's condition that he/she be ever a singer in a strange land, without ever leaving his/her native soil. Of the poets collected here who are now living coast to coast, some return often, others infrequently, to the towns and cities of Texas, drawn back as by a loadstone. Some never felt at home in an atmosphere they basically considered hostile to poetry. Others long to land a job in one of the many urban centers they grew up in or moved to from small communities in search of even a meager intellectual climate. Regardless of which attitude it may be, it is evident from the poems in this collection that Texas has had a deep effect upon her poets. And in return, her poets have responded with a poetry which both does her honor and calls her to account for serious shortcomings.

Dave Hickey, a writer of short fiction who apparently, like many others, gave up the art when he found both regional and national publications unreceptive to his Texas stories, once made an observation about the state that seemed so obvious after he had pointed it out and that struck me as worthy of a Texas poet's constant awareness. He wrote in the University of Texas student literary magazine, *Riata*, for spring 1965, that "it is hard to be a texan, for texas from a given point is always extending." Hickey illustrates this by noting how every area of the state becomes in a sense part of the region on which it borders, though is more than any one of these (Louisiana, New Mexico, Oklahoma, Mexico) by virtue of being something of them all. This may seem merely another basis for a joke on the Texas size complex, but more than just a geographical consideration, it tells us that Texas is indeed rich in a variety of cultures (the plains, Faulkner's South, the Rocky Mountain plateau, and the Spanish and Indian influence of Mexico), and that unlike Illinois, for example, where the state is essentially the same from one end to the other, to be from East Texas is nothing like being from El Paso, although something of all the sections is present in each. So that if, as Steinbeck asserts, "Texas is a state of mind," it is a complex one. This anthology demonstrates such complexity, for these poets have indeed cultivated it. Here a reader will find all the state's contrasting landscapes, with the images and ideas those suggest. The reader also will discover a vast array of styles and forms, from concrete poetry to traditional and experimental sonnets, from narrative and surrealist to lyric and imagist poems, not to mention representation from the prominent minority groups of the region, since every poet is, by definition, a minority group of one.

Unlike the Texas anthologies of the past, this present volume is far-reaching in its implications; certainly it is not the usual cactus and cow-shit collection associated with the Southwest. Its themes, its techniques are those which may be found in the work of the nation's leading contemporary poets, published in such prestigious magazines as *Poetry*, *The New Yorker*, *The North American Review*. And in fact a number of these Texas poets have appeared in those same periodicals. More importantly, such young poets as Charles Behlen and Leon Stokesbury have contributed to many of the smaller magazines. The same holds true for James Hoggard, Seth Wade, and Del Marie Rogers, and this is significant, for as Richard Kostelanetz points out in *Margins* 8 (Milwaukee), "All new directions in serious writing first appeared in small-circulation journals; so have all the American modernism's major writers." On the other hand, poets in *The New Breed* have by no means turned their backs on their own unique heritage. Even though these poets may give the lie to any characterization of Texas writing as simply concerned with ranch life, they remain faithful to a literary tradition which draws on the Spanish contribution to the region, the stoic character of its people accustomed to the land's undependable ways, and through the closeness of earth and sky to a sense of man's nearness to a larger scheme of things. Far from the famous braggadocio associated with Texans, it is this latter aspect of the poet-state relationship which has inspired a poetry well aware of man's lowliness in the presence of natural and cultural wonders. Linked to this is the poets' feeling of both shame and humility before the inheritance they have come into. It is especially the Spanish contribution to their culture that causes them pain when they consider the disrespect shown this ethnic background, at the same time that they are fully cognizant of their great good fortune in having been handed this largesse by the mysterious migration of peoples. The fact, then, that Texas spreads out wagon-wheel fashion to touch on so many and distinctive features of the Southwest, as those of its religions, languages, histories, and arts, may make it difficult to be a Texan, but it also offers, particularly to the poet, the makings of a true enrichment. And it is to this possibility that the Texas poet now aspires.

Although no poet of the past has achieved a composite of these various natural and cultural elements, it is my firm belief that many of the poets here have at the very least begun this valuable process of amalgamation. In the case of a few, such as Peter Wild, this process already has resulted in highly imaginative poems which combine a western tall-tale brand of surrealism with both social criticism and folk wisdom. Several of the poets, among them Robert Bonazzi and Stan Rice, exhibit a sophisticated understanding of trends in poetry of other nations. What many of these poets are doing lives up to the spirit of DB&W's instructions to "have a genius for soaking in and oozing out"; to preserve "a tenderer regard for the whole of the animate world"; and not to be so utopian as to isolate ourselves from what others have done. And if the poets here are "the new breed," this implies that there has been an older line from which these descendants have taken their pedigree, either in imitation or reaction or both. To overlook the earlier poets of the region, or those of earlier generations who are still quite active in the development of a regional literature, would be more than oversight, it would be a true sin of omission, a lack of gratitude for their contribution, and a self-defeating blow. For not to know from whence one has evolved is to understand little about where one is going. I want immediately to acknowledge my own indebtedness to John Graves's *Goodbye to a River*, a sourcebook for many Texas poets; to the Texas poems of Thomas Whitbread and William D. Barney; R.G. Vliet's "Clem Maverick"; a poem on Dobie, "Acrostic," by Tom Sutherland; and William Burford's "South, Southwest." The work of these writers, and that of many others, among them Howard McCord, Judson Crews, Vassar Miller, and Archibald Henderson, has shaped a generation of younger writers by showing how a Texan may find in his region the form and content of fine contemporary poetry. These are the giants upon whose shoulders we hope to have climbed. If we see beyond them, it redounds upon so many pioneers for having furnished us the wherewithal.

Any anthology is limited by time, space, and the editor's own peculiar taste. *The New Breed* is no exception. For this reason there are poets of the present generation who have been excluded, unknown, or simply impossible to contact. Some are, in my mind and in those of many other readers, already strongly identified with other regions. Three of these, who certainly are otherwise deserving of inclusion here, are Betty Adcock (widely published as a North Carolina poet), Lewis MacAdams (known as a New York poet and closely associated with that "school" through its magazines and anthologies), and Paul Foreman (editor of *Hyperion* in California). Two poets in this present collection, Stan Rice and Robert Bonazzi, have been publishing from California and New York, respectively, but both have been closely connected with Texas letters—Rice through his "On the Murder of Martin Luther King" (in *Quickly Aging Here*), with its study of the sources of a Texan's racism, and Bonazzi by reason of his outstanding magazine, *Latitudes*, which he edited for several years in Houston. Such poets as Franklin Haar, John Igo, and Nefthalí de León work in modes which do not exactly fit into this particular collection; nonetheless, they and many others are out there doing their part, and this anthology in no way intends to discount their work. On the contrary, it is the aim of *The New Breed* to encourage more rather than less diversity, at the same time that it calls for a unified effort for the good of a regional consciousness. Another anthology would serve as a corrective to the limitations of this one and would thereby further demonstrate the wide range of Texas poetry.

And what, then, is a "Texas poet"? Perhaps it is, as Steinbeck suggests, a state of mind, but the extreme case of such. Perhaps no such "animal" has yet been bred, with more crossbreeding required before we can arrive at the genuine article. And if this is so, then hopefully this anthology may prove a necessary step toward the creation of such a "critter." For to "breed" a Texas poet, as I envision him or her, would mean that the process of amalgamation had reached a level at which the term "Texas poet" would be synonymous with an awareness of, and respect for, the various challenging and inspiring strains of a line known not for being thoroughbred but for blending such strains in a way that does credit to each separately and to all in combination. This is what any region's poetry, I believe, must aim for, and in doing so will both define its bounds and transcend them.

People, places, and good poetry go together: a truism. But there can be no truth in this statement unless the interdependence of the three components is taken seriously. Always the poetry faithful to the best in man lives with and evaluates where and how he is, has been, and wishes to be, and I trust that this is true of the poems in this collection. What strikes me most about the anthology as a whole is, indeed, its indebtedness to the past and its hope for the future. A young poet like Charles Behlen, dedicated to the art of poetry with all his intellectual and emotional energy (which is great even after painting houses for a living), bodes well for the years ahead. All the poets here are paying their respects to the past, and in looking both backwards and forwards lend evidence of Texas' maturing literature. As a sign of this dual perspective, the anthology has fallen, simply through the fate of an alphabetical arrangement, into that same healthy pattern: the first poem, peering out the back of the bus at the older orders, and the last, contemplating those yet to come. In between these windows and doors to the past and future, the poems here focus, finally, on what it means to be in the 1970s full of song and concern.

Introduction to the Texas Section of
Southwest: A Contemporary Anthology

As much as size, the variety encompassed by Texas—of land-scapes, cultures, hopes, and regrets—has undermined the conscious and unconscious lives of Texas writers.* Most every literary artist who has sought to evoke or probe the nature of the place—its people, its heritages, its languages—has met with overwhelming demands, made on him or her by diffusiveness (in terms both of territory and of the grandiose treatment required), as well as by the necessity of creating with no audience or with a hostile one at best. There always has been a tendency among the natives of the state to distrust and belittle any-thing homegrown, except for beef and barrels of crude. This is even reflected in a drawing from the early fifties—meant to encourage investment in the state's insurance companies—of a cow pictured with its head in Texas, grazing, while New Yorkers milk its udders.

The result of this situation is that many a Texas writer has settled elsewhere, or for a limited view of subject and style, in hopes of achiev-ing even the off-and-on respectable label of "regionalist." In addition to the reluctance of many Texas writers to produce "rooted" material, a haughty challenge is inherent in the heart of the state itself—that *it*, by God, will take more from an artist than it will ever give. Recently, despite the odds, Texas writers have begun to return, in spirit and in person, to a well which seemed eternally dry, and have found even to their own surprise a thirst-quenching source left long untapped. The new writing derives basically from an acceptance of limitations, of the small gains for inordinate pains, from a desire to plumb the depths rather than just to scratch the surface with clichéd drill bits, and from a dedication to making do on what is seen at last as suitably native: the stubby subject that is yet durable as a common post oak; the cedar chopper's furry, rusting, sweet-scented stake which, as he would say, may be crooked as a dog's hind leg but can stand for a hundred years.

---

* *Southwest: A Contemporary Anthology*, ed. Karl and Jane Kopp, and Bert Lanier Stafford III (Albuquerque, NM: Red Earth Press, 1977), pp. 71-73.

Likened throughout its history to hell, both by the transient visitor and the settler here to stay, Texas, with famed heat and monotonous plains, has been looked upon as not even fit for the devil himself. This attitude, along with the typical western image and its wearying burden, has deprived her artists of the ability to come to grips with the truly diverse and deeply fertile character of the region. For the land has proven a magnet of torment attracting peoples as distinct as Scotch-Irish, Mexican, Comanche, Italian, Black, German, Swede, and Jew—and would seem to call for no less than a Dante, a Milton, or a Whitman to tally its account. But it may be that Texas will produce instead a throng of minor voices of every race, raised not in praise of any one vision but as an expression of thanks for each and especially for those lower on the totem pole.

In the state's make-or-break crucible, the new writer faces the same fearful yet inspiring prospects on the literary score as his forebears knew on that of cactus range or oil patch. The healthiest signs are that native writers are taking Texas seriously, are also seeing the humor in many sides of the state taken too soberly in the past. As to any place offering the artist a ready-made pattern for theme and form, it remains true as ever that these the artist must make for himself, inventing in a sense even the place itself. To answer her haughtiest challenges, even knowing that in the end the writing may turn out to be a little-regarded testament to the tight-fisted nature of a place that has ever insisted on the impossible from its inhabitants (while somehow in return promising and even supplying a measure heaped rare as it is real), is an undertaking that offers a potential for creativity unequaled at present by any other region of the nation.

Traveling from Fort Worth in the north (Amon Carter's come-uppance reply to dandified Dallas), through Waco (home of the Baptists and of Brann the iconoclast), Austin (capital city with its industry of "non-polluting," political paperwork and the seat of the sprawling University system), San Antonio (welcome mat for the Chicano-Mexican migration), swinging near but missing sight and sound of killdeer and Gulf at Corpus Christi, passing on to the orange groves of Harlingen and finally arriving at palm-treed Brownsville on the border, the changing sameness, the dry and then humid heat, altered styles of year-long lightweight dress, drawling modes of address, all seem too much for any one author to handle. If he knows those areas lying beyond this narrow strip down the middle of the state, he will feel even more humbled, or rather pulled apart by its procrustean bed, incapacitated in the face of what will strike him as great stretches of the imagination, a beckoning like Scylla and Charybdis on either side threatening to wreck even an enlarged sense of place on the vast reaches of piney woods to the east (where men have lost their ways and never come out alive) or the brush country endless and exhausting to the west.

Looking to the skies near Kingsville, one takes in the long wavering lines of geese written against the billowing clouds above alternating marsh and prickly pear, but how to get them down, how to imitate such alexandrines escaping the coastal page, with that same sweep and grandeur of their going? In fields extending flat to the horizon, bundled hay lies like pungent, compact quatrains the Texas poet can barely dream of penning before the image of mesquite or oil slick breaks in upon his romantic reveries. Just as he has registered his impressions, so many prize-winning Herefords of words, the blatant city lights and urban accents put them down as out of date, cornball, too closely tied to a tradition no town boy in his right mind could ever accept. Yet he must feel that to record alone the hotrod racket of metropolitan streets is to remain too silent upon the ingenuous twang of his country cousin's rockabilly guitar. Listening to the Mexican-looking, native-born Texan at the chain-store register making change in two languages at once, the writer wants to blend his images, his words, his rhythms, but wouldn't that be copying what is natural to the Chicano, cutting in, riding around on a fad? How does one man find it in himself to incorporate such diversity? Where in himself can he honestly discover the right to so much land, so many tongues, at a time when corporate holdings present such a singularly evil aspect?

Indeed, it is this very paradoxical and unsettling state of things that comprises the stuff of his richest writing. And we are back to variety and the question of whether one writer can contain it all, whether he should even worry when he has managed but a meager hold on a minor part of the whole. Today there is no one figure we look to in Texas as laureate or leader, and why should we, when the landscape demands more than a single voice can ever hope to sing, urges its artists to try their hands at every available form, denying none, just as the land would have not a thorn nor a devil's claw less in its array of satanic plants. What is needed, then, and what we are beginning to get, is a harkening (here and back) to the many stories and poems old and new, those of the folk and those of the refined, an encouraging of each in what it would say of a place we can only know once it has been sounded by those who love its ways, its begrudging fields that yield less than we foolishly wish for, yet more than any man or woman will ever need to make it on.

Faced by the vastness of the task, Texas writers may in the long-run come to create a smaller art, one more in keeping with their sense of the worth of each man's contribution in a land where the mythical individualist is seen at last as not so heroic in himself as he is in relation to the grander scheme of true regional representation. The Texas writers of our day indicate that they are on that road by their modest carriage and the authentic message they are learning to bear.

Who's Afraid of the Big Bad Poem?

Certainly Whitman was not, nor was William Carlos Williams, and neither are most of the poets of the 1970s.* Pablo Neruda of Chile was the last of the great bad poets, according to James Dickey, who went over like a lead balloon on saying so before a gathering of Latin American scholars. The idea was not original with Dickey (nor meant the way it was taken), yet serious as the claim has been in some quarters, it seems unlikely to stand the test of time, since the "bad" line of Whitman and Neruda appears due for a long and international respect. Even before the nineteenth century, there were other great poets who feared no evil from writing poems of which the New Critics would never approve. Thanks to Whitman, Williams, and Neruda, today's crop of poets is not intimidated in the least by the prospect of falling short of perfection. This observation is intended only slightly as a tongue-in-cheek criticism of the contemporary poem, for despite certain reservations about the promiscuous poetics of some of our generation, I feel that by and large we should not be cowed by a vision of the perfect poem. The fact is that the recent out-pouring (and publishing) of poetry by poets hardly recognizable and rarely identifiable with any one school is the result of a healthy view established by those three American giants who found the writing of poems a concomitant to, in Neruda's phrase, our residence here on earth. The books, anthologies, and saddle-stitched collections received of late by *The Texas Quarterly* testify to a stimulating array of writing that might be attributed to a disregard for high art but which, considering its quality, seems more the product of a greater love for and fearlessness in the making of poems.

Granted, a distinction must be made immediately between the "bad" work of a great writer and the best performance of a poetaster. What may be justified as innovation in one author (Gertrude Stein noted how the new may be ugly when first attempted) can be simply mediocrity in those who adopt the posture but fail to

---

* *The Texas Quarterly* 20, no. 4 (Winter 1977): 190-199.

render any service of substance. There is a Whitmanesque looseness which is deceptively informal or, stated another way, is subtly formal. Thus, it may be that looseness for its own sake has no place in poetry as such. While the poet may properly require a period for loosening up his lines and for learning a feel for his or her lives, there may be little to justify serving an apprenticeship in public. Nonetheless, if the poet does choose to publish at an early stage, critical judgment may aid in this whole loosening-up process by considering if a work is significantly "bad" or is not yet beyond what Pound called writing poorly out of ignorance and inexperience. Ultimately, I think, it should be clear that the recent explosion of poetry publishing has at least carried forward one aspect of Whitman's vision of poetry-America: "the tremendous audacity of its crowds and groupings and the push of its perspective spreads with crampless and flowing breadth and showers its prolific and splendid extravagance."

Representing the broadest cross section of regions, races, and styles—within the limits of this omnibus review—*The Face of Poetry* (Gallimaufry Press) collects the work (and full-page photographs) of 101 poets, from coast to coast. Perhaps because the photographer and principal editor, La Verne Harrell Clark, is a Texan by birth and for many years a resident of Tucson, there is a fair concentration of poets from the Southwest, in particular from the states of New Mexico and Arizona (a dozen at least), but all deserve to be included, even those who may be less prominent than many others excluded from this selection subtitled the work of "Two Significant Decades—the 60s & the 70s." While there is only one poem per poet, the choices are generally excellent and quite representative, though not the usual pieces which we associate with such figures as William Stafford and Richard Eberhart. Speaking of the photographs of the poets, Eberhart states in his foreword to the anthology that these are not the posed, impersonal portraits we often know poets by but rather are "off-hand, informal depictions" which "increase a reader's interest by doing what LaVerne Clark does so well in this focus on the chance moment, a special moment of being." Likewise, the poems themselves frequently are "off-hand, informal depictions."

If contemporary poets fear anything, it is to be too formal. The conversational tone is, of course, cultivated. The dangers of this studied naturalness are evident in Stephen Dunn's contribution, though he does have better work to offer elsewhere:

My poems are approximately true.
The games I play and how I play them
are the arrows you should follow: they'll take you
to the enormous body of a child. It is not
that simple. At parties I have been known to remove
from the bookshelf the kind of book
that goes best with my beard.

Here even the poet's self-parody is overly cute and self-conscious. A better effort deriving from the "song of myself" tradition is Dan Gerber's "A Fine Excess," which pays direct homage to Whitman and recalls Neruda in its great leaps in sea and space. The title of the poem suggests an appreciation for the epical, even though the speaker admits "I never learn from experience." Gerber's main point is that the excessive in poetry is a fine thing. In his case, the poetry seems to support his contention, though in other instances in the anthology the freedoms taken are somewhat annoying, as in Charles Simic's "Further Adventures of Charles Simic"—a clever analogy involving the question of his being afraid of death, which ends with the line: "His tongue will slash his throat." Fortunately, however, much of the work here is extremely moving and rings true even when it is apparent that the poets are "playing" with, for example, an ethnic theme. Robert J. Conley's "Self-Portrait: Microcosm, or, Song of Mixed Blood" builds a sad commentary on the loss of "the ancient forms" when a half-breed can only hunt "with the channel selector." Leroy Quintana's "Untitled" touches on a similar paradise lost, that of his grandfather's world, where the poet was first taught the four directions:

He spoke their names as if they were
one of only a handful of things
a man needed to know

My favorite photograph is of a friend, Karl Kopp, whose poem, "The Hanging Man," contains characteristic lines from this most hard-looking, soft-hearted of men:

        one cow blunders close
horned like a bull
Look I don't want trouble
Git

        when from the barn a sudden cry
(I'd thought it empty
but a calf of course
not two weeks old so Denver told me)
this its mother with bulk and horn
to brave the man-thing
(and now I see she trembles)

It's okay
I have my own young son to guard
to love so hard it sometimes shakes me too

This excerpt forms part of Kopp's recently released collection, *Yarbrough Mountain* (Baleen Press), a book which recreates the life of Arkansas mountaineers with whom Kopp lived as neighbor and friend.

A really lovely photo and beautiful "last song / i'll ever sing" are those of Joy Harjo. On the other hand, Maxine Kumin's head-erect, Olympic-posture pose goes well with her rather uptight poem, "Body and Soul: A Meditation." Appropriately, a number of the pieces feature autobiographical snapshots we can match up with the facing photographs, as in Richard Shelton's case, where he writes,

you won't have to look close
to see what I am
or what I want to become
or that I'm not becoming it

Another enigmatic poem that makes one look to the photo to try and discover what the poet is getting at is Miguel González-Gerth's

"Tragicomic Conceit":

> Behold here a man at once rapt and afraid:
> Though he is the betrayer, he looks the betrayed.

Since Clark's book is designed as much to showcase the faces as it is to present the poems, it is difficult to do the anthology justice without reproducing both. But for those wishing to see *their* favorite contemporaries caught by the camera's eye, as well as to enjoy many fine poems, this collection will serve as a valuable reference for the faces of poets whose work already is known and admired and for the poetry of those whose work will move readers to want to view the faces that go with it, and vice versa.

Another but more limited collection—restricted to the poets of a single state—is *Travois, An Anthology of Texas Poetry* (Thorp Springs Press). Despite this regional limitation, there is no hint here of parochialism or of narrowness of approach, attitude, or subject matter. What struck me from the first was the great energy this anthology makes manifest. For one thing, there are 156 poets represented (the same number of pages in the book but containing many more poems), and there are still others who could have been included, such as Leon Stokesbury. The sense of a ground swell in Texas writing is clearly evinced by this collection. As coeditors Paul Foreman and Joanie Whitebird so aptly phrase it in their brief introduction, this anthology of Texas poetry gathers "like a summer storm out of the gulf." So overwhelming is the amount of poetry and so electrifying is it in so many different ways that it seems pointless even to mention that there are weaker efforts among a "front" that has moved upon the arid Texas poetry scene (of a few years back) with remarkable power and the refreshing aroma of our own native soils and seasons. To continue with the editors' analogy, a reviewer can only say that the forecast, for those interested in the present Texas poetry/weather conditions, is one of scattered showers—some of the poems hit, others will pass over with hardly a shadow to cool the emotions or to stimulate them with thunderous words. I certainly have my own favorites, but every reader will find his or hers as well. On recommending the book to a creative-writing class, I found my students surprising me by their critical reactions to poems I had not fully appreciated. For the record I would like to say that I found Ryan Bernard's "The Second Coming (of the Flaming Wino)" a particularly intriguing piece, one to which the anthology introduced me. Among those poems I had seen elsewhere and encountered again in *Travois* with renewed pleasure, let me take note of Walter McDonald's "The Hammer," a fine poem from his *Caliban in Blue*, and also Charles Behlen's "Keen Brake." Other pieces that I did not know include Robert Bonazzi's "How I Became a Poet," Richard Sale's "Stilts and Other Vehicles," poems by Les Standiford, Sandra Lynn, Naomi Shihab, and too many others to list. The book is an absolute must for those concerned for the present and future of Texas poetry.

Naomi Shihab [Nye] is probably the leading female light on the Texas poetry scene today. Born in 1952 in St. Louis, she has been a resident of Texas since 1967, working for several years as a Writer-in-the-Schools with the Texas Commission on the Arts and Humanities. Her poetry is characterized by its attention to everyday sights, sounds, and routines. The opening piece from her *Tattooed Feet*, part of editor Dwight Fullingim's *Texas Portfolio* chapbook series (published by B. Weberlein), sets the tone and almost religious attitude of her poetry's "Pilgrimage" to the holy land of the near and diminutive:

> If we have destinations
> they are small,
> they can be walked to . . .

This statement grows out of an interest in "tightly wound cabbage rolls" and "hair braided / so it won't come loose," though the connection between imagery and statement is itself fairly loose. For Shihab this looseness does not seem to bother her, since, as she states elsewhere in comparing her poetry with sunlight,

> It is coming through
> touching plants
> scars on the old wood floors
> in a new light way
> I have everything

to say
I could begin
anywhere

Shihab's theory is that art "is very small, / lives in miniature caves in the hillside / and comes out for crumbs." Her poems are essentially small, start from anywhere, but generally end by winning us over. In one line she can capture what little our repetitive lives come to, surprising us with how rich that smallness really is. Not that she attempts to make anything special out of what she merely presents with simple but subtle music. As she says in speaking of her grandmother's tattooed feet,

They have enough to do without my
making them more than they are.

In "Little Blanco River," Shihab even entreats the small to remain that way:

no one makes a state park out of you
you're not deep enough

little blanco river
don't ever get too big

If these poems verge on the sentimental in their encouraging of the slight and the underdog, this is very difficult to fault, principally because Shihab's manner of expressing such views is fresh and engaging. At times the somewhat mawkish philosophy does become a bit overexposed:

there was nothing obscure about melons
nothing involved about yams

if she were to have anything to do with the world
these would be her translators

More often than not, however, there is just the right amount of imagery and statement. One of the best examples of this combination is to be found in "Night Shift," a poem not included in the present collection but also published by the *Texas Portfolio/Poetry*Texas* imprint. I quote from this piece as an example of one of Shihab's finest to date:

> At 2:00 a.m. the world is populated
> by a mysterious breed.
> Pale-skinned, the creatures shake, sweep, & dust.
> . . .
> Children live for years
> without knowing they exist.
> . . .
> I polish the counter,
> fill each tin canister with sugar & tea,
> stack the tickets on their neat metal spear.
>
> And I know, wherever I appear to be in the world,
> I will always be here first.
> This dark task is tattooed on my heart,
> pure & necessary.
> I will do it over & over
> as long as it needs to be done.

In contrast to Shihab's simplicity, Alison Touster's obfuscating diction in *The First Movement* (Bk Mk Press) has the effect of overkill. A poem with great possibilities subject-wise, "The Cock Fight," never comes to life because the poet is too intent on employing a vocabulary that interferes with any sense of immediacy:

> We sit outside the small house:
> Sturdy, incongruous beside the tall corn
>
> We wait, ourselves somewhat incongruous in the light

This kind of writing does strike me as bad, simply because it is so wordy and so concerned with setting an internal mood that seems neither to matter in the poem nor to be allowed to come into focus on its own, repeating a word ("incongruous") which is more proper in prose fiction, if even there. It may be unfair to characterize an entire book by one poem, yet the rest of this collection is marred by just this type of word choice or phraseology: "avuncular," "curvature," "radical territory," "gradual disownment." There is *bad* writing, as the Black poet would remind us, and then there is simply bad writing, unredeemed by any sort of stimulating, daring, or antipoetic but authentic qualities. What Touster's poems lack is a context for the technical vocabulary, some ironic playing off of poetic and unpoetic, some sensual atmosphere able to absorb the jargon and make of it an integral part of the composition. Until she provides such a context, the words will remain flat and inert, which are other words for bad writing.

Four Bk Mk Poets (Bk Mk Press) is a collection of women writers ranging in age from the early twenties to the early seventies. Represented here are themes and techniques reaching back to Emily Dickinson (in the work of Virginia Scott Miner) and forward to Denise Levertov (in the poems of Jari Dykstra), while the poetry of Joan Yeagley and Heather Wilde speaks for the now generation in its concern for politics and therapeutics. However, even though this book tends to include a wide variety of styles and subjects, there are few poems here that exhibit a rightness of form or expression. Miner's work sounds convincing as structured thought, but in its urge to imitate Dickinson it too often mistakes form for substance. The verses click off nicely but finally far too neatly.

What we have in this volume is complete fearlessness of bad writing. The attitude seems to be not to sweat the bad, just to get to the good and let the rest take care of itself. There is almost no desire to discourage the inept phrase or to cut the gab, rather to let it lie where it happens to fall and to rush on to another catchy analogy, as in Yeagley's title piece from her section of poems: "bureaucracies of crawdads backing into holes." There are good lines at times, but this seems accidental or incidental to the larger effort, which is taken up with piling on pointless, unrelated observations or "meaningful" pronouncements. Yeagley handles descriptions of dances and body movements well, but in the same poem will lapse into a heavy-handed statement of a trite idea. "The Stripper" has many fine touches yet concludes with a stanza that all but cancels everything that has gone before: "Tell me, did Eve / Have such tiny feet / And how did she pass / In the Ordinary world?" Ultimately, Virginia Scott Miner's "old-fashioned" poems outshine her sister poets' Erica Jong-inspired liberated-relevant outcries. Miner calmly renders a version of life in towns where

> It's not hypocrisy, we like to think,
> only impossibility
> of saying, "I am I," and having
> others reply in kind.

Here is the fine first stanza of Miner's "Frames":

> It's a small town where a Latin teacher
> almost got fired by the American Legion
> because she took *The Nation* and listened
> to a Communist speaker on the courthouse lawn.
> It's a go-to-church, skip-the-liquor,
> Woman's Club kind of place, yet kind,
> filled with great O's of goodness
> if you stay inside its frame.

It has been observed that expensive gifts come in small packages. Shihab's poems often attest to this truth. Susan Bright's *Container* is truly a small package (one of three mini-publications from Austin's Noumenon Press), a six-page chapbook composed of three-line, haiku-like pieces, all separated by the repeated word "container" typed in all caps. Read as individual pieces, the tercets are often arresting in and of themselves:

> shape of wooden shoe
> body of peasant
> bend of work

> brown paper bag
> held open
> for the cat

Seen as parts of a larger theme, which appears to be a fear of space and an attraction to shapes and movements that may be slight gestures, fragments, flaws, knots, crusts, or, again, small containers, such as jugs, pots or spoons, these three-line sections present a vast index of the tiny and the nearby that are worthy of attention, as opposed to the grandiose and distant:

> i sleep
> with my back to the stars
> they frighten me

Elsewhere the poet reiterates this fear: "i turn / away from / the stars." Bright discovers instead galaxies in the everyday. Her small packages are indeed rich in returning us home:

> cling to the roof,
> do not blow off
> the surface

If I read her right, there are some fine loaded puns in this little three-line stanza. For those interested, Bright's latest volume is *Julia*, a larger, beautifully printed collection (from Wings Press in Houston), though perhaps no bigger in spirit than her smaller *Container*.

Another six-page Noumenon chapbook is Tamara O'Brien's *Affairs*, a work that moves helter-skelter for me, and unlike Bright's collection it never quite focuses on much that I can feel or with which I can identify. At the end of the title poem, however, the poet manages to evoke a scene I can visualize and to which I am attracted by its "clear" double meanings. At this point the poetry achieves a greater depth—the metaphor, significantly, one of swimming in a pool—and this contrasts dramatically for me with the shallow and overly sound-oriented aspects of the earlier sections of the piece. Other readers may well find O'Brien's rapid-fire writing more successful and appealing than I do.

Carl D. Clark's *Desire, Chasing a Cow* is the third Noumenon chapbook submitted for review, and like the Bright and O'Brien collections it too is a six-page publication. Like Bright's poem, Clark's appears made up of isolate observations which somehow interrelate. With Clark's work, however, it is more difficult to discover a pattern, partly because the cummings-like breakdown of words into unsyllabic divisions too often interferes with the sense and yet seldom if ever adds a visual dimension to the meaning that the poem would, I assume, wish to convey. Like O'Brien's work, Clark's rushes headlong, ending mostly in traffic jams and tie-ups:

        goi

             n

   gona

     he

          ad

Clark alludes characteristically to the chase as "here just a second to say / and no sooner done than / claptrap." There is a definite connection between title and content, for the chase is constantly "goi / n / gona / he / ad," but other than the pure pleasure of breaking up the lines and words into random arrangements, and from time to time offering a curious line by way of relief ("A / roar to buy my eye"), the work puzzles as to where the poet has headed, taken me, or whether there was any "desire" to arrive or to catch the never-imaged cow. For many, curiosity kills the "cow," and in poetry the purely curious may rarely prove long-lived. Given Clark's concretist-dadaist aesthetics, of course, I am guessing that he couldn't fear less. Experiment is often looked down on as no end in itself. But someone should be carrying it on, with all of Whitman's exuberance. Who knows where it will lead. I would hope that Clark continues to chase the cow, even if he himself has yet to catch a glimpse of its tail. Sooner or later he may bring the beef to our tables.

As I have tried here to understand myself, there seems a clear though not easily definable distinction between bad writing—that is, the faulty or mediocre performance—and writing that may fall short of perfection but which, in attempting a more difficult, complex or challenging task, reaches far beyond the merely good poem—meaning the piece that is competent, carefully crafted, and neatly complete. What I miss in much so-called poetry is the poet's willingness to go in over his or her head, even to force relationships which leave him or her vulnerable to charges of going too far, of creating outrageous oxymora. In the small, well-wrought poem, the poet tends to remain satisfied with fitting the pieces so tightly that no objection can enter in, though not much life either. Emily Dickinson and William Blake's short poems are obvious exceptions, for they manage to leave their pieces open-ended and porous with possibilities for interpretation. Likewise, in W.D. Snodgrass's "Heart's Needle," section three of the poem moves us through simple-sounding rhymed stanzas, yet there is nothing easy about the thinking. The analogies are far-reaching as they force us to struggle with political, familial, and poetical implications which involve both a real war and the universal dilemma of giving up for someone else's good, of surrendering pride to allow at least for living, if not for our vision of an ideal life:

> It's better the poor soldiers live
> In someone else's hands
> Than drop where helpless powers fall
> On crops and barns, on towns where all
> Will burn. And no man stands.

Walter McDonald's *Caliban in Blue* (Texas Tech Press), winner of the 1976 Texas Institute of Letters Award for poetry, is a collection based principally on the author's participation in, and his pondering of, the war in Vietnam. For this fact alone the book has had, and will continue to enjoy, a wide appeal. McDonald's sensitive responses, his insightful observations, and his craftsmanship in shaping his experiences into meaningful statements will long elicit our admiration. All of McDonald's poems are short (no more than two pages at the most), for the poet is well able to recreate important moments within a very few lines, as in "Flight Orders":

> It
> has come, the
> pledge
> of all uniforms,
> the

<pre>
flat spin no
        jet
can rudder out
        of,
suction down with
        no
operative ejection seat.
        War.
</pre>

The cumulative effect of McDonald's book is a survey of an historical period. This perhaps is the aim of the imagist or objectivist poet who studies an era through small pieces of large events. The epic poet since Pound has chosen essentially this approach. And most modern readers prefer the shorter poem. Often they will pronounce the long poem a failure but will point to individual, imagistic sections as worthy of being excerpted. Thus, while we fear the bad *big* poem, we can accept the sparkling bits and pieces of which it is composed.

McDonald avoids the epic issue by not attempting a long poem, and the result is that each separate war poem succeeds, though taken together they do not go very far in providing a really penetrating assessment or representation of the war experience. There is lacking here a sense of the universal applicability of the trials and temptations, the enthusiasms and regrets that rise above the subject's inherent message that war is terrible. Somehow the poems remain at a *Catch-22* level—McDonald is a serious student and scholar of this novel—and, while the absurdity and sadness of the political struggle is revealed through a many-sided human involvement, the overall intent of the collection is too limited to sentiment and literary allusion.

Compared with Snodgrass's "Heart's Needle" or even with D.C. Berry's lesser *Saigon Cemetery*—Michael Casey's *Obscenities* has never meant much to me, as I find it overly self-conscious in its playing to contemporary taste—*Caliban in Blue* is too prone to stand outside the events. (It seems to me that to make a nice imagistic poem on a war theme belies the nature of the experience. Stephen Crane only appears to write neat, short pieces on combat, for underneath is an irony that reveals the essential horror or indifference of the war machine. Certainly McDonald at times achieves a similar irony, but it is too clinically removed from poetry's necessary allegorical reflections on any such intense moment that tests man's always conflicting attitudes and qualities—his very soul, as it were.) Perhaps to become less objective, less impersonal, is both a risk and a departure from Pound and Eliot's tenets, but somehow it strikes me as worth the gamble and the sacrilege. Our magazines may be partly to blame for discouraging the bigger, "badder" poem, yet some themes surely call for larger, more unwieldy canvases. Plainly the large and the experimental open themselves up to the greater likelihood of falling apart, but one reason for the abundance of poets today in an age with a decreasing number of significant figures (in our own country at least) is perhaps just this increasing satisfaction with the small "perfect" poem.

While I admire McDonald and Shihab's achievements, I do believe that it is time we quit wading so close to the shore and sailed out farther, as Whitman suggested, recklessly steering for the deepest waters, even if it means sacrificing the ship and all. Nothing ventured, nothing gained, as the adage goes. Or to return to my original metaphor, some critics cry wolf so often that perhaps we *should* ignore their fears of a poem less than perfect.

From "Texas Poetry in Translation"

And why Texas?* Why translate the poetry of a region little thought of within, much less beyond, its borders, a region only known abroad for oil, cattle, and the Kennedy assassination? With Latin American readers aware for the most part of few poets other than those of the Pound-Williams-Eliot-Stevens era and those of the Beat Generation, it would make far more sense to students of contemporary United States poetry to translate the New York poets or those belonging to the easily identifiable Iowa Workshop school. Certainly there are regions and stylistic movements that have produced more popular and perhaps more significant work than that done by Texas poets, yet every region's writing has something to recommend it, irrespective of the level of sophistication achieved or its national or international ranking.

My coeditor, Luis Ramos-García, has pointed out aspects of Texas poetry which he believes will make it particularly appealing to a Latin American audience. He notes that the rural spirit still permeating Texas poetry has given to it a sense of hope and optimism, an openness to the past, present, and future. Luis feels that there is not present in such poetry the anguish characteristic of so many other poetries of the modern world. This seems to me true even of the work of poets living in the bleaker areas of the state, those who have contributed so imaginatively to the new Texas writing. Luis also has called attention to the influence of religion on our poetry, even as paradoxically a number of the poems in *Washing the Cow's Skull* accept as natural the most unlikely attitudes and practices insofar as the religious is concerned. The various ethnic and cultural backgrounds in Texas account in part for many of these characteristics, but the fact that the poets have presented contradictions of the region as vividly remembered events and responses is evidence of the authenticity of their writing and of the sources for it in their Texas experience.

---

* Introduction to *Washing the Cow's Skull / Lavando la calavera de vaca* (Fort Worth, TX: Prickly Pear Press, 1981).

Always the connection of a work of literature with a specific place has determined for me much of its inherent value. Perhaps in recent years this whole idea has been done almost to death, though without its advocates necessarily understanding the essence of place in poetry. There is more to it than simply naming a location or describing a locale. With the broad migration of teachers of creative writing there has been a tendency to exploit places for their quaint or exotic features. With something of the Southerner in me, I find this development comparable to the situation during Reconstruction when the carpet baggers descended like a swarm of locusts to take advantage of blacks and whites alike and to pit one against the other. In this analogy, the scalawags are those in any region who prefer to promote these flashy types from afar rather than to support their own native artists. While this may seem a hyperbolic comparison, the effects of a conscious or unconscious exploitation of place in poetry have been to make of the local a gold mine for those who apply to it an opportunist's clever technique, while those attempting a genuine treatment of place, as native or longtime resident artists, are considered inept and out of touch with contemporary writing. For this reason I find much of what passes for place poetry suspect, and remain dissatisfied with the claims made for the work of poets who lack any real ties with where they are or from whence they come. I sense in such work a groundlessness and an unreality, an overemphasis on cuteness and sheer virtuosity. And in contrast to this general state of affairs, I find that Texas poetry collected in this bilingual anthology is representative of a real and vital expression of what it means to experience the life of a region, to respond to it more deeply than at the level of style or fashionable imagery, and to discover through place one's personal and social history, one's cultural and artistic patrimony, however primitive those happen to be.

But again, why Texas poetry in translation? Personally I left off years ago looking for artistic inspiration to California or New York (except for that city's Louis Zukofsky), much less for a readership. For me a Texan's natural allies in the arts lie south, where Spanish is spoken and where it is being written with ever greater power. Though the super patriot still celebrates over-loudly our independence from the Mexican state, I see our destiny manifest there, our cultural future linked to a chain of nations stretching from the Rio Grande to Tierra del Fuego, and I envision our poets opening a cultural commerce with the descendants of Netzahualcoyotl, to exchange—as the American Indians of these continents did centuries ago—our amulets of words for those fashioned by poets we approach ever closer in spirit, having always been nearer to them by land and sea. It is in fact to a Spanish-Indian presence that we owe in large measure whatever claims our poems may lay to such qualities as warmth and vitality. And thus by way of reciprocation have Luis and I labored long to bring into Spanish these handmade beads of a Texas mind and breath.

The Chile-Texas Connection

It's no secret that Chilean poetry has been a major force in twentieth-century Spanish-language literature, and an influence on poets worldwide, including those of Texas.* The leading lights among Chilean poets are Vicente Huidobro (1893-1948), inventor of *creacionismo*; Nobel Prize winners Gabriela Mistral (1889-1957) and Pablo Neruda (1904-1973); Nicanor Parra (b. 1914), awarded the $100,000 Juan Rulfo Prize in 1991 for his self-defined "antipoetry"; and Enrique Lihn (1929-1988), whose "The Dark Room" is internationally admired. Another Chilean poet of lesser fame but considerable interest is Oscar Hahn, born in 1938 and a participant, during the early 1960s, in an exchange program between the University of Chile in Santiago and the University of Texas at Austin.

In an interview in the fall 1991 issue of *Concho River Review*, poet-playwright-fiction writer James Hoggard of Wichita Falls talks of having taught himself Spanish primarily oo he could read the work of Mexican Nobel Prize-winning poet Octavio Paz; later Hoggard began to translate the poetry of Chilean Oscar Hahn. The Texan's two collections of Hahn poems in translation are *The Art of Dying* (1987) and *Love Breaks* (1991), both from Latin American Literary Review Press. Hoggard comments that in the poetry of Paz and Hahn he finds the "intellective lyric . . . a kind of sensual approach to the world . . . that carries with it the strong stamp of the cerebral, that joins together the contemplative and the erotic." This in itself is something of a definition of the Texan's own writing and explains in part his attraction to such a poem as the Chilean's "Written With Chalk":

> One tells Zero: Nothing exists
> Zero replies: One doesn't either
> because love makes us alike

---

* *Borderlands: Texas Poetry Review*, no. 1 (Fall 1992): 90-95.

Zero plus One we are Two he says
and hand in hand they go through the blackboard

Two kiss under the desks
Two are One near the hidden eraser
and One is Zero my life

Behind all great love nothingness skulks

Ray González, a native of El Paso on the Texas border, has acknowledged on a number of occasions the importance to his own writing of the poetry of Pablo Neruda. In his first collection, *From the Restless Roots* (1986), González reveals in his "Dreams of a Poet, Dreams for Pablo Neruda" that when the Chilean speaks,

I turn my blood in your direction.
Your body meets mine under the earth.
Together, we turn our heads up and
kiss the glistening roots. . . .

In "The Echo of the Voice," from González's third collection, *Twilights and Chants* (1987), the poet goes so far as to suggest that when this century comes to a close, we will all be exiled to "an island of futile sanctuary" where we will pay the price "for not having listened closely to [Neruda]." In certain ways González's poetry "echoes" Neruda's, as when in "Apprentice to Volcanoes," the title poem of González's second collection, the Texan refers to "a blacksmith of blood and lava," uniting in this metaphor both man and earth, as does the Chilean throughout his work.

My own interest in Chilean poetry began when I read in 1965 the translations by Miller Williams of poems by the self-proclaimed anti-poet Nicanor Parra. At that time, very few of Parra's now internationally acclaimed anti-poems had been translated, so that I tried my own hand at a number of pieces that seemed to contain the sort of objectivist poetry that I was then championing, against what I took to be the overly romantic, verbose style of a Neruda. Here are excerpts from four of my translations of Parra poems that appeared in a 1972 issue of *Road Apple Review*:

> Reading my poems puts me to sleep
> and yet they were written with blood.

*   *   *

> And Gloria Astudillo
> to have no superior
> dropped her long panties
> undid her brassiere

*   *   *

> The turtle never wasted so much time
> as when he took lessons from the eagle.

*   *   *

> I think in a fit of rage
> thus passes the glory of the world
> without pain
>   without glory
>   without any fuss
> without even a miserable bologna sandwich

I found Parra's epigrammatic, anti-romantic, and even irreverent verses in many ways more to my liking than Neruda's endless lines full of paradoxical and at times surrealistic images, not to mention his intimidating array of names of unknown flora and fauna, and of what Parra called "'beauty' and her cast of a thousand adjectives."

Even before I published my first translations of Parra, I was surprised and delighted to discover in 1968 that Charles Behlen, a student of mine at New Mexico Junior College, already knew and admired the Chilean's anti-poetry. Behlen, a native of Slaton, Texas, had been inspired by the Chilean's "Young Poets," which the Texan came across in the 1967 New Directions edition of Parra's *Poems and*

Anti-Poems, in a translation by Miller Williams. Behlen took this Parra poem as a kind of manifesto, one that has served him well as a Texas poet and that still offers an attractive creed for young poets everywhere:

> Write as you will
> In whatever style you like
> Too much blood has run under the bridge
> To go on believing
> That only one road is right.
>
> In poetry everything is permitted.
>
> With only this condition, of course:
> You have to improve on the blank page.

Over the past 25 years, Behlen has gone on to develop his own distinctive West Texas voice, and to create a group of poems he attributes to an invented European poet by the name of Uirsche. Taking up Parra's "permissive" invitation, Behlen has even tried his hand at "translating" Rilke, by comparing translations from the German (which the Texan does not know) and coming up with his own intuitive versions.

In addition to the anti-romantic stance of Parra's poetry, another feature of the Chilean's writing that grabbed my attention—and I would suspect caught Behlen's eye and ear as well—is its conversational style, which seemed easy to read and translate and therefore almost demanded that I imitate it in English. Through the years, however, I have discovered how naive I was, how deceptively difficult Parra's language is. In August 1991, on a return trip to Chile after thirteen years from the time of my previous visit, I read in *Atenea* a new Parra poem, entitled "Acúsome Padre," which I translated as "Forgive Me Father for I Have Sinned." Without help from my wife María, and Chilean critic Gilberto Triviños, I would not have achieved even moderate success with this poem, for along with playing on Catholic ritual, the anti-poet responds to a tour of Chile by Arthur Miller and William Styron; incorporates famous historical pronouncements by Chilean heroes during the wars of Independence and of the Pacific; and alludes to Walt Whitman, U.S. gunboat diplomacy, Marilyn Monroe, and the native American Indian. It is this rich blend of motifs in Parra's poetry that has appealed to me as reader, writer, and translator, but which has made any rendering of his work more challenging than it at first appeared to be.

It was the theme of the sea in Pablo Neruda that finally led me to attempt one of my first translations of this cosmic poet's masterful lines. In his "Data for the Tidal Wave of July 25" I found a powerful piece that captures the sea in all its "unruly" beauty, and also exhibits what American poet-translator Robert Bly has called an example of "leaping poetry," by which Bly means that Neruda's

> imagination sees the hidden connections between conscious and unconscious substances with such assurance that he hardly bothers with metaphors—he links them by tying their hidden tails. He is a new kind of creature moving about under the surface of everything.

This same quality prompted me in 1973 to compose an elegy for Neruda and to unify my poem through images I had acquired in reading and translating his work. In particular, I drew on the "Three Material Songs" and his many odes depicting creatures of the sea, such as the whale in his "Ode to the Watermelon"—hence my elegy's title, "Leviathan," as a tribute to "this black fire swallowing schools." In addition, I would connect Neruda's poetry with my own world when, toward the end of the elegy, after having "sailed" with the Chilean through the epical waters of his words, I would enter a

> nutria slough
> and stepping on bank of the Cow-Cow bayou
> find the cattle tracks more my size
> hoof prints & hay cakes easier on eyes
> than readings underneath / beyond the skies
>
> a safe return to the Texas coast
> the shoals & shallows of home

In later years I again found occasion in "Maria's Photograph" to contrast Texas and Chile:

> my Texas beach has held her in
> its most becoming light
> has done its best to measure up
>
> as if somehow it knew
> it must compete
> was up against her vast Pacific
> whose tides take in such climates
> reach to such continents & cultures
> as these poor shores can only dream
>
> could hardly hope to fathom
> her Arabic Sephardic & Araucanian strands
> yet thank my native breeze & inclement sun
> for this lesser glow they lend her still

The Chilean poet whose work I have been translating since I first read it in 1966 is Enrique Lihn, who came to Texas in 1978 as a Guggenheim Fellow and returned in 1985 only three years before his death. On his first visit Lihn wrote several poems on the state, my translation of one of which appeared in 1980 in a special Latin American supplement of *Cedar Rock:*

> Everything in Texas is bigger
> reality has carried out that conceit to the letter
> for in Dallas I saw nothing from the door of my horrid motel
> but cars passing and passing and never ceasing to pass
> from the other identical side of a highway with no landmark
>
> flanked by immense luminous ads
> huge figures there flashing for no one
> under a sky that can't manage to cover such stretches
> One thing always twenty miles from another
> gigantic empty spaces

in the Texan sense of the phrase.

While in Austin, Lihn wrote a poem that employs the city's Lake Travis area as its central metaphor:

> I found that happiness,
> it's always this way, when I was least expecting it
> Like climbing stone steps and suddenly really seeing
> the sea even if it were not: a feat of engineering
> the unmoving river defiant of death
> as eternally as youth

My entire translation of this longer piece was printed in 1989 in a new Austin magazine, *The Dirty Goat*, as were several of my versions of poems from Lihn's *Diary of Death*, his posthumously published collection of poetry written as he was dying of cancer. In his moving *Diary* poems, Lihn, as he says in one piece entitled "Death in the Opera," is like Placido Domingo who "must cry out on entering the house of death / Butterfly . . . Butterfly," and this Chilean poet, like the great opera singer, was never "out of tune," not even when he was *in extremis*.

Unfortunately I cannot say the same for my translations of Chilean poetry created in the best of health. Like Ben Belitt, whose versions of Neruda have often been faulted for going beyond the originals, I myself have made more than my share of mistranslations, mostly in versions of poems by Enrique Lihn. Two will serve as examples. In Lihn's "Monet's Years at Giverny," the poet speaks of the "flor de la pluma" in reference to the wisteria's cluster of grape-like blooms. I mistakenly translated "pluma" as "pen" rather than "feather" or "plume." Although "pen" is one meaning of the Spanish word, it completely misses Lihn's very accurate description of the flowering vine. (My poet-friend, Jon Bracker, who knows very little Spanish, caught this error through his awareness that there is nothing in the wisteria to suggest a pen.) In another translation, which I entitled "Figures of Speech," I rendered the phrase "lucir en el papel" as "lighting the paper," thinking that the poet was referring to the writing of his poem; but in so doing I lost entirely the idea of an actor starring in a "role," another meaning of "papel." Despite my lasting chagrin over these errors in translations published in *Colorado Review* and *New Orleans Review*, I have continued to practice the humbling task of translation, which I believe is a broadening experience for any poet, and in this way I have attained a deeper appreciation for the demanding, rewarding poetry of Enrique Lihn.

The value of translation has even been acknowledged by both Neruda and Parra, whose comments on their own versions of Shakespeare plays offer insight into the meaning of the entire process. For example, Neruda discovered in translating *Romeo and Juliet* that,

> beneath the plot of undying love and unforeseen death, there was a second drama, a second subject, a second principal theme.
>
> *Romeo and Juliet* is a great plea for peace among men. It is the condemnation of pointless hatred, the denunciation of barbarous war, and the solemn elevation of peace.

After translating *King Lear*, Parra reported in an interview in 1991 that when he first saw the play in London, in 1950, he was "bored as an oyster. And now I understand absolutely: It is a work that in essence cannot be acted." More importantly, Parra found in *King Lear* that Shakespeare too was an anti-poet:

> He is not an ideological author: He is at the service of no philosophical or religious end. He practices what is called negative capability, which is the capacity to live with contradiction.

Parra's views are made dramatically apparent in a poem that he wrote in May 1992 and published in the program for the production in Chile of his *Lear rey & mendigo*, a version of *King Lear* that he modestly styles a "transcription." Here is my own version of Parra's poem, which he entitled "Lear":

> There are those for and against
> unconditional admirers
> and topnotch detractors

like Tolstoy
            Gide
                  Bernard Shaw
who declare it's good for nothing
Thomas Rymer says outright
he prefers the neighing of a horse
Patience
while some consider it
the poetic text most epithetic
in all Western Lit
others decide to rub it off the map
accusing it of poetic injustice
Nahum Tate and Co. Unlimited
if Romanticism hadn't interceded
no one today would know it exists
what you are hearing ladies and gentlemen
is that weird stuff also happens in Europe
He's a monster of such magnitude
Charles Lamb warns us
that it makes it tough to fit him into
the setting of the common stage
he's too big for any to direct
it's impossible to bring him off
who has hit the nail on the head
few
one or two but nobody else
It's frightening
to see the poor old tumble-down guy
staggering from port to starboard
in the grand wash of contradictory waves
till he goes completely bonkers
would any of you want to be
in the skin of the one who plays his part?
There's no greater challenge
for an actor no matter how terrific he may be
I don't know
the reliable public will tell us

In any case pluck up your courage
you young ones accustomed
to tragedies that end happily
this one couldn't possibly turn out worse:
in a world deprived of reason
poetry can't be anything other
than the guilty conscience of the times
the rest is Greco-Roman literature
Thanks and have a good night
from here on the director has the floor.

Yet another Chilean poet, Oliver Welden, whose poems I have also translated, once wrote that my own poetry must have been helped along by the Latin American poets that I have known how to translate so well. I would not agree that I have been as good a translator as Oliver has been so generous to think I am, but I do affirm that I have learned much from Chilean poets and it seems obvious that other Texans like Jim Hoggard, Ray González, and Charles Behlen also have benefited from their readings in the poetry of Chile. And certainly in the writing of their own poetry, Hoggard, González, and Behlen have all more than met Nicanor Parra's single condition: "to improve on the blank page."

Generations of Texas Poets

In tracing developments in Spanish and Latin American literatures, critics in these fields have relied heavily on the idea of generations of writers as a way of identifying and defining trends within a given historical period, a concept best exemplified by the Generation of '98, which included Unamuno, Azorín, Valle-Inclán, Antonio Machado, and even Rubén Darío.* This always has seemed to me a useful approach to the continuum of literature and is especially valuable when one would attempt to distinguish between movements or tendencies taking place within a relatively short span of time. Although the distinctions or gradations we observe at close range may disappear over history's longer haul, it is a meaningful exercise to note the ebb and flow of styles and attitudes within a spread of three or four decades, if for no other reason than to recall a few of the more prominent issues and figures of each generation. Such a system of classification also may aid in clarifying the subtle shifts in the poetic strata that exhibit the very makings of a literary evolution. Furthermore, to recognize how a given generation adapts itself to a peculiar environment, which may not exist for the succeeding generations, is to explain in part the reactions of one group of writers to another.

In surveying the brief modern record of Texas poetry (not to return to the first outpouring of verse during and following the period of Texas Independence when, for example, Hugh Kerr published in 1838 what is probably the first book of Texas poetry, *A Poetical Description of Texas*), it is possible to speak essentially of three groups or generations—those of the 1950s, '60s, and '70s. While there was some overlapping from one decade to another, the rise of basic themes and styles is clear within these three ten-year periods, and each new layer of the record can be characterized by two or three individual poets belonging to each of these generations. Recent interest in Texas poetry has focused attention, however, on only two outcroppings, as it were: belatedly, the work of Vassar Miller; and disproportionately,

---

* *The Pawn Review*, vol. 5 (1981-82): 8-17.

that of a group of emigré professor-poets whose presence, beginning around 1976, has received more publicity than has that of any single native poet in the state's history. One emigré poet claimed in 1979 that true contemporary poetry in Texas did not exist until the influx of professor-poets brought professionalism, seriousness, and innovation to the region. I would reply that my own anthologies of Texas poetry, *The New Breed* (1973) and *Washing the Cow's Skull* (1981), amply demonstrate that in fact three strong generations of Texas poets were already at work prior to the arrival of the emigré professor-poets. One review of *The New Breed* questioned the title as misleading, since the reviewer asserted that no other group of writers came before those included in the collection. Yet my introduction to that 1973 anthology clearly acknowledges the importance of a number of figures not present in *The New Breed* because for me they did belong to an earlier generation. Four of those poets are in the 1981 collection—William Barney, William Burford, Vassar Miller, and R.G. Vliet—and one of the major ideas behind *Washing the Cow's Skull* was precisely to preserve their contribution and to present them within an overview of Texas poetry as written by native and longtime resident poets.

Not counting such figures as John Lang Sinclair, Berta Hart Nance, and Lexie Dean Robertson from earlier decades, the first important generation of Texas poets came, then, in the 1950s with the work of Barney, Burford, and Miller. Above all, theirs is a poetry of high seriousness and is marked by linguistic power and mastery of traditional forms. While each of these poets was thoroughly acquainted with the nature of modern poetry, each established his or her individual voice outside the national vogues of the '50s and early '60s. Yet each can be profitably compared with national figures or trends: Barney with Robert Frost; Burford with Denise Levertov; and Miller with the confessionalists Sylvia Plath and Robert Lowell. But it should be stressed that the Texans were creating their ideas and styles independently, and that they either preceded certain trends in the '60s or carried on an existing tradition after a wholly regional manner.

The generation of the mid '60s numbers among its primary figures a poet born before any of those in the previous generation—Joseph Colin Murphey. It was not until the '60s, however, that Murphey discovered his own voice, but by his late fifties he was so successful in achieving a contemporary style and thought that I myself included him in *The New Breed,* not knowing his age at the time that I accepted his poems for publication. Murphey was an early admirer of Galway Kinnell, William Stafford, Gary Snyder, and Anne Sexton, at the same time that he supported the work of Vassar Miller and other Texas poets through his magazines *Whetstone* and *Stone Drum.* In general, Murphey first identified with the writers associated with Robert Bly's *The Sixties,* yet always his own poetry has been distinctively Texan in its content and orientation. Another poet who found his voice in the mid to late '60s, and was published early on in Murphey's *Stone Drum,* is Leon Stokesbury, whose 1976 collection, *Often in Different Landscapes*—the first in the University of Texas Press's now defunct poetry series—represented the truly original work of a Texas poet who had published nationwide in the most prestigious magazines and anthologies.

With the 1970s, some dozen vital new voices began to be heard, although the audience for Texas poetry still remained almost nonexistent. Perhaps the most popular of these '70s poets were Naomi Shihab Nye, Harryette Mullen, Walter McDonald, David Yates, and Sandra Lynn. Charles Behlen, though not so widely known as the others, also created a niche for himself with his strongly regional character sketches in poems reminiscent, according to several commentators, of those of E.A. Robinson. (A poet from the generation of the late '40s and early '50s, Arthur Sampley, has also been studied favorably in connection with Robinson's work, by poet-critic J.M. Linebarger.) Shihab Nye, Mullen, McDonald, Yates, and Lynn all contributed a new look and sound to Texas poetry. It is even possible—and this is no small accomplishment—for the poems of these five poets to be recognized from among those of the thousands of poets active in the United States during the past decade. And although an important figure like William Barney had gone largely unrecognized since the '50s, the prospects for the generation of the '70s to gain a wider audience were vastly improved by a growing interest in the state's earlier poets like Barney and Miller.

Still, one problem that continued to plague native and longtime resident poets of Texas in their search for a receptive audience was the attitude that only writers coming from outside the state had a real grasp of the contemporary poem. Even though I firmly believe that it is quite simple to document the significant contributions made by three generations of Texas poets, there persists even today a very real threat to an acknowledgment of or recognition for these poets because of those who would begin a history of the state's poetry with the present generation of professor-poets. The prof-poets arrived with undeniable credentials both as teachers and as writers; nor is the value of their presence to be denied. And yet, if they alone are to reap the benefits of a slowly developing audience in the state, then any true Texas poetry may well be submerged beneath this flood of emigration. The cultural histories of nations that have suffered from one kind of invasion or another are too numerous even to list, so that to name but our native Indians or our neighbor Mexico should suffice to call up rich traditions overwhelmed in the wake of a foreign conquest. Of course, it has been suggested that many cultures were decadent or stagnant at the time of invasion, though this hardly is the case in Texas. On the contrary. But rather than pursue this issue further, I propose to discuss, in addition to the earlier generations, some of the poets of the 1980s, among them a number of emigré poets, as well as a group of native poets who have begun to reveal another side to the multifaceted crystal that is Texas poetry.

The notion that Texas and poetry do not go together has long acted as a hindrance to a serious readership for the state's poets. Even with the explosion of this popular myth, there remains a feeling among many writers of the '80s generation that anything which smacks of the old Texas is for them and their work anathema. Thus, the school of rough-and-ready, colloquial, or open range writing has been displaced in the minds of these new poets by a need for chiseled diction, for the plumbing of psychological and mystical depths, and for a type of scientific mysticism. Albert Goldbarth, Jack Myers, William Virgil Davis, and Cynthia Macdonald—all of them emigré poets associated in fact or through influence with the Iowa Workshop school—are proponents in one form or another of such tendencies, but an equally good example of this approach may be found in the work of Pattiann Rogers. A convenient representative for several reasons, Rogers is principally so because her career began, in part, with her 1974 publication in *The Texas Quarterly*.

According to the contributor's note on Rogers in the autumn 1974 issue of *TQ*, she graduated Phi Beta Kappa from the University of Missouri (her native state) and returned to writing after a six-year lull. Her poem in *TQ* marked the beginning of an obvious burst of energy that continued with her award-winning appearances in *Poetry* and *Poetry Northwest* for 1981, as well as with publication of *The Expectations of Light*, her 1981 collection from Princeton University Press. What is most striking about Rogers' 1974 poem in *The Texas Quarterly* is its direct link with one of her 1981 pieces in *Poetry*. Compare the following lines from her poem "My Pets" in *TQ*:

> How near am I, my brother,
> Three genes removed and alone
> From the water-fledgling
> Who today for the first time
> Kicked his lovely new-grown appendages?
> . . .
> I am this deep within
> The tiny fur-born rodents
> Who scurry, pause,
> Push their noses thru their wire cages,
> Stop, with glinting eyes,
> And twitching momentarily, my god,
> They wonder.

with these lines from "Being Accomplished" in *Poetry*:

> Imagine the mouse with her spider-sized hands
> Holding to a branch of dead hawthorn in the middle
> Of the winter field tonight. Picture the night pressing in
> Around those hands, forced, simply by their presence,
> To fit its great black hulk exactly around every hair
> And every pin-like nail, forced to outline perfectly
> Every needle-thin bone without crushing one, to carry
> Its immensity right up to the precise boundary of flesh
> But no further. Think how the heavy weight of infinity,
> Expanding outward in all directions forever, is forced,

Nevertheless, to mold itself right here and now
To every peculiarity of those appendages.

In another poem in *Poetry*, entitled "Discovering Your Subject," Rogers speaks of painting "the same shrimp boat / Every day of your life." It is clear from the two excerpts quoted above that the poet certainly has discovered her subject, not only in the rodent but in the analysis of every "peculiarity of those appendages." Rogers' style has changed for the better, but her subject and diction remain the same, as does her highly intellectual, scientific approach to the mystical. All of this is characteristic as well of Albert Goldbarth's poetry, which draws on the works of Newton (see the poet's *Opticks*, 1974) and Linnaeus (see his poem entitled "Blue Flowers" in *Poetry* for September 1981—"The lucid, detailed, inarguable, / relentless cataloguing") as a basis for Goldbarth's own probings for a faith in poetry and the workings of the universe. There is much to be learned from Goldbarth and company, though not everything they do can be considered "inarguable."

Both Rogers and Goldbarth now reside in Texas, yet their work would never be taken as regional by any stretch of the imagination. When Goldbarth has chosen to explore "a Texan's mind," he has picked for the purpose Jean Cocteau's male lover, Barbette, who "escaped" from Round Rock, Texas, and became part of the Lost Generation in Paris. Every generation of Texas poets has had any number of escapees, notable among them Bin Ramke, who shared the 1978 Texas Institute of Letters award for poetry (having already won the Yale Younger Poets Award) for a collection that recounts, in part, the sensitive poet's torment in Texas. (Richard Hugo, who served as judge, found Ramke's escape from Texas a decided plus for his poetry. What is most curious about this and similar cases is that the writer who escapes from Texas always seems to return his or her book for the applause and prize money.) Though many emigré poets have been, for economic reasons, quite happy to make Texas their home, none has wanted to be identified with the place or its poetic tradition. (The sole exception is Paul Christensen, who in his own poetry and through his fine radio program, "Poetry Southwest," has immersed himself in the region's poetic sources.)

The emigré's own writing, like that of Pattiann Rogers, is essentially focused on states of mind, never on the life of a single state of the nation. For this reason, none of these emigrés (with again the exception of Christensen) is concerned with the region as a subject for his or her poetry. In this sense they are closer to Vassar Miller than to any other Texas poet of the earlier generations, and this may explain why Miller and the emigrés are mentioned more often than the other poets of the state. And yet the poetry of both William Barney and William Burford can exhibit a significant use of math and science for psychological and ethical purposes. Barney especially is given to developing insightful mathematical analogies to man's mental and moral problems and his search for understanding of the complexities of existence. Like the epic poet, who utilizes a wide range of sources, styles, and structural patterns, Barney encompasses in his work a variety of elements, whereas the emigré poets tend to limit themselves to painting almost by numbers "the same shrimp boat / Every day" of their lives. Cynthia Macdonald, for instance, has operated on her psyche after the manner of Sylvia Plath, yet only with the result that Macdonald's poems have an anesthetizing effect. Seldom does her work visit, as Barney's does, the great out-of-doors. Rogers and Goldbarth do venture into nature, though frequently what they observe merely serves their obsession with a clinical analysis similar to Macdonald's. Nothing Macdonald has done, however, approaches the power of Plath's "Stones," where the hospital patient sees her environment through a series of ingenious metaphors based on attendants and tools in "the city of spare parts." Nor does Macdonald achieve the depth of a Barney, no matter how completely she devotes herself to self-surgery and personality amputation.

As to native poets of the '80s generation, they too are inclined, like the emigré poets, to focus on states of mind rather than on the nature of a place as such. Five new poets to emerge within the past year are Diane Bertram, who, with her husband Rex Barnett, has established Sleepy Tree Publishing in Fort Worth; Rob Lewis, with the publication by Sleepy Tree of his *The Green Book;* Prentiss Moore, with publication of his *The Garden in Winter;* Rebecca Gonzales; and Jeanette Burney, the last two with collections soon to be published. Bertram's work is available in *Sleepy Tree I*, an anthology of prose and poetry, and her first poem in this collection, "Habitat," can bear comparison with the best of Lenore Kandel's and Erica Jong's erotic work, and may well go those poets one better. The fish/penis analogy in Bertram's poem is developed brilliantly and the diction throughout is completely right. Her other poems contain flashes of deep psychological insight and extremely controlled writing, especially in "Thaw," which describes a melting icicle as a metaphor for her need for love:

> It's true
> I'll be brittle and fragile
> I'll break like dry spaghetti,
> but watch this,
>
> just watch: at the instant
> when the light breaks clear
> of that one small lingering cloud,
> see me dive from the tip of the rainspout,
> bare and potent as a pin.

Readers of the selections in *Sleepy Tree I* will await impatiently the first book by this young "feminist poet."

While Rob Lewis, as a native Texan from La Porte, can allude at times to his presence in or connection with the state, he is in no way concerned with this fact as an issue in his poetry. In "Midnight, a Washateria," the poet refers in passing to "beastly snow pouring down outside / with a will, a puncture in the hot Texas myth." Most of the poets of the generation of the '80s are intent on puncturing the myth that poetry in Texas has anything to do with oil or cattle, though Lewis himself says in the same poem that he wishes he were in those for profit, yet the meaning seems to be that he would prefer even money-making to the painful task of dealing with his memories, his lesions from relationships, "Subtleties to childhood / the networks haven't seen." Certainly Lewis does not back off from exploring the pain of personal relationships. His washateria poem includes a very effective insertion of scenes from a Tarzan movie where the ape-man is swimming to reach his Jane, a cut water flower in her hand (with a constant play on the film itself being "cut"). The effort to reach someone close—even while touching the person—is a subject treated repeatedly by Lewis. "Interface," for example, is the imagined transformation of the poet into the woman he loves:

> A weight, as of your breasts,
>
> pulls on my chest. I feel
> your hips superimpose on mine.
> My face pulls taut, as if, malleable,
> its clay is worked to yours.

The poems toward the end of Lewis's book show the poet at his best and promise much for the future from this young writer. "Polyphony" achieves just that by its juxtaposition of the sounds of tin on tin, cicadas trilling, freight cars clanging, rush hour traffic, and a linseed gin. The writing here is strong and daring. "For You or Some Other" is likewise a fully realized poem, where variations on the words "brush" and "blush" yield

> A chord of ripe sonorities,
> awakened heart, it brushed by me
> like a glancing flurry of wings, invisible —
> but where it touched I blush—

Lewis, like Rogers and Goldbarth, reaches to the mystical meeting of natural and human, and another poet of this tendency is Stephen Harrigan, though this has never been the aspect of his poetry that interests me most. While often I find this whole approach too much of an intellectual exercise, there are definitely in the writing of Lewis, Rogers, Goldbarth, and Harrigan many fine moments when we are brought into revealing touch with the mysteries of the material world.

Prentiss Moore's first collection, *The Garden in Winter*, from the University of Texas Press, has been hailed as a new angle of vision, a poetry close to that of a Zukofsky or Creeley. What the volume contains, however, is more than anything a borrowing from almost every classic literary source beyond the Texas borders, although in one poem entitled "Texas" Moore does tip his hat (not a ten-gallon for sure) to the presence in the state of Moorish fountains "to / honor and enhance / so modestly the sound of water." It is just such a delicate image and sound that Moore aims at in his own work: the calming effect of an artistic design that brings one to a contemplation of natural beauty. One of Moore's favorite sources for tranquility, inspiration, and identification is Zen poetry, with its concern for a still center. But there is neither a new angle here nor an innovative use of the oriental tradition. For an instance of an authentic adaptation of Zen patterns of thought I would recommend rather the poetry of the Chicago poet Lucien Stryk, whose *Selected Poems* from Swallow Press offers the work of a man who not only has translated Zen poetry but has managed to use what he has learned from this tradition for the making of a Midwestern poetry that remains true to itself while it adds the further dimension of a Zen consciousness.

Moore's poems pay homage to every classic poet imaginable, though none of his own can be taken as an advance over or even an equaling of the models. None of the poems in the collection was published previously, and in a number of cases one wonders if reputable magazines would have accepted them, for many are negligible, though this may be my own prejudice against oriental imitations. The diction is frequently archaic, and the straining for restraint or a quiet moment of great intensity grows somewhat wearisome at times and seems a bit too self-conscious. Nonetheless, Moore does create a poetry of delicacy and modesty, in keeping with his sources in Chinese and Japanese traditions. Also, Moore's almost total identification with art itself as a source for his thought and manner may well signal a growing determination to turn away from the traditional subjects for Texas poetry. (Actually, the desire to repudiate any connection with the cowboy or rough-and-ready image of Texas has served as a motivating force behind much of the work of Robert Grant Burns and, according to Paul Christensen, that of Robert Bonazzi.) In a few of his poems, Moore is successful in writing of relationships between others, as in "Divertimento," although the endings of these pieces and of most of the poems in the collection are too often unsatisfying. In "Measure" the poet states that "It is the confusion / of delicacy. / We do not know / where to go. . . ." On the other hand, the risks involved in capturing such delicacy make the poet's even modest triumphs that much more to be admired. It will be especially interesting to note what impact this publication may have on the future practice of poetry in Texas.

Two promising women poets to emerge recently are Rebecca Gonzales and Jeanette Burney. Gonzales may well be the finest Chicana poet (*poetisa* I should say) to appear in Texas, even though her poetry is not characterized by Chicano themes nor by the more popular and more rhetorical verse favored by the leading Chicano practitioners. Gonzales *can* write with great power and imagination of field workers in the Laredo area—where she was born and reared—as she does in an unpublished piece on a watermelon picker who labors under the sun like a man beneath his demanding lover. For the past twelve years Gonzales has lived in Groves, outside Beaumont, and the watery world of this Southeast Texas area also is rendered with great skill and imagination. Witness this opening stanza from "The Second Time," first printed in *Revista Chicano-Riqueña* (autumn 1981):

> The second time to love
> we avoid absolutes,
> as the marsh refuses
> to be either land or water

The acuteness of this analogy startled me, for rarely in Texas poetry has a poet been able to use nature so convincingly in the service of a human situation. William Barney has done so, but not in the same way. This is original work and presages great things for Texas and Chicano poetry. Another piece, "Beyond Our Grasp," first printed in *New Mexico Humanities Review*, demonstrates further Gonzales's fine use of the natural world:

> Even in the rain
> a good racehorse reaches hard,
> runs clean.
> Need flares his nostrils
> till they bleed a bright red.
> His eyes grow wild,
> never even see the wire;
> his need goes beyond the muddy stretch.

The same poem contains a pair of lines that will indicate in passing the "reach" of Gonzales's psychological insight in this complex work: "We hold each other in our eyes, / practice losing each other." Gonzales has only begun to publish her work in magazines, including three poems in the winter 1982 issue of *Cedar Rock*, but already there are readers anxious to see her poetry collected in book form. Hopefully there will be many books by Rebecca Gonzales in the offing.

Jeanette Burney has published in *Shenandoah* and several Texas publications, and her first book, tentatively entitled *The Opening*, will add to the generation of the '80s another voice given to internal analysis. What distinguishes Burney's poetry is that it represents a valid return to Browning's dramatic monologue. Like Moore, Burney is attracted to classical myths and retells several, à la the dramatic monologue, as in her fine "Leda Speaks After the Bath." "Magdalena" and a sequence of poems on Easter apply Burney's dramatic approach to biblical themes. "Man," perhaps an allegory, is, whatever it is, dramatic:

> I found him drinking rain from the roof, right out
> of the spout, the droplets scattering from his beard
> when he shook like a dog. I am first the virgin—touched
> more by hair on a grown man's face
> than by his wit. I know only that I do not know
> this man, and he is grinning to take me in.
> . . .
>   Can this man carry me
> and all I take? His only baggage is his face—an emblem
> of mistake and find, the skin a telling
> of muscle on bone. His eyes, those bulbs in creases,
> speak oceans to my hands: I want to pull his madness near.
> His face is all that I have learned,
> and like a girl I take him, dumb.
> Every line is earned.

It would seem that the new generation of Texas poets intends that every line be earned, that no padding, no dependence on the Texas past (on world literature of the past, yes) will interfere with their quest for the grail of a timeless poetry unrestricted by any reference to the region. While I welcome what is to come, I am hopeful that our earlier poets will be remembered for the important role they have played in getting us where we are, even if much of their contribution signifies for the younger writers a basis for counteraction. For it would be a great loss if Texas readers and poets were to miss the sense of tradition that can come from learning the ways in which Barney, Burford, Miller, Murphey, Walter McDonald, Yates, Mullen, and Lynn, to name but a few, have themselves earned every line without resorting to wholesale borrowing or blatant imitation. If our tradition is not so grand as that of Chile or China, it is still ours, and it is up to us to build on it. If we reject it and follow the pied pipers that would denigrate our difference, then shall we be mice indeed, and none that the universe will mold itself to, as in Rogers' mystical vision.

Knowing of each generation's contribution will help us to ensure our continued poetic evolution. Unfortunately there are still those who find it strange that Texas should have its own literature, but I for one find it even stranger to think that it should not. What is stranger still is the unfounded claim that we have no tradition. The point then is to cease denying its existence and to recognize instead the unique quality inhering in any poetry that belongs to a geographical, historical, and cultural habitation. Seldom has a poetry been divorced from the local, and whatever example is to be brought forward—a Milton, perhaps—must be seen in the end as the exception that proves the rule, for poetry flourishes in the place it knows best, whether it be Greece, England, or even Texas.

A Sourcebook for Texas Poetry

A desire to compose poetry that could be identified as specifically Texan did not come to me—did not in a mythological sense take possession of me—when I first began writing what I hoped were approximations to the real thing read in collections that contained the work of Blake and Yeats and William Carlos Williams.* I do recall, however, that even though one of my earliest efforts was fraught with the heaviest symbolism I could muster as a junior in college, and that although I was right to jettison it in a handy trash can, even that dimly remembered student piece was set among pine trees outside the East Texas town of Woodville. To paraphrase Frost, I knew those woods well, having earned many a merit badge bivouacking there on the needle-covered grounds of Camp Urland. And yet that poem failed to survive, mostly I suspect because it sank in my estimation from an overload of mimicked abstractions.

The makings of truer poems still await me near Woodville, where the loblolly and sweet gum stood by me through that time as a candidate for the Order of the Arrow when I inadvertently broke the required silence and forever lost the chance to dance in that secret order's sacred Indian garb. While that painful adolescent episode has never made its way into a poem, other events at Camp Urland did in fact lead to a piece entitled "Life Saving: Exercises."** Although there is no reference to place in the first section of the life-saving poem, to me it is Texan, unlike the student piece that went down under its own weight of imitative meaning without any effort on my part to rescue it from oblivion. That the events described in "Life Saving" took place in a specific part of the state is not the only reason that for me this later effort qualifies as Texan; however, this fact does determine for me something of the poem's authenticity, just as the setting in the second half of the poem is important to its being an expression of what it was

---

* *The Texas Humanist* 7, no. 2 (November-December 1984): 7-8.
** In later years, I did in fact write a poem about that episode, entitled "Woodville," included in my *Memories of Texas Towns & Cities* (2000).

to live at the time of its writing in the Puebla area of Mexico. Both sections of the poem are "about" life saving, but to me they are also about what places can do for and say to one. Above all, the first section of the poem is Texan because the Texas experience speaks for itself rather than conforming to a formula or resorting to a camouflage of the facts because readers might think them either unfamiliar or commonplace.

In a sense everything I write bears the mark of a Texan. Certainly when I have read my poems aloud, audiences have recognized my origins by the Texas accent, and they have commented that they understood the poems better on hearing them because of the inflections in my voice. There is then a Texan sound to my poetry, at least when I myself am reading it. When others encounter my work on the printed page, they may find no sign of its being Texan, unless perhaps through recognition of its liberal sprinkling of place names. But without such handles, how does a poem deserve or why does it even need to be identified as Texan? Perhaps any explanation will matter to no one but me, and to define a poetry in terms of place may be, as Miguel González-Gerth believes, beside the point of its actual worth as a work of art. The definition may elude me, but still it beckons. For one thing, place poetry derives as much from the people and the buildings in which we meet them as it does from the odor of the air or the look of a locale's flora and fauna. Many of the people in any state have necessarily come from elsewhere, yet knowing them in Texas has been for me part of my Texan heritage.

Three men whose work has become for me a principal inspiration are Stephen F. Austin, Eugene C. Barker of Riverview outside Huntsville, and Lester Gladstone Bugbee of Woodbury near Hillsboro. Immigrant and natives, entrepreneur and historians respectively, these men I never knew alive, but their presence in Texas has shaped my recent conception of a Texas poem almost as much as family, friends, and teachers known on a personal basis. Appearing in one of my poems from around 1970, entitled "Jazz, God, and Freshman English," is another trio of influential men: Harold Meehan from St. Louis; Rev. Elwood J. Birkelbach out of Walkers Creek and Jones Prairie; and Francis Abernethy from Palestine by way of the Panhandle and Altus, Oklahoma. The first of what I think of as "poems on credit," this piece was a breakthrough, since largely from then on my poetry has been about the people of Texas—their names populating poem after poem, their lives stamping my lines with a rhythm and reality missing in my early imitations. Of course, if I have captured their special traits, such figures can be known by anyone, regardless of their residence in a specific time and space. Nonetheless, for me they stand for a Texas life, and this simple fact has spurred me on to record and interpret their lives as representative of what it means to be here in this one place. Those like Austin and Barker and Bugbee came before, yet their impact endures in their writings, in their transmitted grapplings with the issues and the emotional and intellectual needs of those of us who inhabit this same demanding landscape.

Without having consciously set out to be a "Texas poet," I found that the idea occurred to me out of self-defense. On finding that my poetry did not fit into an accepted mold for publication, I felt that it would have to be justified in its own way. If my poems failed by the standards set elsewhere, then they would have to be measured by a different yardstick, one that would register the extent of their faithfulness to a Texas origin, one that would gauge their truth by the accuracy of their depiction of the places and people they intended to recreate and penetrate. Without forgetting the lessons to be learned from the classic writers or such a contemporary as the New York poet Louis Zukofsky, I sought to discover those among my fellow Texas poets who shared with me a vision of the value of a homegrown poetics. From an earlier generation, Joseph Colin Murphey, William Burford, and William Barney were especially important to me. J. Frank Dobie was there only as a writer of prose who had done for folklore what I wanted to see done for poetry: to have it appreciated for being made from sources right under our feet. More recently I have read with great admiration Dobie's "Prose and Poetry" from *Some Part of Myself* and would suggest that it is equal to anything in Larry McMurtry's *In a Narrow Grave*. In Dobie's reminiscence of his school days at Southwestern University in Georgetown, he brings to life his beginnings as a writer and the places and people who made it possible after his own peculiar manner. A poet of Bugbee and Barker's age who had the right idea (from my latter-day perspective) was Hans Hertzberg, a San Antonio product and author of *Lawyers and Laurels* (1891), the "Would-Be Epic and Didactic History of the Junior Law Class" at the University of Texas. Hertzberg characterizes each member of the class in a rhymed stanza of five or six lines, and the portraits are vivid, etched with colorful allusions to the classics as well as to the Texas towns from which the subjects hailed. Even if the poet's style is dated, his technique serves the purpose of revealing his classmates' qualities through reference to such "holes in the road" as Oakland, Waelder, Blossom, and Dresden (originally called Spanky). At its close, Hertzberg says of the members of his class: "Ne'er was a theme so genial to my heart." Though one of the class's number, the poet says earlier that he is not so "vain / As to speak of self, when better men remain." Unfortunately, Hertzberg dropped this native subject matter and went in for love lyrics of the maudlin sort, an aping of fashion-magazine verse.

Fear of staying with what he or she has at hand has been probably the greatest single source of a Texas poet's frustration and ultimate failure. The range of Texas materials is unlimited—past, present, and future. Fortunately, poets throughout the state have begun to realize that this is the case, and the results of their recognition are slowly coming to light, particularly in the work of such Texans as Rosemary Catacalos, Rebecca Gonzales, Harryette Mullen, Sandra Lynn, Naomi Shihab Nye, Walt McDonald, James Hoggard, Ray González, and Charles Behlen. Once the state's leaders awaken to the fact of the value of local literature, they will no longer need to fear that an anthology, an individual collection, or a regional magazine containing Texas poetry will have less to offer than publications featuring work by poets from elsewhere. There will be no need for a Governor Clements to import a James Michener instead of supporting our native novelists and poets. This is but one battle being fought by our Texas writers, who have replaced the Crocketts and Bowies and Travises in holding their mission against our state's own outsized inferiority complex.

Writing Poetry by Research:
From Ragtime and Wrestling to Texas Towns and Cities

The first time that I conducted research for writing a poem was with my "Five Versions of the Twelfth Street Rag," written in 1967.* Before that, in 1965, I had fulfilled assignments in Western American History under Professor John Sunder at the University in Austin without suspecting at the time that such books as George Catlin's *North American Indians* and Cabeza de Vaca's *Naufragios*, which I chose for outside readings, would figure in my poems "George Catlin and the Horned Frog," "Trekking," and *Austin*, the last of these my book-length "epic" composed between 1979 and 1985. It was, however, for "Five Versions" that I purposely visited the Fort Worth Public Library—then at Throckmorton and 9th in its art deco building with a black marble façade—to find what I could on Euday L. Bowman, a fellow native of my hometown and composer of the "Twelfth Street Rag," which in the 1920s and '30s he played in a shoe shine parlor on Main Street between 10th and 11th streets. In 1967 María and I had just married and it was marvelous to have her with me in the library where I had gone as a boy. Her presence on that occasion made me feel even more deeply that I was doing something important as an aspiring poet.

The idea of researching a poem about Bowman and four jazz greats, Louis Armstrong, Duke Ellington, Fats Waller, and Count Basie, who had each performed the famous rag with their bands, was new to me, even though I may have known that writers like Shakespeare had found sources for their works in such historical accounts as Plutarch's *Lives* and Edward Hall and Raphael Holinshed's chronicles. But it probably did not occur to me that this was a legitimate practice. In fact, I earlier had considered T.S. Eliot's poems too scholarly and had preferred those of Louis Zukofsky, not realizing at that point that the latter belonged to the ancient Jewish tradition of hermetic study and learned exegesis. In any event, researching a poem was a thrilling

---

* *Concho River Review* 8, no. 1 (Spring 1994): 54-60.

new approach for me and must have set me unconsciously on a path that would lead to a number of my later poems, following, as it were, in the footsteps of Altick's "scholar adventurers." This was especially true of another piece on a musician from jazz history, King Oliver, the subject of my 1969 mini epic, "The Hero's Fall I Fell For." Although jazz is a spontaneous art in many ways, it also is carefully thought out and developed over time, so that my own research for the sake of a poem on jazz was not contrary to the spirit of that music, or at least I did not see it in such a negative light. But this does raise the issue of research as overly dependent on facts rather than being grounded on invention and imagination. Since I have never been an original thinker nor a person gifted with an ability to create scenes, images, or situations out of thin air, I have had to rely on history and past experience to supply my "creative" materials. Yet even Shakespeare based his plays on historical characters and drew on their outstanding traits, as reported in other writers' accounts, for his fertile descriptions and conflicts, even his key phrases and images and word play. With "Five Versions" I was certainly aware that I was digging into the history of my birthplace, and this in itself would have justified what otherwise might have seemed to me an unacceptable case of cribbing.

The next poem of mine that involved research was "Jacob's Angel," a sequence written in 1968 at the request of my friend Jim Jacobs, who as a commercial artist had been hired to design a publication related to wrestling. When Jim asked if I had any poetry on this subject, I said no but that I would write something for him. Since I knew next to nothing about wrestling, it was back to the library, this time at the junior college where I was then teaching in Hobbs, New Mexico. Even more than the research on "Five Versions," the readings I did for "Jacob's Angel" took me into terra incognita and opened up a whole new world to be experienced vicariously, although it also allowed me to utilize the literature that I already knew, such as *Beowulf,* and to recall the few times during the 1950s when I had seen the laughable matches between Gorgeous George and the Masked Marvel or the staged tag-teams on early TV. This combination of research and recollection enabled me to employ words and images that I never would have thought to use in the kinds of poems that I normally wrote—those centering on my own limited life. Research thus permitted me entrance into the lives of unknown others, and this type of imaginative outreach immediately resulted in a richer language and more to say with it about histories that I had not lived but to which I could relate through the personal memories those called to mind.

This practice of studying a subject in order to discover in it the makings of a poem carried over for me into a similar habit that I began to develop in 1975 when for the first time I visited the Fort Worth stockyards and auction arena and took with me a notebook. In working on the second of two sections for a poem on my hometown, as part of my "Memories of Texas Towns & Cities" sequence, I decided to keep notes that could then be transformed into poetry in much the same way as I had done with the information gleaned from research. Only later would I learn that other poets had worked in this way, in particular Zukofsky, for both his *A* and *80 Flowers*, as well as Robinson Jeffers on his visit to Ireland. Actually it was Robinson's wife Una who had the idea of returning to the land of her people, just as my Chilean María has proposed so many excursions—ironically to my own Texas towns and cities—on which I have just gone along, as Jeffers said, "for the ride," only to profit fundamentally once my notes were turned into poems on such out-of-the-way places as Burnet, Johnson City, and Castroville, or the often passed-through Salado. These visits opened the way for readings in the life and times of the Republic's first president, as well as personal memories of Burnet's nearby Lake Buchanan; meditations on the private and public lives of LBJ; a passage to Alsace-Lorraine, China, and back, through the religious politics of the Sisters of Divine Providence; and a consideration of past and present in the attractions of a popular roadside stop. By looking into the histories of such local towns the universal zoomed into view, as the close-at-hand provided vivid connections with the far-off without my ever leaving home.

The delightful thing about note-taking—which has included facts from travel brochures or local plaques and markers as well as on-the-spot descriptions and snatches from overheard conversations—has been that not until later did certain connections become, from the poem's point of view, "poetic," adding to a thrust that may have been there (in the poem and in the place) from the first, even though specific details did not seem to fit into any particular pattern when they were originally jotted down. Learning to record as much as possible at the time, whether or not a design was apparent before or during the note-taking, would prove an invaluable lesson. However, such a habit was established only after regretting that certain poorly remembered facts or scenes had not been fully registered and could not be recovered when the poem came to require them.

On-site note-taking does differ somewhat from citations copied out of research materials (tracts, journals, newspapers, letters, biographies or autobiographies). To describe a building, a monument, a statue, or a landscape is instantly to respond to these in language, as well as with one's emotions and memories. Research is more a matter of copying out what already has been written and hoping that later the information will be suggestive in some unforeseen way. Little of this kind of material is worked into a poem verbatim; normally it serves more for background that is absorbed into the texture of the poem. With on-the-spot note-taking, the writing is a simultaneous record of data and an immediate response that may take shape on an emotional and/or structural level. Even if on-site note-taking is a purely objective rendering, the writing down of details will necessarily fall into a certain form and will call forth key words, phrases, and images on the spur of the moment. But in either case, whether doing research or visiting a site and taking notes, almost none of the connections made or the vocabulary used would have occurred to me without the act of copying out printed passages or describing a scene directly. Both methods cause me to read or look more closely and to find stimulating diction in another's text or from viewing people and places in situ. Some of what is taken down will survive, while some will be replaced or dropped completely, but always it is surprising what comes to life as or within the poem, which is precisely what keeps me going back for more.

One problem with researching a poem is the same one faced by academic scholars: when to stop and get on with the writing. There is the constant fear that not enough is known or that some really central issue or image may not have surfaced. There is definitely a danger lurking in the fact that research is easier than the creative work to be done and so one procrastinates with the excuse that more preparation is necessary. At some point the writing must begin, and just as some scholars will start before the research is completed and then return to do more when they feel the need to fill in missing pieces of the puzzle, so the poet will go back for more details when there are gaps in the narrative or there is a pause in the poem's emotive drive. In the end there is no substitute for moving through the mass of facts, hooking them up into a line of rhythmic reasoning that has its own inevitable, evolving direction toward which the poem rushes with urgency, even though history may have set down the whole drama as over and done. At the same time that research and note-taking have aided me in constructing many of my poems, they also have instilled in me a sense that I should resist relying too heavily on the facts as I have found them or taken them down. A poem needs to assume its own spirit and not be bound entirely by the historical record. Yet more often than not it is simply a matter of recognizing in rather obvious and frequently repeated facts a new way of seeing them, which for me is essentially a definition of poetry.

But is the object of such writing based on research and note-taking merely to reinterpret the past poetically? In many ways it is an attempt to understand history as an individual, what it means and can mean to one's self. Therein lies the distinct difference between the historian's purported objectivity and the poet's self-confessed bias. While the poet may seek to universalize his or her view of events or of figures in history, it is ultimately a very personal interpretation. For one thing, only certain examples or incidents are selected or, as it may prove, are impressed on the poet's wax-like mind, stamped there by all his or her own experiences and emotional associations. Thus, any research is finally an investigation of the poet's own relationship with the past and those personalities and places with which he or she most fully identifies. The joy of researching a poem derives from the unexpected connections one makes or recognizes between past events, persons, and places and one's own contemporary existence. More than anything else, researching has aided me in coming to appreciate more deeply the people, experiences, and localities in my own life that I could not comprehend or value as I needed to without viewing them through the telescope of past time, seeing them in effect reenact in my own day the heroics of history, under circumstances that can never be duplicated, so that they are not a mere repetition of acts from an earlier age.

In thinking back over my tendency to write about persons who preceded me, those who have been contemporaneous but have remained unknown personally, and those I have had the good fortune to encounter face to face, I am struck by the fact that I have used real names in my poems, a practice that placed William Carlos Williams in legal hot water in the case of his "Five Dollar Guy: A Story." In a few instances the persons I have named who were living at the time—and most still are—expressed their displeasure in one way or another; several have resented my treatment of them in my poems even when the intention was to render homage. Yeats also tended to name specific figures from his lifetime as well as from previous periods, but how much research he did on those only familiar to him through recorded history I cannot say; nor do I know how those he knew firsthand took it when he referred to them as impetuous or proud. In his *Inferno*, Dante identifies by name his fellow Florentines—some still alive when he foresees them in hell. Is this a poet's prerogative? Is the object of poetry to judge its own period or whatever earlier eras it concerns? Or is it rather to report objectively in such a way as to allow for future interpretation and judgment? If the poem places a figure in the light the poet chooses, this is naturally a case of bias, but poetry is not objective history. Each subject can be seen as typical or universal if drawn as such, but I have tried rather to capture the traits that have struck *me* most, or I have sought to identify through research those features or gestures that define what it is that to me has made a figure or place so attractive and perhaps unique.

Even when I have depicted attributes that others may consider objectionable—and that the persons themselves may disapprove of my having brought out—I have not necessarily intended these as weaknesses but more as distinguishing marks, warts at worst yet distinctive, and in some ways the exception that proves the rule of a figure or a place's very real and admirable qualities. In researching or note-taking I would include above all the lapses, the moments of trial and decision when the hero tottered or fell but then recovered and moved on to triumph and glory, small and unheralded though those may have been. At the same time, just as Yeats can speak of his intemperate speech and his fanatic heart and can ask "But what am I that dare / Fancy that I can / Better conduct myself or have more / Sense than a common man?" and Dante can report how he swoons and is reprimanded by Virgil for empathizing with sinners and calling into question God's justice, I have not failed to find fault with myself and have contrasted my own behavior with that of exemplary figures from past or present. It has been a similar urge to identify such qualities as those of soldier, scholar, and horseman which Yeats saw in Major Robert Gregory, the Sidney of his age, that has prompted much of my own writing about Texas and Texans, although restricted by and large to what even I may have considered at first to be unlikely figures and nooks and crannies of my native terrain.

Like any conscientious researcher, the poet gives credit, not only *not* to be a plagiarist but to acknowledge openly and gratefully the sources which have made the poetry possible. After all, one purpose of the poem based on history is to recognize and render tribute to those events and persons who have gone before. This I have tried to do throughout my *Austin* poem, but elsewhere as well I have been concerned to incorporate into the poems, or to give in epigraphs, proper credit for the inspiration and even for the details of the writing. Again, this began with my readings under Professor Sunder, when I first discovered the work of W.W. Newcomb in his *The Indians of Texas*. Later Newcomb would contribute to my "Texas Indian Rock Art" from 1977 and to "Petri in Texas, 1852-1857" from 1979, as well as to the "Corn" section of my "Shoe-dog Rimes" from 1977-78. Naming the sources within the poetry is another part of a larger effort to pay my dues, or to repay those to whom I have been indebted for helping bring the poems into being. Indeed, this form of credit is and has been in most all my writing an underlying theme.

Poetry's Reach for Today, Yesterday, and Tomorrow

This topic was given to me by Peggy Lynch, who tells me that I know something about it.* She also claims that I was the first to advocate the idea that Texas poets should stay in the state and cultivate a homegrown art. It is true that I have had a history of promoting native writers, but I hope that my chauvinism is not interpreted as a provincial view of what it is that Texas writers are accomplishing, have accomplished, and can produce in the future. Let me hasten to add that I would be the last to presume to tell anyone how to write or what to write about. Every writer is prompted by a peculiar need to deal with his or her own subject matter in a way that is self-fulfilling. This does not necessarily mean that the end product will be accepted or admired by the whole world or even by those near and dear. And even if there are readers who respond, the likelihood of their understanding fully our true "genius" is of course quite remote. As I advance in age and look back on my own writing, I think more and more often of a poem by William Butler Yeats, entitled "To a Friend Whose Work Has Come to Nothing."

The problem is that what we envision as our goal in writing and what it is we actually achieve are often not at all one and the same, even though we may deceive ourselves into thinking that we have in fact accomplished precisely what we set out to create. But then the critics enter and ask "What's going on here?" and their answer is usually that, whatever it is, it is wrong, misconceived, or simply unintelligible. I take as an example my own long poem, *Austin*, which I self-published in 1985. This attempt at a type of epic illustrates my longtime fascination with that classic form, and in part the thrust of my extended work was designed to pay homage to the epic poets of many different times and distinct cultures. But as with most of my poetry, this piece begins with the local and seeks to relate it to other places and periods of history and literature. I emphasize my own

---

* This was apparently a talk that I gave at the request of Peggy Lynch, probably for the Poetry Society, but I cannot recall when or where.

intention with regard to the local figures that populate the poem because one reviewer raised the question of who the poets are that appear allusively in the lines of *Austin*. I refer specifically to R.S. Gwynn who reviewed the book in 1986 in *The Texas Review* and found my peopling of the poem with unknown poets and other capital-city figures too privately allusive, mystifying, and finally misguided.

In his review, Gwynn is puzzled as to why he and other readers are subjected to "reading about these people?" Of one unnamed Austin poet—whom I never knew but whose poems live on for me and from which I constructed parts of my own stanzas in memory of her—the critic asks, "who is being talked about? Other than Oliphant's assertion that the dead woman was a good poet, I have no clue. Am I supposed to know?" Gwynn ultimately pronounces my poem a failure and concludes that it "is a thing that has not been *made*; it is a piece of writing. And there is all the difference in the world between the two." In the face of this kind of criticism, I vividly recalled Yeats's poem, yet I was unable to follow his sage advice to

> turn away
> And like a laughing string
> Whereon mad fingers play
> Amid a place of stone,
> Be secret and exult,
> Because of all things known
> That is most difficult.

I have never been good about keeping my mouth shut when I should. And once again I propose instead something of a reply to Sam Gwynn, despite the fact that I'm certain that he is correct, that indeed my long poem is not well made. My response, then, is not to his judgment of my work—i.e., that in Yeats's phrase it "has come to nothing"—but rather to Gwynn's questions concerning who the people are in *Austin* and why any reader should be subjected to hearing about them or their unknown poetry.

In defense of my approach as such, I will note that the technique of recycling others' writings for one's own purpose is a tried and true practice, which we have inherited most recently from such modernists as Joyce, Eliot, Pound, and, in particular in my own case, Louis Zukofsky, author of the long poem *A* begun in 1927 and completed in 1974. In *A*, a contemporary epic poem in 24 movements, Zukofsky incorporates the writings of innumerable authors whose words, images, and/or ideas have been important to his own life and thought, but without his always identifying them directly; instead, he silently absorbs them into the flow of his own poem. This in effect is what I have imitated in *Austin*, though at the time of working on this book-length poem I was not entirely aware of having followed Zukofsky's lead. For one thing, most of my sources were quite other than those of the New Yorker, although a number we shared in common, necessarily, since any writer returning to the roots of the poetic art—and especially to the epic—will ultimately reach back to the Greeks, to Virgil and Dante in Italy, and to *Beowulf* in England. In *Austin*, Homer's *The Odyssey*, Virgil's *The Aeneid*, Dante's *The Divine Comedy*, and Ariosto's *Orlando Furioso* all come into play in the development of the poem's themes and patterns.

A primary difference between my own revisiting of earlier poets and Zukofsky's is my special affinity for Spanish and Latin American writers, many of whom show up in *Austin* in relation to the history of the New World and to our own Southwest. Suffice it to say that the principal epic poets of the Spanish New World appear in *Austin*, that is, Alonso Ercilla of Chile, whose *La Araucana* is one of three books referred to in the famous book-burning episode in Cervantes's *Don Quijote* and spared by the curate who considers them "the best in heroic verse ever written in the Castilian tongue . . . the richest treasure of poetry Spain possesses," and Gaspar de Villagrá, whose *Historia de la Nueva México 1610* recounts in verse the exploration and Indian wars in New Mexico and Arizona in the first decade of the 1600s. Passages from both of those epic poems are interwoven, in my own translations, into the fabric of *Austin*, and in each case there are interconnections being made among my own life, persons I have known, and the various places I have lived throughout the state of Texas. This interrelationship of people, places, and poetry is true of the entire Austin poem. Additionally, all the poets mentioned or alluded to have a connection with Stephen F. Austin, the poem's hero, and to the city peopled by such writers as Austin's biographer, Eugene C. Barker, who himself is compared to the epic hero *el mío Cid* and through this semi-fictional character to the *ur*-biographer of Austin, Lester Gladstone Bugbee. Sam Gwynn was right to refer to my Austin poem as a "civic history," but then isn't the subject of the epic poem generally a city or cities in history—Troy in *The Iliad*, Carthage and Rome in *The Aeneid*, Florence in Dante, Heorot in *Beowulf*? While it may fail as a poem, *Austin* does accord in subject matter with the time-honored tradition of the genre.

Having established the identities of some of the many major poets alluded to in *Austin*, the question still remains, what about such minor figures as Susan Lucas, whose work is in all likelihood totally unknown to any reader outside the city limits of Austin and probably by all but a handful within? Allow me to answer this objection by calling up another name that appears in the pages of the poem: Dave Hickey, who is seen in part as a type of Orpheus, the mythical first singer. At the time of my writing of *Austin*, Hickey's fine short fiction was unavailable to an audience other than readers of the city's small magazines from the 1960s. In 1989 Southern Methodist University Press brought out Dave's *Prior Convictions*, a collection of his work from more than a quarter of a century before that has stood the test of time and was received with regrets that he had not continued as a fiction writer. The point here is that many of the Texas writers gracing the lines of *Austin* were and some still are almost completely unknown, and yet they deserved in my mind a certain recognition, so that my poem sought to credit them with a place in the history of the city and to record their contributions to Texas literature. Other more prominent names surface, but it was the little-known and probably wholly forgotten figures like Hans Hertzberg, Franklin Haar, and Wally Stopher III who stayed with me as vital links to the past history of poetry in Austin. Other local authors who contribute mightily to the Austin poem include Joseph Jones (of *Life on Waller Creek* fame), Thomas Whitbread, Carolyn Osborn, and on and on. Obviously name-dropping does not an epic make, though this sort of cataloging is also typical of the genre. And even though these writers put in only cameo appearances, they are all crucial to the larger design of the work as I, at least, envisioned it.

The few writers named here are but some of the many whose work I have long championed as part of an ongoing tradition of regional writing. Also present in *Austin* is Father Muldoon of the early nineteenth century, and from this same formative period I have spoken and written elsewhere on the German poets who emigrated to Texas. Spanish, Irish, German, Anglo-Saxon—all are central to the history of Texas writing. As for the future, it too will be indebted to and will draw upon the past. At present there are poets like Walter McDonald in Lubbock and Robert Fink in Abilene who are mining their experiences there and in the Vietnam war. Who can say what is to come? My notion in *Austin* was to suggest the important poets who had already appeared in Texas—particularly in the capital city—and to predict that more could come as a result of discovering in the local the stuff of poetry's universal concerns. The links with classical epics were intended to underscore the potential for heroic poetry in Texas, for the far-reaching connections possible through looking at something near and thinking about its archetypes in literary history, or the reverse—reading the classics and recognizing them as alive as ever in our own everyday existence. For even in the technological age, the poem is still the truest, most enduring, most meaningful form of space travel. Through the wonders of language we can retell and relive the stories of Odysscus, Aeneas, Dante, and Beowulf from bygone epochs, revisiting their lands and lore while sitting in our own air-conditioned living rooms. Likewise, through our reimagining of their imagery and adventures, we can foresee for Texas literature the endless possibilities promised by an awareness of the continuum of poetic expression.

While not every writer will rely on the classics for his or her inspiration or as a model for a local scene or situation, there is no doubt that the past will influence the future. A contemporary poet like Walt McDonald depends often and effectively on the Bible for his parallels and parables of modern life, as well as on such a fairy tale as Jack and the Beanstalk. Poetry, then, is by nature a rich blend of today, yesterday, and tomorrow, never confined by the limitations of space or time, in Texas or anywhere else.

History in the Texas Poem

The ties between history and poetry are a matter of the literary and historical records.* Much of what we now know of the ancient Greeks is owing to Homer's poems, just as our knowledge of the early lives of Italians, Spaniards, and even American Indians is owing to some extent to Dante, the anonymous author of *El mío Cid*, Alonso Ercilla in Chile, and Gaspar de Villagrá in New Mexico and the epic poems those poets left behind.[1] Likewise in our own time, the poetry of T.S. Eliot, Ezra Pound, William Carlos Williams, and Louis Zukofsky has recorded the history of twentieth-century life from the literary point of view. In creating their historically revealing poems, poets from all ages have necessarily depended on firsthand experiences or on sources close to the events which they report and through which they develop their characters, themes, and poetic structures. The relationship between a historical time and place and the poetry on which it is based has produced an impressive range of masterpieces, from Homer's *The Iliad* and *The Odyssey* to Pope's "The Rape of the Lock," Joel Barlow's "The Hasty Pudding," Wordsworth's *The Prelude*, and Whitman's "Song of Myself."

Although Texas history has fired the imaginations of countless movie producers, as well as inspiring a Whitman, who alludes to the Alamo and then retells the battle of Goliad and what he calls "the murder in cold blood of four hundred and twelve young men," it is perhaps too soon to say which of our contemporary poets' works will live on as important chronicles of Texas life. And while no Texas poet has yet achieved anything to approach Whitman's epic vision and revolutionary poetics, there is little in section 34 of "Song of Myself" that can lay claim to the kind of meaningful evaluation of the Texas experience that we would expect from poets significantly connected with the state. Whitman's views as expressed in section 34 are too

---

* This essay originally appeared in *Stone Drum*, no. 4 (Spring 1986): 64-81.
1. Alonso Ercilla, *La Araucana* (1569); Gaspar de Villagrá, *Historia de la Nueva México, 1610* (1620).

closely associated with manifest destiny, as are those in a poem by the second president of the Texas Republic, Mirabeau B. Lamar. In 1846, during the Mexican-American War, our poet-soldier used his verses to offer a gentlemanly apology to one of the many Mexican ladies with whom he delighted in socializing:

> But wo is me thy love to lose,
>   Apart from thee abiding;
> Between us roars a gloomy stream,
>   Our destiny dividing.
> That stream with blood incarnadined
> Flows from thy nation's erring mind,
> And rolls with ruin to thy kind,
>   O Donna Carmelita.[2]

Lamar may be aping Macbeth's use of the word "incarnadine," but even as he demonstrates his knowledge of Shakespeare (which was considerable, as evidenced by a poem composed some fifteen years earlier in his native North Carolina and entitled "New Year's Address"), he also reminds us of an era in Texas history which he himself experienced, and which caused in him both a sense of self-righteousness and of regret. The fact that Lamar's poem records this historical period and its effects on him is perhaps more interesting than anything else about his verses. For one thing, there seems more involved in the situation than even he may have cared to recognize. Certainly the questions raised by his lines are with us still and continue to plague us with self-righteousness and regret that differ only slightly from those felt by Lamar.

Homer's, Virgil's, Ercilla's, and Villagrá's balanced estimates of the qualities of their opponents are more in keeping with the type of poetry Texas may one day hope to produce. As to the contributions of those like Lamar who have done their best writing elsewhere before coming to Texas or have continued to base their poems on a background and experience in other places, such poets may represent superior talents, but what they have said on Texas and its history

---

2. Philip Graham, *The Life and Poems of Mirabeau B. Lamar* (Chapel Hill, NC: The University of North Carolina Press, 1938), p. 251.

(with the possible exception of William Carlos Williams' poem on El Paso, "The Desert Music," and Ronald Duncan's "A Short History of Texas") has yet to carry the weight of even the lesser works of native poets or those truly rooted in the state's way of life. Like Lamar's lines to Donna Carmelita, Father Michael Muldoon's verses from the days of Stephen F. Austin capture for us an historical time and place, in this case the scene of a big barbecue and the festivities following a baptism and marriage performed by the poet-priest at the Abner Kuykendall home circa 1830:

> To see whole steers on spits a turning!
> The dropping grease on embers burning!
> The whizzing stews, the broiling sound!
> The air perfumed all around,—
> No, no such feast was seen in Spain!
> Where he could cut and come again,—
> Where every one could gorge and swill!
> The Governor might his belly fill.
> The fiddle plays, all dancing go!
> Upon the light fantastic toe.
> Vermillion cheeks, and many faces,
> Seemed angels dancing with the graces.
> The wrestling waltz with arms entwining
> And heart and soul to love inclining,
> No stop, no pause the long lived night!
> 'Til Phoebus put the stars to flight;
> When cheeks from red to white as snow,
> Vicissitudes of beauty show.[3]

Father Muldoon's Milton-inspired couplets register an event from Texas history that is still very much a part of our contemporary life, just as are political and military differences. To find that we have changed little in our lifestyle and to hear it described in a lively manner by an early observer is rewarding even when the verses are imitative of an outmoded tradition. The value of Lamar and Muldoon's

---

3. Quoted in Mary Whatley Clarke's "Father Michael Muldoon," *Texana* 9, no. 3 (1971): 204.

versifying lies essentially, then, in the historical connections it reveals and the kinds of realizations about ourselves as present citizens of Texas that such verse makes possible.

Despite the view in some quarters that contemporary Texas poets are, like Father Muldoon, still working in outmoded traditions, as compared with poets in other parts of the nation, such native poets and those who have long resided in the state provide their readers with perspectives on Texas' natural and human histories that make of their writings an important basis for understanding the thoughts and feelings of a region's people—past, present, and future. A useful starting point for a discussion of contemporary Texas poetry and its role as a recorder of and commentator on Texas history is a poem by Dwight Fullingim, entitled "Poets of Texas":

> Not here, but in Gonzales, the Texas troops
> dragged their smoking cannon to a shallow creek and
> cooled its bore for a hundred years, the bronze barrel
> forming only the thinnest layer of patina.
>
> In that time, also, many church bells were
> buried in the wet sand along our coast, so that
> now there is great excitement when someone chinks in-
> to the flaking metal with an iron pick.
>
> Many of our poets are lost in the forest of neon
> palms, drinking for a time with the crowd of blond
> girls who will shed their lamé pants only hours
> before they're due at the office. Our sun is
> too strong and heartless; both blue and brown eyes
> squint at the least drop of water.[4]

The contrast and simultaneous comparison here between contemporary life and the period of Texas' struggle for independence are utilized by Fullingim to suggest that "the thinnest layer of patina" has settled over our lives. This analogical handling of Texas history is unusual

---

4. Dwight Fullingim, "Poets of Texas," in *Washing the Cow's Skull*, ed. Dave Oliphant and Luis Ramos-García (Fort Worth, TX: Prickly Pear Press, 1981), p. 236.

among Texas poets, but there are contemporaries of Fullingim who have made an equally impressive use of personal and not-too-distant events to reveal much about the nature of the state and those who have inhabited its landscape. Each area of the state has now given rise to articulate voices, and these in turn have rendered for us something of the part of Texas they have known most deeply.

Two poets from the Lubbock area have set down in stark but artfully crafted lines the hard lives endured by those who first settled West Texas and attempted to scratch a bare existence from its begrudging ground. The marks left on these people and on their descendants are symbolized in Walter McDonald's poem, "Adapting," by the rare magnolia tree that was knifed in the night out of a perverted sense of revenge.[5] The poet has found in such an event a troubling need for violence, and in McDonald's "Settling the Plains," he hints that West Texas was settled out of desperation:

> Families came creaking
> in wagons. Some
> ignoring all reports;
> some intending
> only to pass through:
> broke down
> and had to stay.
> Some, simply lost.
> This flat land was nothing
> then but prairie grass.
> What have we done,
> they must have thought, what
> have we done.
> The children likely
> waited near the loose
> wood spokes of wagon wheels.
> Their mother may have
> hugged her arms. Their father
> likely shrugged. Shook

5. Walter McDonald, *One Thing Leads to Another* (New Braunfels, TX: Cedar Rock Press, 1978, p. 31.

his head. Said hell. Said
help me hitch up the plow.[6]

The desperate nature of West Texas life comes out repeatedly in poems on this section of the state, but always there is a certain heroic quality to the stoic lives of those who have taken root and accepted the challenge of a place they may have meant to pass on through.

In the poetry of Charles Behlen a sense of hopelessness and despair pervades the lives of people who have survived as broken, haunted figures. Behlen's images of women—one wife "dazed by 30 years / of pressing clothes"; another with her hands scrambled in her useless lap as she is carted off to the rest home—are powerful emblems of the damage and desperation inflicted by overwork and a lack of love. In "Cora Stroud" Behlen gives us a grim portrait that is drawn with the aid of references to oil pumps in a realistic landscape that corresponds to a human insensitivity the woman has known and suffered from:

When Burns, your husband,
laughed at the way
he'd throw your shrivelled
leg aside and thrust into you as
you wept and pleaded,
all of the farmers
in Boyce's Grocery
turned to the window
and counted boxcars
swaying to Lubbock.

When we came for you,
Burns stood in his yard,
clutched his rage in
his folded arms and
grinned at his windmill
leeching the dust,
grinned at a twister

6. Ibid., p. 26.

ten miles from Waco
that thrashed the power lines,
blinded his house.

Mamie, your sister,
followed the wheelchair
tracking the dust as
you inched your wired hips
from room to room and
sorted by flashlight
the heaps of old clothes
for the long journey.

Vaporlocking
through oilfields
into Abilene,
the Chevy jerked
past the black pumps
that pulled and shoved
in the August heat.
Wide-eyed, wordless, you
stared as the potholes
scrambled the hands
in your useless lap.

At the Golden Age Home
we emptied your bags
into the stained bureau,
hung your Christ
on the blankest wall,
pumped your shrivelled
hand goodbye.[7]

Not all the poets living in the western reaches of the state have
emphasized the harshness of its existence as a source of desperation.

7. Charles Behlen, *Perdition's Keepsake* (Fort Worth, TX: Prickly Pear Press, 1978),
pp. 34-35.

In El Paso, Robert Burlingame has in fact found in his surroundings the stuff of a positive poetics. His poem "Desert, Not Wasteland" begins much as does Ralph Waldo Emerson's "Hamatreya," by listing what the land produces, with the difference that the New Englander's apples, hemp, hay, and wood are replaced by "Squaw-thorn, devilsclaw, and Joshua; / Sunray, bullhead, and Spanish bayonet." Burlingame goes on to say that

> These are the plants of the desert,
> A hard, curt, unpretentious poetry
> Put down in the margins of bloodshed.
> They need at most an inch this side death
> To reach the rude drop hidden like love's wink
> Inside a trim pelvis, perfect but unlavish.
>
> They prevail. Each root a beak, each pore
> A womb, each stem and leaf thorn-arbored
> Beneath a sky blandly immaculate.
> Here love is solemn, a strict icon of thirst;
> And birth a blind tear in a sun-chiseled font.
> Here no sound but wind scales the dry heights.
>
> And what, one asks, can man's damp brain
> Take from such wealth speared without greed
> To this light-cisterned land? What parable?
> Nothing. Against lip old peace engods first silence.
> Soundless, rock ripes on rock.
> From beardtongue's flame no speech save flame.
>
> In grails of heat life guards its grace, quiet.[8]

Burlingame's "hard, curt, unpretentious poetry" defines succinctly the poetics of this region. Although such a positive note may be fairly rare among the unsentimental poets of the western parts of Texas, even in poems that present histories of "quiet desperation" there is always something celebratory and near-religious in the treatment of those

8. Robert Burlingame, "Desert, Not Wasteland," in *Washing the Cow's Skull*, p. 66.

who have endured such a rock-bed existence. At times there can be a touch of sympathetic satire implied in this braving of an often rugged environment, as in Joseph Colin Murphey's "Crop Duster Disaster":

A Tri-Pacer, an Apache
a Pawnee and a Bellanca
burned in the small town
airport fire here last night

One of them, the livelihood
of the once-dare-devil-P-47
World War II Ace now faced
with living dangerously only

over wheat fields, corn and maize
Sitting at Duffers over coffee
the next day, the Gothic wrinkles
of his face reveal

only what he wants to show
The blue haze of his eyes shield
the heart. His cowboy hat, jeans
and boots accent the lean hips

of the dream self his blond wife
dresses him toward each day
warming herself at the fire of his
hard core death defying smile[9]

Murphey's contrast of his pilot's exploits in World War II with his present lifestyle captures much of the nostalgia in Texas for a macho image that dies hard.

A poet who echoes Charles Behlen's empathy with the elderly and Joe Murphey's subtle sense of humor is David Yates, who could write in more of a surrealistic vein. In Yates's "Snickersnee," the

9. Joseph Colin Murphey, *A Return to the Landscape* (Fort Worth, TX: Prickly Pear Press, 1979), p. 37.

seemingly senile uncle plays out the narrator's fantasy of revenge on the indifferent family members. In blending references to cutlery, a cutting winter wind, bayonets, fighting with knives, and a brandished sabre, Yates expertly develops his commentary on our slighting of the aged who like old horses are considered "not much use anymore," which goes as well for Uncle Stafford's word "snickersnee." Here the history of World War I serves as part of this poem's far-reaching pattern of symbolism:

> Mom just finished saying, "Bless this food," when
> Uncle Stafford cut in with, "Do you know
> what 'snickersnee' means?" Mom hurried her
> amen and told us all that we could eat.
>
> Daddy carved the turkey with his electric
> knife. Thin slivers of white meat curled down like
> Swiss cheese and his knife hummed like a sewing
> machine. The wind cut through cracks in the window.
>
> "I'll give you a clue," said Uncle Stafford,
> and I passed the cranberry sauce over
> to Uncle Reno. Aunt Dickey ate scalloped
> potatoes. She likes to chew the crisp ones.
>
> "It comes from the Dutch word *steken*," he revealed.
> "Eat your oat meal. Eat it," Daddy told him,
> but it was pasty and needed more milk.
> Through the window panes I could see snow,
>
> and I thought about the times Uncle Stafford
> told me about the Germans, how he fought
> them in Alsace while the snow covered the dead.
> Their bayonets were sharp. Like icicles.
>
> "It's archaic now," Uncle Stafford added,
> speaking of snickersnee. Uncle Reno
> gobbled on an ear of white corn. Aunt Dickey
> told him to chew softer, to slow up some.

Daddy told Mom the snow bothered him, cut
through him to the bone and he was glad
he put the horses in the barn. Old Red Boy
has digestive troubles, so Daddy provides him

with crushed oats, sometimes mixed with chaff and mash.
He's not much use anymore. When he moves,
his nostrils whistle, but Daddy says he
can't bear the thought of turning him out.

"It means 'fighting with knives,' though we never
use it anymore," Uncle Stafford says
and I see him rise from the table until he
hovers above us, brandishing a saber.

He shakes that saber at Daddy and stabs out
an eye. He plunges deep into the heart
of Uncle Reno and severs Aunt Dickey's
head. He slashes Mom in her left side.

But they never stop. They keep on. Dad, with
one eye gone, asks Reno what's the best
fertilizer. Reno wipes blood from his chest
and says horse manure. Aunt Dickey, her head

on the floor, chews another potato,
and Mom, her whole side bleeding, says Reverend
Draper's preaching tonight and shouldn't we go?
Daddy finally reaches up and grabs

Uncle Stafford by his snow white hair. He sets
him back down in his chair. "Eat, Stafford, your
oat meal. You hear?" This time Uncle Stafford eats.
I see milk trickle down the wrinkles of his chin.[10]

---

10. David C. Yates, *Riding for the Dome* (New Braunfels, TX: Cedar Rock Press, 1979), pp. 34-35.

One of the most frequent motifs in any poetry is that of loss, either personal or communal. Texas has been witness to the rapid rise and virtual withdrawal of the cowboy as representative of a way of life (except, of course, on the movie screen), and the nostalgia for this horseman's passing has dominated much of Texas writing, at least in prose. A less romantic version of this aspect of Texas history was treated by Glenn Beaudry, a one-time teacher at East Texas State University, in his poem entitled "A View of Older Horsemen from the Back of the Bus." In this piece, Beaudry not only alludes to the disappearance of an older Texas but to its replacement by a newer, more sinister Texas symbolized by the oil industry:

> Past *Midland* the skies slide side-
> ways off the derrick peaks like a dry
> gravel off cracked saddles on a hot night.
> The metronomic heads of cows collide
> as they up-and-down for water white with alkali,
> the plunging tongues beside them sleek and bright,
> lapping out largesse left and right
> from those lolling pools whose gross slick eye
> bulges up from the root of its dark nerve.
> There is a jolt, a hairpin curve,
> you bear closer in to where, with a swerve,
> the probing looks up to gnomic taproots
> sucked up by great leeches along with raw hide
> and atomic sutured bones and baggage and boots
> and thick black blood stained on panama suits
> as the bleached-brown cows dip past you as on you ride.[11]

Larry McMurtry, whose *Horseman, Pass By* is the classic novelistic treatment of the theme of the new versus the old Texas, has called for writers of the state (and by this he really means novelists) to focus on urban life rather than reworking the same tired soil of ranching days.[12]

---

11. Glenn Beaudry, "A View of Older Horsemen From the Back of the Bus," in *The New Breed: An Anthology of Texas Poets*, ed. Dave Oliphant (Malta, IL: Prickly Pear Press, 1973), p. 19.
12. Larry McMurtry, "Ever a Bridegroom: Reflections on the Failure of Texas Literature," *The Texas Observer* (October 23, 1981): 10.

Until fairly recently, however, most writers grew up in small towns or even in makeshift oil camps, and these experiences have been the subject of many contemporary Texas poems. The poets of this rural upbringing often sought to escape what they felt to be the small town's cultural deprivation; on the other hand, they have lamented the loss of its close family or communal ties, with the cause of this loss being traced—if only by implication—to the poet's move to the big city. A number of poets like Michael Anderson have thought to discover by revisiting their "roots"—if with only questionable success—a missing link in their lives that seemed an essential part of their narrow existence, in Anderson's case in a Phillips Petroleum Trailer Park. Returning to his former home in the title poem of his collection *The Road, The Eye*, Anderson finds "only a veiled evacuated / space, all the trailer houses long / gone, the gas and water connections, / twisted from split concrete slabs . . .," metaphorically implying his own broken connections with his "birthing place" and the emptiness of his quest.[13] A more typical piece by this poet, entitled "Relativity," concerns a familial loss:

> A bloody beechwood tree
> dropped into the swamp,
> sinking leisurely beneath
> the spring-green ooze,
> and a million years later,
> decayed, drilled, distilled,
> that wood—now gasoline—
> gave my mother's Chevy
> the speed it needed
> to bang a concrete bridge
> and veneer her wrinkles
> with a make-up of steel.[14]

Here the poet has achieved—through a type of cosmic irony reminiscent of Thomas Hardy's in "The Convergence of the Twain"—a synthesis of scientific thought, geological time, the refinery process,

13. Michael Anderson, *The Road, The Eye* (Dallas, TX: Texas Center for Writers Press, 1978), p. 18.
14. Michael Anderson, "Relativity," in *Chawed Rawzin* (Lubbock, TX: n.d.): [1].

and personal loss. Like the best poetry of any age, Anderson's poem "distills" his subject by presenting in few lines much history and its telling effects.

In keeping with McMurtry's call for an urban Texas writing, but written long before he issued in 1981 his public summons, I myself attempted to recount the impact of urban life on those coming from rural areas of the state, as well as on those coming from other states. The history in "Houston"—from my sequence "Memories of Texas Towns & Cities"—is both personal and communal in its recollection of the social, cultural, and political dimensions of urban life.

> The air is heavy with wet,
> heavier on a hot muggy day.
> Out of the bayou mouths
> mosquitoes float
> in thick humming breaths,
> swarming so, you nearly choke,
> or if not, then gag on chemical clouds
> of the fumigator's nightly spray.
>
> It's a weather sticks with you
> more than men. Everything
> is close: clothes in summer
> sucking the sweat, gray sky kissing
> the morning mist, closets of damp and mildew,
> apartments compact as hives,
> though honeyless. Everything close, except the lives,
> those, more often asunder.
>
> A stadium of voices from every state,
> urgent accents from East and West,
> a U. of Michigan graduate
> once linebacker on a Rose Bowl team
> turned a 9-to-5er in a bruising Bank and Trust,
> or the man Prudential Insurance moved,
> with wife and kids, from their Connecticut dream,
> reshowing the Hartford slides, hoping it somehow soothed.

Come to a complex from the country, the only Texans there,
our pup, a few months old, blown apart
by the dogcatcher's high-powered legal weapon,
the church bazaar and cakewalk
on an asphalt court of St. Vincent de Paul's
when our allowance went for naught,
the junior high dance when I wouldn't dare
hold her near, all the days it wasn't fun.

Rules seemed harder to learn.
Multiplication tables bored.
Swimming nude in a school pool made cheeks burn.
In games only the bullies scored.
And then, any lessons were lost on weekends
when nothing made so much sense
as trading the kid with a Mohawk strip for Batman comic books
or watching on our first TV "Boston Blackie" catching crooks.

In neighboring woods we knew how red and black
is a friend of Jack,
how red and yellow
can kill a fellow,
but on the streets or in the halls
we couldn't quite distinguish,
all—red, black, or white—seemed corals,
cold snakes of injustice.

Even knowing the names of trees,
memorizing dates, i's before e's,
made nothing right or easier.
The girl with rheumatic fever,
who could never leave her room,
only the half-wit spoke with her,
mashing his nose against the screen.
Once recovered, she found him a bother.

But enough of this.
Every ledger has another side,

and on it I can list
people have made it a matter of pride
I spent eight months in this metropolis, though known
more for NASA and artificial turf of the Astrodome
than for those converted to our countless gain
their long nights of loneliness and pain.

I think of Bracker, my faithful friend,
who wrote of life with his father there
in a simple four-line poem that pays
true homage to the man, his tender ways;
recall how Vassar Miller's sonnets mend
a broken spirit's beauty, taking care
the boney wisdom—the metered touch—offset
a body born in the red;

hear Stokowski and the orchestra
heap the city's treasure store
with an Ives or a Villa-Lobos score;
after Barbara Jordan's puissant speech, hurrah
for the election gave her a seat, more for the vote she cast
to bring men closer than a coastal climate—
enter them all as accounts receivable, a balancing of hate,
a summing in solvent black what once but appeared a
      bankrupt past.[15]

Just as Anglo poets in Texas have interpreted personal events in the context of historical time, so too such minority poets as Carmen Tafolla and Harryette Mullen have done the same for Chicano and Black experience. In Tafolla's "Memories," she makes connections between her family history—her own racial and personal heritage— and past eras associated with the Medina River.

Medina Magiadora.
My campmeeting-preacher grandfather

---

15. Dave Oliphant, *Lines & Mounds* (Berkeley, CA: Thorp Springs Press, 1976), pp. 52-54.

used to wash souls here
baptizing them
in the name of.

My fronteriza-fuerte great-grandmother
washed clothes here
washed clothes here
scaring the stains away
from her loved ones' clothes.

I only wash memories
of lives and times I never knew
dipping them delicately
in the soft water of the shady
Medina
softly polishing them clean
until the faces of the past are clear

. . . hello, great-grandma,
in your 1867 norteña vaquero jacket
and your tiny unconquerable
face and frame.
. . . the frozen crisp image of a little boy
guiding log-laden mules
through the icy mountain morning,
dreaming of running far away
from his dead parents' graves,
dreaming of being far away
from the cold and the death . . .
. . . A bugler in the Civil War
who didn't speak English.
. . . Indian chicken-thief taking
out his anger on the small farms
around San Antonio,
taking his tiny brigade
on a joy-ride chicken-shout celebration
bareback around their civilization

taking what was his.
... A worried family offering a white horse instead
so Pancho Villa wouldn't take their youngest son
as soldier.
... A widow crossing an unimportant river,
later to become the Greenback-Wetback Curtain ...
... A Basque street urchin flippantly jumping aboard ship
for an unknown world
easy to conquer
in his young
pickpocket mind.
... una india, maidservant in the colonizer's house,
desired and daring, too efficient, too beautiful, too smart,
chased out after she bore his child,
alone but strong,
still studying, still too smart.
... quiet centuries of sailors and seashore dreamers,
quiet farmers, loud gypsies, songmakers, and metalworkers,
flow here from the ocean.
... star-scholars, hunters, potters, dream-workers,
curanderas, earth-workers, drum-dancers,
sun-worshippers and river-followers
pour here from the land.
... vaqueros, fronterizos, rebeldes, and
as always, dreamers, poets
grow here,
breathe here now,
drinking from the waters
of the Medina.
Medina Magiadora.
Aquí estoy,
lavando mi herencia.[16]

The poem ends in Spanish with a phrase that summarizes the object
of Tafolla's work as a poet: the washing of her inheritance in an effort
to bring back its clarity and significance.

---

16. Carmen Tafolla, "Memories," in *Washing the Cow's Skull*, pp. 326-328.

The work of Harryette Mullen is similar in this regard, especially in poems based on her own family history. An unpublished piece entitled "Generations" celebrates the risks taken and the miracles performed by Mullen's forebears under much harsher circumstances than she and her fellow Black writers have experienced since the advent of emancipation and integration. Mullen suggests, however, that even with all the freedom the later generations have enjoyed, their lives have not produced the admirable qualities, attitudes, and accomplishments of those who endured slavery and segregation. Here the gaining of greater freedom ironically has brought with it the loss of a meaningfulness that was the inspirational mark of those earlier lives. In her poem "For My Grandfather, Lowell Paxton Mitchell," Mullen draws many parallels between her grandfather and Christ, at the same time that she comments subtly on the history of racial prejudice through her natural use of color imagery:

> I remember you, Granddaddy, in shades of black and white.
> On weekdays working in carpenter's overalls
> striped like mattress ticking,
> with a hammer swinging at your side.
> Tall, strong man who could lift me up to touch
> the crystal chandelier,
> you would raise up a house on a solid foundation,
> hammering together the upright ribs of the frame,
> holding the nail in a deep-creased, hard-calloused hand,
> between two fingers and a grim, tortured thumbnail.
>
> On Sunday mornings you stood in the pulpit of Greater
>   New Hope,
> preaching a meat-and-gravy sermon,
> wearing a serious, scowling black suit.
> Your shirts came fresh from the laundry,
> "washed whiter than snow"
> and folded around stiff sheets of white cardboard
> perfect for your grandgirls' homemade paperdolls.
> Leaning out over the congregation
> you mopped your face with a starched white handkerchief

that, by the end of the sermon, was soaked with sweat.
After church we climbed into Betsy, your black Chevy,
and you took us for Carnation ice cream,
poured pennies in our palms,
and tossed us packs of Juicy Fruit gum.
Your pockets jingled like the collection plate.

There were black rubber hip boots
you wore fishing on Saturdays
and also for first Sunday baptisms,
where white robes of reborn Christians
spread wide like nets in the water.
I always thought you liked to go fishing
because the apostles were fishermen,
who became "fishers of men."
I thought you worked as a carpenter
because that's what Jesus would have been.

I see you after blackouts and strokes
sunken in a hospital bed with white sheet
tucked up to your chin.
Your big strong body shrunken
until your huge head leaned
like a heavy dark flower on a thick stalk.

And when you died, you appeared a final time
in black and white,
in a newspaper clipping
I keep between the pages of a black-bound Bible.[17]

History is indeed alive in the Texas poem, even when all is not well with the past or present that such poems bring to mind. The purpose of much Texas poetry is in fact to recall personal, regional, and world history in order to aid in the growth of our sensitivity and intelligence, and as a means of expanding our consciousness and of

17. Harryette Mullen, *Tree Tall Woman* (Galveston, TX: Energy Earth Communications, Inc., 1981), pp. 14-15.

appealing to our conscience. There are many poems that could be cited as examples of a tendency to remind us of and to distill for us the events and trends that continue to shape our lives. William Barney, of Fort Worth, has certainly produced some of the most profound writing in Texas, and his "Threshold," a poem which he first published in 1962, still offers a powerful vision of natural history and the evolutionary potential in the simplest forms of life. By extension, this poem suggests as well the vast potential for Texas poetry, which in many ways has already been realized by such figures as Barney, William Burford, and Vassar Miller. Indeed, these and other poets like them have taken Texas poetry beyond the "threshold" and into the realm of a distinctive contribution to our national literature, as can be seen by the artistry and the universal scope of this thought-provoking poem by William Barney:

> An eyelid of the sea can stretch,
> a film slide inward till it fades, till it stains
> the sand with shining. On this long-drawn beach
> a bird of orange bill precisely planes
> the highmark of the wave, a connoisseur
> feeding upon parabola.
>
>   Here burrows
> that armorless snail with dexterous toe
> desperately into sand, as though
> caught out of wet he shrivels (does this
> deftly: the disappearing quick finesse
> would marvel a badger). One moment discovered,
> nude in pure air without skin of sea
> or sand, he panics in extremity
> back into mothering muck.
>
>   Something is severed
> by his delving: he fears too much the sun,
> keeps silence. Only in well-bred books
> break lamentations. No peril provokes
> these tidal blobs into suspiration
> bitter for saving sound. Utterly naked,
> stripped-of-all-shell race, of shelter

and adequate roof for hiding, backward
clan, they await the helter-skelter
stroke of shaping history;
the wave, the underplowing scroll,
the rote, scratch, brazing abrading push-pull
that reduces (it pumps there in the skull,
in the heart, whatever cockpit of destiny
governs our going—there's no other mangle
to spoil and sprawl them other than that
milled in the mind's whorl). Let them learn to exult
for a weather managed; snails too may shudder
counting the wind.

                              Yet there's order,
learning to burrow. This anonymous
slick mollusc coming from the sea
has got his footstep on the threshold
of magnificent stairs. Suppose he learns
to keep his lust for salt controlled,
in generations to walk tall, breathe free?
Will he be justified to seek a turn
at the roulette of self. We ask a question
without answer: the skimmer sweeps the beach
unceasingly, the surf diminishes to gloss.
Safe in his sump the snail may reach
his own extravagant conclusion:
momentum locked in stars may ride his genes,
from meaningless ends to sort enduring means.[18] .

18. William Barney, *The Killdeer Crying: Selected Poems*, second, expanded edition
(Fort Worth, TX: Prickly Pear Press, 1983), pp. 32-33.

II.

Coming Home

to

Texas

A Yankee Poet in Texas

Ubi sunt? is a poet's constant question, not only the romantic's but the classical and the contemporary's alike.* In a Spanish version of Heraclitus, the philosopher states that no man bathes in the same river twice. Thomas Whitbread has both lamented and celebrated this fate of things, standing, poetically speaking, where he "half-reaccepts the intricacy of living." His own poems are simple-sounding but intricate designs which

> seem greatest [when] some major change
> Comes of the evening, such as a reformed mind,
> A new sense of limits and of wider range.

As a former student who has returned often to fruitful re-readings of such poems as "Motorcyclist" and "Breakings," I acknowledge the enduring lessons Tom Whitbread has taught me: to accept limitations of our own making or those imposed by nature, while yet thinking it possible "to change the music of the stream / By dipping an idle finger into it." Ringing his changes on the mutability theme, Whitbread has achieved a body of poems full of sympathy for the common fate of place and flesh, forming thus in his poems a bond between the two. The sonnet form is made for such a meeting of mutable and immutable, and in Whitbread's crafted stanzas there is grasped an understanding and acceptance of time's sculpting hand.

Perhaps the truest paradigm for Whitbread's method and meaning is found in one of his favorite images, that of the pond. As a poet, Whitbread is the captain in his "Captain's Pond," the man who believes "when there's nothing to be believed," one who dives into the muck of romance, of a bloody Argentine rite, of the rubble of civil war, of a friend's suicide, of any pond where "antagonisms meet," bringing back to life "credence as our constancy." Despite his questions as to "who can bare / scar-piercing changes in his central

---

* *Lucille*, no. 10 (Summer 1978): 8-9.

cells?" Tom Whitbread has long been willing to risk the depths and dangers awaiting just below the ordinary surface where "extremes meet," breaking from poem to poem the "bloody pond" and the "silent miles" in hopes we grow "reminiscent," "to feel whole," to find our way "Towards warmth again, away from emptiness."

This is much, and we are fortunate indeed that this New York-Massachusetts Yankee came to Texas to share with us how at Fresh Pond "as the world grew dark" he and his friends "drew together."

Nye's *Eye-to-Eye* and *Different Ways to Pray*

Like *Tattooed Feet*, Naomi Shihab Nye's earlier chapbook from Texas Portfolio, her *Eye-to-Eye* is a catching piece of work—infectious as laughter and as welcome.* Not that these are comic poems. Many touch on the dark side of our lives—the death-in-life of the elderly, the slide show where "lives pull apart like old cloth. / You mend and mend so long, then make rags." Yet always the theme of darkness "like a heavy coat / I didn't want to put on" is balanced by the lighter one of "breaking into song." A number of poems attempt to survive "all those dark hours" by dreaming, remembering, or dancing:

> We danced. And everyone loved us
> because we did what they maybe felt,
> but didn't do. I carry this with me,
> that sometimes things happen
> which no one could have planned
> and they are, beyond everything,
> true.

In another piece (dedicated to William Stafford, who took the cover photo of Nye), she speaks of how her poet-photographer friend can "Leave us that small place where a stone / enters the water, / the feel of a chair in our dark." Much of Naomi Nye's work concerns itself with just such a search for small places (of integrity, of feeling, of "a delicate enterprise / of eyes") within a larger world of darkness or unseeing.

Aside from the thematic content of this collection—though significantly linked to it—there are the stylistic and technical aspects of Nye's work which merit attention as well. Even when the piece is a playful love poem, as in the case of "How It Is," the poet by means of fine understatement makes the lightest subject carry a fairly heavy load, as she ends this piece on separation of lover-friends with "Now comes the hard part." Similarly, in writing of an "Address Book," she

---

* *Lucille*, no. 10 (Summer 1978): 68-69.

creates an analogy between book and house in order to achieve in the final stanza a more serious statement than the subject might have seemed capable of offering:

You handed me a pencil and let me move in
O what an intimate evening, you and I,
propped in the same catalog like fence-posts
linking the distant regions of the earth

Although many of Nye's metaphors (or similes) are quite fresh and engaging, others seem too easy, too sentimental, too catchy, as in "San Antonio":

I remembered the old men
in the west side cafe,
dealing dominoes like magical charms.
It was then I knew,
like a woman looking backwards,
I could not leave you,
or find anyone I loved more

The metaphors of the first and last poems of the collection ("Eye-to-Eye" and "Arriving at a Fish") are some of the strongest, but the analogy of westward movement in "The Saddest Cowboy in Texas"—

For days something inside him
pushes west, farther than the land
or his own skin can let him go

—strikes me as too surrealistic in a clichéd sense, a reaching for the ineffable solely for effect. At such times the effort fails to convince, despite the value of the object reached for.

On the whole *Eye-to-Eye* is an easy book to read—the lines moving as smoothly as the rivers that inhabit Nye's poems, with water being equated with the free flow of feelings (though at times the poetry gagging us like her "stick caught halfway / between a river and a sob"). What is most attractive in her work is Nye's ability to maintain an openness to the simplest events and to celebrate them with a matching candor and with an uncommon freshness of expression. And while her poems move in the mind with a natural ease, her openness to her subjects and her accompanying naturalness of treatment are not at all easy for a writer to manage, and for this reason we cannot help but find her performances infectious, something like the child's brief vacation-providing illness that any sibling would love to catch.

Naomi Nye's third volume, *Different Ways to Pray* (from Breitenbush Publications), takes her readers along with the poet on travels to Palestine, to Latin America, to bakeries, and into the lives of volcanoes, fish, tables, streets, and relatives, to discover, once again, the miracles of small events and memories:

> I found the table at a store called
> "The Hand and the Heart"
> I was not looking for tables
>
> The table sat in the center of the room
> leaves like wings folded at its sides
> a single drawer with a runner that stuck
>
> Now I am learning the comfort of wood
> as I place my head on the table
> as I fold my hands over the scars
> (from "The Comfort of Wood")*

Nye's use of simile here and elsewhere is for purposes of making things appear sacred, and her metaphors are always integral and aid in her effort to achieve the emotional or philosophical statement. Although she often employs comparison, she mostly seems intent on presenting objects and people as they are. Nye's poems are essentially caring, yet the poet does not at all ignore the sad side of life:

---

* *New Letters* 48, no. 2 (Winter 1981/82): 105-107.

Before you know kindness as the deepest thing inside,
You must know sorrow as the other deepest thing.
You must wake up with sorrow.
You must speak to it till your voice
catches the thread of all sorrows
and you see the size of the cloth.
(from "Kindness")

Nye's work is marked by its search for and discovery of such "regions of kindness." In "A Survey of Breads in Popayan, Colombia," she writes of a policeman who gives her "half his breakfast and we smile, clear signals in the traffic." In "At Otto's Place," she finds "a therapy in fields," and in the poem already cited, "the comfort of wood." As in "Kansas," Nye constantly responds to situations with hope:

I'm lost, you moan, I have no idea where we are.
I pat your arm. It's alright, I say.
Surely there's a turn-off up here
somewhere.

No matter where she is, at home or abroad, Nye emphasizes the positive, the open, the accepting, and the hopeful:

More and more I understand what people do
I appreciate the daily braveries   the clean white skirts
morning greetings between old men
(from "What People Do")

And she handed me one perfect pink rose,
because we had noticed each other, and that was all.
One rose coming into Cuzco and I was thinking
it should not be so difficult to be happy in this world.
(from "Coming into Cuzco")

For some this may prove a bit too much sentiment, too much sweetness and light, but for others I suspect that this will suit them perfectly, those in need of therapy and comfort.

The most impressive poems in this third collection are too long to quote in their entirety: "For Mohammed on the Mountain" (a fine piece on an uncle in Palestine who chose to go alone and live on a mountain for the rest of his life); "Negotiations with a Volcano" ("We need dreams the shapes of lakes, / with mornings in them thick as fish"); and the title poem, which contains a passage that may serve to sum up Nye's poetic vision:

> There were the men who had been shepherds so long
> they walked like sheep.
> Under the olive trees, they raised their arms
> Hear us! We have pain on earth!
> We have so much pain there is no place to store it!
> But the olives bobbed peacefully
> in fragrant buckets of vinegar and thyme.
> At night the men ate heartily, flat bread and white cheese,
> and were happy in spite of the pain,
> because there was also happiness.

Two Cedar Rock Poets

One development—perhaps the most important—in recent Texas small-press history has been the rise of *Cedar Rock* magazine with its concomitant chapbook series from Cedar Rock Press.* Editor David Yates has not only established a nationally recognized magazine outside the metropolitan areas of the state but has given to columnists, poets, fiction writers, and correspondents throughout Texas and the nation an opportunity to engage in a wide range of literary expression, unrestricted to any one school or region. Even though all the columnists are in Texas, with the exception of Judson Jerome, the contributors of poetry and fiction are located from coast to coast. The mark of every issue of the magazine is its catholicity of representation—from prison poetry to a homemaker's dishpan verse, from prose poems to one of R.S. Gwynn's brilliant columns in Pope-like rhymed couplets! The editor's taste leans heavily toward natural lines that express a lively attachment to the things and occasions of contemporary life. This same general view of the magazine's contents holds true for the poems found in the press's chapbook series (with again the exception of a hardback edition of Judson Jerome's collected poetry). Of the half-dozen titles published under the Cedar Rock imprint, the most outstanding are *Riding for the Dome* by Yates himself (his second chapbook—the first, *Making Bread*, also from Cedar Rock Press) and *One Thing Leads to Another* by Walter McDonald, his second of three published volumes.

Designed by Dwight Fullingim along the lines of his own earlier chapbook series from *Texas Portfolio*, these are attractive publications, with the cover art of Yates's volume remaining its only real disappointment, and this apparently not Fullingim's but the poet's idea, since the former always prefers a photograph of his authors, as in the very striking example on the front cover of the McDonald chapbook. As with the tasteful choice of format, the poetry included in both collections is appealing, and it is representative of each poet's strongest work to

* *The Pawn Review* 4, no. 1 (Winter 1980-1981): 90-97.

date. While the poems in each chapbook belong together as a group, they are limited neither in form nor in subject matter. Indeed, both chapbooks signal the coming of age of two essentially unlike, though authentically regional, stylists.

David Yates's work contains the necessary ingredients to make of him a popular poet in the tradition of Carl Sandburg and Vachel Lindsay. His poetry is lighthearted and meant to be read aloud to an audience, which Yates does often and always with success. And yet there is substance to the poetry; it holds up well on the page. A perfect example of the poet's ability to combine pop humor and artistry is "Sex," with its almost hilarious opening lines:

> I think about it
> every time I'm in Mentone, Texas,
> way out there in
> lonely Loving County

In this poem there is a vital use of old material (a "making it new") in Yates's handling of Texas' unpredictable and extreme weather. The analogy between the atmospheric conditions above the Permian Basin and human sexuality is true at once to West Texas life and to the universal response of lovemaking. Although the ending is somewhat unrelated to the carefully worked out conceit, it is typical of Yates's tendency to settle for a fairly tame conclusion after a rather wild, attention-getting start. The point of many of his poems is ultimately on the side of sentiment or is left open, perhaps as a way either of minimizing, in his playfully unassuming manner, what has gone before, or of emphasizing the ongoing nature of his subjects. One reason the cover design of the book falls short of the volume's high level of writing is that its amateurish drawing of a hooded skeleton seated at the steering wheel is so uncharacteristic of the poet's basic point of view. Yates is all for life, not death, and even when his poems come to endings less vivid or memorable than one could wish, what is presented along the way does evoke and celebrate everyday incidents, dramatizing them through a durable, imaginative diction.

Thematic concerns in Yates's second volume vary just enough to maintain the reader's enthusiasm from poem to poem, despite a certain repetition of such topics as the poet on poetry, the longing for escape or for a return to the good old days, and the century's lack of human communication. To summarize Yates's themes in this way, however, does not do justice to his undeniable rightness of tone in poem after poem. We are won over again and again by the urgency of the speakers in his poetry and their intense desire to have their say. Above all, Yates should be recognized, and is to be commended, for his creation of a cast of unforgettable characters who may talk of a same obsession—mostly of how to flee our wasteland of indifference—yet who do so in winning lines that hold us breathless up to the end (perhaps another reason a Yates closure eases off a bit compared to the rest of the piece). Uncle Reno, Uncle Stafford, Dickey and Aunt Dickey, Daddy and Mom—all of these and more are figures with whom any reader cannot help but identify fully. Whether tender or absurd, their declarations are destined to move and delight us each time we return to Yates's beautifully modulated narratives. Here is a favorite already with many readers:

> Dickey hollered to us all
> but to no one in particular
> that he was no longer for sale,
> that he was nobody's real estate any longer,
> that he was tired of chasing
> stray cows and breaking wild horses,
> that he was on his way to Dallas,
> where he'd be the Lone Ranger
> and not have to answer
> to nobody:
> not his sisters or his mother
> or Daddy or Aunt Dickey
> or the big-assed ranch foreman
> or the earth the sky the rain
> not anything, not anybody!

All this declared, of course, before he passes out in the middle of the street from a night out and is carried home and put to bed by his friends.

Structurally Yates's work is varied just enough to satisfy our need for the formal aspect of any poem worth its salt. In "Watching the Super Bowl in Uncle Reno's Home in Dallas," the poet alternates the man's and woman's voices to a wonderfully ironic effect as each speaker concentrates on his and her immediate object. (Walt McDonald has tried this sort of alternation in "My Neighbor Who Kept Pigeons" but fails to bring it off nearly so well.) The man in Yates's poem wants his football team to win, while the woman wishes the man would pay attention to her. By turns the situation is funny and touching, the writing pulling us both ways at once. Here the ending functions artfully as it drives home the final phrase, "don't take a chance," which bears significantly on the hopes and fears of both speakers in the poem. The poet shifts points of view deftly, both here and in the finely wrought conversation of "Snickersnee." In the latter Yates mixes colloquial language with allusions to a dictionary meaning and to a bayonet fight in snow during the First World War, creating simultaneously in his measured quatrains a realistic bit of table talk and a thrilling moment of surrealistic revenge. References to the wind cutting to the bone, to what kind of feed is best for an old horse, and to carving the turkey—all are blended into a metaphorical episode in which "senile" Uncle Stafford gets back at the family for ignoring his explanation of the word "snickersnee":

> I see him rise from the table until he
> hovers above us, brandishing a saber.
>
> He shakes that saber at Daddy and stabs out
> an eye. He plunges deep into the heart
> of Uncle Reno and severs Aunt Dickey's
> head. He slashes Mom in her left side.
>
> But they never stop. They keep on. Dad, with
> one eye gone, asks Reno what's the best
> fertilizer. Reno wipes blood from his chest
> and says horse manure. Aunt Dickey, her head
>
> on the floor, chews another potato,
> and Mom, her whole side bleeding, says Reverend
> Draper's preaching tonight and shouldn't we go?

The unobtrusive and only occasional rhymes add irony to the formal structuring of an outrageous scene. In at least two other poems Yates employs rhyming in an equally effective and subtle manner. Generally the look of his poems and the way they read so clearly and flow so naturally disguise the fact that the lines are internally and terminally shaped and tuned by a fine eye and ear. Again, the pure sound of the poet's work makes it a sure hit with any audience, while on the page it rewards the closest reading and rereading.

Walt McDonald has also staked out for himself a poetic territory for cultivation and harvest, in his case the unlikely area of Lubbock and the Llano Estacado. In *One Thing Leads to Another* (1978), the poet may have gathered his finest group of poems, even though he has two other strong collections to his credit: *Caliban in Blue* (1976) and *Anything, Anything* (1980). Both Yates and McDonald share with a number of other contemporary Texas poets the production of important bodies of work that are impressive for their volume alone. McDonald has himself gone from being an occasional poet to one approaching the prolific Emily Dickinson of 1862, the year in which she wrote 366 poems—McDonald having written more than 100 during 1977 or thereabouts. At times poets are criticized for writing too much, as when the individual pieces cannot justify themselves, and McDonald's work may be open to such a charge. Yet his collection from Cedar Rock Press suffers only partially from the effects of an obsessive writing habit. It may be that most of these poems came prior to his *annus mirabilis*, for some appeared in magazines several years earlier. One point in this chapbook's favor is its length—only twenty-seven pages of poetry. The selection is divided into five sections and each offers a mere handful of poems, but most stand on their own. All work well within the sections and some are as good as McDonald's best. The poet may have poems equal to many of these and better than several, but as a whole this collection introduces strengths not present in the poet's first book and performances rarely surpassed, if at all, in his third volume.

For the first time a McDonald collection contains a section of poems devoted exclusively to the poet's native region, though he has since written numerous poems on West Texas life—where it seldom rains, where trees are at a premium, and where most people stopped for "good" after finally giving up on finding El Dorado. McDonald sees his people as adaptable, a quality he obviously admires and celebrates in poems that treat of those who arrived, looked around at the godforsaken place, said "hell" and "help me hitch up the plow." The crop yield is as grim as the life that brought it forth:

> plants with bones
> for stalks survive the wind
> and grow red fists of flowers.

McDonald has recorded with a natural objectivity the violence that has also grown from such a tightfisted existence. An increasing number of the poems refer to his people's essentially unsettled ways, which seem the result of the region's severe strain on their emotional systems. Some adapt but others take to getting back by knifing the priceless trees in a strangely perverse revenge.

Paul Christensen has referred to a Texas poet's rites of passage as a typical theme, and in McDonald's work one can easily find a representative instance. Yet a poem like "The Year She Turned Sixteen" is not simply characteristic of a Texas upbringing but speaks of that age when the young awaken to the "glory" of sex:

> Her eyes sheened
> Gloria would come late to homeroom
> clothed in cologne.
> Glory, someone would groan,
> with all rows moaning Glory
> Glory.

(This opening stanza *might* be seen as a Texas version of Herrick's "Upon Julia's Clothes.") Later in life McDonald comes to experience this same awakening in the lives of his own sons who cannot believe he once tracked down the magic of love like a Jack and the Beanstalk bringing back the goose that could lay the golden egg. And then in "Cindy at Vallecito" McDonald describes his daughter's excitement at fishing and beating her brothers by snagging the biggest catch. The need to find magic at all ages is beautifully rendered in the best of

McDonald's work, where one poem after another leads us to a discovery of those memorable, if painful, moments of youth.

In *Anything, Anything*, McDonald's poems have grown more sinister. Two of the finest pieces in the Cedar Rock volume are reprinted in this collection from L'Epervier Press; others which carry through with similar interests, such as retellings of biblical stories, regional sketches, and family relationships, represent a continuation more than an advance. Yet this is certainly no small accomplishment, given the high quality of McDonald's previous work. But by and large it is the sinister nature of this new book that makes it what it is—a further commentary on the desperate lives of the region. If this is intended as a metaphor for contemporary life, it is even more disturbing than if it merely speaks of the desperation born of a "wasteland" existence in the American West. Three poems at the heart of the book are especially powerful and sum up the situation: "Signs and Warnings," "At the Human Development Center," and "The Girl in the Mackinaw and Panties."

As in the earlier McDonald book from Cedar Rock Press, tortured cats serve as a symbol for the cruelty of those who somehow hold a deep-seated resentment. (Curiously, and perhaps revealingly, a book entitled *Kitty Torture* was published in Austin about the same time as *Anything, Anything* and was extremely popular in certain quarters.) Cats that are decapitated and dropped on the speaker's porch (in "Signs and Warnings") or that have been beaten in the head and are mercifully shot with a B-B gun by the man who finds them (in "Overheard")—these suggest a perversity inherent in the region, or again, throughout our entire contemporary world. In his moving description of the Human Development Center the poet remarks that

> Nothing
> about this place seems like a hospital.
> They must not think they're sick.
> Only unlucky. That, they can understand.
> Here what they get is luck: methadone,
> valium, the address of AA, whatever
> it takes to get them by, sometimes
> no more than fifteen minutes of crying

in a room with someone who doesn't
beat them.

McDonald has descended into this hell and returned to report on its
suffering with oppressively ironic overtones. The message is almost
too painful to bear, yet the poet must be praised for the truth of his
vision. Here it seems undeniable that the reference is to man's inhu-
manity to man, in or out of Texas. And though I must admit that my
own squeamishness in these matters may prevent me from finding
the new writing in *Anything, Anything* superior to McDonald's earlier
achievements, clearly it is strong medicine.

One hang-up I have is with the use of the pronoun "you" in
place of the narrative "I" or a third-person pronoun, a practice I find
presumptuous and typical of the Iowa Writers Workshop approach.
Still, I can see how McDonald has made good use of this device in
his poem on picking up a hitchhiker, the better perhaps to distance
himself from the embarrassed narrator who finds himself caught
up in another person's fearful flight. The poem is a telling one and
epitomizes the sinister nature of McDonald's recent work. Written
in three-line stanzas, the poem is carefully crafted—with line breaks,
similes, and conversational excerpts all controlled for the final effect
of the poet's subtle suggestion that there is some unseen figure or
force threatening the girl's very existence. Here, however, the menace
is not the same as that hinted at in "Especially at Night" or "On the
Farm," where death and the unknown flash their malignant "signs and
warnings." For "The Girl in the Mackinaw and Panties" is probably
just showing her boyfriend or husband that she won't take any further
abuse. In some ways melodramatic, the poem is masterfully constructed, with internal rhymes calculated to underscore the uncomfortable
feeling experienced by driver and rider alike, their situation at once
laughable and unnerving:

> You open the pickup
> door and she climbs in,
>
> her panties showing. Hi there,
> you say, shifting up as you go.

You live around this way?

Just take me the other side of Slaton,
she says, her words hard as her knees.
You try steering your eyes off her

bare legs to keep from killing
you both. Lose something
in a poker game? You try

to joke. Listen is all she says,
shut up and drive. She keeps
looking back. Faster, she says.

Between David Yates and Walt McDonald, two of our important Texas poets, there may lie a world of difference in terms of their
points of view, but both share similar techniques and both have
written on similar themes. More significant is the fact that together
they have brought to the state a vital new writing with its roots in
the region and its branches extending beyond to all readers who can
appreciate the genuine article. If the one can chill us with versions of
our deepest fears and darkest deeds, the other will warm us with his
deeply human portraits of aging men and love-starved women. Both
deserve a sensitive readership, for each in his way has created poems
to which all can respond, just as McDonald's son responds, in "At the
Football Stadium" from *Anything, Anything*, on looking through his
binoculars at the moon,

> a round orange tunnel
> in the east.
> . . .
> Silent, under the savage crowd noise,
> beneath the lens and his fists
> he mouthed an O.

From the Foreword to *Two Gulls, One Hawk*

With the title poem of this volume, James Hoggard has created a long, dialectical piece that is unique in Texas letters.* And
while it is the authentic expression of a native poet, "Two Gulls, One
Hawk" draws upon a wide range of biblical, classical, mystical, and
Southwestern strains in building up and counterpointing its themes
of family love, a sense of place, and the mind's act of imagination.
Weaving his images and motifs—of sticks, snakes, birds, grasshoppers,
the weather, miracles, and human ties—Hoggard presents a warp and
woof that is at once Southwestern and Greek, prophetic and poetic,
contemporary and classical. The poem's alternating voices are rich
with linguistic play and moving in their emotional responses one to
the other. Much of the work's multilevel impact is owing to the poet's
skillful manipulation of his image and motivic patterns in a poetic line
that is his alone. As a poem that concerns husband-wife and father-
son relationships, it is the work of a mature artist who has come to
sing of universals in a local idiom that includes the lowly sights and
sounds of mesquite and cicada.

On the other hand, "Tornado's Eye" is a poem that recalls the
poet's origins, his early journey into the caves of mystery and meaning.
In his search for a self-image, the boy in Hoggard's autobiographical
piece stumbles over one impression after another, only vaguely aware
of a trail that will eventually lead him to poetic invention. The awk-
wardness of the youth is paralleled by the poem's fumbling effort to
discover a voice and a means of recording the significance inherent
in the poet's past. Even though such an interpretation constitutes a
pathetic fallacy, "Tornado's Eye" serves nevertheless as an important
complement to the title poem—the one revealing Hoggard's struggle
to create a viable and vital art, the other paying witness to the fact that
the poet has, as D.H. Lawrence proclaimed, "come through." Without
the first there is not the second, and to have them both is evidence

---

* James Hoggard, *Two Gulls, One Hawk* (Cedar Park, TX: Prickly Pear Press, 1983),
pp. [i]-ii.

of the necessary ground that has been covered, not only by James Hoggard but by other Texas poets of a generation that promised much and has now delivered.

Coming Home to Texas:
The Poetry of R.G. Vliet and Betty Adcock

On a PBS television program written and narrated by Bill Moyers, this native of Marshall, Texas, returned to his hometown to interview its people and to review the history of a place that had left an indelible mark on him and his generation.* In speaking with a descendant of one of the area's cotton barons, Moyers discovered that two Blacks who had once been slaves there, but who had moved away on being emancipated, left a request that their bodies be returned for burial at the site of their former enslavement. It was suggested that a family closeness could account for this homecoming, yet to Moyers there seemed something in such a wish not to be explained by this or any other fact.

This same enigma of place magnetism is apparent in the work of two Texas poets, R.G. Vliet and Betty Adcock, the latter a native of East Texas and the former a product of his sometime education and residence in a state that has continued to inspire his award-winning books of prose and poetry. As writers who have lived outside the state for most of their writing careers, but whose works are imbedded in Texas as a place and an idea, Vliet and Adcock share participation in a phenomenon that is becoming more and more evident: what Joseph Colin Murphey, another native East Texas poet, has called "a return to the landscape." In a number of cases, this attempt at coming to terms with a place that means more than can be fully understood or expressed has taken the form of a prolonged imaginative response by those who have left the region yet return to it through the written word. Aside from what these writers specifically tell us about the Texas experience or the translation of a Texas mythos into poetry, their need to retrace their steps and to decipher through symbolic language what they knew in this state suggests that a given place as subject often endures beyond our being there and can provide one of the most vital sources of our writing.

---

* *The Pawn Review*, vol. 8 (1984): 105-121.

The recent reprinting by Shearer Press of Bryan, Texas, of R.G. Vliet's poem, "Clem Maverick," as a separate book publication, is call for a general assessment of this writer's work as a Texas poet. Vliet's three previous volumes of poems are *Events & Celebrations* (Viking, 1966, which included "Clem Maverick"), *The Man With the Black Mouth* (Kayak, 1970), and *Water & Stone* (Random House, 1980). Both the 1966 and 1970 collections won awards for poetry from the Texas Institute of Letters. For my money, however, *Water & Stone* is the strongest volume of poems Vliet has yet published. Although the book publication of "Clem Maverick" promises greater recognition for Vliet's talents, *Water & Stone* represents the fullest expression of this poet's art as regards its aesthetic preoccupations and proclivities as well as its debt to sources in Texas. By way of discussing Vliet's achievement in *Water & Stone*, it is fitting on the twentieth anniversary of the first appearance of "Clem Maverick" to review the poet's work as it has developed during these past two decades.

Two years before Viking Press released *Events & Celebrations*, Vliet's first volume of poems, *The Texas Quarterly* printed the poet's "Clem Maverick" in its autumn 1964 issue, and at that date this poem was truly an "event" to be "celebrated." Now in 1984, Shearer Press has reprinted the poem sequence in a beautifully designed book with woodcut illustrations by Barbara Whitehead. From the first section of this long poem, the reader is gripped by the accuracy of detail and the skillful handling of sound and sense:

> Today in the capital it's Clem Maverick Day.
> High-stepping, white-crotched majorettes gambol.
> Corps of twirlers prance away,
> tails snapping in the sun like shrimp for gumbo,
>
> boots cut tall and skirts cut short.
> The entire legislature's adjourned for the day
> to watch the apple-kneed twirlers sport
> as twenty-seven hand-picked school bands play
>
> Dixie and Aggieland and Semper Fidelis.
> Today in the capital it's Clem Maverick Day,

the governor a-saddle, the queen in her trellis,
the thousand-gallon stetsons of paper maché,

the rose-wove floats of Texas-size guitars,
the cowgirl duchesses in bannered cars.
The whole damn crowd just stomps and roars,
and tonight there'll be a host of recording stars.

Told in various voices from country-music singer Clem
Maverick's past ("the characters depicted here have no relationship
to actual persons"), the poem follows the recording star's rise and fall,
with each of the twenty sections shaped into a different verse form,
which in itself makes of the piece a tour de force. Essentially the
work has stood the test of time, for the story line is still intriguing,
the verse forms are artfully crafted, and the sound and imagery are
an effective blend of folksy talk and figurative touches. For all this,
however, the music star himself comes off as a rather stylized creation.
The verse as well is by and large contrived for the purpose of tracing
the musician's dramatic climb to fame and his inevitable decline to
disillusion and drink. Fortunately, the speakers in the poem reveal as
much about themselves as they do about Clem Maverick, although
each contributes some insight into the causes for his unique manner
of performing:

> Clem climbed black branches
> to give the tree a shake, but it come
> a rotten branch. Clem's arm never
> did set too right. It's how come
> he helt his guitar so peculiar[;]

his popularity: "It was the wild and the lonesome / and the hurt.
Women loved it"; his romantic nature: "He poured ketchup / on
everything he et. Yep, and one minute / be bawling like a baby at a
purty sunset"; and his exploitation by "Top Notch Music."

The most moving sections of "Clem Maverick" are those narrated by his mother and the women who knew him, especially sections

IV and XV, which recall the death of one of Clem's sisters and the climactic drive from Kansas to Texas when the singer puts a scare into a university co-ed before she realizes "all he wanted was me to ride / on his back." Section IV makes effective use of country imagery, with its blend of quotidian life and religion, and both the occasional internal rhymes and the credible bits of dialect combine to produce one of the high points in Vliet's poetic output:

> And I had one
> daughter onct. Name of Augusta.
> I ain't never lost her face. I tell you
> it'll take the steers of Hell to drag her
> from my breath. Her dear small breath
> I kissed it. She was perfect of light
> and gentleness. It was a Wednesday she
> took sick. She turnt such shining
> eyes and fever cheeks. She burnt
> along her hair. Days and days. She fair
> went like kindlin. Then got so strange
> and peaceable, like settlin of ashes and past
> her hurt. Wanted up from bed. She said,
> Mama it's so *light*. Her pore daddy
> helt her thin as sticks in his arms
> and she said, Put on my bonnet. I put
> the little fresh muslin bonnet
> on her head. She werent but five. I said,
> Gussie do you want to see God? Yes
> Mama. Do you want to see Rudy? Yes . . .
> Mama.

The weakest sections involve a rather artificial use of hick expressions like "That liveoak puredee *thrives*" or "the crowd so allfired thick / a puredee stick / couldn't stir it." I must admit that this use of dialect was highly attractive when I first read it in 1964, because it did sound like certain people I had heard. Looking back I can see how Vliet's work was an influence on my own thinking for half-a-dozen years afterwards. But this kind of stereotypical narration can be used only for special effects, and in the long run it sounds mannered, regardless of how real it may be in and of itself.

"Clem Maverick," positioned at the center of *Events & Celebrations*, was the heart of Vliet's first book. The rest of the volume was less impressive, less memorable, and yet both the centerpiece of the collection and many of the shorter poems are representative of Vliet's persistent concerns and techniques. Likewise, in *Water & Stone* the strongest writing appears in the two long sequences, "Passage" and the title poem "Water & Stone," which carry the collection. Vliet's major achievement as a poet is to be found, then, in his three longer pieces—"Clem Maverick," "Passage," and "Water & Stone"—and it is also in these three works that he has most clearly relied on Texas sources and has most fully commented on his own Texas experience.

In "Clem Maverick" and "Water & Stone," Vliet has hit upon an original use of Texas material through his creation of dramatic monologues for a gathering of regional voices. In "Passage" he reports on personal moments that led to his becoming a poet whose dramatic and aesthetic concerns are essentially extra-regional. Although he has continued to write poems grounded to an extent in Texas settings, Vliet has attempted through such sources to speak with the sensibility of a Matthew Arnold, which has resulted for the most part in Vliet's brand of hybrid poetry. For while his poems approach the real lives of the various speakers in "Clem Maverick" and "Water & Stone," ultimately Vliet's work lacks a convincing vision of Texas life and experience, just as it lacks a poetics that is comfortably at home in Texas.

Vliet's tendency to combine a type of sensual-poetic drama with very human moments of natural tension was demonstrated early on in the section entitled "Ballad" from "Clem Maverick," which is the only section of the sequence later reprinted in *Water & Stone*. "Ballad," section V, concerns the murder of a rancher's wife who has been left alone with a Mexican hired hand. Vliet is attracted to such a ballad theme because it offers a heightened moment, the kind of effect he is usually after in all his poems (as well as in his novels, which also involve sensuality and murder).* Vliet also has an attraction to such "realistic" violence as this ballad situation provides for his writing:

---

* See "Violent Beginnings," my composite review of Vliet's three novels, *Rockspring*, *Soledad*, and *Scorpio Rising*, in *The Texas Observer* (February 12, 1993): 16-17.

he knifed her until her own heart's blood
ran down her milk white knees,
ran down her milk white knees.

A similar piece from *Water & Stone* is entitled "Penny Ballad of Elvious Ricks" and concerns another murder, here of lovers shot by a jealous boyfriend. (Vliet considers this poem a parody, but if this is so, then it may be equally the case with much of his other work in this same vein, though it seems unlikely that such pieces are simply parodic.) "To Die By Daylight" is still another instance from *Water & Stone* of Vliet's fascination with an event that contains what he terms, in this poem on the death of a Mexican child, the "climactic, wellnigh sexual." (Vliet's treatment of Mexican subjects in this light is more believable than when he applies it to Texas settings.) Perhaps the most effective of the shorter poems involving violence is "Legend," also from *Water & Stone*, which recreates the slaying of three brothers:

> the pursued
> caught, the smoking knife
> and naked bone, the bloody,
> folded clothes,
> an immense
> energy hangs suspended,
> consummate, its motion no longer
> forward, a stain in the air.

Vliet's use of ballad and legend in his titles would seem to underscore his need to stylize a dramatic moment, whether by turning it into myth or into parody.

This same type of dramatic moment, with its after-effects on the lives of those involved, is also the subject of the title poem of *Water & Stone*. Constructed after a Japanese Noh play, "Water & Stone" treats of an accidental drowning of a youth whom two male picnickers, watching at a distance with their female companions, choose not to rescue. As in his ballads, Vliet employs a landscape reminiscent of Texas to set up the poetic backdrop against which he will play out his historical-sounding event. (It might be noted that both "Penny

Ballad" and "Water & Stone" seem to derive from incidents in or conceivably connected with the town of Comfort, Texas.) It is in his writing of such consciously poetic backdrops that Vliet would raise the "facts" to a level of high drama:

> Again and again and again. Sudden rain
> lashes the ground. The river rises,
> foams. Sap rises from the root,
> hurting us with its power, hydraulic
> power that crams the buds. Can you hear
> the pain?
> Can you hear the noise of the pain, pink
> butterfly-crowd [*sic*] flowers?

The combination of "hydraulic / power" and the "noise of the pain" places the poem at a pitch that is hyperbolic. This same heightening of the scene can be found in the narration of Lee Benbow, the drowned boy's brother, with its "O the redbuds! Pale / as a brother's drowned heart." Even though the landscape is at times rendered realistically—

> Brush scrapes the runningboard
> here in the cedar-choked pastures where
> armadillos snuffed among roots at dusk
> and a boy lugged a birdgun after doves

—this is the voice, supposedly, of an unsophisticated truck driver, and thus the sound of the writing is out of keeping with the way we would imagine the character to speak. Ultimately, however, the power of "Water & Stone" is not to be denied, and it represents the strongest work in this book and, in several ways, a more significant achievement even than "Clem Maverick."

"Water & Stone," like "Clem Maverick," is a poem made up of speakers from the Texas past who report the effects on their lives of, in this case, the young boy's drowning. The dramatic monologues by this group of speakers (male and female) are more penetrating as psychological studies than those in "Clem Maverick." The language is essentially that of a poetic play, and as such there is greater verisimilitude in its portrayal of the speakers' sense of remorse, of their memories haunted by the realization of a tragic failure to act. Nevertheless, Vliet's penchant for what he must take to be aesthetically fine writing frequently mars a subject that is naturally charged and, whenever he allows it, can speak quite expressively for itself. Vliet prefers instead a stylized approach to his subjects, and the result is often the forcing of his sense of aesthetics on an inherently poetic context, a type of gilding of the lily. Thus, there is a tendency for the poet to end a speaker's monologue with heavy-handed symbolism:

> I never married.
> I taught school for twenty years
> and will for twenty years more.
> I wish I were one of my children
> standing on the schoolhouse steps,
> washed faces, fresh shirts
> and pinafores, waiting for the camera click
> with wide, innocent stares.
> Nights I dream of redbud pods
> churning in the wind, hissing like foam·
> Judas' face
> > purple on the tree.

The redbud image is repeated throughout the poem and the sound made by the wind churning like the river that produces foam suggests in the word "hissing" something of nature's disapproval that reflects the speaker's own sense of remorse. But the reference to "Judas' face" is too blatantly symbolic and jars against the naturalness of the speaker's previous lines. Because of this tendency to overstate the case, Vliet's poems necessarily falsify at some point the crucial experiences of his speakers. In his attempt to elevate the subjects into an air of aestheticism, the poet lifts them out of the reality that gave them life.

Although "Clem Maverick" largely avoids the sort of self-conscious poeticizing found in "Water & Stone," even in that earlier sequence Vliet could lapse into such lines as "hummingbird / caught / in a web / beating / like a piece / of green / fire / like a satiny / daymoth thing." In the shorter poems, Vliet is almost always after the aesthetically conscious effect. His revisions of poems from *Events & Celebrations* for inclusion in *Water & Stone* are an example of this, in particular the poem entitled "Invocation," which closes the earlier book and in the later has been reworked so that the more natural line lengths have now been shortened in order to heighten each phrase (or at least this seems to be the intent). A comparison of the two versions will reveal that the change has only weakened the impact of the poem's statement. Vliet's shorter pieces are overly precious and generally sound a false note that has marred his work from the beginning and is at odds with his claim that he would call a spade a spade. In part this is the case because he continues to reprint the same aesthetically conscious pieces from his first collection; in part because many of the new pieces are more often than not equally ineffectual by reason of their artsiness. There are exceptions in *Water & Stone*. "The Peaceable Kingdom" is a slant-rhymed, utopian piece with a persuasive integration of imagery and meaning unusual in Vliet's shorter works:

> Then men sleep. Space
>
> grows mineral and quiet. The tools
> of theft and death hang
> in the barns. Into the inhuman sweet
> silence groundhogs and moles
> ascend and feed. Rabbits
> range for kernels along
> the close-order fieldcorn rows. . . .
> Beasts possess the field.
> Mice climb the cane
> spears and deer browse
> on swords.

"Muscovy Duck," an even shorter, tighter poem, is built on a number of striking analogies drawn between the "latent images" of "Strange, weak, reptilian / hatchlings" and a variety of natural and man-made objects—a realistic/poetic rendering that is Vliet's trademark in most of his shorter pieces, as in "Games, Hard Press and Bruise of the Flesh" and in "As if *karew karew*" (the latter from *Events & Celebrations*). In these last two poems, however, there is realism of descriptive detail but an unreal pressing for a sensual contrast or connection that again works against the ultimate effect of much of the writing. This has always struck me as a desire on Vliet's part to escape into a realm of aesthetics quite removed from the realism of his subject matter. This reaching for the "poetic" is unconvincing and tends to contradict the reality of Vliet's vividly regional subjects.

Many of the defects apparent in Vliet's shorter poems are also found in "Passage," which is the central poem-sequence in *Water & Stone*. Yet here Vliet writes autobiographically, and so long as he permits an experience to stand on its own, the effect is moving, and convincingly so. Especially powerful is section VI, subtitled "Running, And How I Learned to Fly." Even here, however, Vliet cannot resist a need to poeticize, to bring in what he refers to in "Poetry (If It Must Come)" (also reprinted from *Events & Celebrations*) as the "insubstantial air." The opening of the section recounts dramatically his bout with cancer and simultaneously a race he ran as a boy:

> Now, after surgeons' knives, cobalt's
> basilisk stare, the destroyed blood,
> I dream of running. Rounding the curve,
> my breaths relaxed and fat, strength
> gathering as it never does in fact,
> once more I pull ahead of the runner
> from Houston. I did one day
> of crucifixive breath,
> locked thighs and knotted back,
> breaking through the wall of iron victory
> into the arms, nearly, of death. But now
> his is a complementary flesh, our pain
> joint animal joy, motion
> the orison of being. I am
> the god of the nine-foot stride.

After this gripping start, Vliet begins to relate his development as a poet to an adolescent desire to rise above schoolmates who made fun of his big ears. There is something incongruous about the leap from realism to this sentence:

> From that it was an easy matter
> to glide pterodactyl-like from roofs
> and trees, to grow feathers and fly.

Perhaps he is correlating his own poetic development with man's evolutionary stages, but this fanciful leap removes the experience from any actual growth process. The connection seems too far-fetched for a section of the poem concerned with "breaking through the wall of iron victory / into the arms, nearly, of death." The next line, with its allusion to Icarus, does recover the intensity of the parallel between his struggle with cancer and his boyhood race, and does relate to the desire for flight or a rising above his schoolmates: "I have come too close to the sun / of disease." This section ends superbly and in its direct handling of the subject achieves the highest form of poetry in Vliet's best book of poems:

> Sleet ticks
> on the window, and again I feel the nausea
> lift its curdled head. Outside
> in the dark the numb, bent trees
> explode, shattering ice onto the crusted
> snow. A gun cracks. In the green
> heat of my sickness I run, this time
> past dusty leaves, up an incline
> on a dry, country road.

Section VII of "Passage" is a tender love song for the poet's wife, and in this lyrical, at times almost sixteenth-century movement, the heightening that Vliet seeks so often seems fully justified:

> When
> we shall not be
> may this song
> stonecrop

flower of a small gift
ever cherish thee.

In the end, however, "Passage" is a disappointment, for the last three
sections of the poem fall flat in their attempt at transcendence and
transubstantiation. Section VIII is a mishmash of the realistic and the
ritualistic, where a naked girl "moons" in a river and "is taken up / into
another language, another country." These three sections epitomize
Vliet's weaknesses as a poet, and even though they also represent his
most ambitious effort, the results are not compelling either in their
manner or in their message.

If Vliet's aesthetics are somewhat easier to take in his autobiographical sequence, it is because the subject is his own development
as a poet. In other words, he is discussing and describing an aesthetics that is natural to him but which for the most part belongs more
appropriately to an Edwardian, an Elizabethan or a Mycenaean age.
When he applies such self-conscious aesthetics to themes and subjects from the country days of an earlier Texas, there is an unreality
about his writing. The modern narrator of an excerpt from Vliet's
novel, *Scorpio Rising*, published in *The Pawn Review* in 1983 and then
entitled *Another Country* (like the phrase in "Passage" cited above), is
on his way back to Texas from New England.* Vliet himself lived in
the Vermont-western Massachusetts area for many years but returned
to Texas as a Dobie Paisano Fellow to work on this last novel. At each
of the narrator's stops along the train route, he discovers that he is
going backwards in time. A calendar reads "1902 July 1902" and at
the final stop in the excerpt he has boarded a horse-drawn "conveyance." The youth in *Another Country* sounds suspect when he says
"it well-nigh hypnotizes you" and then uses such words and phrases
as "conveyance," "placed in strategic places," and "a gigantic, high-
ceilinged concourse." Just so, Vliet's mixture of Texas downhome with
sophisticated phraseology is an indication of how distant his writing
can remain from an authentic Texas past or present. In much of his
poetry not only does Vliet frequently fail to approach a real Texas,
but the language he and his speakers employ is often inappropriate

---

* See "Violent Beginnings," my composite review of Vliet's three novels, *Rockspring,
Soledad,* and *Scorpio Rising,* in *The Texas Observer* (February 12, 1993): 16-17.

to the person or situation, is spoken (if at all) in "another country." Even though Vliet was educated in Texas, has written often on "Texas" subjects, and has returned to the state for inspiration and support, in certain ways his conception of poetry has not gone hand-in-hand with a Texas habitation. Only when he has come at his own experience and that of others more directly—minus the adornment of poeticisms— has he written with the authentic ring of a man alive to reality more than to a spurious set of aesthetics.

By contrast, the work of Betty Adcock provides both subjects and approaches of real significance to a developing Texas poetry. Adcock's return to her native ground is extremely revealing as a method and as an exploration of responses—her own and those of others—to a particular people and place. Like Vliet, Adcock is aware of a visionary, mystical quality to her subject matter, yet unlike Vliet's, her handling of this surreal aspect is convincing and is not impaired by poeticisms that cannot do justice to the actual observations or insights being offered. Adcock has recalled with great sensitivity the scenes she saw and lived through in East Texas, and by means of a precise rendering of sense impressions she has discovered the deeper meanings of her regional experience.

By way of calling my attention to the fact that I had not in previous review-essays noted the work of Texas writers living outside the state, Adcock sent me her latest collection of poems, *Nettles*, published in 1983 by L.S.U. Press. In reply to my news that I planned a review of her book, she responded in turn with what for my purposes proved a highly instructive letter. I excerpt this passage with her permission:

> It is quite true that I am known, insofar as I am known at all, as a southern poet. That's partly because the experiences I write about [in] east Texas are common to southerners everywhere.... Landscape is everything, finally. Still, east Texas was something besides southern, some difficult something I hope someday to capture. My part of the redlands was a strange mixture....

Born in St. Augustine, Texas, in 1938, Betty Adcock has revisited her redlands part of the state in two fine collections of poems, both from L.S.U. Press. Her first book, *Walking Out* (1975), contains a number of exceptional pieces that would seem to derive from her Texas experience, although rarely are they identified as such. Among these would be "Identity," "Things Left Standing," "Louisiana Line," "The Sixth Day," and "Water." What is particularly remarkable about these poems is that, for me at least, they speak more clearly in her own voice than do those pieces that I take to be of non-Texas origins, and at the same time they foreshadow the later development of even more powerful work in *Nettles*. This difference between the Texas and non-Texas pieces is most evident in the first poems in *Walking Out*, which sound overly indebted to Anne Sexton and her witch/mother obsession. Stylistically such a piece as "Gretel Now" recalls Sexton both in its imagery and its diction:

> When I sleep I dream a threat
> to push into the oven's throat.
> I wake to a tickle of mice who ate
> the careful road of signal bread.
> How much longer can I wait
> with the secret house inside my head?

Although the Sexton influence does seem obvious, the theme of identity is one that also figures significantly in such a poem as Adcock's "Identity," which concerns her own mother who died early in the poet's life. Much of the writing in Adcock's first collection is extremely private in nature, and for this reason its metaphorical meaning tends to be fairly difficult to interpret. Nonetheless, in what I am hypothesizing is work based on her Texas years, the poetic sense comes across more plainly and the metaphors function as part of a world that can be shared more directly. It is definitely in the "Texas poems" of *Walking Out* that Adcock moves beyond the Sexton influence and into her own country, the one where her shaping voice seems more at home.

It is perhaps partly due to the types of experiences recorded by Adcock from her redlands upbringing that she is better able to communicate a vision of time and transcendence which seems at the heart of most all her poetry. An example would be "South Woods in October, With the Spiders of Memory," the first poem in *Nettles*, which refers to the poet's baptism:

> that silent passage through breaking
> unbreathable circles of light
> where you were caught quaking and brief
> in the fingers of clarity.

Such luminous events are evoked for their visionary nature, but often even the simplest objects—as in her poem "The Farm," also in *Nettles*—lend to Adcock's imagination a profound sense of human and natural relationships:

> Melons in grandfather's field
> had always one paler side
> from touching earth, remembering that dark
> with a little loss.

Light, loss, and memory are constants in Adcock's poetry, even to the point that they become somewhat predictable, especially the image of light. Nevertheless, the range of revelations the poet achieves through these three motifs is quite impressive, as she recovers the lost through returning in memory to explore its meaning. As she says in "Things Left Standing" from *Walking Out*, her own writing is like a child "who was left or whose ghost stayed / to study the seasons of corn." In a pine grove she discovers a gutted house that she had not seen before, and in it she finds that "children / grown tall and permitted / their will among the unused" have left their names

> cut deep in three walls,
> and shapes: every sexual part, all things
> male and female carved outsized,
> whole new animals
> in a wooden impossible book.
>
> In the movement of shadow, that place
> trembled with ritual, with the finding

that always is personless.
I spoke to the fields
severed names, fragments, forbidden
words notched crookedly, correct.

I lay down near a tree, slept,
and my dream shaped a man,
made simply of summer and grass,
who would take on a face, who would hold me
speaking the tongue of the touched.
I woke with the grass on my dress,
sharp stain that would stay.

The ghost that clouds any window
only at one angle of vision
was gone when I turned for home.

That which is given once
or thrown like a curse or a weapon
came both ways in the ruins of August.
I knew the dead child in the glass,
knew the sun with its open knife
and I stood up in the smell of the future
to wear as time had given
the green, deep scars of the light.

Here and elsewhere in her work, Adcock vivifies her memories through such images of indelibility as the green stain or—in this same poem, as well as in "Water"—of "dead paint" that falls off and leaves an outline of the house, or of various photographic prints like the box-camera snapshot in "The Elizabeth Poems" from *Nettles.* Frequently the indelible is a paradoxical imprint of loss, as in "The Swan Story," the deeply probing sequence that ends *Nettles*:

> ... *in woods and churchyard,*
> *houseyard, abandoned orchard ...*
> *There burns the green to be crushed,*

to be spun in earth's turn,
the garment our bones wear
weaving itself of humus,
of light the dead are.

Much of the strategy and intent behind Adcock's poems is characterized by this sentence from "Water":

In the dark
she had made, she worried the object in her hands the way
the mind catches at memory, trying to place a scene.

It is in placing a scene that Adcock's mind catches at what her memories mean. In "Roller Rink" from *Nettles*, the poet recalls her East Texas childhood through yet another outline—this time on the earth—that has in turn left its mark on her mind. Adcock's memory sets the scene, and though it involves another of the losses she has suffered (like that of her mother), in placing the memory in words and images, she coaxes forth the largest meaning possible:

That summer it just appeared,
like a huge butterfly
pinned to McNaughton's field . . .

In August the old man who'd taken our change
hefted sections of floor and his tent
and his music into a truckbed and left. . . .

Of course it never came again.
There was the round brown place
where grass wouldn't grow in that field,
but would grow next year with great ghost wheels
of queen anne's lace.
That summer was a line we'd stumbled over,
and so we were free to fall and gather
the dear, unskillful, amazing losses
departure needs. . . .

The reality of Adcock's remembered world furnishes her with such vivid images, and through these she finds words to match. Reading her work is to walk, as she says in "The Sixth Day" from *Walking Out*, "in heat that clings like a history." In fact, a place and the emotions that it registered is the history that haunts her poems and casts a spell over the reader. Not that Adcock has come to record this history without questioning the romantic urge behind it. In "Redlands Journey" she asks herself pointedly:

> What could going back there claim for me
> under the generations of trees,
> among shadows thrown like dishwater
> from the porches that are left?
> Rags of red dust spin in those backroads
> like the small storms of Sunday children
> raised by nothing but wind.

The details here place the scene through the poet's use of both real and metaphorical imagery, yet beyond this there is no clear answer to the question posed. But wait, it will come, if only in the person of a "girl with dark copper hair ..."

> Her presence among the stories,
> the ones we never told,
> is perfect the way one weathered board is
> remembered without reason,
> a play of surfaces so ordinary
> it can only stay.

It is the ordinary that Adcock recreates for us and that turns miraculous before our mental eyes. Her poetics for this recreation are contained in an image in "Two Words" that is at once natural and wholly mystical:

> Imagine the lives of such words.
> Subtle as the interiors of antique jars,
> they shape their enclosed dark

because we hold them to be;
and name after name, they give us the many.

Adcock's poems are indeed antique jars (reminiscent of Wallace Stevens' jar in Tennessee) that are full of histories that mean because our minds are permitted to hold them, to see into them through her lucid lines and images.

There are so many examples of this poet's success in capturing a sense of time, place, and people, and the words they offer, that it would be possible to quote from almost every poem in *Nettles*. Again, Adcock's poetry is largely personal, whereas Vliet's is for the most part impersonal. However, Adcock, like Vliet, can enter the lives of others with both objectivity and empathy. In "Poetry Workshop in a Maximum Security Reform School," she reveals the hatred and hope of those who are "sick of the artful / part-time in their time that is whole." In a poem that recalls James Dickey's entrance into the world of hunters and their prey, Adcock writes of her father's death from a hunting accident. While she may only approach Dickey's ingenious poetry in this vein, Adcock's writing strikes me as more genuine, if less brilliant, than that of her fellow southerner, and perhaps in part more genuine for that very reason. Witness these lines in particular:

> I cannot guess your careless thought,
> how it unfolded in pine scent,
> some strand of memory or need unwinding
> too taut and suddenly
> broken just *there* on a buried edge,
> your father's father's gun taking on
> a weight that shifted utterly
> because of a low branch
> rock underfoot or a root
> the stumble because the world does
> turn over   turn over and kill because
> the world does and the sound of it
> dies out and dies out
> in the hot thick light, and ground

can shake like the hide
of a thing enormously alive.

You got to your feet for hours
holding your opened belly,
cicada-hum braiding through red
pain   hope   love   terror
gripping the backbone.

You were standing when strangers found you.

I who am daughter and stranger
find you in every weather of sleep. . . .

And to me you have given a history . . .
now that the weapons are given away.

Poised in any prayer I make for light,
to catch the way it glances off the world,
your ignorant knife is
praising the river, praising
currents of canebrake, pinewoods,
thickets under the wild sky—
whatever lives there lost,
whatever is helped to die.

Adcock's lyrical poems are both delicately crafted and enlightening on psychological and philosophical levels. Her longer sequences are equally effective as a combination of craft and meaning; they also illustrate once more her ability to make of the ordinary an outlet for thought and insight. "The Elizabeth Poems" are a case in point and display Adcock's gift for taking such a simple event as a child playing on a bed with pickup sticks and marbles and making this, as she puts it, "be other, out of her hands":

Bumps on the bedspread have marked her thighs.
She rubs how the skin knows

where it's been.
And the grandfather comes through the screendoor streaming
late sun off his shoulders.
Coming a rain. Heard the east thunder.
She knows there can be no weather
until he tells it.

In section III, the child has asthma, and here the poet finds in the illness a real/mystical quality with which she invests her descriptive/ suggestive lines:

Before dawn, the stick-child
thinned out like a rosebush,
woke crying again. *Hush.*
Accept what the steam kettle offers.
She choked and took in rounds of air.
She gave them back.

It is just such an acceptance and a giving back that Adcock offers her readers. And even though I have asked myself if I find her poetry so meaningful only because I am close geographically to its sources and can identify its settings and the lives of its speakers, can identify *with* the environment and her responses to it, I feel bound to believe that any reader anywhere can receive with gratification the work of this native Texas artist.

Despite a clear vote here for what I consider Betty Adcock's more natural writing, in no way would I wish to go without the services of R.G. Vliet. For in maintaining a long-distance relationship with Texas, both of these poets have brought this place and its people closer to us than they would have been even in our living with them day in and day out. To read their books is to be blessed with the pain and joy of a regional life that means more than any of us can fully know, certainly less than we would without such poets to grant us the gain from their luminous scars and their losses that still live on.

Three San Antonio Poets

1984—George Orwell's big year—saw the publication of three collections of poems by three San Antonio poets, and with two of these the inauguration of a poetry series from the city's Corona Press.* In launching what will hopefully be an ongoing enterprise, Corona appropriately looked in its own backyard and found two local poets worthy of publication: Arthur Muñoz, a former San Antonio policeman, and Bryce Milligan, editor of San Antonio's *Pax* magazine. The third collection, published by Tooth of Time Books in Santa Fe, New Mexico, is the first full-length collection of poems from Rosemary Catacalos, one of the finest poets San Antonio and the state have to offer. Muñoz's *From a Cop's Journal*, Milligan's *Daysleepers & Other Poems*, and Catacalos's *Again for the First Time* are three very distinct kinds of books, yet there are some curious features shared by all three, quite apart from the fact that these poets live in the same city and have appeared in some of the same regional magazines, including *Cedar Rock*.

One striking feature of Muñoz's poetry that is found at times in the work of Milligan and Catacalos is the use of sea imagery for poems written in a landlocked metropolis. More than a passing metaphor, the sea represents in the poetry of all three poets a reaching out to larger bodies of myth and meaning than any one place may furnish in and of itself, or that remain unnoticed without the aid of a wider perspective. While there are references in these poets' poems to the San Antonio missions, to specific streets and shops or buildings in the city, and to well-known characters who inhabit its urban landscape, the range of these three collections is more universal, more concerned with timeless issues. Though these may be landlocked poets, their imaginations are neither limited nor isolated, as their visions and literary allusions vividly attest.

The most identifiably local of the three poets is Muñoz, whose book begins with "Street Poems," the first of its four sections, which

---

* *Cedar Rock* 10, no. 1 (Winter 1985): 6-8.

presents scenes witnessed by the ex-policeman during his twenty-three years as a San Antonio patrol officer, investigator, and homicide detective. Street names and locally recognizable figures or shopkeepers are alluded to often in these pieces that read for the most part like journal jottings, for which the title of Muñoz's book has modestly prepared us. At times the poet manages a moving sketch, where both sound and sense are the work of a conscious craftsman, as in "Lady," with its opening and closing lines that capture the sight of an abandoned mother-to-be:

> Eight months into time
> where's your man
> to help you up those steps?
> . . .
> two steps
> rest,
> and smiling

At other times Muñoz's choice of verbs, his phrases, and his closures are questionable. "23rd Street" is an effective piece until the last two lines, which contain an unnecessary comment about urban blight—"On 23rd Street / the city is dying"—since the idea has already been suggested through the fine image of fences "trying in vain / to keep out the weeds / and the shoving of time." Other poems are, again, little more than journal entries, with almost no attempt at structure or musical phrasing. An example would be "Mr. Garza's," a nostalgic visit to a store where "signs still read of goods / that sold for nickels and dimes," which may be the best lines in a piece that lists objects without making them come to life or serve any very meaningful purpose. Several poems on prostitution suggest the profound emptiness of the "profession" as experienced both by the buyers and the sellers, with the former hoping for more for their money than the latter are able or willing to provide: "leaving their love / in rooms dead of light, / and their groans unanswered." Muñoz is best in these epigrammatic scenes where the simple, natural metaphor is most effective in rendering the poet's very human insights. The least interesting section of the book is the 4th, which offers a group of "lyrics" that fails to sing because of a too straightforward talkiness. Sections 2 and 3 continue a nostalgic strain common in the "Street Poems," but there are also some especially strong pieces among these middle sections that indicate Muñoz's larger, Hardy-like vision, one hinted at even in the journalistic offerings of the first section.

Two poems in section 1 that recall the work of two of this century's master literary artists are entitled "Extra!" and "Did You Know?" Like William Carlos Williams' "The Term," Muñoz's "Extra!" laments the state of man through a metaphor based on yesterday's newspaper:

> What little difference
> . . .
> when you see both
> at the mercy of the wind,
> crumpled in a doorway

Muñoz's power of observation is greatest here, and his use of the word "crumpled" for man and paper is a convincing double entendre. Compared with Williams' "The Term," Muñoz's "Extra!" achieves a similar sad irony, yet there is little evidence of Williams' artistry that makes of that master's poem more than the sum of its statement. For Williams not only discovers an important *difference* between man and a piece of newspaper, but in doing so he suggests the possibility for man to imitate the inanimate, or at least to admire in it a quality for imitation:

> a car drove down
> upon it and
> crushed it to
>
> the ground. Unlike
> a man it rose
> again rolling
>
> with wind over
> and over to be as
> it was before.

If nothing else, the sheer sound of Williams' poem leaves us with a feeling of triumph, of something positive even in the face of man's limitations, almost a suggestion of hopefulness for those who would attempt to rise again from disappointment or yesterday or today's bad news.

A point of comparison between Muñoz's rather objective journalism and the objectivism of James Joyce appears for me in the ex-policeman's "Did You Know?" where the latter reports bits of gossip to set up a type of epiphany, which may also remind other readers of scenes in Joyce's "Araby" and *Stephen Hero*. In the novel, Joyce in fact discusses his theory of objectification and illustrates it with a "fragment of colloquy" between a young lady and a young gentleman who are flirting in much the same way as the salesgirl is in "Araby." Muñoz employs this same technique to reveal not shameless flirtation, but simply the idea that those involved in gossip fear to be the first to leave the circle of conversation, knowing that once gone they too will be talked about in the same sniping way. Even if overall Muñoz's poetry does not approach the range or depth of works by Williams and Joyce, it is notable that the San Antonio poet can utilize some of their literary devices for his own particular ends.

Journalistic though Muñoz's poems may be, some of those in the first section of his book do exhibit the wide lens of his vision. In observing the games that children and adults play, the poet demonstrates how these pastimes often develop into tragic realities. From children's games of catch or hide-n-seek, adults grow into their opposing roles as cops and robbers. And even the idea of murder is too closely linked—for the poet's comfort—with mothers in the baseball stands yelling "'KILL 'EM!'" This vision of the tragic turns that life takes from games to the real thing is consistently and effectively driven home in the "Street Poems." But perhaps nowhere is the poet's view of life so fully drawn as it is in "I, Ocean," where the ocean stands as an emblem of a superior force in man's world that "can / with just one wave / return [his] might to sand." Here as elsewhere in his poetry, Muñoz has a clear and steady sense of the topsy-turvy nature of existence, with every push being answered by a corresponding shove.

Throughout the book, Muñoz's use of sea imagery suggests the in and out of the tides of life and his awareness that the two sides in any situation can be reversed from an earlier order and that the reversal of roles or attitudes may happen at any time, leaving a judgment as to right or wrong nearly impossible, as if man were simply a pawn in a Hardy-like naturalist scheme of things. A poignant example of Muñoz's own change of mind is found in "The Marchers of the '60s," where the extremes of those times—represented by "an undertow of words"—pulled him both ways; now, however, he must acknowledge the eye-opening nature of those protest marches that brought him and the nation to a new perspective. In spite of his earlier rejection of "their fists raised in anger," he comes to admit that

> Today, we must say,
> "I'm sorry,"
> having lived
> before they marched
> with eyes and heart
> not knowing.

The maturity and fullness of Muñoz's vision is indeed admirable. More than a local colorist, this poet sees beyond the immediate events to their larger meanings. His ability to weigh the value of experience in the scales of a universal context does not exclude, however, a regional base. In "The Old Breed," Muñoz has "read America" in the faces and talk of migrant workers who are "bent and tired / from years of picking and weeding." The poet finds their experience—"the sand / in their throats / from both shores"—has resulted in a balanced view, a way of survival:

> in their eyes
> there's laughter
> that can't be silenced;
> it's what got them
> through the Texas valley,
> 110 degrees in Indio,
> and the dirt of Idaho.

It would be difficult to find a poet more different from Muñoz than his neighbor Bryce Milligan. If Muñoz is in the line of Williams and Whitman (indebted to the latter by his own admission in a poem from the "Personal File" section of *From a Cop's Journal*), Bryce Milligan is a Dante and Eliot man, by way of old Irish and Anglo-Saxon poetry and myth. The echoes of Eliot predominate in Milligan's "Daysleepers," the title poem of his collection, even though this piece is based in part on the personality and circumstances of "the 14th century Irish poem, 'Buile Shuibe'." Such phrases as "Through the thicket" and "still point upon which the garden turns" are conscious borrowings from Dante and Eliot, and Milligan follows his Virgilian guides in a renewed search for "the divine twilight," believing that "Only the moment out of time endures" and that the one way is "the way of Logres and the grail: / renunciation and fruition, / the way of the goddess, / of and to Cerddwen [the Welsh name for the Celtic muse]." Never having been an Eliot man myself, much of Milligan's work leaves me cold, yet even in "Daysleepers" I can find intriguing sections and can frequently fall under the spell of his runic quest.

Before discussing the title poem, which Milligan considers his most important effort, I would like to begin with two shorter pieces, "Continuity" and "Copano, 1834," which concern one event from the 5th century A.D. in Britain and another from the period of nine-teenth-century Irish immigration to Texas. In "Continuity," a Celtic boy speaks of a rivulet that emptied into the sea, describing its water as having turned to a fine rain that looked like "the diamonds and bit of the gods' color," which he relates to his own sense of the mysteri-ous and mystic: "It was almost holy, the running water / that never hit earth; the old men / gathered for talk below it." The boy goes on to describe a pier that slowly lost touch with the shore as the ocean rose:

> The old men sat every night and watched,
> an old friend gone wicked:
> they had trusted their souls to it
> for fish, sport, and manhood—
> and I could see that distrust moved among them
> as what was foreboding became real. . . .

Later the old men accounted for the ocean's sudden rise by attributing it to "a great worm / long asleep in the north" awaking and "slipping its bulk into the sea." Eventually the boy of the poem and his family moved to higher ground, not really thinking "the world would last." But in keeping with the poem's title, we find that the speaker married and carried on, "bearing [his] own spear." Although I am not certain of the larger meanings behind the various images in this poem, I can respond to Milligan's combination here of realism and vision more immediately than to much of his Eliot-inspired work. My sense is that Milligan is onto the possibility for more significant discoveries when he chooses actual rather than mythological situations.

The other poem, "Copano, 1834," deals with a local event, beginning with a storm at Aransas on the Texas coast, "the channel churning and full of muck." (Milligan's use of sea imagery is almost always effective, as in certain phrases in his "Kii Suido," and such imagery recalled for me Ezra Pound's version of "The Seafarer" through the Texan's very realistic description of the "heaving diamond spray / like ten thousand shattered mirrors" and the "heaving stomachs, / as we felt the sea through our steel skin; / ankylosed joints groaned and sighed / like ancient rigging.") In "Copano, 1834," the inauspicious introduction to Texas for "Two ships full of Irish" escaping famine is followed by the ravages of cholera, which "took them / one by one / until the bay was littered." The survivors end up at the battles for Texas independence, and surviving those experiences live to forget the pain endured both in Ireland and at their arrival here. The conclusion of the poem fails to offer much in the way of meaning, though the realism of the scenes depicted is in itself remarkable. Milligan has the capacity to bring historic events vividly to life, but there is a tendency in all his work to leave the issues up in the air. Nonetheless, I suspect that the ambiguous nature of Milligan's writing will be highly attractive to those who find the symbolist tradition more to their liking than I do. Such ambiguity is particularly prominent in the poet's title sequence, "Daysleepers."

As a reviewer, I find myself on extremely shaky ground with Milligan's longish poem. Since I must confess that only the sections with a touch of realism come through for me to any degree, I will limit my comments to those, believing that even those few can indicate the poem's central theme—of a spiritual quest undertaken by a janitor—fully enough to evaluate the poet's effort and its special achievement.

Opening with a "Prologue," the sequence identifies the speaker as one of the night workers who inhabit the

> blackest holes
> as watchmen,
> sweepers of concrete
> washers of tile
> with ears and eyes open to the
> emptiness
> of vacant steel and concrete shells.

The suggestiveness of the language here is quite inviting, as it anticipates some paradoxical insights. Like Muñoz in his occupation, Milligan's speaker in his keeps a journal which is presumably the poem that we are reading, though obviously more consciously literary than the cop's jottings, with the janitor's written "on washroom towels . . . observations / annotated on / course brown paper." So far so good, but then the next section slips into Milligan's inclination toward Dante-Eliot myth and diction: "Currency unredeemable in time," its "archaic wood nymph," and its "still point in the tumbling song."

With the third section Milligan returns to an image of the "mop and pail," but quickly loses me in a ritual dance with "a willow and pale apparition." The speaker's quest for a Beatrice-like figure is saved only by his occasional references to the real walls and halls of "an old hulk we remodeled, / modernized, made sterile." The contrast between his spiritual search and his nightly job keeps me interested, even though I have little desire to follow the particular apparition he is after. When the speaker refers to the destruction of a building where he had seen her vision, the allusion is too mythic for me: "Driven from the garden / by ball and crane." Still, this section continues to work out the wrecking image to good effect, and were it not for such phrases as "ascending an empty purgatory" that hit me over the head, I could almost go for the grail.

Ironically the most satisfying section for me is entitled "Empty handed." Here the speaker is employed in what appears to be a basketball arena: "In the hall among the giants." The analogy to quests involving larger-than-life trials is more subtle in this section, and the references to mopping vomit and dusting the boards at half-time set the scene almost dramatically. The picture of the hero as the man "with the keys: / power to bind and loose in the locker rooms" is at once wonderfully natural and mythical. The description goes on to build nicely on one of the poem's central contrasts:

> My empty cubicle echoes
> to monotonous cheers, pounding,
> stomping,
> agonized
> > orgasmic
> > > screams.
> Nothing but time and dust on the hands;
> one novel a day, a little history,
> Nennius or Gildus,
> and the staples:
> > one half-gallon coffee,
> > two packs of cigarettes.

Sitting "below the stands," the speaker once again envisions his lady, but it seems this may be a false femme fatale, or is his Beatrice more in keeping with today's "new morality"?

> Doe-shy virgin,
> aimless vestal in denims,
> I entreated you formally,
> > your presence at least,
> screaming down these
> > our subterranean haunts—
> I prostrate my soul;
>
> > and you demand copulation.

From here on the poem for me is a labyrinth of Eliotic allusion and "unmajestic griffons." Certainly the more realistic parts that I can follow would be little without the larger poem's golden bough structure. Nevertheless, Milligan's poem works for me only when it unites "real experience" with the mythical quest. And yet this is in no way to detract from what is truly an exceptional poem for a Texas poet. The conception, while not original, is brought to life at times through Milligan's artistic handling of mythical and realistic elements, the one played off against the other dramatically and meaningfully. That the meeting of these two aspects of one man's vision can be a subject for poetry is owing to its timeless occurrence here and everywhere. That it happened in San Antonio should come then as no surprise, but that it was recorded in such an ambitious poem should be an occasion for rejoicing. If nothing else, this first book by Bryce Milligan makes clear the potential for a visionary poetry in Texas.

Not that we do not already have in Rosemary Catacalos a poet who can see beyond the simple event to "something more than everything." But even Catacalos has not attempted a long poem of mythic proportions; instead, she has slowly come into her own as a spokeswoman for the "daily returns" of a life that, through her writing, offers in itself mythic relations to unsuspected worlds, past, present, and future. Given her dual heritage as a Mexican and Greek descendant, it is natural that Catacalos would draw in her poetry on the rites and myths that characterize her two cultural strains. The first half of her *Again for the First Time* focuses more on the Mexican side of her nature, while the second half reexamines such Greek mythological and/or literary figures as Ariadne, Penelope (the subject as well of a fine poem by Bryce Milligan), and Odysseus, seen in the light of the poet's own modern sense of what those mythical forebears have to say. In "Ariadne to Dionysios," the poet clearly identifies herself with the woman who is,

> even if a princess, a simple weaver
> of spells. Sometimes of faith that
> there will be no more mazes, no more beasts.
> But hold me, Nyounios. We are making time
> with our bodies, our old ties.

Catacalos, whether writing of her Mexican or her Greek side, is concerned throughout her book with "old ties." In "From Bolivia After

All This Time," the ties between the speaker and her cousin-lover are found to reach back "From so very far away . . . past ancient cities . . . whose entrails of doorsteps . . . long ago swallowed all time, all hope, / all desire from so many lives. . . ." But in the survival of the lovers' relationship there is cause for the speaker "to mourn and castigate / and celebrate all in the same breath." Much of the richness of Catacalos's poetry lies precisely in its blend of agony, elegy, and joy—frequently, as the persona suggests, "all in the same breath." And what lends this poet's work its vital power is in great part the very blood relationships which are the source of her anguish and gladness, her guilt and pride. Yet just having two lines that furnish her with mystical and mythical connections can in no way account for the achievement of Catacalos's poetry. As she has her version of Odysseus put it,

> I keep telling you
> we worked hard for it.
> Anyone who aspired to being
> lighter than air
> faced the prospect of everything
> from sirens to being turned
> into a dog [sic?] for his trouble.
> . . .
> Let them say we can't couple with time.
> But look what we stand to gain.
> The chance to make all this past
> we reach across
> tremble and explode with newness.

The signs that Catacalos has worked hard to achieve a new kind of poetry—for Texas and for the nation—are found everywhere in this book. For one thing, the poet never allows herself to use sources for selfish or clever ends. "Paying Respects," for example, is a self-critical piece in which Catacalos sees herself as "only flirting with the living, / only flirting with the dead." Her visit to the cemetery concludes much more convincingly than does Muñoz's "Perpetual Care," mainly because the "I" in Catacalos's poem is honest with herself, whereas Muñoz remains too coldly observant and ends his poem with a heavy-handed image of gravediggers urinating "on the sleeping faces." Catacalos never resorts to such a shock treatment, even though her facts are in themselves more shocking than Muñoz's. Concerned with a spiritual life that is constantly being judged by the highest standards, Catacalos is equally dedicated to her own writing performance, holding it up to a demanding but realistic appraisal. In "Poison in the Eye of the Beholder," she exacts harsh criticism of herself for having accused the old men of being slow and dilapidated, recognizing that she has betrayed those same old men who gave her "songs and lessons and hope."

A number of the most powerful poems in Catacalos's book depict characters in her neighborhood who have taught her truths to live by. One of these is found in "One Man's Family," which eulogizes the "Dog Man," with "his bunch of seven dogs / and his clothes covered with / short smelly hair." This mysterious figure, who may once have been a college professor, teaches the poet

> About how those seven snouts bulldozing
> through neighborhood garbage and memories
> give off a warmth that's just as good
> as all the breasts and apple pies and Christmas trees
> and books and pipes and slippers
> that a man could use on this earth.
> But mostly about how they're dogs.
> Friends that don't have to be anything else.
> About how nothing could be more right
> than for a man to live
> with what he is willing and able to trust.

From Lupe, who sweeps the floors "at the J & A Ice House" and who for a long time "has been operating on what some people / call dim," the poet learns endurance. And from homesteaders she drinks in the lessons of the Edwards Aquifer:

> They made houses of limestone
> and adobe, locked together blocks
> descended from shells and coral,

houses of the bones of the water,
shelter of the water.
And they swallowed the life
of the lime in the water,
sucked its mineral up
into their own bones
which grew strong as the water,
the gift of the water.

In turn, there are several of Catacalos's own courses in which prospective writers would do well to enroll. However, the poet's finest teachings are difficult to imitate, just as her best poems will remain truly her own. Even when she seems to ramble, as in "(There Has To Be) Something More Than Everything," through talk of

growing old . . .
the new camper . . .
how electrical engineers have impatiently
taken over the functions of real watchmakers
without having an inkling of how to order
the true passage of time

the poet keeps us knowing that kinship and the loss of a family member are to be celebrated and mourned simultaneously as "something more than everything." Indeed, it is through talk that Catacalos believes we arrive at a renewed awareness of the worth of those we have lost and to a greater sense that we should hold close while still together. In "Final Touches" she offers a type of *ars poetica* as well as a very personal and powerful account of what I take to be the end of a relationship. Here the poet calls up the past (she believes, she says, "in the ultimate triumph of memory") to recount how, during the last three days, the two of them rode "past the open mouths of astonished stars." Mourning the end of the romance, she yet manages to celebrate its memorable moments. In "Tongue-Tied," another poem that comments on her own poetics, Catacalos justifies her talkiness by suggesting that she speaks for so many selves that "They clog [her] lungs and tongue / with their possibilities." In acting as a spokeswoman for others and for self, Catacalos in fact expands the possibilities for poetry as a way of saying "how much / has been lost or forgotten or left unsaid." In so many ways, she speaks as few poets do today—she expresses our deepest pains and our highest hopes in a world that "is not always / as we would have it."

For all these reasons it is impossible to say too much about this book by Rosemary Catacalos. There are poems in her collection that will astound, and not merely because they manipulate myth and reality so artfully, but because they are spoken with the strength of a person who has learned to lament and to give thanks at once, to keep "doing and undoing the whole cloth" even as her "fingers bleed all over the loom." Like her fellow San Antonio poets, Catacalos has a vision to share with her readers, and while Muñoz and Milligan both deserve consideration, it is Catacalos who must be accorded the laurel, not alone for the truth of her lines, nor for the wonder of how she makes them, but for the fact that she has endured to speak so eloquently "in the service of memory," no matter how painful remembrance can be.

R.S. Gwynn at the Drive-In

There are five or six poems in R.S. Gwynn's *The Drive-In* that are as fine as anything being published anywhere.* This "Breakthrough Book #50" from the University of Missouri Press is not only beautifully designed and printed but adds to the press's series a distinctive voice as original as that of Wesley McNair, whose *Faces of Americans in 1853* (#42) introduced another of today's truly remarkable poets. As George Garrett and X.J. Kennedy note on the back cover of Gwynn's book, this is the work of an accomplished poet who combines craftsmanship and passion in poems that achieve power, resonance, and even outrageousness.

Although there are satirical and parodic poems in the collection that at first left me all at sea with their unfamiliar allusions and distant situations, even these pieces are impressive as formal and linguistic designs, and after repeated readings I found them just as rewarding as such thoughtfully made poems always are. As Gwynn's poetry often does, "A Short History of the New South" sets an earlier era's phraseology and concerns ("The cause, / I fear, is lost, Suh"; "pass the yams"; "Y'all come") against those of the present day ("pass the pizza") in order to parody them both: "We cashed the insurance and bought us a TV and rotor, / Which we used to improve our minds and accents." Gwynn frequently retells biblical, classical, historical, and literary tales in contemporary terms, as in "Horatio's Philosophy" or "Among Philistines," the latter of which blends Samson's Old Testament predicament with an updated version of the star "Hebrew Hunk" entrapped by his own weakness for a Delilah's

> perfect breasts, her hips and slender waist,
> Matchless among the centerfolds of Zion,
> Which summoned to his tongue the mingled taste
> Of honey oozing from the rotted lion;

---

* *Texas Writers' Newsletter*, no. 44 (November 1986): 5-8.

For now his every mumble in the sack
(Bugged, of course, and not a whisper missed)
Would be revealed in lurid paperback
"As told to" Madam Sleaze, the columnist.

These satires are fun and convincingly rendered, but compared with some half-dozen pieces in the collection, even they seem mere warm-up exercises for the big game. For in poems like "The Drive-In," "Three Versions of the Young Poet," "In Place of an Elegy," "The Simplification," and "Mimosa," Gwynn reveals a tone and intent that are simultaneously playful and deeply moving. These poems successfully employ objective and subjective levels of meaning that are not so remote as the poet's allusive parodies.

In the collection's title poem, Gwynn develops through strict tetrameter couplets a view of family relationships that is paralleled by scenes from the movie *Union Pacific*:

I know it, know it frame by frame,
The tyranny of separation,
The lack of all communication
From shore to shore, the struggle through
Smashed chairs and bottles toward the true
Connection of a spike of gold.
I fall asleep. The night is cold.

In his creation of this almost metaphysical image (reminiscent of James Dickey's intercontinental railway metaphor in "Adultery"), Gwynn achieves an emotional impact that is at once impersonal and personal. The reader is drawn into the child's family situation through the connections the speaker once vaguely made at the out-doors movie—between a film's historical setting and his own home life—and through the contrast now presented by the adult who has objectified that painful experience by means of a tightly controlled poetic structure.

"In Place of an Elegy," a poem that originally appeared in James P. White's *New & Experimental Literature* (Center for Texas Writers Press, 1975), has been changed slightly from its earlier printing to intensify the self-criticism the poet-teacher directs toward himself for having given a "C" (here an "F") to his dead student's "last bad essay." Now that she is gone, the speaker senses that he was wrong to judge the girl's writing so harshly, for her death in a car accident has forced him to reconsider it with greater sensitivity. The poet-teacher italicizes one of her trite sentences—"*For lasting friends can see right thru you but / Still see you thru*"—to emphasize the change in meaning for him that has taken place as a result of her death. The fact that *she* has not lasted to respond to his grade now makes the sentence both poignant and accusatory, with the "elegy" turning ironically upon the metaphor of the teacher being lined up before a firing squad. For the poet feels that he is now being punished for having "singled out / A word as 'clever'," for having executed all the victims of his writing class. The most telling line in the analogy reads: "A shot / With no report." This is a poem full of Gwynn's finest devices, all employed for the highest possible emotive effect.

"The Simplification," a love poem, exhibits Gwynn's best oblique style—his ability to speak unemotionally about something very dear to him, a practice he shares with another poet whose work Gwynn greatly admires: that of Leon Stokesbury In "The Simplification," the writing manages to hide Gwynn's true feelings, but only on the surface, for underneath he is revealing how genuine his affection really is. The title is aptly chosen, and the final lines of the first of two long stanzas are memorable: "Then, that day, / You taught me what I knew: I would be the man / To make the most of you. Then we made love again." The closing lines of the poem are lovely and follow from a series of sentences that "simplify" the relationship by healing "of all your hesitations" and "fears" and giving "the simplest thanks" for the way "*the sunlight melts like copper in your hair.*"

The poem I most admire in Gwynn's collection is "Mimosa," which I heard him read in Austin around 1982. I liked it then, but not until I saw it in print could I fully appreciate its artistry. This is a poem any writer would be more than proud to have produced, whether for its flawless rhyming pattern or for its sure-handed and unsuperfluous statement. The poem must be seen in its entirety, but here is the stanza that caught my attention on hearing it read by the poet:

True to self-seeking plans
You flaunt your gaudy show-
Girl powderpuffs and fans
Until the plants that grow
Beneath you, even the weeds,
Submit before the needs
That rob the hours of day-
Light from my wrinkled green
Pepper and blighted bean
So you can have your way.

Other stanzas now mean even more to me, yet all are building toward the overwhelming conclusion—the final line with its tremendous pun—which carries through with a highly philosophical thought on what a man or woman must do to survive in a hostile world, as suggested by this tree with leaves that fold

Each day with the late sun
. . . as if to hoard
Your unexpended powers
Until those lucid hours
When all will be restored.

This is not the end of the poem—there are two more *more* powerful stanzas yet to come! I highly recommend them, as well as the rest of this impressive collection by Sam Gwynn.

Foreword to *Three Texas Poets*

The three poets gathered in this mini-anthology—Charles Behlen, Sandra Lynn, and Joseph Colin Murphey—have at least three things in common: all are native Texans; all were first published in book form by Prickly Pear Press; and all have achieved distinctive regional voices.* Essential to their achievement has been the ability of all three to interpret through vivid imagery and personal insight those parts of Texas which each has known most intimately. In the case of Charles Behlen, this has been West Texas, and his ongoing definition of this section of the state follows here from his earlier work in *Perdition's Keepsake* (1978). Sandra Lynn, on the other hand, has shifted attention away from her girlhood years in the piney woods of East Texas—the starting point for much of her writing in *I Must Hold These Strangers* (1980)—to an almost religious observation of the Rio Grande area of the Big Bend. Similarly, Joseph Colin Murphey has gone from remembering his years in East Texas and in the Panhandle—the basis of the poet's work in *A Return to the Landscape* (1979)—to a penetrating look at his more recent days spent in the north-central part of the state around Gainesville. Since the first collections by these poets were all published half-a-dozen years ago, the new work included here reflects the maturing skills and visions of each, for all three have grown more subtle, more incisive and/or more responsive in their perceptions of place and its peculiar influence on their lives and literature.

With each of these poets there is perhaps a key perspective that has determined the thrust of his or her previous and present writing. Charles Behlen's poetry, for example, often describes the people of West Texas as staring into space, which is understandable "given the ground" with its open stretches and nearly treeless plains. But more than merely a reaction to the landscape itself, the word "staring" indicates that Behlen's West Texans are frequently left dazed and debilitated in the face of the natural and human events

---

* *Three Texas Poets* (Cedar Park, TX: Prickly Pear Press, 1987), pp. 9-11.

that characterize their existence in such a "barren" environment. Yet after staring in dismay, they return almost heroically to swinging their hoes or to recalling a difficult past that lives on as a reminder of the stoicism which they knew in others who are now deceased and which they would emulate if only by holding on to their names and their sayings. The poet himself is responsible for maintaining the very memories of those he failed to understand or to appreciate at the time, or of those who either ignored or misunderstood him. Through his way with words, the poet has come to serve as their most faithful guardian and their lasting means of recognition or redemption. In a sense Behlen achieves for such figures a metaphorical existence that transcends their actual lives. He has done this most effectively by seeing in the simplest tools used by his forebears the symbolic values that they held to and represented. In depicting their lives on the level of everyday drudgery and despair, Behlen has paradoxically elevated his West Texans to a higher plane than even they would have thought possible. This is indeed proof of the saving power of a poetic gift.

In the poetry of Sandra Lynn there is a direct reply made to those who find the wide-open spaces of West Texas either empty or fearful. Through her communion with the Big Bend "gaps" and "gulches"— a "body broken before you"—Lynn has recognized for herself and her readers a spirituality formed of forthrightness and the "eternal / lure of stones and sticks," of "holy light," and the inviting hands of water. Lynn's work has always been able to uncover the unsuspected strengths inherent in the most inconspicuous scenes or objects, and this is particularly true of the poems chosen here from her Big Bend sequence. Her identification with the flora and fauna—from prickly pear and sun-bleached grasses to rattlesnakes and lizards—is more than the mark of a nature lover; it is the signature of a poet who has discovered in the natural world the measure and message of her own writing. In asking to be taken into the fellowship of rock fissures and lichen, Lynn has acknowledged her desire to have her poetry bear witness to the less gaudy and more fundamental side of existence that is represented for her by the landscape of a semi-desert.

Joseph Colin Murphey's voice—one of the most self-confident but casual and reassuring in all Texas poetry—has deepened in its deliberate trusting of "the frame" in which this poet has found himself. By accepting a subject matter close at hand as proper for his conversational yet finely crafted stanzas, Murphey has moved beyond the trickery of much contemporary poetry into a realm of music and wisdom that can best be compared with those of William Butler Yeats in his last great period. Unlike the figure in Murphey's "Sitting in the Porch Swing Reading on a Saturday Afternoon," this Texas poet did not lose his way but has rather stuck with the road he started on—one that has led him to an artful understanding not only of his own inner life but of the macho types driving past his home, young girls dressed in their "death-defying" Levis, the woman serving him coffee at the local cafe, or the one he has called elsewhere "the miracle of my life" walking with him among a cemetery's tombstones as soft rain falls on the hopeful epitaphs. Whether writing on love or 100-year-old fence wire, Murphey returns us to the most enduring landscape of all: that of the human heart with its good and bad in every season and weather.

While these three Texas poets share many of the same "stomping grounds," they are still very different and very special artists, whose work is distinctly their own. And even though each has developed a uniquely Texan kind of poetry, all three should speak clearly and meaningfully to any reader anywhere. For above all, these three are wordsmiths of the truest sort—poets attuned to the expressive and musical capacity of language and to its means of observing and evaluating the deepest urges and regrets forever experienced by men and women wherever they have happened to live.

Prize Texas Poets

Ten years have suddenly come and gone since the first collections of poems by Leon Stokesbury and Walter McDonald were published by Texas presses and vied for the 1976 Voertman poetry award of the Texas Institute of Letters.* During the past decade both poets have continued to publish their distinctive brands of poetry, and with the publication of Stokesbury's *The Drifting Away* (The University of Arkansas Press, 1986) and McDonald's *Witching on Hardscrabble* (Spoon River Poetry Press, 1985), it is more evident than ever that these two Texas poets have created uniquely original Southwestern voices.

While the differences between the strategies and intentions of Stokesbury and McDonald are indisputable, the two poets have been linked in the minds of some readers ever since their first books competed for the Voertman prize. McDonald won that year's poetry award for his collection *Caliban in Blue* (Texas Tech Press, 1976) and has won it again for *Witching on Hardscrabble*. Stokesbury lost out to McDonald for the Voertman, but he was subsequently the winner of the Porter Fund Award for Literary Excellence and was before that a co-winner of the first Associated Writing Programs Poetry Competition in 1975, which resulted in the publication of his *Often in Different Landscapes* (University of Texas Press, 1976). Critical response in Texas to the first books of poems by these two poets was, in part, a reaction against the one as a way of preferring the other. To consider them together after their ten years' production provides an opportunity to see why, regardless of preference, we are fortunate indeed to have them both.

Two reviews of Stokesbury's work appeared in the *Texas Writer's Newsletter*, a vital outlet for critical commentary published by the Texas Association of Creative Writing Teachers, founded by James P. White. In the February 1977 issue of the *Newsletter*, James Hoggard reviewed *Often in Different Landscapes* and was immediately the

---

* *Vortex* 3 (1988): 33-37.

object of angry denunciations for having asserted that Stokesbury "hasn't found a voice capable of letting him race beyond the strictures of timidity binding so many poets these days to efforts which are meager." Hoggard did go on to say that "in several of these poems . . . [Stokesbury] admits his dissatisfaction with this logy load; and the sharpness of his self-criticism suggests a capacity for growth." In the January 1980 issue of the *Texas Writer's Newsletter*, Lloyd Parks reviewed Stokesbury's second collection, *The Drifting Away of All We Once Held Essential*, published in Denton in 1979 by Trilobite Press. (It is inexplicable that neither this book nor Stokesbury's third collection, *The Royal Nonesuch*, published in Tallahassee in 1984 by Anhinga Press, is credited by the University of Arkansas Press for important poems reprinted in *The Drifting Away*.) In Parks's review, Stokesbury is lauded as

> a regional poet, but chiefly by virtue of style and rhythm, not because he uses Southwest place-names, which he does, nor because he dwells on pioneers, pinto beans, and barbed-wire, which he doesn't. Especially in the title poem, the reader will detect the Texan love of the long-winded, thigh-slapping narrative and hear vowels bent out of shape and accents preferably in odd places.

In the course of his review, Parks praises Stokesbury's sense of humor, his Einsteinian relativity, his Picasso-like ability to create art out of throw-away objects, and his Frostian universality. This last estimate was shared even by Hoggard's earlier review, which found Stokesbury "depicts with a finely comedic, though gentle, mode the forces of things remembered disorienting him while at the same time giving him a sense of touch with certain particulars of family life, details whose sources and effects are more universal than parochial." It is Hoggard's observation of the "forces of things remembered" as simultaneously "disorienting" and putting Stokesbury in touch with family life that interests me most, and this because the critic has suggested what was and still is for me the greatest attainment of this poet's writing. Within days after the appearance in 1979 of *The Drifting Away of All We Once Held Essential*, I was invited to give a talk on Texas poets for a Poetry Society meeting at Texas Christian University, and as my subject I chose "Leon Stokesbury as Elegist." Reading now in 1986 *The Drifting Away* from the University of Arkansas Press, I find that my remarks made seven years earlier contain much of what I would still say about Stokesbury's work, and so I include them here, followed by a few additional comments.

* * *

Contemporary poetry and what some critics have identified as its prose tradition began with Ezra Pound, though the relationship of Texas poetry to such may be considered by most a mere coincidence, if even so slight a familiarity be granted to it at all. An outline of the characteristics of the prose tradition in poetry must include the use of colloquial language and of an objectivity associated with scientific investigation. Neither of these features would seem to bode well for the production of a poetic line, yet taken together with more traditional elements of the poem—imagery, irony, and stanzaic and rhythmic patterns—the colloquial and the objective have resulted in some of the finest offerings in the field of the contemporary poem. And it may not require a quantum leap of the imagination to find in the best of Texas poetry this same combination of prose and poetic traditions, since Texas as a place has naturally affected her contemporary poets in such a way as to encourage a use of the colloquial and the objective, and to discourage the overly poetic, though not the artful inclusion of ironic and structural elements capable of yielding the true visionary poem. The Texas poet who has proven most inclined to work within the prose tradition is Leon Stokesbury.

As the title of Stokesbury's latest book, *The Drifting Away of All We Once Held Essential*, indicates, he is an elegist. In the poems where he makes his most important contribution to contemporary poetry he has shown himself both a compleat student of the prose tradition and an astute manipulator of such timeless poetic elements as form and irony. Above all it is through the elegiac mode that Stokesbury most fully demonstrates his felt harmonization of the prose and poetic traditions. The very fact that he consciously controls and patterns his emotions is the sign of an authentic poet at work; that he employs a highly colloquial language in conjunction with an objective, almost clinical, presentation of details places him directly in the mainstream of modern poetry. While much of Stokesbury's manner is perhaps too predictably the product of our age's need to remain aloof and disillusioned, his artistic handling of the elegy redeems him from such an otherwise damning tendency. For it is by means of the elegiac mode that Stokesbury maintains an emotional commitment, even as he achieves the distancing necessary to a contemporary poem that his ironic, colloquial, and objective treatment makes possible.

Without being in any way a self-conscious regional writer—he has even repudiated his part of Southeast Texas as "a land of nod" with its small town "boobs and boobies"—Stokesbury has rooted his elegies in a regional reality, which he has yet moved beyond in mourning that most universal loss: the death of a loved one. In "The Lamar Tech Football Team Has Won Its Game," Stokesbury refers to a fact of his everyday existence in the college community of Beaumont, where football, as in most of the state's towns and cities, is a way of life. The poet, however, treats this "great" event ironically by placing beside it—literally in the next line of his verse—news of his grandmother's death. Without any further comment on either event, the poet proceeds to catalog the colloquial maxims offered by his father as a consolation. The facts pile up in the poem as so many headlines in the newspaper, among which is the sports news of the football team's big win. The father, like King Claudius in *Hamlet*, offers a matter-of-fact truism: "Time is a great healer." This attempt to console is, however, as unreal as the great meaning suggested by the headlines announcing a football victory. Truer to the mark is the unlikely headline that reads: "Siamese Twins Cut Apart, One Lives." More exotic than the usual sports headline, this piece of news obliquely reveals the emotional state of the poet and its very real cause: two like-spirits have been separated by death and there can be no healing of this wound, just as the scalpel mark will remain with the surviving twin. By approaching his loss in this indirect manner, Stokesbury intensifies the emotion and makes of prosaic events a means to poetic power. That is, the objective, prosy statements ironically underscore the emotional impact of the grandmother's death.

Another quality of much contemporary poetry is its simultaneous tone of humor and high seriousness. Stokesbury is as often a comic as he is a cynic, and in his elegies he is regularly both, which again places him in the contemporary camp—a pun accidentally apropos, since some of Stokesbury's antics are at times overly cute. An extremely successful instance of his blend of clowning and cynicism is the entirely appropriate case of "The Death of Harpo Marx," where that master of Dada humor is remembered elegiacally through another series of off-beat facts. Here the newspaper items parallel precisely the kind of zany mixture typical of the movie star's comedic flights. Yet again the tone throughout is as serious as it is in the elegy for the poet's grandmother. Indeed, the list of incidents occurring at the moment of Harpo's death alludes to the tragic thinness of our times, to the "screaming and scratching" that characterizes its lack of anything meaningful to say. By contrast, the man who ironically said so much by practicing as a mime artist has left us to our racial prejudice and money-grubbing, our empty words and living death.

If not intentionally regional, Stokesbury can be self-consciously contemporary. In "Why I Find Myself Immersed in Few Traditions," the poet writes an elegy for dreamers, or more specifically for those like Christopher Columbus who have not found what they were seeking but still long "for tickets to non-existent lands." Stokesbury is too much the cynic here and in fact is even contradictory, for he *is* immersed in many poetic traditions, the elegiac for one and that of the sonnet for another. Stokesbury's sonnets are again quite contemporary because of their use of the prose tradition, and yet the fact that he expresses his cynicism in this predictable form makes him an old-fashioned poet even as he affects a modern tone. His second collection testifies to a continuing attraction to this traditional form, and in "The Lover Remembereth Such as He Sometime Enjoyed and Showeth How He Would Like To Enjoy Her Again," Stokesbury even demonstrates his attempt to parody the very form he utilizes so often. The inversions both in the title and in such a line as "Almost, I drank a pint of Sunny Brook," plus the use of the "thou" form, are intended to establish that the poet is aware of how hokey and old-fashioned his form and theme really are. Reducing love to luck is also a mark of the poet's urge to remain above a theme he wants us to realize he knows is sentimental. Mostly, however, it is the line-up of prosaic activities he recalls that makes of this a contemporary piece. But here the effective irony of his other elegies fails him, for he works too hard to convince us he is not committed, whereas in those poems where he infers his emotional attachment, he allows the oblique references to add to the sad state of affairs. While the technique is similar, it differs basically because the "I" here is too self-conscious and feels it necessary to parody the form *and* the feeling.

One of Stokesbury's most successful elegies is "To Laura Phelan: 1880-1906." As in the sonnet just discussed, here too the poet employs inversion and a repetitiveness characteristic of that form in order to set an elegiac tone, to emphasize the serious, traditional intent of the poem. Here also the poet is ironic, but this time effectively so, for while he is near comic, he is deeply moved by a meditation on the unknown person buried in an Arkansas cemetery. Having carried off Laura Phelan's tombstone as a prank—he and other college students having set it on a professor's front lawn during their all-night drinking binge—he has now returned it and faces what he calls "the loam's maw," a deadly serious phrase and one that helps point up the irony of his suggesting that he is more drunk now, from this contemplation of death, than he was when he played the graveyard joke. The most powerful passage is indeed sobering, yet sends us reeling from its reality:

> when the thought comes at last
> that people fall apart, that the things we do
> will not do. Ends. Then, we come to scenes
> like this.

If the poet only rarely reaches this pitch of intensity, it is due perhaps to his contemporary play for aloofness but also to the fact that, as Emily Dickinson knew, peering into the abyss of death too deeply can drive us into an intoxication that can turn suddenly to mental breakdown.

The title poem of Stokesbury's second collection contains examples of both his strengths and weaknesses. Elegiac in essence, "The Drifting Away of All We Once Held Essential" presents itself as a mere stylistic exercise, in another attempt to play down the seriousness of its theme: the loss of even a belief that remorse for our failings "can be called up for purposes / of flagellation, from the darker regions

/ to rip and tear at the pink soft underbelly of thought." There is much hoakum and some minor hilarity in this parody of "a comparative study of / masturbatory techniques and tendencies of / certain southern oral interpretation of literature / professors and South Texas redneck barflies." Stokesbury can always be clever, with his witty references to the Lone Ranger, peanut brittle, and the Baby Leroy Look-Alike Contest, but at times he goes too far and ruins a good thing. In this poem it may be justified somewhat when we consider how mock-serious he is in recalling a kind of Mark Twain version of a George Washington tale of confessed dishonesty. Stokesbury reports to his family his confession of the "crime" of having spent the funds raised for his Boy Scout troop on a movie, candy bars, and chocolate shakes, but instead of remorse there is a vague resentment against his parents. Any desire for forgiveness in the midst of a moving allusion to "Father and son, driving along. So close. / Real pals" is destroyed by the colloquial interjection "My God! What a load of crap!" Here the clever handling of all the elements of a prose tradition in poetry is perhaps less satisfying than it might be, and yet the obvious pain involved in Stokesbury's recalling of such an episode makes his poem a triumph of this same contemporary balance of the poetic and the excruciatingly objective.

* * *

There is little I would add to or change in this earlier "review" of Stokesbury's work, other than to say that in reprinting from his three collections, the University of Arkansas Press's 53-page gathering of his poetry leaves out a number of excellent poems, notably "The Death of Harpo Marx" and "The Graduate Assistant Tells of His Visit." However, there are several new, previously uncollected pieces that deserve special comment, in particular "Renoir" and "Day Begins at Governor's Square Mall." An elegy for the poet Frank Stanford unfortunately falls short of the high standards set by other Stokesbury elegies. In the Stanford tribute, Stokesbury finds no ironic way to approach the subject, which has been his most effective strategy in the past. Here, somehow, Pound's purely "direct treatment of the thing" does not move; it merely depresses. As for "Renoir," in this poem

Stokesbury adds another of his insightful interpretations of works of art—a fine example from his first book being "This Print of Durer's," as is "Gifts," a satirical variation on a type of "art criticism." Even though "Renoir" ends weakly, the poem manages several touches that bear the Stokesbury trademark, especially his tendency to combine farce and feeling:

> Then, as the eye roams over the rest
> of the festive scene, the quiet joke of the artist
> begins to emerge. For, although a half dozen
>
> conversations continue on, half of these people
> are not even seeing the person looking at them.
> They are looking at somebody else. It is a sort
>
> of visual quadrille, the theme of five hundred
> French farces, except in this case the painter
> must care very much for them all, for he has soothed
>
> their wants and aches in a wash of softness.

"Day Begins at Governor's Square Mall" is a poem that captures our day and age as accurately and sadly as anything I know:

> . . . But these trees, now,
> climb up through air and concrete never hot or cold.
> . . .
> Everyone is waiting though, as before a storm—
> anticipating something. Do these leaves never fall?
> . . . And in the center, at
> the exact center of the mall, a jet of water spouts
> in a shallow pool where signs announce that none
> may ever go. O bright communion! O new cathedral!
> Where the appetitious, the impure, the old, the young,
> the bored, the lost, the dumb, with wide dilated eyes
> advance with offerings to be absolved and be made clean.

Just to have written these passages must surely place Stokesbury from now on among our most prized poets.

To return to Lloyd Parks' review of Stokesbury's second book, it is evident that to the reviewer "his" poet should have been declared the legitimate winner long ago. The first sentence of Parks's review declares: "Incredible that [*Often in Different Landscapes*] did not win the Voertman prize, considering what did!" The reference is to Walt McDonald's *Caliban in Blue*, and the whole problem with art prizes is pointed up by Parks's undisguised resentment. That two such original works will have to be chosen between is always unfortunate, yet in the long run it is clear that McDonald's work has proven deserving not only of the T.I.L. poetry prizes for 1976 and 1985 but of more readers than even his six volumes have brought to his well-crafted poems. By my count (and I may be missing one or more), McDonald has published the following collections: *Caliban in Blue* (Texas Tech Press, 1976), *One Thing Leads to Another* (Cedar Rock Press, 1978), *Anything, Anything* (L'Epervier Press, 1980), *Working Against Time* (Calliope Press, 1981), *Burning the Fence* (Texas Tech Press, 1981), and *Witching on Hardscrabble* (1985). This in itself is a remarkable record, and doubly so considering the consistently high quality and originality of McDonald's writing.

Since I have reviewed three of his six volumes previously, I will primarily limit my rather brief comments to McDonald's latest collection, *Witching on Hardscrabble*. Like all his other books, this new collection contains part of one section that is devoted to the poet's experiences in Vietnam (the subject of almost two-thirds of *Caliban in Blue*, with one particular exception worthy of mentioning once again—an elegy for his grandfather entitled "The Hammer"). Like his more recent collections, this latest book also contains a majority of work given over to McDonald's native landscape—the country in and around Lubbock where he teaches at Texas Tech University and where cattle and irrigated crops are the focus of many of his poems. At least two pieces on his father are, as with all of McDonald's tributes to family members, tastefully done, convincing from their blend of sentiment and manliness. "In Times of Fever" is an epiphany of the sort that McDonald favors: an event in life that brings dramatic change. Here the mother is ill and the father, who has a drinking problem, will be cured of his own illness:

> For days,
> for weeks he sat up turning cold cloths
> on her forehead like seven veils.
> . . .
> Huge fingers shaking, fingers that could lead bulls
> to slaughter, unfolded the cloth like a pearl
> and placed it in earnest on her face.

Most of the poems in *Witching on Hardscrabble* concern the poet's observations of life in the raw on a land that is characterized poignantly in the book's opening piece, entitled "Black Wings Wheeling," where a calf has probably tumbled "down an arroyo / alone and bawling, bone snapped, / stumbling, unable to stand." A similar poem, "On Earth Where We Live," obviously serves as an *ars poetica* for McDonald and is one of his finest recent efforts. Like an earlier piece in *Caliban in Blue* entitled "Flight Orders," "On Earth Where We Live" employs an effective line-movement that slowly leads the reader to an overwhelming conclusion. McDonald's artistry is fully apparent here and elsewhere by the way he starts a poem with the most strikingly right approach and then carefully and clearly carries us along through always multiple levels of meaning that work toward an impressive and memorable ending. Like many of McDonald's poems that are aerial views, "On Earth Where We Live" utilizes a bird's-eye vision of the world, and more particularly of the poet's specific place of habitation. This same point of view is presented brilliantly in "Going Home" from *Burning the Fence*, but here the poet has achieved both a view from above (in this case that of some predatory bird) and an emotional reaction from below (that of a lizard, comparable to the human mind that also must "survive / on hardscrabble"). The final two quatrains bring together these three elements in a powerful statement of the poet's philosophy of art and life:

> The object
> is never to take off,
> caught in the talons
> of whatever fancy

          snatches you,
          but to stay down,
          scuttling over
          the workable sand.

Any interpretation of this poem should be qualified, however, by the
fact that McDonald still finds flight irresistible.

    In "Growing Up Flying," the poet accounts for his fascination
with flight:

          I'd hear the car and run
          crashing through the door, take off
          from the porch and fly
          to Daddy. Around and around
          he'd swing me over his head
          up to his shoulders, a wild
          spiral that always worked.

There is something about McDonald's own art that always works,
and will go on "working against time," as his 1981 book title so aptly
puts it. While there is little that is radically new in McDonald's latest collection, it does show his slow and conscious development of
themes peculiar to his writing. With each new volume the poet has
deepened his hold on the subjects he knows best. Like his native
mesquite, which it has been said can put down a 40-foot root to reach
its needed moisture, McDonald's poetry keeps on penetrating to the
depths of his habitation and of his own being. And with each new
volume his readers are enriched beyond any wealth of oil or real estate,
since what his water witching reaches to is our deepest need for the
change of perspective that can produce an epiphany of understanding
and empathy.

In Search of Tomás Rivera

From the beginning of the Chicano movement, poetry played a prominent role in motivating *la raza* and in publicizing its need for political muscle to effect social and economic change.* A poem by Tino Villanueva in the September 16, 1990, issue of *The Texas Observer* (printed in Spanish with a facing-page translation by James Hoggard) recalls the year 1959 and the situation then existing when Chicanos suffered in silence from the biased textbooks that branded their people as "more treacherous than Indians." Ten years later, in 1969, Ricardo Sánchez looked forward to leaving prison and forming part of the Chicano movement, ready to "pick up a gun" for *la raza chicana*, "to fight our common enemy." The poem containing these lines by Sánchez, which dates from the last year of a violent decade, is included in his *Selected Poems* from Arte Público Press, which has just brought out *The Searchers: Collected Poetry* of Tomás Rivera, the author of the now-classic "*. . . y no se lo tragó la tierra / . . . and the earth did not devour him,*" winner of an award for the best Chicano novel of 1969-70.

While Tomás Rivera (1934-1985) shared with Villanueva and Sánchez the vision of a better day for *la raza*, with all three having experienced the evils of prejudice and exploitation in their native Texas, Rivera did not express his anger so directly or vehemently as his fellow Texans. Instead, Rivera, in both his prose and poetry, employed a subtler art in his struggle against those who denied the Chicano's human dignity, his abilities, and his cultural values. Not that Rivera did not at times resort to an open attack on those who made him "eat shit / in a taco—laughing, all laughing." Certainly one of the most disturbing sections of the title poem of *The Searchers* levels a searing indictment against misguided public school regulations and the treatment of migrant workers:

> We are not alone
> if we remember and

---

* *The Texas Observer* (September 28, 1990): 19-20.

recollect our passions

. . .

We are not alone
when we were whipped
in school for losing
the place in the book
or for speaking Spanish
on the school grounds
or
when Chona,
dear Chona,
a mythic Chicana,
died in the sugar beet fields
with her eight-month
child
buried deep within her
still

Yet these are the exceptions, for Rivera's poetry is more often given to an internal quest for meaning, to a concern for an understanding of abstractions associated with traditional Spanish poetry: solitude, the self, memory, poetry itself or the power of the written word, love, hope, death. These and related themes predominate throughout the book and testify to editor Julián Olivares's claim that "Poetry was for Rivera a very intimate experience . . . [He] writes . . . for and to himself." Even so, Rivera has much to say to his readers.

Among the finest pieces in *The Searchers* are several that were frequently reprinted during Rivera's lifetime, including "The Overalls," a moving tribute to his father that ends: "the overalls, hanging / in the garage / never to be filled again"; "The Rooster Crows en Iowa y en Texas," a poem on Rivera's experience as a migrant worker with its memorable lines describing the poet's birthplace of Crystal City: "to walk the holes / full of street / of my town"; and "M'ijo no mira nada," one of the most successful bilingual poems by a Chicano writer. This last piece is especially instructive, for in it Rivera does not merely show that he knows both Spanish and English but uses the two languages for a significant dramatic purpose. In a dialogue between father and son, the boy speaks English instead of Spanish, a sign of the younger generation's rejection of the older generation's cultural tradition, brought about by societal and economic pressures and the natural need for the son to find his own way. The vision of the father is questioned by the son, whose interests lie beyond the actual scenes pointed out by the parent. While the father sees the beauty in a downtown fountain, the son only thinks about needing to go to the bathroom. Ultimately the father loses patience with the boy's responses and tells him in Spanish, let's go home, you don't look at anything. Although this conflict relates to such an ethnic issue as preservation of one's inherited language, it goes deeply as well into generational differences as to meaning and significance. Furthermore, Rivera does not take sides, but simply presents the dialogue as an indication of the complexities involved. It is this wider kind of insight that Rivera brings to bear on his subjects.

Rivera's writing often moves away from the basic concerns of the Chicano movement to consider the nature of poetry as a means of comprehending the continuity and connectedness of life. In a previously unpublished poem entitled "Eternity," the poet observes that "The living will always be dead / as the dead will / always be living." In another previously unpublished piece—this one in Spanish and entitled "Palabras" ("Words")—Rivera claims that he has deciphered the eternal secret of immortality, which he says was so easy to uncover: Behind his words he will remain forever to follow with his eyes those who read his poem. He exhorts others to do the same: "¿Por qué no me siguen? / Métanse conmigo entre las palabras" ("Why not follow me? / Plunge with me into the words"). Rivera concludes the poem by referring to his words left on the white sheet of paper as being pieces of his bloodstained brains that smell of life and will know how to live. Despite the limited number of poems collected in *The Searchers* (and there are quite a few which are the same poem written by Rivera in both Spanish and English and which exhibit some curious variations), the reader cannot but feel the truth of the poet's assertion that there is something timeless about the mind behind the words. What goes on inside the mind is suggested in the following passage from yet another previously unpublished poem, "Searching at Leal Middle School":

We talked of thinking
of inventing ourselves
of love for others
of love to be searching
for ourselves.

In introducing this welcome collection of Rivera's poems, editor Julián Olivares and Frank Kersnowski, whose foreword recounts his publication of Rivera's first book of poems in 1973, have together provided valuable accounts of a man who remains an inspiration to those who knew him, to those who have read his prose fiction, and to those familiar with his various public appearances as a speaker. As Olivares and Kersnowski make clear, Rivera was a warm, sensitive, thoughtful, and sincere figure who by his own academic example— he served as vice president of administration at the University of Texas at San Antonio, executive vice president at the University of Texas at El Paso, and chancellor of the University of California at Riverside—led the way for those of his own generation and for generations to come. The group of previously unpublished poems included by Olivares in this collection, comprising about half the book, reveals the kind of thoughtful man and writer Rivera was. In particular, it is enlightening to have a piece that describes something of the sources of the poet's early awareness of history and literature. Entitled by the editor "In the dump" (after the first line of what is apparently an unfinished poem), this piece concerns, as Olivares points out,

> an adolescent who discovers in the dump that which has been thrown away as refuse, objects of beauty. In the dump the subject endeavors to find the search but it appears to elude him. Yet the final line suggests a liminal state, the entrance into that creative solitude that augurs the process of discovery and rebirth. It is clear that the dump, that mountain of refuse into which la raza had been thrown, is a symbol of search, of discovery and self-discovery.

In "Searching at Leal Middle School" Rivera also refers to

the dump yards
where smoke curled and
with long sticks we turned and turned and
found half-forgotten fruit
to be washed and eaten
and books.

This image of the dump proves an important key to the reading of Rivera's entire oeuvre. In fact, this same episode is central to Rivera's novel, as it appears in the section entitled "It's That It Hurts," which depicts the narrator's fear of having been expelled from school—from the learning he comes to know is crucial to him and to his people.

Just as the poet found in the dump nourishment for both body and intellect, so Olivares has performed a similar service for present and future readers by digging into what the editor refers to as the poet's wastebasket and rescuing work he might have wanted to discard. Fortunately, Olivares saw fit to include such "refuse" in his collection of Rivera's poetry. As perhaps the finest Chicano writer to appear on the scene from the beginning of the Chicano movement, and still the closest to the affirmative spirit of that effort to recognize and credit the qualities of the Mexican-American mind and culture, Tomás Rivera is and will be a figure about whom we need to know as much as possible. This collection of Rivera's poems aids in preserving the work of a man who deserves a readership not only for his creative expression, but for all that he has meant and will continue to mean to those convinced of the rich potential of our multicultural heritage.

To Mow or Not to Mow

Of four recent collections of poems by Bryce Milligan, John Herndon, Del Marie Rogers, and Wendy Barker, the first three were sent to me by their authors with the request that I review them and the last I selected because I had seen some of Barker's poems in such magazines as *Poetry* and *Cedar Rock*.* As usual, I know these writers personally, and as a result, I had second thoughts about taking on the task of commenting on their work in public. Even though I have been doing this sort of thing for years, more and more I find I hesitate and wonder with J. Alfred Prufrock, "And how should I presume? . . . Do I dare to eat a peach?" But always I have gone ahead, though increasingly less certain I have anything to say worth being heard. What convinces me in the end is the notion that I will once again be—in life insurance parlance—the primary beneficiary, and this occasion proved no exception. What strikes me now is the fact that in reading these four collections—*Litany Sung at Hell's Gate, Poems from Undertown, Close to Ground,* and *Winter Chickens and Other Poems*—for purposes of writing a composite review, I have necessarily discovered themes and patterns among them that probably I would not have noticed otherwise. For me, at least, the exercise of reviewing has once more brought unexpected rewards.

One common denominator I found among three of these collections—Milligan's *Hell's Gate,* Herndon's *Undertown,* and Rogers' *Close to Ground*—is the democratic image of grass, an extension of section 6 of Whitman's "Song of Myself." These three Texas poets have seen different meanings in Whitman's "hieroglyphic" that sprouts "alike in broad zones and narrow zones," from one another and largely from those offered by Whitman. On a negative note that is sustained throughout his book, Bryce Milligan cites the "drought wracked dry cracked soil / . . . the seals and birds drowned in oil"—that is, the absence of grass, the effect of "developers who develop nothing." Milligan's *Litany Sung at Hell's Gate* is an apocalyptic vision of the

---

* *Texas Books in Review* 11, no. 1 (Spring 1991): 30, 32-33.

modern world, "a place where love has never been." The collection contains no relief from its unrelenting indictment of America's fall from a Whitmanic dream of brotherhood and of communion with strength-giving nature. Only in "Hair," where Milligan recalls that

> Daddy and I walked the long blocks north
> after the Saturday mowing to be mowed ourselves
> where Old Joe shined shoes as black
> as his own bald pate and I laughed
> not knowing his pain or my own shame,

is there a touch of humorous nostalgia—bitter though it may be—in the poet's recollection of going "where Baker's tonic filled bright red bottles," where "every week without reason" they strapped him in, hoisted him "mirror-high" to trim and wax his crew-cut "in perfect imitation of a surreal wheat field." Other than in this one poem, Milligan's work in his second collection is rarely satisfying as poetry, either in sound or shape, but his litany, in the wilderness voice of a contemporary Jeremiah or a Dante at hell's gate, reminds us of our shortcomings, and this still remains a vital if disturbing function of one type of poetic utterance.

John Herndon's *Poems from Undertown* opens with a similar vision of a chemically and spiritually tainted "america," with its "dark thoughts vented behind / and buried underground," as it is phrased in the first poem entitled "Tell it to Dante: one for the framers of Hell." The scatological imagery in this initial poem is certainly reminiscent of Dante's *Inferno*, and progressively the book develops the satanic side of things, climaxing with "Mutual Benefit Life" and the lines

> In the Age of Technological Terror
> we have forgotten the usefulness of feces,

which are followed by an excerpt from the Lord's Prayer (similar to a parodic use in Milligan of the *kyrie eleison*) and an ironic catalog of

> vestigial and polluted powers
> who yet will not be denied:

Stercutius Cloacina Tlacolquani Suchiquecal Baal-Peor
Gods of the Dirty Mouths
Coprophagi   abundant eaters
responsible for the fertility of crops.

All of this relates directly to the poet's view in "Explanation to
Thomas" that "the grass is all alive, but we don't / understand the language of grass." Mostly Herndon finds that "Your everyday Resident
of Undertown" performs

certain housekeeping duties, chief among which
is the tending of lush, green waste-lots
as expiation for the sin of gluttony, outward sign of piety and
    wealth,
distress signals, prayer flags.

There is nothing in Herndon's book of Whitman's grass as "the
flag of my disposition, out of hopeful green stuff woven." Rather,
Herndon rebels against his neighbors' constant watering and mowing
and lets his own lawn go thirsty, declaring that it "seems by avoiding
pointless and thankless drudgery / I've backed into the right path"
(in "Excuse for Not Mowing the Lawn"). The poet finds that he has
discouraged fire ants by leaving his grass long, and that deeper grass
"soaks up less gasoline." He concludes: "This then is not an excuse,
but an exhortation." Through about half his book, Herndon exhorts
us, and then turns to providing us with a glimpse of paradise, once we
have been through a hell of inappropriately prescribed antibiotics (in
"Versus anti-Biosis") and a purgatory of diminished expectations (in
"A Spell to Forget Scientific Farming"), leading us

into a bewilderment of rock and root . . .
the running lifeblood of water
that gives [nature] all shape and meaning . . .
the miracle of water in a dry place.

From Undertown's wasteland, the poet emerges in "Cypress" with a
belief that "Stumps heal over, push out new shoots and branches," and

that "Everyone should have a compost pile, / even if only as an object of contemplation."

Herndon's idea that ecology is a source of "linguistic inventiveness" is also something of a theme in Del Marie Rogers' *Close to Ground*, the latest collection from Corona Publishing Company, which has previously issued fine books by Robert A. Fink and Charles Behlen, among others. Like Milligan and Herndon, Rogers presents a rather gloomy perspective on America, characterized in her work as "The Great American Loneliness," the place where "Children are left at home to save themselves." But like Herndon, Rogers also finds meaningfulness in the natural world, in mountains (compare Herndon's view of "lovely Jémez . . . blue in the distance" with its "mighty cloud full of lightning . . . like the symbol of a new age") and in "Birds, wind, grass." As Rogers says of this world, "It's all I know. It's enough." Also like Herndon, who writes in "Toward an Understanding of Trees" that "You must climb a tree to know it. Embrace the scaly alligator bark," Rogers asserts in "Letter to My Mother": "I am happy. I will live in a tree." This closeness to nature is epitomized by her poem "In the Mountain Cabin":

> Waking close to the trees
> in a cabin of rough wood
> we can feel their presences.
> Even before we are fully awake
> our sleep goes branching upward in a lake of light.

While sharing some of the bitterness over contemporary life with Milligan and Herndon and some of the latter's attraction to the enduring environment as "the right path," Rogers exhibits greater "linguistic inventiveness" in writing of her contact with the natural world. A single line by Rogers can contain more punch and poignancy than whole poems by the men, as when in "Antler" she says of deer, "Wherever they go, there is grass," or in "Dry Arrangement in a Domed Jar," a poem for her daughter, where she writes,

> Now you have these open fields, grass,
> each stalk in air, long survivor.

Over our heads, a rich river of stars.

Also from Corona Publishing is Wendy Barker's *Winter Chickens*, a collection which, instead of complaining broadly, tends to celebrate home life and the quotidian imagery of garden and kitchen. Barker's poems, like "Kitchen Fever," focus on the small details of her woman's world:

> Furiously cutting carrots.
> Round slices.
> You can see the sun inside, small
> spokes yellow as butter in the pan,

or in "Canning Season," where simmering tomatoes with their "skins peel[ed] off, expose pink / veins tracing over / glistening flesh." In her poetry Barker takes delight in the wonders of everyday existence, but there is also an ability to make us feel the hurt in life, a sadness at things not being as we would have them to be. Never, however, is there any attempt to appeal to our consciences, and yet the effect of Barker's book is quietly to return us to an awareness of our better selves.

As might be expected in a book concerned with home life, there are poems in *Winter Chickens* on relationships within the family, as in "Love Poem," where the wife recalls to the husband

> You told me not to worry,
> I'd fit the pieces together sometime,
> couldn't do these hard ones on rickety tables.
> . . . You never interrupted
> while the dark trees in the puzzle
> found each other, lifted branches into sky,

or in "Deer Running" where the parents seek to instill in the children a sensitive response to the world. This latter poem contains the moving account of a doe struck by a car,

> When she crawls
> into the safety of cedar brake . . . only to fall

on her side, and fall
again, again,
before she moves off
and loses us
among the dry leaves.

What is particularly effective about this poem is the poet's juxtaposition of her son's piano lesson against the later scene of the deer leaping and trying desperately to escape the oncoming traffic, as well as a remembered fearful episode in Chicago when the speaker walked "like hell" to get away from twenty or thirty figures "moving straight for us." The piece ends with this simple stanza that draws together and unifies the various emotional strands of Barker's poem:

For knowing the music
David's teacher gave him
a plastic bust of Brahms.
She's teaching him to use
the right fingers
on the right keys,
not to rush the tempo.

A similar technique is employed by Barker in "Saturday Kitchen Requiem," where the speaker combines in her mind the plucking of a chicken and its smell of death, her son's "first concert" when "third grade sopranos / gave their regards to Broadway, / Chicago, places they've never seen," and thoughts of her husband off in Ithaca at his father's funeral. With little commentary from the poet, Barker's poems allow such scenes to work their cumulative effect on the reader, and time and again they hit their emotive mark.

Comfort and Native Grace

Among some dozen collections of poems by native Texans to appear in 1991, three from university presses at Carnegie Mellon, Texas Tech, and Louisiana State have—through their compelling narrative lines—continued to haunt my thoughts.* Gillian Conoley's *Tall Stranger*, Walter McDonald's *The Digs in Escondido Canyon*, and Susan Wood's *Campo Santo* are all attractive publications and feature on back cover or dust jacket a photographic glimpse into the personality of each poet. None of these is a first book, and the assured individual voices make this obvious even without the publishers citing Conoley's two previous collections, McDonald's eleven earlier volumes, and Wood's book as her second and the year's prestigious Lamont Poetry Selection of The Academy of American Poets. What immediately struck me about these three collections was the identifiably Texan or regional tone and subject matter of much of the poetry, though this is not what stuck with me or impressed me most deeply. For these writers have depended upon but transcended the occasions or settings of their poems to recreate scenes that speak of every man or woman's timeless places: memories of childhood, moments of discovery when the world proves different from what parents or society deem it to be, days that bring loneliness or loss, the need whenever or wherever for hope and a belief in love and forgiveness.

Reading these collections for their common ground, one can find such poems as Conoley's "Country Music," McDonald's "Leaving the Middle Years," and Wood's "Rhythm and Blues," which all attempt to interpret the relationship of music to a time of life. In each case, the style and general point of view of the respective poet is reflected in his or her treatment of this particular art form. With Gillian Conoley (born in Taylor in 1955) music serves to bring together a woman who "slips her wedding ring / from her finger" and "walks inside a bar" and a man who

---

* *The Texas Observer* (March 27, 1992): 18-19.

leads the woman backwards
to the dance floor

as though she were the last of a kind,
as though she were capable of releasing
the stranger inside him.

As in most of Conoley's writing, this piece ends on a somewhat melancholy note, as would be expected from the situation and the sentimental nature of the music. But Conoley's highly imaginative narratives all have at their core a positive feeling, for they are told by a speaker who is not disillusioned by what happens to her or by the consequences of her choices. A key phrase in "Country Music" may be this: "the floor creaks comfort," or as the next stanza has it, "the world has been cruel / but they've come to sing it politely. . . ."

In "Leaving the Middle Years," Walter McDonald (born in Lubbock in 1934) tells of a sawdust dance floor "almost deserted," where a couple past middle-age is beckoned by a "slow blues" to "join sad others" and glide to

fiddles and steel guitars
sentimental enough for lovers bound
by more than rings and wrinkles
deeper than any scars.

The poet's description of "lazy smoke layered like haze / in the mellow glow of the jukebox" is at once musical in itself and suggestive of the "golden years" with their acceptance of change but also of the couple's attachment that is unaffected by time. McDonald's book is full of such moments when the poet accepts his environment, his past and present, or as he says in "The Barn on the Farm We're Buying": "dust / we're growing used to, our other odor, / the earth we're beginning to call home."

In "Rhythm and Blues," Susan Wood (born in Commerce in 1946) recalls the teenage years when

we fled the family's satisfied table

to cruise those country roads in twos or fours
or tens, whatever kept us not alone.

Fear of being oneself or someone we do not want to be is a theme running throughout Wood's book, as in a remarkable piece entitled "Eggs," where the speaker says

I hated myself, hated the egg
growing in secret deep in my body,

the secret about to be spilled
to the world. . . .

In "Rhythm and Blues," as elsewhere in her book, Wood knows more about life—how with each generation the sun will "still be / going down like teenagers in the backseat / of a father's borrowed Chevy"—than she did in those teenage years, but she knows such knowledge would not have helped since "the object changes / but desire persists." One constant desire in Wood's poetry is to console those like herself who have suffered the loss of a loved one or of some fundamental dream, even though the poet realizes, as in "Dear Everyone" and in "Campo Santo," that "there are those who suffer, even unto death, / and are not me, and cannot be consoled." And yet Wood's poems comfort in the way they work through the most horrendous experiences (as in "Matinee," where during the movie a childhood girlfriend's father exposes himself to the speaker), emerging fully aware of the pain of loss or disillusion but still ready "to show . . . how much love matters," despite the fact that in "Rhythm and Blues" she remembers how as a teenager "love / was only misery" and as an adult she understands that love is "a secret life," an "ache / that can't be filled." Ironically, even in a poem like "Hollow," which revisits the Black section of her hometown and recounts the hollowness of her response to the "Coloreds," Wood *fills* her reader through an ability to reproduce period and place with all their smells, looks, regrets, mysteries, pities, and revelations, weaving them together in conversational but telling lines that move powerfully from stanza to crafted stanza.

As for Gillian Conoley, she seems intent on standing on her own without collapsing under the pressure of others' desires or demands—as when she writes of "The Singer" who

> learns
> to hold each note,
> though the roads curl
> like paper from her hair,
> the rooms full of who and why
> she chose the wrong nights
> to stay out
> late. . . .

Conoley's poems may be characterized as "Unchained Melody," the title of one piece in which the speaker declares that with

> the rose in her hand
> drooping and gently hurt,
> she eats dirt if she has to
> but drinks from her own well.

In "The Farmer's Daughter and the Traveling Salesman," perhaps the most striking poem in her collection, Conoley—like McDonald—has her speaker accepting what life brings and living with it, even finding inspiration in hardship, or as McDonald terms it, surviving on "hardscrabble." Retelling the traditional tale of the farm girl who has the "humdrum" wooed out of her life by a traveling salesman, Conoley does not present any bitterness on the part of the speaker who had "her forehead cleansed of dreams," who the neighbors reported had drowned herself (presumably out of shame), and who "was beginning to know good / from evil." This persona remains "unrepentant as a pillar of salt" and announces in the end that she "had been chosen / to live on / and on in the mortal soul / of the wayward tale." Or as Conoley says in "Native Grace," "There's nowhere to go but on," and her poetry does just that. And this is not meant in a pejorative sense, for Conoley's inventive poems are unperturbed by mistakes and full of forgiveness for herself and others, even, for instance, of "Lee Harvey" (and Dallas) because, as the speaker says in the poem of this title, she had a cousin looked "a little like Oswald" who no one claimed on either side of her family, while she has taken him in along with so many other souls she seems to have encountered along the way, such as history's Belle Starr, in the poem of the same title:

> My only son
> so loved me
> in an open field
> with the same hands
>
> he shot me, and in the back,
> three times. The pain in my spine
> I was glad for;
> it kept me alive to the bone[,]

or Alma in "The Last Aunt":

> a red brag
> in the middle of the road
> shattering bits of Depression glass
> as if to snap your fingers
> at the world, oil rigs
> rusted in the background
> like monkey bars.

The theme of acceptance is treated with particular poignancy in Walter McDonald's "Eighteen," which refers to a son the speaker in the poem "cannot bring back." The apparent conflict between teenager and father is hurtful, and yet the speaker comes to an understanding that he must accept the fact that his son "has too many scars / to be a child again." If the father has contributed to the son's staying away, he also knows that he once held him on his lap,

> taught him

> patty cake, cat's cradle . . .

how to walk, how to make fire,
how to bed down under stars.

The speaker pleads with himself for patience, and is perhaps some-what comforted by knowing that at a certain age some sons must make their own way, against all the father's teaching, love, and suf-fering. Accepting this view is no easy task, but McDonald's poem is evidence of his artistry and wisdom, of his view of the need to face up to a bitter experience and turn it into a thing of beauty through the miracle of measured speech.

Likewise, Susan Wood in her poem "Nineteen" has not forgot-ten "it's so hard to be" that age with its "powerlessness, all that sexual / longing that makes you feel as if you're burning / from the inside out," when one "can't separate / personal freedom, responsibility, from the good / of the state," when one suspects like Hamlet that "there's something wrong / at the heart of things." But in the end the speaker asserts that even though she can fully empathize with her young stu-dent, she still knows "the grammar of desire, how the heart longs / to fill and to be filled," and it is this "grammar of desire" which drives Wood to accept that even if "description is the best" a poet can do—though "not enough"—it at least offers, as she says in "Hope,"

what saves us ... something small, the thing
so insignificant we hardly notice. ...
It was there
all along, had we seen it, the way
the constellations are always
in the stars.

Susan Wood's poems often remind me of the writings of other Texas poets. "Sunday Nights" ("Still, I can't help thinking how that movie might end: / the train stopped just in time by a telegram"), "Campo Santo" ("every grave is piled high like this / with paper flowers, so gaudy / and touching the hills bloom / all year long"), "Immersion" (with its depiction of baptism), and "Too Good To Be True" (with its reference to "That sign hung for years above the courthouse: / 'The Blackest Land, The Whitest People'")—these in particular recall for me Sandra Lynn's "Happy Endings" and "Mexican Cemetery," Carolyn Maisel's "Witnessing," and James Hoggard's "Tornado's Eye." Lines in "Campo Santo" ("they call it *holy field,* / and even those without belief / say it is blessed by the dead who lie there") echo English poet Philip Larkin's famous "Church-Going." At times Wood's poems ramble a bit and lose their focus and impact, yet her work is neither derivative nor pointless; indeed, Wood's poetry has achieved a renewed and profound treatment of regional settings and themes and has done so in a voice wholly her own, one that is both appealing and convincing in whatever it has to say.

Along with Walter McDonald, Gillian Conoley, and other Texas poets, Susan Wood has penetrated to the "Bedrock" of the Texas experience, which Conoley infers (in her poem of that title) is telling us "we live in this world / and the last, and the next, / now or never." All three of these exceptional poets are, in McDonald's words, "Digging on Hardscrabble," seeking to quench us by their consoling springs. And while they know "three wells out of four / are sand," they have yet lowered themselves into their own depths, in an effort to spin us up out of Wood's blend of love and awe and shame into McDonald's "almost liquid light."

Poems From the Texas Plains

In his dust jacket blurb for Walt McDonald's *All that Matters: The Texas Plains in Photographs and Poems*, Steve Harrigan has declared of the Lubbock native and his thirteenth collection of poems: "Walter McDonald is one of the best poets in America, and there is no better place to encounter his work than in this haunting album of words and pictures."* I can only second this substantial claim by pointing to individual poems that remind me of the work of major American poets, for *All That Matters* contains writing that can be compared favorably and on the same footing with the poetry not merely of today but from earlier, perhaps more profound, periods of American literature.

Along with a number of fine pieces reprinted from McDonald's previous collections, this "New and Selected Poems" includes work that I had either forgotten, overlooked before, or that is in fact new to me. An example is "Goat Ranching," which called to mind the following lines from section 32 of Walt Whitman's "Song of Myself":

> I think I could turn and live awhile with the animals. . . .
> They do not sweat and whine about their condition,
> They do not lie awake in the dark and weep for their sins . . .
> Not one is dissatisfied . . . not one is demented with the
>   mania of owning things,
> Not one kneels to another nor to his kind that lived
>   thousands of years ago,
> Not one is respectable or industrious over the whole earth.

While McDonald echoes Whitman's sentiments (especially in another poem, "After the Flight Home from Saigon," where he says of his sorrel that "He's never killed a bull, keeps no money / in the bank, sings no soft gospel songs / at sundown"), he does not entirely agree with the other Walt, for certainly the Texan seems to find his animals

---

* *Texas Books in Review* 12, no. 4 (Winter 1992): 20-21.

"respectable" and "industrious"—as he says of cows in a hailstorm, they "go on grazing / afraid of nothing but hunger." More importantly, McDonald finds in animals, as Whitman did, admirable qualities to be appreciated and learned from. In "Goat Ranching" the Texan begins by asserting that he "could let go and live with goats," moving on to observe that "They've never killed a kid by kindness // or neglect, never had to put their kids' / old dogs to sleep . . . I've never / seen a goat afraid of trouble."

This same poem also reminds me of Robinson Jeffers' "Hurt Hawks," as do several of McDonald's poems that enter the world of animals to reveal their fears, dreams, and beliefs. Jeffers declares in his poem that he would "sooner, except the penalties, kill a man than a hawk," and yet he does so because the bird "is strong and pain is worse to the strong" and because it asked for death but "not like a beggar." In another poem entitled "Death of a Dog," Jeffers confesses that he let someone else eliminate his vicious pet and that "if I had had the courage / To kill him myself I would think better of myself." McDonald's own relationship to his animals—goats, horses, cows, dogs, cats, bulls, and even such creatures as cottonmouth water moccasins, rattlesnakes, buzzards, and mice—is equally moving in its way. Throughout this collection, McDonald identifies deeply with the life around him, learning from it so many lessons that are—as with the case of the goats and their kids—crucial to men and women and especially to those "living on the open plains."

The lessons McDonald picks up from sentient, intelligent animals—even those he refers to as dumb—strike me as one of the most impressive features of this collection, even though the poems on various relatives (Uncle Murphy "The Honey Man," "Uncle Bubba and the Buzzards," "Uncle Rollie and the Laws of Water, " and in particular Uncle Oscar in "After a Year in Korea") are also of a kind with the animal pieces in the insights they reveal. From the first poem, "Wind and Hardscrabble" (where steers remain calm "as long as there is wind" to spin the windmills, "believing there is always water"), to a poem like "Deductions from the Laws of Motion" (where "cats on the farm / never need for long what we offer, proof / they're not alone"), McDonald obliquely touches a number of very human nerves. This is most effectively achieved for me in "Sundown," a portrait of an old bull presented with all the poet's brilliantly telling details that capture the animal as he

> listens to his farm, the last hens
> clucking, the snort of horses
> in the barn, the faint
>
> swishing of cows' tails,
> and somewhere far off
> a dog's persistent barking.

As the poet says, the old bull is "not alone" and in fact holds sway over all that surrounds him—a knowing reply to Whitman's "not one is demented with the mania of owning things" in that the bull possesses a whole world of meaningful sound. Another poem of this sort is "Where the Trees Go," in which McDonald becomes one with "leaves brittle, branches / twisted like fists . . . stumps seared dry by snow" in order to learn from the surviving trees "to go on / without them"—survival of what withers or is cut off from us being one of the lessons McDonald might say is "all that matters."

Like Robert Frost and Wallace Stevens, this Texas poet has looked closely into the world of nature and has found both his subject matter and his message. As McDonald states in "Wildcatting" (in his plain, unadorned language, which yet can be balanced by lines that are richly metaphorical and musical), "Nothing is there until we find it." McDonald has indeed discovered an inexhaustible well of words and images to be drawn from a seemingly barren terrain, with its sandstorms, treeless spaces, tornadoes, and rattlesnakes. But landscape is not McDonald's only forte, for in a love poem like "A Woman Acquainted with the Night," which would seem to be the Texan's version of a Frost piece of almost the same title, the regional motif of a storm cellar is turned into a memorable image of his wife, who, when the lights are knocked out, "goes on mending clothes by feel / while I sweat and rage / to make the spare fuse fit." Like so many of McDonald's poems, this one ends with an unforgettable lesson:

> When storms short out

the relay stations, she knows
how to touch me, how to make
romance of failure,

knows like blind friends
how many steps to the candles
so if our children wake and cry
for light, there will be light.

The photographs from Texas Tech University's Southwest Collection add an important visual dimension to this volume, beginning with the dust jacket image of an irrigation hydrant pumping out the region's life-giving waters. Janet M. Neugebauer has selected a group of photographs that supports McDonald's poems both literally and thematically, from cemetery to ice storm, from a bee swarm on a fence post to slaughtered hogs, and from weathered farm buildings to cotton fields and a man kneeling in the wind-blown dust. In many ways, despite the austerity of the landscape, the photographs and poems in *All That Matters* answer the question asked in McDonald's "Mercy and the Brazos River"—"How could they [Quakers from Iowa] leave their families for this?"—by documenting the mystery and miracle of life on the poet's beloved "open plains."

Surviving a Silenced Lamb

In 1960 Alfred A. Knopf, Inc., published John Graves' *Goodbye to a River*, a classic Texas work of meditation on a passing way of life—a common theme in Texas letters.* In 1992 Knopf has published—so far as I am aware—its first collection of poetry by a native Texan: Stan Rice's *Singing Yet: New and Selected Poems*, the harrowing chronicle of the effects of a single passing away—a death in the family. Another beautifully designed and printed Knopf edition, Rice's book features on the dust jacket a full-color reproduction of a painting by the poet: possibly a symbolic depiction of death raping innocence. This vivid and disturbing piece of art seems to relate directly to the central section of Rice's collection, "Some Lamb" (1975), which is in two parts, subtitled "During" and "After," and concerns the death of the poet's daughter from leukemia. An excruciating, moving, and even heroic series of poems, this section of Rice's book presents a situation and its impact on the poet that may be characterized by a phrase from the collection's final section of "New Work" (1983-1990): "I take the nursery rhyme into the slaughter house." In many ways, the poems from "Some Lamb" (with its epigraph from William Blake's "Infant Sorrow" out of his *Songs of Experience*) pervade and permeate the rest of this powerful book, one of the most important collections of poetry by a Texan ever published.

Born in Dallas in 1942, Stan Rice was for many years at San Francisco State University as a professor and the assistant director of The Poetry Center. One of Rice's poems from the 1960s first appeared in the outstanding anthology, *Quickly Aging Here* (1969), and was then entitled "On the Murder of Martin Luther King" but is included in *Singing Yet* as "Whiteboy." Section 3 of this piece recalls a practice from earlier years when, as the original subtitle has it, "The Young Texan returns to the Texas State Fair and sees the source of his racism sitting in a glass cage over a tank of water." The object of this particular sideshow "attraction" was to dunk the "nigger" and "pay him

---

* *The Texas Observer* (October 2, 1992): 19-20.

back for his sensual blackness," but he keeps "staring at you through the glass tank / like an animal that you can't kill." Section 2 of this poem was probably written before Rice's daughter was diagnosed with leukemia, but it too, like the poems on her condition and its devastating effects on the poet and his wife, is about children, in this case "suave children black and brown" whose bodies are

> full of echoes,
> scary as Death in the ivy standing
> knee-deep in the green ivy,
> beating on the mouths of bottles with their palms,
> grieving and smiling.

Despite the tragedy at the heart of Rice's book, his poetry can bring smiles as well as grief, for this collection ultimately celebrates the fact that the poet is "singing yet."

A lighthearted piece like "The Skyjacker" is told in the voice of a cowboy singer-movie star:

> I am carrying a pillow into the cockpit on
> which is embroidered
> I am Tex Ritter. Howdy.
> A calm falls over the cockpit.
> The co-pilot takes off his extra ears and I tell them,
> Relax. . . . That this is not Eldridge Cleaver
> This is Tex Ritter talkin
> and . . . We are going to Havana forever!

More representative of the book's black humor is "The Allnight Hamburger Stand in the Dangerous Neighborhood" from the "Texas Suite":

> The Murder Burger
> is served right here.
> You need not wait
> at the gate of Heaven
> for unleavened death.

You can be a goner
on this very corner.
Mayonnaise, onions, dominance of flesh.
If you wish to eat it
You must feed it.
"Yall come back."
"You bet."

But even such sinister humor is the exception, for *Singing Yet* is the equivalent of "the bust of my dead daughter in marble" that is being carved in movement 7 of the "Texas Suite" by the poet's father-in-law.

Many of the book's central images and motifs are introduced in "Elegy," the first poem in the collection. Written during the daughter's illness, this piece is a very private acknowledgment that the speaker's pain cannot be escaped, but it is also an effort to face death through offering "Detail by detail / the living creatures." Throughout Rice's book, there are wondrous poems on animals—cows, cats, birds, a "tragic rabbit," a "goofy gold, ever hungering" dog who complicates the poet's life ("I can't move with you. / I can't bear the guilt of getting rid of you"), and, in one very significant case, a "dying goldfish"; in this last poem of the same title, Rice contrasts an oriental philosophy that sees death "as a continuity," with his daughter's goldfish resisting it "like crazy." The poet seems torn between these two views, faced as he is with the expected death of his daughter. Much of the tension in the book comes from Rice's constant struggle with two opposing sides, two incompatible philosophies pulling him apart. In "Elegy," enigmatic lines hint at pain or provide frequently a type of existential consolation: "If I bleed I must exist / Only hanging hogs get kissed." Since the daughter's disease is one that often attacks the blood, death and blood are everywhere in "Elegy," and the penultimate movement of the poem, number 20, concludes with one of many references in the book to savage sacrifice. In a passage written some twenty years ago, Rice evokes the then Los Angeles riots, ritualistic sacrifice, and his own sense of personal ruin:

And Durer gasped on first seeing Inca sun
six foot wide gasped silver moon . . . perceiving all men

had Craft & Giant Heart & who is savagery? Lost,
my friends, they took the metaphors literally, lost
in ramshackle moonlight kicking meat
the bus pulls up they stand in its headlights
the 7-Eleven manager cries out MUCH MUCH MUCH
my business is ruined . . . ketchup, all the ketchup broken . . .
           . . . they didn't want
to *eat* anything they just wanted to *have* everything . . .

Another allusion to human sacrifice is employed by Rice in "Time in
Tool," one of the most impressive single poems in the collection. In
this piece from the "New Work" section, Rice makes an oblique reference to savagery while he and his parents are in a Dallas shopping
mall:

The beauty and safety of the Mall is our forefathers' gift. . . .
The sun is setting but we are immune. We
go down into
manpower, humor, debt. We look at shirts.
We buy shirts. This is the moment
the flint knife digs out
the jumping heart of the sacrifice
slave. Then we sit calmly on the lip of the planter,
fulfilled.

The scene here is reminiscent of sometime Texas poet Leon
Stokesbury's fine "Day Begins at Governor's Square Mall," which
suggests how shopping in the artificial confines of a mall has become
in some ways a form of escapism. Rice's use of the mall, however, reso-
nates with his inability to escape reality, in that the shopping recalls
his book's many references to sacrifice, all deriving from the poet's
personal attachment to an innocent victim.

Other images and motifs central to "Elegy" and to Rice's later
poetry concern eating: of flesh, by shadows, "a white moth" by a frog,
and "the gypsy's dream" consumed by the lion in the Henri Rousseau
painting. Lamentation and bloodletting, "filthy grave" and "much
morgue," are motifs that combine with details from life that, accord-

ing to an old Japanese, cannot be ignored, in order for "godly sperm" to leap "from silkworm." Again, a type of existentialism enters the poem: "No joy is merely a handhold on something less. / What it squeezes, it is." Squeezing, bleeding, meat, eating, cannibalism, and death are image-motifs around which Rice's poems revolve, creating in a kaleidoscopic technique the heart-rending grief at the loss of a loved one, but also achieving a deeply felt philosophy for survival.

A number of the poems confront the impending death of the daughter by seeking to recount the experience as it happens. Although later in "Time in Tool" the poet will confess that "it is not clear when autobiographical data should be suppressed," in the earlier "The 29th Month" the speaker declares "I want to make it be in words, because / to get the poem right / is to have another baby / while the real one dies." In another poem from Part I of "Some Lamb," entitled "Trying to Feel It," the speaker again attempts to endure the experience through writing: "So I write this. So I / Try to give birth. Me, / a man." In poem after poem, the poet peers unflinchingly into the jaws of his daughter's death, as in a piece named after her, "Michele Fair," which elaborates the imagery of death feeding on the young girl, even as the poem concerns how "Naked Knowing" is "the Substance Beast" that "keeps check on me / To see that I have fed it me / Just as policemen like to see / A proper show of humility in those they rule." The most horrifying vision of innocence eaten is in "The Last Supper," with its image of a child dropped like a watermelon on concrete by the "crusher of children," the "Baby-eater."

Along with such oppressive but artful pieces in Part I, there are, among others, two magnificently uplifting poems that even as they register the horror of loss record a visionary coming to grips with life and death: "Only two choices / To stress: go on, or give in." In "Testimonial," the occasion of death has heightened the poet's senses, as it always does, and the poem manages to capture the paradoxical nature of this disheartening yet maturing experience: "My capacity for belief increased / As my number of beliefs diminished . . . I care so much / I don't care any more." The poet discovers that "Nothing mattered therefore / But the ambivalence of accurate / Illusions: art." For Rice the function of his own art is to employ verbal charms as a magic ritual of exorcism. And yet what is involved in the four sections of "Incanto"—which begins with an allusion to Blake's dichotomy of lamb/tyger ("Time / hath made off with the last lamb left"; "Which tyger shall eat the reflection?")—is that the poet weds "Clarity & Vividness, both miracles," by simultaneously depicting the death scene in all its overwhelming detail and by asserting that "If I'm to go on / the terms of the slaughter must be known," that such "cannibalism" of a precise art's clarity is necessary for there to be "No more death." Ultimately the poet believes that "To write this right is to cope with the corpse."

The second part of "Some Lamb" deals with "After," which brings with it repeated and painful remembrance, drunkenness, guilt, loss of marital sex ("Her thighs are tight. / My cock's no cure"), insomnia, and, in the next section ("Body of Work"), near madness, as the couple "Now in disquiet / . . . slowly, slowly thrive / On what [their] luggage closed upon and ate." However, even in these poems the poet is "singing yet," as the last line of "Singing Death" affirms. And in "Anne's Curls" the poet struggles with his guilt feelings— "Maybe / if I'd sought out a better doctor in Houston / Mouse would've lived longer. / Like you wanted to. Every / death's a murder. A million maybes"—and arrives at a new understanding of his relationship with his wife: "To die of fear of revealing yourself / to the person who loves you is murder." In the "Body of Work" section the poet has survived the "wreckage of remembering . . . Burying the never-to-be-forgotten bone" and is now "Singing along with the wrecking ball." Here he recovers "Tenderness" in the poem of that title: "To learn not to hate the original tenderness / that rendered you helpless." At this point the poet seems to return to his own childhood and to rediscover the thrill of sexual difference in "What Happened in the Hallway." And even though he can still experience a death wish—as in "The Fishing," the final movement of his "Texas Suite," where he says

> Again I ache to slide from my body.
> The lures lie naked in the tackle box.
> I envy them. Above me the [electric] tower to which I am tied
> is "singing." I slip over the edge of the boat
> into the cold water and wait

for one of the gods to take me by the hair
and pull my body off me like a nightgown

—in "Madness: Fullgrown" he can announce: "Madness . . . we have been, we have done. / What you have given is what I've outgrown."

There are so many profound and finely constructed poems in *Singing Yet* (like the Whitmanesque "America the Beautiful" in which the poet pledges allegiance "this time to the vivification of our lost Body Politic, / nerves and follicles and arteries / ablaze in the suaveness of night") that it is impossible to cover even a fourth of this collection, which runs to 226 pages. The sound and sense of even a shorter piece like "How Keep Dark and Pattern Off" cannot be appreciated unless the complete poem is reproduced. For me one of the most amazing pieces remains "Time in Tool," a more prosy narrative—than Rice's tighter lyrics—which builds cumulatively through eleven pages of "the most mundane things" to ask several crucial questions, such as "How is it possible to know when to stop remembering things?" Something of an urban version of Rice's more nursery-rhyme-like pieces, with their often grim reminders of the cruelties visited on the innocent, "Time in Tool" defines to some degree its own masterful achievement: "Though the tone wanders / the intent is song. / Sometimes it may sound like the cowboy song of a child." As a selected poems from a major publisher, Stan Rice's *Singing Yet* stands as a monument to the truth of the poet's own life and writings as proclaimed in the first four lines of this compelling book:

All life
has song. Tho the ear be sad
still it sings songs.
Men cannot be so gone.

In Memoriam: Joseph Colin Murphey

Toward the end of 1993, Texas lost one of the most important poets the state has yet produced.* Born December 13, 1915, in Lufkin, Joseph Colin Murphey died on Thanksgiving Day in a Denton-area nursing home where he had been taken only weeks before when cancer had reduced this tall, gentle man to a shadow of his vigorous, vital self. As in all such cases of prolonged suffering, the end came for those who knew him as a mixture of relief and regret. Both as a man of warmth and compassion and as an authentic Texas poet, Joe Murphey had meant much to many of us, and to commemorate these two inseparable sides of his life, a memorial poetry reading was organized in Austin, where Joe had received a doctorate from the University of Texas in 1963 and where he had returned to live for nearly a year before moving to Fort Worth to undergo radiation treatment.

A group of Austin writers associated with the capital city's Mexic-Arte Gallery, in particular Sue Littleton, Néstor Lugones of Argentina, and Thom the Poet from Australia, invited Joe's fellow poets and friends from around the state to participate in a reading at the Gallery on December 10th. Among those to make the trip to Austin and to read in homage to Joe Murphey was William Barney, the Fort Worth poet who had grown closer to Joe during his final days. Local writers in attendance were Miguel González-Gerth, Joanie Whitebird, Foster Foreman, C.A. Wiles, Albert Huffstickler, Grady Hillman, John Berry, and Herman Nelson. It is gratifying to be able to report that this gathering paid a high and moving tribute to the poet whose work will long be remembered and read by those who appreciate the music and wisdom of such a native Texas artist.

From her last conversation with Joe, Sue Littleton recalled the saddest anecdote of all. When she asked him if he was writing any poetry, Joe, who by then was not always cognizant of those around him, replied that in the night he was composing many poems, but

---

* *Re: Arts & Letters* 19, no. 2 (Winter 1993-1994): [63]-67.

when he awoke in the morning he could not find them anywhere. As Sue pointed out, Joe Murphey had always been writing poetry, and the evidence for this is to be found in his numerous handwritten journals full of his daily poems that are now preserved in the Special Collections Library at Texas Christian University in Fort Worth. On a happier note, Sue announced plans for publishing some 250 poems by Joe Murphey in a volume he himself entitled *The Perfection of Beauty*, which contains many of the pieces he wrote during the approach of death and his contemplation of what he called "the final journey." Certainly, as he says in one poem from the '80s, Joe Murphey was no "tea and toast geriatric," for he would "not go gentle into that / Procrustean, nurse-home bed!" Sue Littleton read one of the poems from Joe's unpublished manuscript, and Herman Nelson gave an affective reading of Joe's poem, "Kites Flying on the Bedpost Overnight," which had been published in Mexic-Arte's *Poesía y calle* (1992/1993), edited by Sue Littleton and Néstor Lugones. Others in attendance read pieces written especially in memory of the poet.

All felt the presence of Joe Murphey in spirit as we listened wistfully to the placid accent of his recorded voice from a tape issued in 1988 by Prickly Pear Press. Sue had selected from this recording one of Joe's most widely admired poems, "The Short Happy Bloom of Lurline Scruggs," which contains the lines San Antonio poet Cynthia Harper has said that she would give anything to have written herself:

> But at fourteen
> she was tall and straight like the pines
> and her flesh smooth as new pears,
>
> a tinge of pink everywhere and in the
> secret intimacies clean as spring clouds.
> She ran wild as the muscadine vine
>
> that grows (profusely) over the low trees,
> her arms always reaching, her body
> fragrant as a laurel sighing in the wind.

In contrast to this almost idyllic portrait, the poem recalls that after the war the young girl had become

a bent design,
a question mark with child,

carrying under the straight, high pines
a soon sought weight of guilt to swear at
all her life through twisted teeth.

Joe Murphey's own life was long and fruitful and unblemished by resentment. During the Second World War he was stationed in India; afterwards he graduated with a Masters degree from Southern Methodist University, where he became poetry editor for the *Southwest Review* under Decherd Turner and Margaret Hartley. In Huntsville, where he taught at Sam Houston State University, Joe founded *Stone Drum*, a magazine that published many of the leading national poets of the 1960s, including Robert Bly, Robert Creeley, Galway Kinnell, and Houston poet Vassar Miller. Some fifteen years later, while living in Gainesville and teaching at Cooke County Community College, Joe revived *Stone Drum* and encouraged many of the younger generation of Texas writers by editing and publishing their work in the pages of his distinctive magazine. A daughter, about whom Joe wrote his poem, "Walking Linda to Sleep," contributed the artwork for one cover; his brother Jack of Corpus Christi provided an Easter Island-like head for another; and a painter friend, Chris Burkholder, with whom Joe camped and took long walks in the Davy Crockett National Forest, supplied a Neches River landscape that graced the cover of an issue in 1986. Joe also enjoyed playing the piano, and could read music as well as perform any tune by ear, preferably in a jazz style, the fingers of his large hands spreading and rippling across the keys. In addition, he took up the writing of novels during the last decade of his life, completing three of these based on the intriguing lives of his Irish-Texas and American-Indian forebears. At the memorial reading in Austin, John Berry recited passages from one of Joe's plays, his version of *Sir Gawain and the Green Knight*, which Sue Littleton had premiered in Austin at Mexic-Arte two years earlier.

But above all, it was to poetry that Joe Murphey devoted himself most fully and eloquently. His poetry journals reveal the easy flow of his lines and thoughts, for there are few false starts and only occasional changes in word choices or phrasing. From the beginning of a poem, his lines trace out a thought or narrative whose point is wholly unsuspected, the reader's sense of direction being suspended as the subtle sound patterns (end or internal rhymes, natural but poetically heightened speech rhythms) move the eye and ear to the surprising yet inevitable closure. There is hardly another Texas poet who has written within the same structural framework (often a type of villanelle or lined musical effect achieved from stanza to stanza) or with the same ceaseless, run-on imagery and diction that are always so clear and yet so profound. Only Walt McDonald shares with Joe Murphey some of this same penetrating artistry, but in the end they are two quite different poets—partly because one is rooted in the arid, true-grit West Texas terrain and the other was in tune with the slower-paced, laid-back climate of the East Texas piney woods. Both, however, plumb in their poetry the depths of modern life in the Southwest and do so in a plain style that dramatizes their insights into the alternately violent and tender natures of the region's people and places.

The progress of Joe Murphey's career as a poet is not at this time so well documented in print as it should be. Early poems appeared in *The Texas Quarterly* and the *Southwest Review,* and his work was included in *Southwest: A Contemporary Anthology* published in New Mexico in 1977. More recently his poetry has been published in *New Texas '91* and *New Texas '93,* and is forthcoming within the state in several anthologies and magazines. But like so many poets who have been as prolific as Joe Murphey and Walt McDonald, single poems fail to indicate their range or vision, for in this regard only larger collections can do them justice. Joe's one representative volume is *A Return to the Landscape* from 1979, although a dozen newer poems were included in *Three Texas Poets* from 1986, both from Prickly Pear Press. The edition planned by Sue Littleton should present Joe Murphey as he needs and deserves to be, and perhaps with the availability of a fuller sampling of his poetry it will be possible for readers to understand why he merits a much wider audience than he enjoyed during his lifetime.

Clearly those who came to Austin to read in Joe's honor were well aware of his poetry and demonstrated its very real impact on their minds and on their memories of the man. While it is ever to be lamented that a poet must go uncelebrated in his own day, it remains appropriate to render to a figure like Joseph Colin Murphey the belated recognition he was accorded at Mexic-Arte Gallery. All who were there agreed that Joe, who was always a modest, unassuming person, would have been pleased by the reading and by the reminiscences of his life and writing. Such a eulogy should have been heard by this Texas poet, but then, perhaps it was, for Joe himself believed in visions and in visitations of angels and ghosts, for in "Storms, Presages, and Prophecies" he has written

> The wind brings my father
> his hard, dark face handsome
> > riding now in death
> > with the King of Texcoco, proud
> > and leather-handed on a horse of gold

Texas History Revisited

From Hide and Horn, a sesquicentennial anthology of poems compiled by Peggy Zuleika and Edmund G. Lynch and published by Eakin Press, is a heroic attempt by 150 poets variously to retell, interpret, and exorcise or live with the remote and more recent Texas past.* Given the nature of this project—in which each poet was asked to write on one of the 150 years being celebrated—it should come as no surprise to readers familiar with the state's record, stretching from "independence" through "reconstruction" to the present bloody century, that the poetic effort has often been unequal to the task. Here and there a poet has perhaps been "fortunate" in the date assigned— finding in him- or herself a truly responsive chord struck by an event or figure from that particular year. But many of the finest writers of Texas poems are not represented here simply because they do not work in such a way. That is, the idea of researching a period as a source for inspiration is alien to their approach to the art of poetry. Those who accepted the assignment have had the "pleasure" of discovering the sorrowful along with the instructive in the history of genera- tions who came, and saw, and conquered, were driven here as slaves, exploited if here already, stolen from and looked down upon, who yet endured the godless acts of men and the fickle weather to erect the foundations for a democratic land.

Among the viewpoints some of these poems take is the one found in Chuck Taylor's piece on Ma Ferguson, the first woman gov- ernor of Texas:

> Right or wrong, you and your husband
> gave the impression at least
> that you cared for the little man.
> I remember you saved a young Chicano

---

* If this book review was previously published, I have been unable to recall or dis- cover where or when.

from the electric chair because it was
his first offense.

In bringing back the moments of understanding and baring for all to witness those of prejudice and injustice, many of the poets have obviously been moved by this return to the near or distant past. Their words in turn manage at times to communicate a sense both of the praiseworthy and the shameful that are present in the Texas story. In some cases the burning issues of another day have yet to be resolved, as Thomas Whitbread's poem ruefully and playfully observes:

> The end
> Of Governor O.B. Colquitt's four-year term
> Saw alcohol cussed, discussed, and swallowed down. . . .

In the year before (1911), Roland Sodowsky finds one of the many ironies inherent in man's rulership of earth, as reported in the Pecos *Daily Times* for May 21 and contained in these lines from Sodowsky's longer poem full of wry juxtapositions:

> a river of oil burst from Electra
> *Rinche* burst through border children's nightmares

A number of the poems here are more intimate sketches of persons or happenings. Lynn Novak's portrait, "Eleanora in El Paso, 1884," takes us into the romantic world of a young girl seated at her vanity after having suffered from the fever of a disappointed love. Walt McDonald's "Texas, 1849" contrasts political and historical headlines with the death of B.F. and Sarah Jackson's youngest son, laid to rest "under the cool pine clay, / all gold in California / nothing to them. . . ." Daryl Jones brings vividly to life the tornado in Wichita Falls of 1979:

> in a whirl of glass,
> the mannequins at Sikes Center mall
> recoil, as if in a tableaux of terror,
> their wigless heads askew

Jones' use of the objective correlative here is unusual in this collection, as most of the poems tend toward more subjective, rather superficial techniques characteristic of mere versification. As would be expected, however, William Barney's masterful "Judson Thrash" is both poetic on the surface and philosophically penetrating. Through a series of analogies drawn from nature, the poet dramatizes the gruesome effects of World War Two on boys who "had no quarrel with fish, nor with water, nor with anything."

The range of styles is in keeping with the broad sweep of the anthology's subjects and themes, although in the handling of the historical patriots and their contributions or questionable practices there is more often than not a greater tendency toward the superlative than the subtle. Texas poets have much to learn from the state's history, as well as from classic and contemporary poetry. Let this process not end with the sesquicentennial, for the sake of a place whose past and present its writers should come to know better and, thereby, to appreciate more fully and to cultivate as a literary resource.

III.

BEFORE & AFTER ROUNDUP

A Canadian Poet in Texas

Publication in 1994 of David Wevill's *Child Eating Snow* comes thirty years after the appearance in 1964 of his first collection, *The Birth of a Shark*, published by Macmillan in Toronto.* In addition to his 1964 volume, Wevill had written five other books before his 1994 volume: *A Christ of the Ice-Floes* (Macmillan, 1966); *Firebreak* (Macmillan, 1971); *Where the Arrow Falls* (Macmillan, 1973); *Other Names for the Heart: New and Selected Poems* (Exile Editions, 1985); and *Figure of Eight* (Shearsman Books, 1988). The unsigned blurb for *The Birth of a Shark* states concisely what is true of all Wevill's books: his "poems are attempts to trace his experiences back to their roots, to recreate them from the senses. He writes about many things: his family, the tender and the violent side of love, separation, exile and travel, reunion, and the arrival at an identity not yet final. . . . Above all, he can convey the will of living things to survive without despair in the face of violence and death." A note on the back cover of Wevill's 1985 *New and Selected Poems* declares that the poet is "a compassionate survivor" full of "meditative depth and strength of spirit" and that he "has remained steadfastly Canadian both in nationality and outlook." This last statement is made in light of—and in spite of—the fact that Wevill was born in Japan, educated in England, and since 1970 has been on the faculty of the University of Texas at Austin.

The title poem of *The Birth of a Shark* is probably the single most powerful piece the poet has produced. Here Wevill enters the consciousness of a young shark as it experiences the first attraction to blood. A later use of this shark image is found in a poem from *Firebreak*, entitled "For Nefertiti," where the sea creature represents the swirling and thrashing mind of the poet. Much of Wevill's meditative writing concerns in fact his inner thoughts, as he struggles with past, present, and future, with a search for wholeness or "orderliness which is forever / breaking and scattering" (section VII of "Figure of

---

* *Texas Books in Review* 15, no. 2 (Summer 1995): 15, 17.

Eight"). The poet's most fully developed and realized work to deal with his quest for a meaningful center that will hold (to borrow an image from Yeats) is perhaps *Where the Arrow Falls*, in particular Part 1, which is divided into 46 sections and covers 71 pages. This extended self-conversation is, like the rest of Wevill's poetic production, something of a paradox, in that, as the speaker states in section 17, "we move to discover ourselves / in silence, only," or as the poet comments in section 1 of "Figure of Eight" from *Firebreak*: "eventually the stories get told / yours, mine, in whispers or through / that silence which is terrifying." Elsewhere in Part 1 of *Where the Arrow Falls*, the speaker remarks that

> words always fail the ego
>
> to the quiet, words come
> as a kind of listening.

A limited number of sections of Part 1 of the 1973 volume emerge as independent pieces that can stand on their own. This is the case with three sections that were written for particular reasons other than the speaker's search for self: to pay homage to Stravinsky, who "farmed the air / for thunder" and created "nerves of roller-coaster suns"; to question a Robert Bly performance as "an act," "a slush of simplicities"; and to critique memoirs on D.H. Lawrence as "mindless eyewitness accounts" by "dead people" who "talk about a living man." These sections are clearly the exception in Wevill's work, which is largely devoted to monologues that never arrive, as the blurb writer for the poet's first volume observed, at a final identity. While at times Wevill's poems can lack a satisfying closure, it is ultimately through the poet's own dissatisfaction with any easy ending or resolution that his writing achieves its greatest impact.

In a sense, David Wevill's poetry must be read in its entirety to appreciate fully the small gains he has made as a poet, which by quiet accumulation have resulted in a solid body of work. A piece like "Paracentric" from *New and Selected Poems* illustrates the growth of the poet's thinking as he has become "less clever and more personal":

the old

crazy connections fade
before some need to survive, to feel
the gravity of the long invisible line I have been
walking
        which I perceive now
to have had its
fatal colors, misdirections, smells
I attached to those I loved
and thought my own.

As early as "Prayer" from the 1971 volume, Wevill wished for his new-born son "the nerve / to face his own failure / the darker face behind the face in the mirror // which is his substance, all else being ghost." From the same collection, the poet in "Sickness" refers to himself as one of those "who have no gods but keep returning." This willingness to survive, to move on, to endure and face one's real self is epitomized by a passage in part 11 of *Where the Arrow Falls*: "my duty to dream, not sleep, not / ease like a snake into the hole / of knowing, without eyes." Aside from his early "The Birth of a Shark," perhaps no other Wevill poem so unblinkingly stares into "the hole / of knowing" as does a beautiful but disturbing piece in *Child Eating Snow*. Entitled significantly "Things That Can't Speak," this piece demonstrates Wevill's ability to look deeply into life and discover its predatory nature, which for the poet symbolizes each man's "need to feed and survive / that long moment when a life cries no." This moment is dramatized by Wevill's poignant description of a lizard, its claws

dug hard in dirt.
Then suddenly it jerked back
as if pulled from behind
and I noticed that a long snake
had caught it by one leg
and was dragging it back, back
with infinitely slow irresistible pressure
to its lair under the rock. . . .

On a lighter note, *Child Eating Snow* offers a fairly unusual Wevill poem that captures the talk of a local Austin laborer who has been called in for a bit of "Home Improvement." This delightful piece reproduces the workman's reminiscences of the D-Day landing on Omaha beach. As a survivor, he is obviously, for the poet, an attractive subject. Relating war experiences to the projected job, the speaker mixes up the two as his mind blends past and present:

> Should take about a week
> to get that drive graded proper. That old dozer there
> ain't exactly a Sherman. That your dog I see
> staring out at me from that jasmine bush
> or is it a big old cat? I reckon it could take
> another week before we get to Berlin.
> That is if it don't rain and the ground ain't hard.
> We'll talk about the cost when we get there, friend.

While unrepresentative in style, this piece is but one example of the wide-ranging material Wevill has treated throughout his career. More characteristic is a poem in the 1994 volume entitled "Conversation," which opens with the lines, "I have this habit of talking to you / when you're not there. Your absence gives me time / to explain why it is I love silence / as much as you need voices," and concludes

> I knock three times on wood
> for the shadow who lives in our bones
> grants three wishes. The first is memory.
> The second is that the secret you remember
> is worth your life. The third one has no face.

Readers here and wherever can be thankful that David Wevill's silent thoughts have continued to be committed to paper—for the past 25 years as a resident of Texas. While his work may remain identifiable in terms of an alleged Canadian outlook, it is undeniable that *Where the Arrow Falls* was inspired by the poet's habitation in the Southwest—based specifically on a trip during the Vietnam War from Austin to Arizona, as was his "Polonaise" in *New and Selected Poems* with its marvelous image of "the prickly pear / this effigy with pins stuck in its heart / which stands for patience." Prior to his important 1973 book that broke away from the more measured, even forced, early poems and features a flowing, stream-of-consciousness style in keeping with his "endless thought," there was "The Surgeon's Tale" from the 1966 collection, where La Salle leaves "Texas in a desperate attempt to reach Canada." The surgeon, a party to the explorer's murder, wonders "what power / Drives men to finish what they most regret / in the doing, and afterwards." No one, least of all Wevill, should regret that this "poet in exile" has been driven by some internal need *not* to finish but just to move on. In "Late Sonnet XII" he puts it this way: "Delicately the light // steps over us who are / temporarily fallen. When we get up again / we leave these shadows as reminders of where we have been." Ironically, through his books published over a 30-year period, Wevill, as he puts it in "Spain," has—like that country whose landscape and culture he goes on absorbing—"earned the silence," which proverbially is golden.

Unignored Plunder:
The Texas Poems of Walt McDonald

In 1978, Bin Ramke, a native of Port Neches, Texas, won the Yale Series of Younger Poets Award for his collection of poems, *The Difference Between Night and Day.** In the Foreword to Ramke's book, Richard Hugo refers to a poem entitled "The Feast of the Body of Christ in Texas" and suggests that, to illuminate "both the work and the poet's life," a critic "would probably take more than casual note" of this piece. In it Hugo finds evidence that by age twelve Ramke was developing "personal escape routes," since he realized that "the chances of heavenly redemption" seemed "remote," that there were "cities to go to, Chicago, Los Angeles. . . . Already the poet has begun . . . to create a world of other possibilities he can escape to." More recently, Mary Karr, who was born in Groves, Texas (a few miles from Port Neches), writes in "Coleman," the first poem in her 1993 collection, *The Devil's Tower*:

> When I finally caught a Greyhound north,
> I wanted only to escape
>
> the brutal limits of that town,
> its square chained yards, [oil] pumps
> that bowed so mindlessly to earth,
> the raging pistons of that falling
> dynasty.

Bin Ramke and Mary Karr share a number of similar themes and attitudes which may or may not have grown out of a desire to escape what they saw as the mindlessness and prejudice of Southeast Texas. Both poets were apparently educated in Catholic schools, and

* *Concho River Review* 10, no. 1 (spring 1996): 50-62; reprinted in *The Waltz He Was Born For: An Introduction to the Writing of Walt McDonald*, ed. Janice Whittington and Andrew Hudgins (Lubbock, TX: Texas Tech University Press, 2002), pp. 80-91.

much of their writing is in the so-called confessional mode. In "Nuns in Sunshine," from Ramke's 1981 collection, *White Monkeys*, the poet recalls Sister Francesca in her

> full habitual splendor
> striding through classrooms
> winged and wafting the sharp-
> edged smell of starch,
> black and white as the answers
> in the Baltimore Catechism.

In "Nuns in Sunshine," Ramke also observes that

> It is hard to remember surviving
> childhood in Texas, the heat: it's hell
> they said gleefully, on women and horses.
> But think of the nuns!

In "Hard Knocks" from Karr's 1987 collection, *Abacus*, she remembers Sister Angelica, who

> banged
> her ruler, and we printed the same confession
> a hundred times, her shadow crossing
> our spiral notebooks,
> her eyes like old
> spiders.

Karr's black friend Coleman—with whom she "straddled the [oil] pump as it bucked / a slow-motion rodeo" and watched "dawn breaking / in chemical-pink sky, refinery towers looming / like giants from a fairy tale"—"made the papers as a hunting accident" but was clearly the victim of "vigilantes" who had spotted him playing chess with a white girl. Despite the critical tone in most of these poems on their Texas experience, both Ramke and Karr yet return in memory to their native state, as in Karr's "Diogenes Tries to Forget," where she wants "a slice of pecan pie, some life /

sweeter than this, like my childhood in Texas." In "The Legion" in *The Devils' Tower*, Karr even acknowledges of her father's comrades "[t]hat they should never leave / the Lone Star State had been / the fondest wish of each." Nonetheless, for those like Karr, who was "preoccupied with books," and Ramke, who, as he says in *The Difference Between Night and Day*, "would not eat for days / because I liked / the strange dark feeling," Texas was essentially a place to quit for "other possibilities."

Bin Ramke and Mary Karr left what is known as the Golden Triangle area of Beaumont, Orange, and Port Arthur and achieved considerable success as poets—Karr even publishing a best-selling memoir, *The Liar's Club*. On the other hand, after earning a doctorate at the University of Iowa, serving in Vietnam, and teaching at the Air Force Academy, Walt McDonald of Lubbock returned to his hometown to stake out his claim as the most prolific and profound poet in Texas history. His first book, *Caliban in Blue*, was almost entirely devoted to his war experiences, but one of his poems in that collection, "On Planting My First Tree Since Vietnam," forecast what would come to be a ceaseless outpouring of poetry focusing on McDonald's native landscape, its flora and fauna (or lack thereof), its hardscrabble existence, and its people, like the singer of a country-western song who vocalizes, in the title poem of McDonald's *Where Skies Are Not Cloudy*, "as if these plains are all she needs." Even though West Texans may need more than the plains provide, just as Ramke and Karr required more than Southeast Texas seemed to offer, the impression created by the sixteen collections of poems published by McDonald since *Caliban in Blue* is that his Llano Estado (Staked Plains) area of West Texas has proved more than sufficient to inspire a wide-ranging and penetrating poetry of the highest artistry and insight.

McDonald's fourteenth collection, *Where Skies Are Not Cloudy*, contains what is but one of many key poems among the more than 1,900 he has published in an amazing variety of magazines both here and abroad. Entitled "The Barn on the Brazos," this piece recalls another prophetic poem in *Caliban in Blue*, "The Hammer," an earlier instance of the same retrospective power found in these later lines on a grandfather who

pounded on mustangs,
filing their hooves, fitting the cooled shoes
and sinking the beveled nails, his hammer swung
by a bicep hugely bulging. When I touched that arm

my fingers couldn't reach. I rose on his arm
toward heaven.

The poem concludes with two stanzas that return to the theme of a
missing past, or of not paying attention to what is always around us
until it is too late:

my knees and old boots creak as I bend
to pick up nails. My wife doesn't laugh
at my cocked ear, tuned for the clang of steel,
the puff and sizzle of an iron shoe doused,
something to last until a work horse threw it,

lost forever in weeds, unless some boy
with a cane pole on his shoulder found
and cleaned the shoe with his hand, spat on it
for luck and tossed it over his head
behind him, not looking back.

In the second stanza of this poem, McDonald, after finding that
the grandfather's barn has been rifled, that "[e]ven the anvil's gone,"
remarks that he does not "blame anonymous neighbors for plunder
/ I've ignored." In surveying this poet's career, one would have to
say that in fact McDonald has not at all ignored the valuables of his
Texas life, that indeed he has mined them for all they're worth, and
that following from his first collection where he planted his first tree
after Vietnam ("scraping memory down through crust"), the poet has
come, in such poems as "Setting Out Oaks in Winter" from *Rafting
the Brazos*, to thrive in a place where "no trees stay green all summer .
. . / heat-stressed, blighted, / full of drought," to learn and to teach the
appreciation of where one is and what little one may have, to "swing
[trees] overboard like treasure" and to soak them "over and over with

water / pumped from our own deep wells."

Unlike Ramke, Karr, and many other Texas writers, McDonald has not settled—at least not entirely—for the traditional view of Texas as hell or a fallen dynasty but has risen toward heaven on the arms of its people in whom he has discovered simple faith and strength of character. This West Texas poet also has forged a poetry of high seriousness from seemingly the most unlikely subjects. Taking the standard western movie scene of a lynching for stealing horses or rustling cattle, McDonald, in "Someday"—from his fifteenth book, *Counting Survivors*—sees a particular tree with "grooves in the bark like rope burns" and imagines "a thousand thieves / swinging the same ballet" as he hears "the twist of ropes under tension." Along with the notable diction of "ballet" and "tension," his alliterative sounds recreate the drama of such a Hollywood scene but go far beyond it in letting the reader mentally see and feel the full ironic and cruel effect of this dance of death. (Mary Karr's "Lynched Man," in *Abacus*, also contains some moving moments, as when she writes, "He twirled like a tire swing / in the breeze that stirred the sugar cane.") More moralistic, perhaps, is McDonald's "The Tap of Angry Reins," also from *Counting Survivors*, for here the poet refers to quarrels between friends, which he likens to the bones of dinosaurs, to tongue-lashings that only bleach the tongue "like cow bones," and to little words that turn men into bulls gorging "all night in the mind's silo." The poem concludes with a call to "[b]ury the dead / and let good fences save us, if they can," an allusion perhaps to Robert Frost's "Mending Walls." More especially, McDonald's poems on his Texas experience summon up a passage in Book XI of John Milton's *Paradise Lost*, where the angel Michael reports that, after the postlapsarian world has gone to "universal rack" and God brings on the Flood, which only Noah and those on his ark will survive,

> then shall this Mount
> Of Paradise by might of Waves be moved
> Out of his place, pushed by the horned flood,
> With all his verdure spoil'd, and Trees adrift
> Down the great River to the op'ning Gulf,
> And there take root an Island salt and bare,

The haunt of Seales and Orcs, and Sea-mews clang.
To teach thee that God attributes to place
No sanctity, if none be thither brought
By Men who there frequent, or therein dwell. (*PL* 11.829-38)

Since 1978 when McDonald published *One Thing Leads to Another*, he has concerned himself with his origins, how he came to be in West Texas and what it means to those who live there. In "Settling the Plains" from that second collection, he gives an account of a family arriving in a covered wagon, breaking down perhaps, wondering "What have we done" to come "ignoring all reports," but then, after the mother has hugged her arms, the father shrugs, shakes his head, and says "hell . . . help me hitch up the plow." Another poem entitled "Settling the Plains" appears in McDonald's 1992 *All That Matters*, and here the poet delineates the faith of those who "worked and sang" "[f]or here and for the after-life," believing "whatever they put in the dirt / would live, if it was God's will / and the wind blew," the latter an allusion to windmills for water. The very fact that McDonald has revisited many of the same themes (such as settling the plains) without depleting their possibilities for aesthetic expression and human insight is a testa-ment to the inexhaustible fund of his region as a source for artistic inspiration. After the 1992 volume, the poet once again, in his 1993 *Where Skies Are Not Cloudy*, plumbed the depths of meaning in the lives of those who came to Lubbock's treeless plains. In "Steeples and Deep Wells," from the 1993 collection, the poet observes that on the Llano Estacado there are "no stones to hide behind," going on to comment that

If any came blameless,
here their faults were plain.
No wonder they shoveled dug-outs first,
Somewhere to sleep out of sight.

His interpretation of the realities of a West Texas existence leads him to assert that "[n]o sense of guilt: that must be / what they sought," and for this they risked being

stranded like crippled buffalo
a thousand miles from Kentucky loam
and lakes, pleasures of the flesh
where sin came easy.

As part of his imaginative versions of the lives of his Texas forebears, McDonald offers a sense of their sacrifices, their hopes, their frustrations, yet always he reveals how they faced the truth of their circumstances—"one crop away from being meat for buzzards"—and how they would neither leave nor renounce "a land so flat they dug deep wells / and raised plank steeples fast, / as lightning rods."

Even though McDonald has clearly accepted the place he inherited from his ancestors, he has in no way denied that he is drawn to other landscapes and climates. In "After Years in the Mountains" from his 1981 *Burning the Fence*, the poet remembers how

In Colorado we had four seasons,
real snow, always other rocks to see. . . .

Always we found
another trail or others like us
packing in, climbing for Eden.

In a piece from *Manoa* (fall 1990) entitled "After a Week in the Rockies," which it seems has not been collected in any of McDonald's published volumes (although he frequently changes the titles of his poems after they have first appeared in magazine form), the poet contrasts "a drizzle trickling gallons overnight" and "the odor of green pines" with "[h]ours of flat miles . . . the same dry sage and cactus," and wonders

are we here by choice? Were our squatter fathers
banished from regions where it rained?
Our children have moved away, seeking their fortunes

in cities. We'd do it a different way,
if we made prairies. Rain like children would visit

more often, buzzards like domestic dogs would lead us
to calves before they starve, the summer sun

would squint, not a hot, hypnotic stare
enough to drop a bull. If we stand in one unshaded place
too long, our boot soles burn. Lift up your
faithful head and look around: it's home.

This very fine variation on the typical infernal view of Texas—close
in its depiction of burning boot soles to Milton's description in
Book I of *Paradise Lost* of Satan's "painful steps o're the burnt soyle"
of Hell—reveals McDonald's wish to recreate his fated place more
in the image of a Golden Age or utopia. But in the end he sees it
for what it is: a merciless habitation that can yet reward the faithful.
And certainly this and countless other poems by McDonald have
justified his belief and trust in his Staked Plains. Perhaps in a way
this poet has adopted Satan's point of view, that it is "[b]etter to
reign in Hell, than serve in Heaven" (*PL* 1.562), at least to the extent
that if Heaven only means mountains with plentiful rainfall and lush
vegetation, Hell in some ways may inspire more imaginative, more
thought-provoking poetry.

Still another example of McDonald's contrast between Texas
and the appeal of adjacent states like New Mexico and Colorado
appears in his poem entitled "Colonel Mackenzie Maps the Llano
Estacado," which seems also to be an uncollected work, published
only in *The Texas Review* issue of spring/summer 1989. This piece
presents once again the hell motif in a fine combining of historical
and poetic dimensions. In addition, the poem creates with a sense of
humor the desire for escape, incorporates an allusion to the nomadic
Plains Indians who never settled in any one place, develops through
simile the hell motif, and builds with internal sounds and dramatic
line breaks a formal design that bears the majestic McDonald ring and
rightness of style and meaning:

Chain by chain they dragged these plains, ten rods,
ten rods, sometimes forgetting to count,
not really caring how wide hell is,

prairie flatter than desert good for nothing
but native cunning enough not to settle.

Soldiers rode for nothing but pay,
knowing hell like enlistments can't last
forever, ten rods, ten rods nearer the bars
in Santa Fe, women and mountains,
something to look at that wasn't flat.

With his 1995 collection, *Counting Survivors*, the poet once
more considers how and why he and his people ended up on the prairie. In "Rocking for Days in the Shade," McDonald asks,

are we here by choice?
Great-grandfather left the cavalry
for this? After renegade bullets and arrows

he stayed in Texas where topsoil was sand
and free. He said he needed sun to heal . . .
enough water to bathe in,
far enough from others
to build a shack with a back porch

and do whatever he wanted, rocking for days
in the shade, watching buzzards thirsty
for his blood, daring anything
to make him leave.

In a poem from *One Thing Leads to Another*, entitled "To Derek, Still
in West Texas," McDonald agrees that on the plains "there's little /
to see . . . [i]t bores me, / too." Nonetheless, he goes on to observe
that "[o]nly the people count. Someday you'll / know how much that
means." Indeed, the poet has filled his poems with a sad but unforgettable gallery of figures: Uncle Edward who survived World War
I and having his gangrened, diabetic legs amputated, a wife who left
him, and a son who went to prison; "Billy Bastard" who was given to
cruelty to helpless creatures, slicing up a centipede till "all that lived

were stumps"; and the owner of a corner grocery store who "marked each item up / however much he thought / would sell," cursing those around him for his disabilities suffered on the Bataan death march— all from *Burning the Fence*. Many of these same types of characters also appear in the poems of Charles Behlen, a native of Slaton, a town near Lubbock which McDonald often mentions, as in his sinister but amusing "The Girl in Mackinaw and Panties" in his 1980 *Anything Anything*. In the best Faulknerian tradition, both Behlen and McDonald describe vividly those who have managed to endure.

Not unexpectedly, then, McDonald entitled his 1995 collection *Counting Survivors*. In the title poem of this volume, he exclaims, despite the long list of names on the Vietnam wall touched by the poet's own fingers, "I'm stunned to see so many of us home." In collection after collection, McDonald has recalled the survivors among his neighbors and kinsmen (all or many of the latter apparently invented), as in "Uncle Philip and the Endless Names," from this same volume, where the poet pays tribute to the man who "hated work, walked off a dozen jobs / before thirty," and won the war against the Kaiser

> over and over, his doubled fists like tanks.
> . . . [T]he pension he never got
> stuck in his craw, his quarrel with the war
> all that saved him from steady work.

From this figure, as from so many others in his various books, the poet has learned a form of survival, a type of trust and belief. And through his empathy with the numerous animals that populate his poems, McDonald unceasingly creates such exquisite lines as the ones about Uncle Earl's Saint Bernard, found in the poem entitled "Coyotes and Dogs," also from the 1995 collection:

> Cowboys taught him
> to howl sad tunes with the jukebox. Girls tossed him
> quarters, the only dog on the dance floor,
> waddling past couples locked in each other's arms.
> Lapping draft beer, he lay down by blondes

and cowboys tugged off leather gloves
and let him lick stiff knuckles busted in rodeos.
Fists that shot wild dogs and coyotes
burrowed into folds of fur and made
his massive paw keep time, thumping the floor.

I remember how he howled and tugged outside
after the sheriff left, the moon no jukebox,
a dozen pickups but not one fist to pet him,
sniffing packs of coyotes miles away,
dragging the stiff chain tight.

A related piece is entitled "The Last Saloon in Lubbock," from McDonald's 1999 collection, *Whatever the Wind Delivers: Celebrating West Texas and the Near Southwest* (with photographs selected by Janet M. Neugebauer). Here the poet envisions the life that went on inside the walls of a building which, as he passes by, he sees being torn down by a wrecking crew. Mainly he imagines what cowboys, "bulky in coats," who came to the saloon after breaking their backs herding cattle, needed in such a tavern, concluding that they went there "to get away / from skies more lonely than [themselves]." The poem focuses on "rouged women," "the swing of their crystal earrings," "girls in spot-lights moaning songs / I longed for." In the end, this bit of nostalgia achieves a kind of permanence for those who came before, "ghosts with throaty tunes / and the flash of starry earrings." The poet too has needed what he calls here and elsewhere "the old songs," and he brings them back along with the vibrant imagery of a past that has given way to a "call for order on the plains." McDonald seems determined not to lose entirely that early life that shaped his own, but to capture its poetry that he glimpses in simple objects like a set of "starry earrings." This is true as well of "At the Stone Café," where the poet portrays a typical short-order waitress, "rouged, perfumed," and exposing "a flared / white cleavage" as she "waltzes off, // humming some coun-try and western tune / that makes her human." It is McDonald too who "makes her human," bringing to life such people of his region by revealing them vividly through characteristic touches, like the one in this poem where a cowboy "rises and whispers in her ear. She winks

// and flips his hat, leans back and sips her coffee." As is so often the case with McDonald's work, the poet has rendered a rich complex of imagery and human interrelationships, uncovering them in an everyday Southwestern scene. At the same time, the writing is subtly poetic, the internal sounds (flips-sips, hat-back) adding wonderfully to the overall impact of this typical Southwestern vignette.

In addition to poems with a cast of colorful and moving West Texas characters, McDonald has written innumerable pieces on the many farm and ranch animals of his region, as well as every imaginable creature from snakes and prairie dogs to deer, fish, hawks, buzzards, cicadas, and scorpions. One poem that epitomizes the acute ear of the poet is his "Where Seldom Is Heard," also from his *Whatever the Wind Delivers*, a beautifully-constructed piece in cadenced and mostly rhyming lines, whose title alludes to "Home on the Range," the famous western song by Brewster Higley. (The title of McDonald's *Where Skies Are Not Cloudy* also derives from this classic cowboy song.) Here the sounds of the prairie and its dramatic life-and-death struggle are picked up by the ears of cowboys and the keen hearing of hawks, rattlesnakes, and tarantulas. The concluding line even alludes to Mozart's *Eine kleine Nachtmusik*, through a description of the tarantula and its prey, "a careless squeaky mouse," whose emitting of "a little night music" gives its whereabouts away and provides the arachnid's need for "at most one meal a day." McDonald has also written an impressive array of poignant pieces on flying, the airmen who died or disappeared in war, and those survivors who, like "The Food Pickers of Saigon" from his 1988 *After the Noise of Saigon* and "The Children of Saigon" from his 1989 *Night Landings*, scavenged at an airbase by climbing smoldering heaps of bulldozed food and discarded goods (another kind of unignored plunder): "the dump was like a coal mine fire burning / out of control, or Moses' holy bush / which was not consumed." But then, this Texas poet has never been limited to his experiences in war or to the themes related to his own region. Even when he has written poems on the same subject, even giving them the same title, as in the case of "War in the Persian Gulf," in both *Where Skies Are Not Cloudy* and *Counting Survivors*, McDonald has resorted to little or no repetition, for each piece presents a new and engaging perspective.

Like Bin Ramke and Mary Karr, McDonald also has been a close observer of the world of human art. He and his fellow Texans have all written poems that allude to classical music, and McDonald has devoted especially trenchant lines to painters like Rubens, Rembrandt, and Picasso. In "The Women under Rubens' Thumb," from *Climbing the Divide*, the poet says this painter "made flesh / magnificent, no way to save it, / nothing to do but capture it in oils." In "Rembrandt and the Art of Mercy," from *Counting Survivors*, McDonald probes beneath the Dutch master's work to reveal that, contrary to the claim that the artist painted for money or for a lusting after painting itself, it was flesh that Rembrandt "loved and pitied most," "flesh // that's caught but never saved by canvas." The Rembrandt poem shares the same biblical scene employed by Wallace Stevens in his "Peter Quince at the Clavier," but McDonald's version exhibits the Texas poet's own very distinctive style—direct, sure-handed, and full of sensual details that all contribute to the poem's clear and striking effect:

> Consider
> his florid elders astounded by Susanna bathing,
> his naked Danaë with her god of gold. Behold
> the fragile, eggshell flesh of sad Bathsheba,
> her toes and thighs scrubbed slowly
>
> for a king. If only he could capture those
> in ocher, rub her troubled eyes so they could see.
> Notice the gold, pig-bristle swirls that touched
> his dying Saskia's neck, her honey lobes,
> the sweaty radiance of her breasts.

This same theme had already been developed in McDonald's "Picasso and the Art of Angels" from *Where Skies Are Not Cloudy*. But once again the poet does not in the later piece simply repeat himself, since in the earlier poem, Picasso is shown to have felt the frustration of not being able to paint what he envisioned the day he died: an angel

> marvelously complex,
> the skin tones perfect,

her flesh angelically erotic,
nothing at all like humans,
the skewed, cubistic angles
of the actual.

In the end, McDonald suggests that what the artist saw was "his morning nurse, a local woman / working for pay." This is a dramatically different point from the one made in the poet's poem on Rembrandt and demonstrates once more the far-reaching, imaginative range of McDonald's writing.

Above all, this brief survey of the poetry of Walt McDonald proposes that here is a writer who has in no way been hampered or confined by the place in which he lives and from which he has drawn his unfailing creative impulse. Although he more frequently reproduces the insides of dance halls and the country-western tunes that whine and twang their predictable sorrows, he also has given evidence in poems like those on Rembrandt and Picasso that a Texas poet need not be restricted to popular culture but can interpret as well the work of the world's greatest artists whose themes were often drawn from literature, especially the Bible. Time and again, McDonald has manifested his ability to penetrate to the meaningful core of whatever object or idea he happens to take for his subject. Most commonly he has come to his wise and empathetic insights while contemplating his immediate surroundings, as in a representative piece of West Texas poetry entitled, delightfully, "Rig-Sitting," from *All That Matters*: "On the derrick, I twist this wrench tight / as if the oil pipes of the world depended / on it." Could this be McDonald's wry plains reply to William Carlos Williams' "The Red Wheelbarrow"? Somehow, like that New Jersey poet, the native of Lubbock recognized early on that his own writing should work with the tools he found lying about him, and like his familiar cactus, which "grows a quarter of an inch / each decade," to devote himself to the slow but conscious development of the local, elevating it to the universal. The remarkable result has been that, as McDonald says in "Rig-Sitting" and "Wildcatting" (the latter echoing "The Snow Man" of Wallace Stevens), the "drill bit" of his Texas poetry has managed with persistence to bite "miles through the bedrock" in order to discover that "[n]othing is there until we find it."

Facing Down Fear and Dread

With a second volume of poems published by Alfred A. Knopf, Dallas native Stan Rice attests that not only is he "Singing Yet," as the title of his earlier collection affirmed, but that he is doing so as movingly and artfully as ever.* Appearing in 1995, three years after *Singing Yet: New and Selected Poems*, Rice's *Fear Itself*, like his previous book, features on the dust jacket a striking four-color reproduction of one of the poet's own paintings—in this case a yellow-eyed fish swimming against a red background laced with green aquatic plants. Just as the painting on *Singing Yet* alluded to the death of the innocent—a theme developed throughout that volume—the painting on the jacket of *Fear Itself* would seem an oblique reference to Roosevelt's famous "All we have to fear is fear itself" by way of the idea of isolationism versus being part of "the fishfry," a phrase found in section 12 of a sequence of poems entitled "Deadletters." In its fourteen sections, "Deadletters" sounds many of this new book's primary motifs: fear, anger, and memory without art—all related, as is much of *Singing Yet*, to the poet's daughter, who died of leukemia and who is described in Deadletter 1 as a marble statue "the color / Of a glass of milk / On which the shadow / Of the head of the drinker / Has fallen."

Rice repeats his image of a fallen shadow in Deadletter 6 in order to question the ability of art to deal with loss—a theme carried over from *Singing Yet* that still accounts in large measure for the poignant power of this poet's finest writing.

> It is not an art at all,
> Watching the shadow of the building
> Fall on the roses. Not an art to note
> Color crumble from wall
> Scarlet in inches to orange.
> Crickets chirk in the dark.
> They, also, are not art.

---

* *Texas Books in Review* 16, nos. 3/4 (Fall/Winter 1996): 8-9.

I have tasted the sweetness of the mental sugar
And ruined it by coughing thereon.
Clogged the colander of stars. Yuk.
Soon the whole courtyard will be in shadow
Like the roses, as before,
And I will go home to more
Of these irrational songs.

Preceding "Deadletters" is an epigraph taken from canto 12 of *A*, Louis Zukofsky's book-length poem: "What more happy song than one's lot?" Obviously aware of the irony of Zukofsky's line in the context of his own poem, Rice both mocks his fearfulness and accepts it and the event that created it as the fundamental sources of his sadly joyful music. Likewise, even while Rice denies that his observations are art, they nonetheless take on a complex of meanings by their choice and arrangement in settings that communicate emotional, psychological, intellectual, and aesthetic dimensions. As he acknowledges in "The Interruption," a poem with an image of "bugeyed goldfish" rising to eat,

Water plunges always downward.
Chocolate cake ablaze with candles.
This is more proof than Dread can handle
That what matters is what we make.

He goes on to assert that "The oil paint in the tube isnt the same / As the oil paint of the oilpaint rose." At the same time that this piece addresses the issue of making or being or not making or not being art, it also alludes to Coleridge's "Kubla Khan," a dream-poem cut short by "a person on business from Porlock." Rice's own poem ends, after the phrase "oilpaint rose," with the line "—poem fatally interrupted by a phone call." References in *Fear Itself* to poems, paintings, and sculptures all bear in one way or another on Rice's basic theme of a need for the transformative force of art to counter debilitating fear and dread. Ultimately, such allusions all seem to derive from the fact of the daughter's death; and even observations in poems apparently unrelated to this event can suddenly evoke the poet's never-forgotten loved one, as in a line from "Not in New York": "The yellow cabs move like cancer cells in a bloodstream." Consistently, then, Rice's artistry is inspired by his efforts to confront his fears of being unable to go on with his life and art in the face of tragic loss.

Fear Itself opens with a tourist poem—"Two Weeks in Haiti"—in which the speaker confesses that he was always afraid: "I was the only white man / I'd see for days / And I didnt like it. / I had done nothing wrong / But felt constantly guilty." In the end, he discovers that the change of scenery was not "wasted," for he found that he "was the nigger." Rice's poems often place the poet in a position that causes him to see life from a radically new perspective, and despite his fear of experience, he exhorts himself in Deadletter 2 to

> Eliminate fear that experience is dangerous.
> Lock stork in dark.
> Undergo Woolworths.
> Vomit the skeleton and feel lighter, wiser.

He also tells himself that the "Piano peels lid to its harp. / Each tension, tenderness, offered." For as the poet declares in "April Again," he is "truly / In admiration of being / Human," and goes on to ask, "Who can gather / And adequately praise / The details?" Rice himself shows that he at least can make the attempt, as when he describes how

> The newly
> Leafed crape myrtle
> Softly shivers. Almost
> Instantly the frost-burnt
> Banana leaves unfurl
> New leaves from
> Their stumps.

Unlike T.S. Eliot, Rice welcomes "the cruelest month," saying of the gods, who are in league through "The greenery, the dustmotes / In the sunbeams," that in order for him to be "Blinded by variety" he will "bend to their needles. / This won't hurt a bit."

Just as the poet identified with the fear and cruelty suffered by the Haitians in 1978, he also can empathize and even draw strength from the homeless in New York. "The Religious Life" may allude to Milton's sonnet with its closing line, "Those also serve who only stand and wait," for Rice's poem observes that "The beggar, also, works. / Though some sit slumped like Rodins." The persistent theme of doing versus not doing is underscored especially in a poem entitled "Censorship," where Rice reminds his friends to beware of "Self-censorship / For the book unwritten / Is the book burned." The poet remarks that censors may have seen Satan and may "mean well," but "They beat the gate / To the same old tune ... And they are the goons." In a poem entitled "A Boy's Satan," Rice recounts a tale of his fear of a rooster that the Devil offered him fifty cents to bring out of a "narrow space between / Our garage and his fence, with no way out." In the end, the boy sees the rooster "as uncatchable / As a ball of flaming razorblades," but the Devil tells him "It'll come out or starve, / And I knew that even / Though he had toyed with my life / The Devil was right." Throughout *Fear Itself* the poet learns and in turn teaches such memorable lessons, but above all he reveals how, in spite of fear, self-pity, anger, and guilt, he will, as he states in Deadletter 4, "walk back to the fire," acknowledging that even the Devil may be right when it comes to the choices for those who are "truly / In admiration of being / Human."

While *Fear Itself* is largely unified around the volume's title theme, there are many poems that seem to stand apart from this central motif. "Isaiah Speaks: Lust" is a remarkable analogy developed between lust and yard care, and "The Jewish Virgin" is an intriguing depiction of a young woman who "By doing as little as one possibly could do / ... has completely dominated the living room." But more typical of the way nearly every poem in Rice's book reflects on its focal motif of fear are the humorous "Former Life," with its western "horror of horses"; "Sheer Fears," with its off-rhymes and its tight, fully-packed lines, such as "Dread red thread, erect. / Nakedness urges aside / Edible delicate shreds; / Unless dress rise"; "The Sea and I," with its view that the poet's dread of the sea does not keep him inland; and, most impressively, "H.D.," a marvelous piece on a poet to whom Rice admits being irresistibly drawn as a "goatman" to an "ice nymph," and in which he announces that

There is no Hell.
There is only separation
And selfish fear, there's only
Difference, that delicious pull
Of the opposite
For its poisonous prey.

Finally, there is "The Proud One," an autobiographical sketch that closes Rice's attractive and highly original volume. In this poem, based on the Greek myth of Pentheus, which is employed as an analogue for the poet's own life in Los Angeles and Berkeley during the turmoil of the 1960s, Rice openly blames the loss of his daughter on his own arrogance. Even though this allusive—yet very direct—self-indictment is unusual in Rice's new collection, it has been fully prepared for, and the effect is, while devastating, both cathartic and totally in keeping with the poet's unblinking vision and its expression through an unflinching artistry.

Foreword to Joseph Colin Murphey's
Waiting For Nightfall

Born in Lufkin, Texas, on December 13, 1915, Joseph Colin Murphey died on Thanksgiving Day 1993, leaving most of his poems unpublished and largely unknown.* Those readers and fellow writers around the state and beyond its borders who were aware of some of Joe's poetry mourned his loss, even as they gave thanks for his life, his writings, and his editorship of his little magazine, *Stone Drum*, in whose pages many older and younger poets had received their encouraging start. Two selections of Joe Murphey's poetry were issued previously by Prickly Pear Press: *A Return to the Landscape* of 1979; and a dozen poems included in *Three Texas Poets* of 1986. His poems also formed part of Prickly Pear's two anthologies: *The New Breed* (1973) and *Washing the Cow's Skull* (1981), as well as its *Six Texas Poets Read From Their Work*, a tape recording from 1988. The present collection of Joe's poetry covers for the most part the period from 1985 to 1991, with a few poems that were possibly written after August 1991 and are reprinted from undated typescripts or from posthumous appearance in magazines. Aside from the few exceptions, this selection was made from entries in Joe's handwritten journals, which he kept for over 40 years, as revealed by a poem that he wrote on March 6, 1988, entitled "The Paradox of Being Neither One: What the Journal Made the Other Has Undone." Joe Murphey's journals are now housed in the Special Collections Library at Texas Christian University in Fort Worth, where much more of his unpublished work survives and deserves to be unearthed.

One remarkable fact about Joe Murphey's poetry, which is apparent from his journal entries, is that this poet thought naturally in verse form. The lines flow directly from his pen and shape themselves more often than not into stanzas of the same length, whether three-, four-, or five-line units—and this with rarely any change of word, line,

---

* Joseph Colin Murphey, *Waiting For Nightfall* (Cedar Park, TX: Prickly Pear Press, 1996), pp. 9-11.

or stanza. The thought moves through stanza after stanza almost un-interruptedly to an elucidating, musical closure. The conversational sound and sense seem effortless, and yet one is astonished to discover the masterful stanzas that evolve with their subtle echoes and internal or occasional end rhymes. We can follow easily the poet's stream of thought as it meanders through a meditative field to carry us in the end to larger and deeper discernment. Most amazing, perhaps, is Joe's use of the villanelle form, with its repeated lines that accumulate greater meaning as he works his way through the five three-line stanzas to the closing quatrain with its affirmation of faith. In this regard, it should be noted that in his last years Joe was dying of cancer and that many of these poems were written as he was "waiting for nightfall." Yet this poet did not succumb to what he calls in "The Never Be" a "wait and see" attitude that "keeps us from any joy / that possibility may hold / in store." Joe continued to write and to assert the power of love and poetry and to affirm, as in his poem entitled "The Armada," an image of his own mystery.

One of the most powerful expressions of Joe Murphey's visionary faith is found in "There Comes With Pain," which may remind readers of Emily Dickinson's "After Great Pain, A Formal Feeling Comes." Joe's poem, however, offers quite a different viewpoint. Rather than resulting in a giving in, the experience of pain and approaching death lends to him, as the poet says, a "strength // that releases in the mind / a wisdom and a knowledge / of vast unfathomable things." This is seen in his poems on mountains, flowers, birds, and, repeatedly, "the marvelous mechanism of the kiss." It is also evident in the way his poems are often a continuation or linking from one piece to the next, as in the case of "Yet in This Present," whose last line and a half—"our little / cycle of time's decay"—serve as the beginning lines of "For What Has the Good Man to Fear." The poet's writing gains added force and insight from his manner of carrying forward day by day, just as each individual poem pushes onward in an effort to voice the affirmative thought in spite of a sense of loneliness and impending doom.

The arrangement of the poems in the present collection follows in general the chronological order in which the work appears in Joe's various dated journals. To read the entries in sequence and to see the clippings or other items that Joe pasted or laid in from time to time—reproductions of paintings, on which some of the poems are based, photographs or leaves or flowers—is to experience more immediately the sources of the poet's thematic concerns. Choice of the poems included here was subjective, even though an overriding motif was suggested by the collection's title poem, which was not of Joe's choosing, since his own final, more retrospective compilations differ almost entirely from this selection that concentrates on the poet's last half-dozen years. At times the poems printed here bear distinct titles and some slight revisions of lines or stanzas in the journals and reflect changes located in later typescripts. However, such modifications are not adhered to consistently, as in the case of "Nostalgia For a Finished Novel," whose subsequent title, "For Stephen Shannon and Meg Lambert," was not adopted but certain of whose revisions were incorporated into the journal version.

It is fortunate that Joe Murphey's journals are preserved at Texas Christian University, for they testify to the fact that here was a man whose natural form of utterance was the poem, each arising from his day-to-day existence, his constant coming to grips with the reality around him, and the perspectives he achieved from witnessing the death of his cat or his ruminations on his own inevitable demise. What makes Joe's poetry so moving and enduring is not simply that he faced his end with courage and kept writing even in pain, but that he created lines and stanzas that speak clearly, beautifully, and poignantly of what it means to be alive to the world, to cherish being inside history rather than escaping into self-pity or whatever narcotic dulls us to love, imagination, and a desire to understand the mysteries of the universe and one's own relationship to past and present.

As a poet of the local, Joe Murphey discovered in his immediate environment a means to wisdom and spiritual growth. This was not necessarily in any religious sense; rather, his citing and explicating of biblical passages were more in human terms. It is clear that as he approached his death, Joe, like many other writers, came to contemplate the nature of God and to look more closely into the idea of an afterlife, either as a necessary punishment or as a state of grace for those like his mother, from whom he had inherited his love for the arts. Relatedly, a theme that runs throughout Joe's work is his relationship with his father, who appears to him in visions and with whom he identifies despite his absence when the poet needed him most. Through years of feeling neglected by some of his loved ones, of self-doubt as a writer, and of the disregard of all but a limited readership, Joe Murphey continued to keep track of his inner life, never forsaking the meditative mode that produced so many of his memorable poems. There is much to learn from his lyrical thinking, his probing of past and present, and his staring wide-eyed into the maw of death. But above all, music and imagery abound in Joe's leisurely flowing lines that arrive again and again at "ends and meaning" we "will always be a part of."

Remembering the Alamo in Rime Royal

Michael Lind, in creating his epic poem, *The Alamo*, has aspired to the highest literary genre, and his performance is perhaps all that a devotee of this form could hope to see accomplished.* In short, this work contains writing and thinking of the first order, and for my taste no other Texas author has produced anything to equal its literary and historical scope. Lind's mastery of the epic tradition is evident throughout his 6,006 lines, which, as he points out in his thirty-two page essay appended to the poem, is approximately the length preferred by Aristotle. Simply to follow the epic formula and parallel the famous episodes created by Homer and adopted by writers from Virgil to James Joyce for their own purposes would not ensure a successful poem; a truly artistic synthesis must take place. While Lind obviously did his homework in reading his predecessors from Homer to Tasso and even Joel Barlow's *The Columbiad*, this Texan also has constructed a grandly imaginative, unified, and universal poem that is uniquely founded upon the history, language, and landscape of his native state.

Lind does not explain in his essay why he chose the seven-line rime royal stanza pattern for his traditional twelve books of *The Alamo*, yet it appears but one indication of how well the poet conceived his epic poem. (Another more crucial and unerring decision that resulted in a work of the first order was Lind's choice of William Barrett Travis as the visionary, hubristic hero of the poem.) Lind's handling of the rhyme scheme is both ingenious and satisfying. Obviously not intimidated by the fact that rime royal was employed by Chaucer and Shakespeare (as well as Milton in his youth), Lind has filled the form with naturally flowing sentences that end perfectly with a final rhyme in one stanza or run on to the next; descriptive passages that move logically and powerfully to their conclusions; extended similes that complete their comparisons pointedly; and speeches by characters who hold forth with verisimilitude whether they utter their thoughts in literary figures or the colloquial phraseology of a western yarn.

---

* *Texas Books in Review* 17, no. 2 (Summer 1997): 2-3.

In finding the necessary rhymes for each stanza, Lind repeatedly surprises the reader with his splendid diction, which is appropriate to every occasion. In Book 4, such word choices as "avulsion," "bight," "flyting," and "putsch" are accurate and effective in each stanzaic context. The poet clearly enjoyed writing in rime royal, for it is a sheer delight to hear and watch him at work, as in Book 2 where he rhymes police/peace, allegiance/legions, and lunatic/brick, or in Book 11 where he develops during the battle scenes his "epic simile" of

> troops
> of Matamoros. Dozens there collapsed;
> across their speckled comrades, remnant groups
> now scrambled, chickens scooting from the coops
> a shattered truck has scattered on a road.

Some readers may object to the leaps in historical time, but this is a traditional technique and provides perspective even as it allows the poet to create his striking, fitting analogies. The fixed form has paradoxically freed the poet to indulge in an imaginative transformation of his research materials into a dramatic, incisive work of art.

Lind has taken his epic theme directly from Virgil's *The Aeneid*, Book I: "It was so hard to found the race of Rome" (in Allen Mandelbaum's translation), which in the Texan's version comes in his Book 7, where he announces: "No easy thing it is to found a state." Other central Virgilian parallels include: a prophecy in Book 6 (based on the shield made by Vulcan in Book 8 of *The Aeneid*) of scenes to come in later American history engraved on Davy Crockett's Colt six-shooter (the pistol an anachronism according to some critics but perhaps, since Colt's early models of a five-shooter were being developed in 1835 and 1836, merely an example of what Lind refers to as "probable impossibility" sanctioned by Aristotle); the simile in Book 7 of Santa Anna like a wolf "prowling round a bleating pen," which derives from an episode with Turnus in Book 9 of *The Aeneid*; the escapade of Charles Despallier and Robert Brown in Book 7, which recalls the nighttime foray of Nisus and Euryalus in Virgil's Book 11; the destiny of Texas in Book 9 "to touch the planets . . . teach the tongue you speak / to sing," which alludes to Virgil's famous passage in Book 6: "Roman, these will be your arts: / to teach the ways of peace to those you conquer"; and, of course, the *de rigueur* epic catalog, which is especially fine in Lind's description of the Mexican troops crossing the Rio Grande. The poet's comparison of pennons to butterflies is representative of some of his most remarkable writing. Two stanzas in particular foreshadow the tragic death and destruction of the impending battle:

Hillsides will flame
sometimes, when mobs of orange pennons jam
together, flimsy cymbals silently
percussing in a summer symphony,

a smokeless, heatless lava. Birds will scream
above the tender flames, drop from the skies,
and learn too late the meaning of the gleam:
whatever tastes the monarch butterfly's
emblazoned wings inevitably dies.

Lind has contributed to Texas letters a tour-de-force epic that will stand as more than a "modest monument" to those who died at the Alamo, on both sides. One reviewer characterized Lind's writing by quoting Sam Houston: "That's not rhetoric, it's rant." It appeared the reviewer knew Houston better than did the poet, but it was in fact Lind who inserted the phrase in Sam Houston's mouth. Instead of crediting the poet, the reviewer made clever, no-quarter use of the quote to belittle a writer who knows well the difference between rhetoric and rant. While Lind can imitate Homer's and Virgil's brutal descriptions of the carnage of war, he does not—as he asserts in his essay that the epic should not—"idealize nor vilify war" but treats it as "a perennial part of the existence of human communities, in which what is best and worst in human nature is shown in sharp relief." Lind's poem portrays the poignant scene of wives, friends, and sweethearts watching their "menfolk" leave to defend the Alamo; and he evokes the sights of death on both sides that are effective and artistically inventive, as when a rebel is run down like "a drunk man on a carousel that glows / and grinds within a midway, carven manes / ascending to the hammering refrains." But there is humor as well, as in Book 6 with Crockett's tale of the two-headed girlfriend, and subtle links between the Homeric imagery of flying geese and the carved silver goose in Virgil's Book 8 commemorating the warning that saved Rome from attacking Gauls, both related to the rebellion stirred up by Travis at Anahuac. The range of Lind's writing is impressive from start to finish, and in setting a Texas subject in his chosen form Lind has notched for the state a rightful place in the epic line. Some forty years ago in his sonnet "Texas," Jorge Luis Borges compared the defense of the Alamo to Thermopylae, but it was left for Michael Lind to dramatize this epic metaphorical connection.

In section III of Lind's encyclopedic essay, "On Epic," the poet-essayist answers historical criticism of Homer for influencing those who took his heroic treatment of militarism as a guide to their own barbarities. In citing examples of "this viewpoint . . . in the early United States," Lind might have gone further back than John Quincy Adams to Cotton Mather's "Manductio ad Ministerium" of 1726, which objects to Homer not only for "first exhibiting [the Greek] gods as no better than rogues" but for "the ill impressions of this universal corrupter" that were felt by "that overgrown robber, of execrable memory, whom we celebrate under the name of Alexander the Great, who by his continual admiring and studying of his *Iliad* and by following that false model of heroic virtue set before him in his Achilles, became one of the worst of men. . . ." But then Mather's indictment of Homer is merely additional evidence in support of the essayist's valid argument that the epic has been wrongly condemned because it extols "arms and the man" and that in fact this classic genre reveals that "martial virtue in the service of legitimate ends by liberals and republicans must be accompanied by an unflinching acknowledgment of the costs of war."

I must admit, however, to disappointment that Lind has excluded from his discussion of the epic tradition Louis Zukofsky's *A* and William Carlos Williams' *Paterson*, which fulfill in part the type of poem Lind excoriates Emerson and T.S. Eliot for being too elitist to write, "one whose heroes were Jewish immigrants or Irish longshoremen." But this is a minor point, for after all, Michael Lind has written a learned, well-considered statement on the nature of the epic that will send many of us back to an overlooked writer like Tasso. Not only this, but Lind has created a "modest monument" that not even "the ten rivers [that] marble Texas"—much less carping critics—can erode or wash away.

Roundup Time in Texas

Twenty-five years ago it was not clear to me—or to those whose work I was gathering for Prickly Pear's first anthology, *The New Breed*—that there were so many accomplished or promising Texas poets in the Lone Star State.* After the appearance of that anthology in 1973, many of the poets included in the publication reported that they had thought that they were laboring alone in the poetry vineyards of Texas, that *The New Breed* had made them aware of one another, and that it had given them a sense of community, which supported and encouraged them to go on with their work. Nearly half the twenty-two poets in that anthology would later gain regional and/or national recognition. From an occasional writer of poems, Walt McDonald would develop into a prolific award-winning poet with now seventeen books to his credit, while Leon Stokesbury would be published in numerous national anthologies and now in 1998 has garnered the Poets' Prize, awarded by the Nicholas Roerich Museum in New York City. James Hoggard has since 1973 distinguished himself as poet, translator, essayist, and president of the Texas Institute of Letters. Stan Rice has had two collections of poetry published by Alfred A. Knopf, and Joseph Colin Murphey carried on until his death in 1993 as the highly regarded editor of *Stone Drum* and a much admired poet of poems set in his native Piney Woods, the high plains of the Panhandle, and the Hill Country of Central Texas.

In 1976, another anthology, *Travois*, gathered an even greater number of Texas poets, with editors Paul Foreman and Joanie Whitebird describing the burgeoning poetry scene in the state as "a summer storm out of the gulf." Five years later, Prickly Pear would issue its bilingual anthology, *Washing the Cow's Skull/Lavando la calavera de vaca*, which brought together some of the poets of the earlier generation excluded from *The New Breed*—William Barney, William Burford, Vassar Miller, R.G. Vliet, and Thomas Whitbread—and added

---

* Introduction to *Roundup: An Anthology of Texas Poets From 1973 Until 1998* (Cedar Park, TX: Prickly Pear Press, 1999), pp. 10-14.

them to a more recent group of outstanding younger poets: Naomi Shihab Nye, Rosemary Catacalos, Carmen Tafolla, Harryette Mullen, Ray González (who since 1981 has edited seventeen anthologies and has had five volumes of his own poetry issued by regional and national presses), and David Yates, editor of *Cedar Rock* magazine, from one of whose poems the bilingual anthology took its title.

The present 25th-anniversary anthology represents an attempt to assemble all the poets previously published by Prickly Pear, either in the 1973 and 1981 anthologies, in poetry volumes by single authors, or on one of the two tape recordings released by the press in 1988 and 1993. Most of the poets responded to the invitation to submit their more recent work, but some did not and others could not be located, while a few were not invited because it was felt that during the past quarter of a century they had no longer been associated with Texas either in terms of habitation or of their poetic production. (I readily admit that my criteria were not applied consistently.) In place of those who were left out there is a group of poets who have either lived in Texas for many years or who, like Betty Adcock, have continued from afar to write of their native state. The work of this last group of poets, although not previously published by Prickly Pear, had been promoted through reviews that I had written for various publications. Certainly there are many poets in the state whose work I have also reviewed and could have included in this anniversary anthology, just as there are many whose work I have never commented on in print who are worthy of appearing here. However, time constraints necessitated that limits be placed on the number of poets that I would try to contact and work with in choosing a representative poem and in eliciting from each poet a prose commentary to accompany his or her selection. Unfortunately, not every poet produced a commentary—in the case of Carolyn Maisel, for example, I was simply unable to discover her whereabouts. My hope had been to publish only poetry written during the final decade of the millennium, but that was impossible from the first, since Harold Beeson, David Yates, Tomás Rivera, and R.G. Vliet had not survived beyond the 1980s. For this reason, I had to settle for other means of conveying a poet's critical thinking, either by offering two poems, one of which may suggest something of the poet's thoughts on the art of poetry, or, in the case of Harold Beeson, a sample of his late prose. Overall, however, it was gratifying to see that most of the poets had persisted into the 1990s with unabated power, and consequently it was immensely exhilarating to be in touch once again with such inspiriting, still flourishing writers.

The idea behind *The New Breed* had essentially been to make evident to readers—primarily those within the state—that Texas poets were doing significant work that could be favorably compared with poetry being produced elsewhere in the nation. If that notion was ever in doubt, surely today it is indisputable. As for *Washing the Cow's Skull*, the intent there was to introduce Texas poetry to a Latin American readership through translation into Spanish of the work of some two dozen poets. Even though the U.S. State Department purchased and distributed 400 copies of that bilingual anthology to binational centers throughout Latin America, it is not clear whether the publication made any wide-spread or even a limited impact on Spanish-speaking readers. The press did receive a few letters from persons who came upon the book and expressed their delight in finding a world of poetry whose existence they had never suspected nor expected. With the present anniversary anthology, the aim has been to revisit the poets and to catch up on the kinds of work they are doing or have done since 1990. At the same time, it was hoped through the prose commentaries to learn how the poets saw their work in a retrospective light, whether their approaches or attitudes had changed or not, and what tendencies they observed as constants in looking back on their writing careers.

It became evident to me as the material came in that, even though many of the poets had gone on writing about the same subjects, their insights had deepened. For instance, Stan Rice's "The Proud One" necessarily returns to the unforgettable death of his teenage daughter, to whom his "Elegy" in *The New Breed* was dedicated. Rice's more recent poem focuses on the continuing effect of that loss, on his life and thought, but also reflects on his thinking prior to that tragic event and compares his own hubris to that of Pentheus in Euripides' *The Bacchae*. Carmen Tafolla's "This River Here" is a combination of two earlier pieces—one of those her "Memories," included in *Washing the Cow's Skull*—from which she has fashioned a new blended version that offers a richer, more profound music. And Ray González's "At the Rio Grande Near the End of the Century" harks back, as his first book phrased it, to "the restless roots," to the cottonwoods, the river, and the desert that he now says he is "so tired of writing about"; and yet it is out of an obsession with the El Paso landscape that the poet has "molded," as if from his often imaged clay, an ever more penetrating, paradoxical wisdom. Such poetic maturation will be noted in many of the younger poets collected here, while those from earlier generations—like Betty Adcock, William Barney, and Robert Burlingame—will be found as observant and sage as ever.

What for me has been especially satisfying about this reunion—aside from its having given me a chance to stay abreast of the poets' more recent work—has been the opportunity it has afforded for the reading of discerning prose commentaries from the poets themselves. Many have never before written about their own poetry, and while this in itself may make their comments here of special interest, the value of such prose statements lies for me in their revealing not so much any particular "meaning" in a specific poem but rather in their providing access to the very process of creation itself, the poets' attachments to or reactions against their subjects, their views on techniques or intentions, their sense of failure or their abiding pleasure in having accomplished what they set out to achieve. The pairing of poem and prose commentary is certainly nothing new, but as Robert Bonazzi expressed it in one of his letters in response to the idea behind this anthology, there is the hope that, by Texas poets airing their views, this will lead "to some serious discourse on poetry and poetics."

The title of this third Prickly Pear anthology follows from the titles chosen for the two preceding anthologies. *Roundup* may well be objected to as an unfortunate choice, as was the case with *The New Breed*. Jim Jacobs, Prickly Pear's designer and my friend of thirty-four years, saved that first title from a too literal or limited association with cowboys and cattle by adding a third eye to the boy on the anthology's cover photograph. David Yates's "Washing the Cow's Skull" was safely surrealistic enough to appeal to readers despite my continued attraction to a bovine or equine motif for books of Texas poetry. But at this writing, without knowing what Jim's visual wit may do to rescue readers from my penchant for the cow-based appellation (my first two chapbooks having been entitled *Brands* and *Taking Stock*), I feel called upon to say a few words in self-defense.

After having in my own mind settled on the title for this anniversary anthology, I was pleased when Del Marie Rogers, unprompted by anything that I had said about a title for the book, asked unwittingly if I was "rounding up the poets." In compiling this anthology my title became even more meaningful to me as I struggled to "corral" the many "mavericks" who were scattered across the state and from coast to coast, California to New Mexico, Oklahoma, Minnesota, Massachusetts, Virginia, North Carolina, Georgia, and even Saudi Arabia. As Frost would say (and a number of the poets here have quoted that New England bard), the metaphor falls apart, and especially since I was in no way planning to "break" this group or "drive" it to an abattoir. The title for me reflects rather the idea of cowhands coming together at the end of winter to swap tales, sing and celebrate having made it through to another spring. The atmosphere of camaraderie, the sense of sharing in a work none would trade for any other—this contrasts dramatically with the type of ruthless roundup described so movingly in Tino Villanueva's poem on the Holocaust. Although I can admit to the clichéd nature of the title on grounds of its stereotypical connection with a Texas industry, I still find that the cattle man and woman's tradition of roundup is appropriate to a gathering of poets who know one another's work, joy in its imaginative open ranges, and are ready to recount the long nights of riding herd on straying words, their pegasean stumbles in unforeseen holes, scars from barbed wire or thorn, and their comet, moon, and starlight visions set to the measure of a 1990s song.

The Audacity to Edit Texas Poetry

In preparing the anthology of Texas poets entitled *Roundup*, to mark the 25th anniversary of Prickly Pear Press, I experienced again the pains and pleasures of reading, selecting, rejecting, editing, and proofing the work of poets that I had long admired.* As with past anthologies and individual volumes from Prickly Pear, I found once more that I made some of the poets happy and others I irritated by presuming to suggest that their poems could be improved by reconsidering a word here or a line there. How it was that I ever took it upon myself to judge the work of others and to conceive of myself as an editor is surely too long and tedious a tale. But even when I have recognized that such must be the case with my reminiscent stories, I have never been deterred from going right ahead and telling them just the same.

R.G. Vliet, whose classic Texas novel, *Solitudes*, was reprinted by TCU Press, wrote to me after I included some of his poetry in Prickly Pear's 1981 bilingual anthology, *Washing the Cow's Skull*, to say that I should give up writing poetry and should dedicate myself to editing the poems of other writers. I was grateful that Russ approved of my work as an editor, but for me writing my own poetry and editing that of others had always gone hand in hand. Some may think that I became an editor and continued as one because it enabled me to publish my own poetry in the anthologies that I compiled, as well as my introductions written for both the Prickly Pear anthologies and the press's individual volumes by other poets. Some may believe that my being an editor was simply a power trip, a way of pushing my little weight around and lording it over better writers than myself. All of this must contain a grain or even a gross of truth. Certainly I took great pride in being associated with the many superb poets that I have published through Prickly Pear. At the same time, I was drawn to the

---

* A talk given at Texas Christian University on October 9, 1998, on the occasion of the 25th anniversary of the founding of Prickly Pear Press and an exhibit of its poetry publications.

role of editor in order to present what I viewed to be significant Texas poetry and to place it in the most becoming light possible. Some poets, I have found, do not necessarily recognize their finest work, and as a result they do not, so to speak, put their best foot forward. As an editor I wanted to help them appear in public looking their spiffiest.

No matter what one does, there will always be detractors, among both writers and readers, but especially among writers who resent being rejected by or uninvited to contribute to a publication. When I first began to edit in 1964, and as editor of *Riata*, the student literary magazine at the University of Texas at Austin, announced my plans for an East-West, or Orient-Texas issue, I was satirized in a letter to the student newspaper. I was so shocked and disappointed that I considered resigning on the spot, but fortunately for me I went right on and through editing came in contact with some of the wisest and most stimulating minds in the Lone Star State. After my first issue of *Riata* appeared, another letter to the newspaper attacked me for producing a piece of work more suitable as a Christmas tree ornament than a literary magazine. The writer of this letter would later announce in the newspaper that he and others were organizing their own publication, to be called *Pegasos*, because under my editorship "the official campus literary magazine" did not "supply the primary creative literature for University needs." Even after I had garnered a good deal of praise for my work as editor and included, in the two issues that I edited, some of my own poetry as well as one of the few short stories that have ever written, I was told by a member of *Riata*'s faculty committee, which oversaw the magazine, that I should give up on writing poetry and should concentrate on prose fiction. By that time, however, I had become inured to criticism and was determined to continue writing poetry and editing that of others, regardless of what was thought or expected. More recently I have been told by writer friends that I am not a good poet and how dare me to edit their own poetry. It seems that detractions will never end.

Looking back on my career as an editor, I believe that the idea of editing a magazine and later establishing a small-press imprint was owing in large part to another editor-writer who was born, as I was, in Fort Worth. Dave Hickey attended TCU in the 1950s, as I did very briefly in 1963, and was published in *descant*, the University's literary magazine, edited for many years by Betsy Colquitt. Although I did not know *descant* in those early years, it too was indirectly influential on my decision to found Prickly Pear Press, for in 1969 I bought a copy of *31 New American Poets*, an anthology that included a poem entitled "Jigsaw" that had originally appeared in *descant*. The poem was by a Maine poet, John Stevens Wade, and I liked that piece very much and was impressed that it had first been published in a Texas magazine. At the time I was living in Illinois, and in that same year, Betsy Colquitt edited *A Part of Space: Ten Texas Writers*, which included the poetry of William Burford and William Barney. While a student at the University in Austin during the early and mid 1960s, I had known and held in high regard Burford's widely published poems, but Barney's poetry was new to me and quite appealing in his handling of form and Texas flora and fauna. As I would acknowledge in 1977 when I wrote an introduction to Barney's *The Killdeer Crying*, Betsy Colquitt's editorial work had encouraged me to bring out this first collection in some 25 years of Barney's poetry. To be able to do so, I was forced to incorporate Prickly Pear, which I had begun in 1973. Only by obtaining tax-exempt status as a non-profit corporation could the press qualify for funding from the Texas Commission on the Arts (TCA) and thereby fulfill Mr. Barney's wish for a hardback edition of his selected poems, *The Killdeer Crying*. Through the press's non-profit status it was subsequently awarded eight grants from the TCA for a total of ten books and one cassette tape recording of Texas poets reading from their work.

I want to say at this point that I remain indebted to Mr. Jay Vogelson, of Dallas, who offered his legal services free of charge to help Prickly Pear obtain the necessary tax-exempt status. Later Mr. Vogelson continued to promote Texas literature as Vice Chairman of the TCA. Thus it is that a number of people—other than the Texas poets published by Prickly Pear—contributed to the success of this Texas imprint. I will mention one other person, Mr. Decherd Turner, an internationally respected bookman and during the 1980s the director of the Harry Ransom Humanities Research Center in Austin, who generously supported Prickly Pear for almost two decades. Without the backing of Mr. Vogelson, Mr. Turner, and the TCA it would have been virtually impossible for Prickly Pear to have produced the number or quality of publications that it did during its 25-year existence.

But to return to Dave Hickey, whom I first met in the late 1950s when I went with him and a mutual Cowtown friend to what was called The Cellar, a coffeehouse in downtown Fort Worth during those heady days of the Beatnik era. Later I ran into Dave again in Austin when he was editing *Riata*. In 1963 I was thrilled to be published by Dave in *Riata*, and the following year I would be chosen to succeed him as the magazine's student editor. Although I would try to do my own thing in editing *Riata*, I was definitely following in Dave's footsteps, as I bore in mind the unsigned manifesto that he most likely wrote for the January 1963 issue of the magazine. Among the nine types of material the editors of *Riata* would not accept were the following: number 2—"Poems written at 3 a.m. and not revised. (First drafts should be submitted to the Rare Books Library, not *Riata*)"; number 5—"Poems by girls who state that the soul of a Maenad lurks beneath their bubble hair style, or that their last boyfriend was a louse. The editors will probably call up the authoress but are not about to print her poetry"; number 8—"Idolatrous articles about Eliot or Hemingway"; and number 9—" 'New Criticism,' especially in the form of A- course essays with professors' comments still written on them." The manifesto ends with this brief paragraph: "Outside these limits, there is no subject or literary form *Riata* will not consider sympathetically. Though all pieces written in ordinary English prose will be stringently blue-penciled according to Strunk and White by the editors and their advisors; there is no censorship of subject matter or language (except, of course, *that* word)." In preparing the *Roundup* anniversary anthology, I myself was faced with "*that* word" in a poem by one of the Texas poets. When I asked that he replace it with a euphemism, this ruffled poet refused my editorial suggestion, so I selected another, perhaps a lesser, poem in its place. As one of my critics told me years ago, I can be unbelievably squeamish.

Humor, as I have been reminded more than once by different friends and family members, is not my forte, so I could never have written a manifesto of the Dave Hickey sort. Nevertheless, in other respects I did go to school to Dave and his fellow editors. For one thing, my idea for the issues of *Riata* that I edited in 1964 and 1965 was to seek out work not limited to any one style or subject matter but which would exhibit the highest literary quality possible, without being restricted to any predetermined style or content. Like Dave and his associates, I did not hesitate to wield a stringent blue pencil, which Dave himself had used on my own prose when, in 1963, I had submitted an essay to *Riata* on Gertrude Stein. Also like Dave, I was interested in treatments of regional scenes and themes, which accounted for pieces that I solicited on Texas folklore and Stephen Crane's Texas short stories, but like Dave I was equally attracted to the modernist tradition, represented for me by the poetry of William Carlos Williams and Louis Zukofsky. One difference between the earlier *Riata* issues and the ones that I edited was that I felt the layout of the magazine could be improved, and I was fortunate to find in Jim Jacobs the ideal designer, who would subsequently design most of the Prickly Pear books. Another prophetic difference between Dave's issues of *Riata* and my own was that I emphasized poetry over prose, although I did include stories and personal and critical essays, as well as translations, discussions of music and art, and a full range of graphics, for which Jim Jacobs was responsible. But above all, I was from that first experience as an editor determined to promote regional poets, a number of which had been published in earlier issues of *Riata*, including William Burford, Thomas Whitbread, and Joseph Colin Murphey, all of whose work would later appear in Prickly Pear volumes.

From the beginning of my career as an editor, and especially during my years as a graduate student in Illinois, I saw the need for more outlets for Texas poets. Very few had been published in *The Texas Quarterly*, another magazine at the University in Austin that had profoundly influenced my sense of what a literary publication should be: full of high-quality writing, well-designed, and inclusive, particularly in terms of an eclectic gathering of culturally distinctive traditions. Even though *The New Breed*, the first anthology produced by Prickly Pear, was, as one reviewer noted, "rough, typed, uneven, and limited," it did draw upon, as the same reviewer phrased it, "a rich variety of publications" and was ultimately justified by "its absence of stereotypes." This reviewer went on to say that "More important than any one poet or poem is the impression that the art of the state, like the state itself, cannot be summed up in one image or metaphor." This was precisely what I had set out to demonstrate through Prickly Pear

Press. And surveying the record of the imprint over the past quarter of a century, I must say that I believe that Prickly Pear's publication list represents the kind of wide-ranging poetry that I had hoped to find and promote through the press.

Essentially my idea had been that Texas poets had developed innovative, imaginative ways to present the world around them, whether through realistic depiction of hardscrabble existence, which is characteristic of the work of Walt McDonald and Charles Behlen, or the cynical-satirical-sometimes-sentimental conceptions of Leon Stokesbury, Stan Rice, Dwight Fullingim, Richard Sale, and Jim Linebarger, or the mystical evocations of Ray González and Del Marie Rogers, or the older and newer approaches of such pairs of poets as Vassar Miller and Harryette Mullen (each into religious imagery after her own unique manner), and William Barney and Joseph Colin Murphey (with their opposing tight and loose forms that offer similar and subtle insights into regional people and places). A poet like William Burford, whose 1966 collection was entitled *A Beginning*, had indeed pointed the way and was emulated, though perhaps unconsciously, by such younger poets as Robert Bonazzi with his minimalist techniques and Michael Anderson with his technological metaphors. From the concrete poetry of Seth Wade to the narrative poems of R.G. Vliet, Betty Adcock, and Rosemary Catacalos or the conflicted voices of James Hoggard and Tino Villanueva, Texas poetry has been impossible to characterize as any one method or matter, and this is what Prickly Pear Press sought to establish through its publication. I will leave it for readers to judge if the press has made its point effectively and/or convincingly.

There are those who will say that I never should have had the effrontery to edit Texas poets, who are by nature mavericks to the core. But despite the grief that any such undertaking ever brings with it, I would do it all over again, and thank even the poets who have declared that I had no business questioning the diction of their deathless poems.

Three Distinctive Voices

Texas poetry has always come in many shapes and sizes, just as Texas poets can hail from any part of the state.* Take, for instance, three new collections by poets B.H. Fairchild, Stan Rice, and Walt McDonald, born, respectively, in Houston, Dallas, and Lubbock. All three are fairly thin volumes, but all are filled with distinguished work. Fairchild's *The Art of the Lathe* and McDonald's *Blessings the Body Gave* have both won prestigious prizes (the former garnering four, including the Texas Institute of Letters Award for poetry, and the latter the Award in Poetry from Ohio State University Press). Just the distinction of publication by Alfred A. Knopf places Rice's *The Radiance of Pigs* in the running with the best of any year.

All three volumes revisit scenes of childhood. The first sections of McDonald and Rice's collections are devoted to such memories as baptizing a dog (McDonald thinking "he'd rise / and talk like Balaam's donkey, but he thrashed as if drowning . . . I had to drag him out, his glazed eyes hopeless") and catching a rabbit (which Rice leaves alone and goes to tell his folks to come see: "Stupid to think a rabbit would stay"). Fairchild's adolescent memories are mostly about wishing he were somewhere other than unromantic Kansas or the machinist's shop described in a number of his poems (including the title piece), in contrast to a longed-for world of beauty and art.

Fairchild's work is intriguing because of the casual way he can begin a poem. His first two pieces, "Beauty" and "The Invisible Man," both open by setting the imagined scene with the same two-word phrase:

> We are at the Bargello in Florence, and she says,
> what are you thinking? And I say, beauty, thinking
> of how very far we are now from the machine shop
> and the dry fields of Kansas.
> * * *

---

* *The Texas Observer* (September 3, 1999): 26-28.

We are kids with orange Jujubes stuck to our chins
and licorice sticks snaking out of our jeans pockets,
and we see him, or rather don't see him, when the bandages
uncoil from his face and lo, there's nothing between
the hat and suit.

These almost offhand beginnings introduce powerfully probing meditations on the discovery and meaning of beauty, appearance vs. reality,
the "embodiments / of good and evil," embarrassment and perversity
in the use of a word like "beautiful," and of stumbling "blind into daylight and the body of the world." The subjects inspiring Fairchild's
fresh imagery and penetrating thought include baseball, basketball,
cigarettes, an airlines stewardess dreaming of the Himalayas, a burn
ward, a machinist named Keats, a personal account of the historic facts
behind the film *Chinatown* ("A Model of Downtown Los Angeles,
1940"), old women (among them a "garbage picker, hag of the alleys,
/ the town's bad dream scavenging trash cans ... the terror of love"), a
machinist teaching his daughter to play the piano, a Latin professor,
Edward Hopper's paintings, and a Book of Hours. *The Art of the Lathe*
is a well-crafted collection, and the great irony is perhaps that the
world of work and the

                                        treeless horizons
        of slate skies and the muted passions of roughnecks
        and scrabble farmers drunk ... at the darkened end
        of the bar

should prove the very sources of the book's profound artistry. "At the
Excavation of Liberal, Kansas" contains a moving summary of the
poet's principal theme of beauty, as revealed by a feed-store calendar
with its

                                picture
        of golden trees, a stream, an ancient water wheel.
        Such common beauty was a daily reminder, of course,
        of the hollowness of measurement,
        the ephemeral lushness of the world in its flight toward oblivion,

the sterility of abstraction and calculation
and everything beyond the caught moment.

Those unfamiliar with B.H. Fairchild's writing will find in *The Art of the Lathe* the haunting poetry of a native Texan who has come along "to expand the possibilities of contemporary verse."

Stan Rice's short poems are deceptively simple. Consider "When I Grow Up," with its allusions to Yeats' "Sailing to Byzantium." Rather than wishing to be "eternal and all," a "salmon / Turning hook-nosed and scarlet / As I rot in fertilized roe," or "a roasted gold brown turkey," Rice's speaker declares in the final line (with a typically witty off-rhyme) "I want to be mercury." In "Long Life" the poet says,

> I always thought importance would not be my fate,
> That I would be, like my father, a plumber of poetry,
> Under the house, with the black widows, melting a pot of solder.

While Rice is as discerning as Fairchild, he is more laconic, more given to what his speaker calls being "cursed with ten thousand angers / And the small vision / Of what's wrong with things." Rather than being addicted to cigarettes, as Fairchild implies by saying they are "the only way / to make bleakness nutritional, or at least useful, / something to do while feeling terrified," Rice confesses that he "had to go to Hades / Because I wanted a dark beer." In "My Trip to Hades," he recounts how he finally got "tired of being sick in the mornings" and "quit." His colleagues elected him chairman, treated him as if he were Satan, thought he wanted power.

> All I wanted was to be desired.
> But I was sober, and so moved on.
> Being drunk is like being dead,
> And a death to fear.
> But there's one thing I'd like to make clear.
> In Hades they brew a great dark beer.

The ever-present touch of black humor in Rice's writing serves both as comic relief and as a means of deepening the meaning.

The Radiance of Pigs is Rice's third collection from Knopf, and it contains much that is characteristic of his work. One new piece, "Doing Being," is notable for its length (running over 400 lines), but also it is vintage Rice in that it "Deals with the structure of experience," prefaced true to form by the phrase "I hope." "Doing Being" is full of leaps—from a consideration of Ezra Pound's "ear, his timing," to leaving the speaker's son at a university dormitory, contemplating Winslow Homer at the Metropolitan Art Museum (Rice's own paintings grace the dust jackets of all three of his Knopf books), Jesus ("Cracketh no jokes"), Nazis, grief, God (the poem somehow follows the seven days of creation), "the religious experience of the atheist," Job, "Pound and Picasso, their footprints / Darkspots in dew"), the thought that "Perhaps / All experiences are bug-eyed green plastic / Fishinglures, with hooks dangling down," the poet's former habit ("When the music stopped being / Its own explanation the booze and the pot / Had to stop"), "The Theory of Dissipative Structures," a carousel in Central Park, a sculpture of Alice in Wonderland, the speaker's looking forward each day to working on the poem, the injunction to "End all long poems with a monkey," Adam, and finally "The gods / are the slaves of our prayers, poor babies." The stream-of-consciousness works well to juxtapose seemingly unrelated incidents and thoughts, unified by "the structure of experience"—or at least that of a poet who can even include the consideration that "It is / Impossible to know when the lines are too long / Or when autobiography is a crock."

For newcomers, *The Radiance of Pigs* is a good place to begin in reading the work of Stan Rice, since it offers representative poems which, as the jacket correctly asserts, "are outside the circle of conventional poetry in their adherence to the strong, expressionist drive that makes his work so interesting, as well as entirely his own."

Far removed from Rice's surrealism is Walt McDonald's realist Llano Estacado and Vietnam War poetry in *Blessings the Body Gave*. Yet certainly both West Texas and the "facts we compiled about a war / already being lost" can, in McDonald's hands, turn, if not surreal, startling and even astonishing. This poet's knowing way with common words, familiar images, and rather matter-of-fact structures makes his writing surprising and extraordinary, even when we recognize some of the same scenes and phrases replayed again and again.

"Sleeping With the Enemy" alludes to the biblical image of "the holy bush / still burning," by way of a nightmare about being at home but remembering the war. This will remind some readers of a passage from "The Food Pickers of Saigon" in McDonald's *After the Noise of Saigon*: "Moses' holy bush / which was not consumed," in reference to an earlier depiction of Vietnamese urchins digging in garbage heaps. The biblical allusion is repetition with a difference, and revisits a timeless image even as the meaning changes with each new context. Another instance in McDonald's latest of sixteen volumes is "Uncle Earl's Wind River Ranch," which begins, "It's salt, not rain, fat elk cows need." This recalls a similar line in his "Wind and Hardscrabble" from *The Flying Dutchman*: "It's wind, not rain, dry cattle need." It is natural enough that a poet might repeat himself over the stretch of sixteen books of poetry (and some 1,700 published poems), but the amazing thing is that McDonald can employ a handful of images for such a variety of thought-provoking observations.

Most strikingly different about *Blessings the Body Gave* is the large number of strictly rhymed poems. McDonald has always been a master of a naturally flowing plain style, and that is still the case here, except that now the pieces are made perhaps tighter and more acute, even more satisfying in terms of sound, owing to the off and pure rhymes that unobtrusively frame his narrative lines. Just one of several fine examples would be "Gardens of Sand and Cactus." Again the poet presents familiar western imagery, but here the subject is primarily the poet's wife, who takes whatever she finds in the seemingly limited environment of West Texas—chipping "chunks from a salt block mired in sand, / that tongue-rubbed marble artwork of the West"—to fashion her own works of art. In the first stanza, the word "left" is an off-rhyme with "West," and "tree," the last word in the final stanza, is an off-rhyme with "cream," just as "tumbles" in the same quatrain is a slant rhyme with "mobiles." The rhymes help generate a subtler music, and McDonald successfully concludes the poem by bringing his various images together in the last line to reveal that the wife has turned "this desert we call home" into "wind chimes and swings, bird feeders in every tree."

McDonald also begins his poems with just the right tempting bait. This is certainly the case with the controlling metaphor of "Marriage Is a Bungee Jump," which continues from the title: "off some box canyon." The poem-long analogy ends by tying tenor and vehicle of the comparison naturally and convincingly together:

> Hand in hand we stepped up
> wavering to the ledge, hearing the rush
>
> of a river we leaped to, a far-off
> cawing crow, the primitive breeze of the fall,
> and squeezed, clinging to each other's vows
> that only death could separate us now.

Many of McDonald's poems are concerned with West Texas, the Vietnam War, his moving relationships with his family: mother, father, grandfather, son, daughter, wife, and grandchildren. (See in particular the wondrous "With Mercy For All" about his mother; the villanelle "The War in Bosnia" about his son; the tribute "Anniversary: One Fine Day" about his wife; and the touching "Catching my Grandson" about playing baseball and observing the effects of time.) "Stones Grandfathers Carved" is partly about England, and what is special about this piece is how well and concisely the poet summarizes English history:

> Is London burning? Do natives over fifty
> still hear the bombs in their sleep? Is the blitz
> handed down like titles, like the Tower
> and chopping block? They still ride after foxes,
> open castles to tourists who swat at aphids
> trapped in tapestries . . . a city sober
> as its name, thousands of actors writing plays,
> always a tower announcing London time.

Notice too the marvelous sounds of McDonald's subtly musical diction.

For those who may think they have heard everything Walt McDonald has to say, *Blessings the Body Gave* will change a few minds. For those who have not read him before, this book is as good a place to start as any, and will prove once again, as in a previous McDonald title, that he can write on "Anything, Anything" with power and insight.

William Barney's Fort Worth

Last year, on the occasion of Fort Worth's 150th anniversary, Browder Springs Books of Dallas published William Barney's *A Cowtown Chronicle*, a thin, elongated volume filled with masterful poetry.* Divided into three sections—The Arts and Ardors, Some of the People, and The Town—this collection of fifty-seven poems depicts a number of public features and figures of and visitors to Fort Worth, as well as some of the poet's more personal encounters with the sights and sounds of the city that have inspired his writing (as has his pianist wife Mary) for over six decades. Tastefully designed by the graphics studio of Margie Adkins, edited by poet-critic Betsy Colquitt, and with separate forewords by Colquitt and Joyce Gibson Roach, the book is a fitting tribute to Cowtown and a worthy sampling of Barney's poetry from across the years.

Born in Tulsa in 1916, Barney has lived in Fort Worth since 1928, employed there for thirty-five years by the U.S. Postal Service. Although active intermittently with the Texas Poetry Society, Barney in large part has practiced his art in private and has remained a rather self-effacing man of letters. However, his talents have been recognized within and without the state and were honored as early as the fifties when his first two collections, *Kneel From the Stone* and *Permitted Proof,* won awards from the Texas Institute of Letters. In 1962 Barney received the Robert Frost Award from the Poetry Society of America for his poem "The Killdeer Crying," with Frost himself making the presentation. In 1977 I had the privilege of publishing Barney's *Selected Poems* through my own Prickly Pear Press, with a second, expanded edition printed in 1983. In 1993 the University of North Texas Press issued *Words from a Wide Land*, a compilation of entries from Barney's notebooks, one entry for each of 365 days, taken from various years in each decade from the thirties through the eighties. Here is an entry from July 2, 1971:

---

* *The Texas Observer* (March 17, 2000) 36-37.

I like to sit watching Bermuda grass
spring back into place where my foot has crushed it.
Blade by blade, stem by stem, like clockwork,
it regains its original condition.
Being stepped on interlocks it
into a three-dimensional jigsaw mix
which it has to solve, piece by piece;
a blade must give way here
before the one beneath can click into place.
Over the width of a shoe motions take turns,
now at this side, now another yonder.
It is a picture of resurgence,
of life fighting back after taking a blow.
Watched long enough, the grass will return
to its fullest deployment.
The cost of observing this heroic struggle
is practically nothing.

Other collections of Barney's poems and a gathering of his observations on poetry and nature (*A Little Kiss of the Nettle*) have appeared from small presses like Counterpoint and Thorp Springs, and his work has been anthologized often, most notably in 1969 by Betsy Colquitt in her *A Part of Space: Ten Texas Writers*, from TCU Press.

A Cowtown Chronicle is fully representative of Barney's keen eye for detail and his ability to make connections between the natural world and the activities of humankind. In "Mr. Watts and the Whirlwind," Barney wonders if a phenomenon like the tornado that touched down outside an auditorium might have been jealous of pianist André Watts as his "hands . . . delicately touched Scarlatti" and later produced a "perfect storm" when he "cleanly and powerfully . . . smote the stays / and timbers of the Steinway / until it moaned with joy." Similarly, "Rider and Sea" parallels the movement of longhorn steers and a lightning storm: the "lone rider" is "frozen in a sea of bronze," a sculptured "tempest of horns . . . lashed into turbulence," twisting "lank flesh till it screams," "great heads" flashing "as if lightning / set fire to bone." Like Frederic Remington (whose work is on permanent display at Fort Worth's Amon Carter Museum), Barney also "works to paint crisis in the air," or in "The Cranes at Muleshoe" (from his *Selected Poems*), he struggles in his poems like those birds which

> make order where they rise
> in staggered thousands gabbling,
> try, try again a drift toward design,
> scrawling their trail of loud calligraphy
> on vacant sky. With no more skill than men
> can they arrange a right society,
> resolve their noisy dithering. . . .

A quieter, more reflective side to Barney's art is found in "A Few Leaves from Lindheimer," which derives from his visit to the Botanic Research Institute of Texas. For Barney, the relationship between man and nature is one in which the former seeks to discover in the latter "a brooding knowledge waiting to unfold." Lindheimer, the German naturalist of the 1850s who named so many Hill Country plants, came to Texas originally as "a hothead meaning to fight" in the revolution but "arrived too late," and subsequently became a friend of Comanches,

> who in awe
> watched as he gathered medicine.
> A man with a cart and a trained eye,
> wandering in hardship and in joy
> for a work of love.

It is clear that Barney identifies closely with Lindheimer as an observer of nature, especially of birds, their habits and habitats. Barney also has spent much time at the Fort Worth Nature Center and Refuge.

In "The First Cliff Swallow of April" the poet recalls a day in the thirties when he and his father walked to a bridge under which returning swallows constructed their nests. The birds still return, and the poet posits a meaningful link between man and the natural world, this time between himself and his feathered friends:

> I've lived most of my life in this place,
> as much a sanctuary as any could ask,

a place to dream of fabulous voyage,
a port to come back to after flight.

In "The Ginkgoes at the Water Garden," Barney imagines that the trees native to China must feel like

strangers in this land,
they not of this epoch;
always they hear the mountain streams,
the howling monkeys, the rustling bamboo
muffling the traffic's grind.

Like Keats, Barney is a poet of "negative capability," able to enter imaginatively into everything he sees, becoming the plant, creature, or thing he observes so faithfully and so feelingly.

Barney's "chronicle" of Fort Worth includes myriad aspects of his Cowtown: the stockyards and slaughterhouse, where "the deed was done / turning live beast into food"; airplane factories, whose "great gray planes" went "clambering the stair / upward to flight," mumbling "in the dark of a grim dread"; and the site of the Van Cliburn piano competitions, where the poet listens in awe of "the chemistry, whatever bond can be / that ties together finger and brain / in instantaneous prodigy." And there is the state and city's principal livestock exhibition and rodeo, depicted in the poem "In the Cattlebarn," where

boys grooming the fat steers,
. . . hands fondling the hair
dread what is coming;
even in the moment of pride they tremble,
knowing that boys have to be men,
that steers, inevitably, make meat[;]

and where, as in "Bill and Clown,"

The bull has no sense of humor;
he is not in a mood to be messed with
by one more two-legged tormentor.

Barney also portrays the city as once the destination of the trail drive, whose "strung-out herd moved and bawled . . . a music dark, part rage, part fear; / body to lumbering body called"; as now the home of the renowned Kimbell Art Museum, where a wine vessel from "buried centuries" was "flawlessly wrought . . . in the timeless metal of a mind / and hand . . . an age / when out of nothingness came sudden design"; and as the land of the sawtooth daisy, whose leaves and "upright stance" the poet much admires, "standing golden in loose sheaves . . . garish tops, giddy in the summer wind."

Captured in this cross-section of Fort Worth is both the city's past violence and death and its ongoing remaking of its image into that of art collector and music advocate. Barney often brings these two facets together, as in "The Drovers," which combines the bawling of cows and the cries of the killdeer he "drives" before him like cattle in his walks across the fields, for he is "a listener with cool ear" who knows "a raw harmony in [his] head" and recreates it on the page from having leaned "close to hear / the resonance of [the killdeer's] quaverings."

There are many poems in *A Cowtown Chronicle* deserving of notice; my personal favorite is "Once the Ear Wakes to Listen," which contains some of the finest examples of the poet's sensitivity to his surroundings, and his care in rendering them vividly through his metered diction. As a boy growing up in Fort Worth, I would hear nightly the trains nearby passing or shunting on parallel sets of rails; Barney evokes this aural image, which I always associate with my native city. At the same time, this poem catalogs many other sounds typical of the place, and then brings the piece to a subtle, touching close, uniting most intimately the world outside the poet's home with the human warmth and affection inside. This poem exemplifies the artistry of William Barney, whose work for much of the past century has brought together the best of two worlds, that of nature and the environment and that of humankind's senses and intellectual endowments:

> Once the ear wakes to listen, night
> fills with a thousand sayings:
> the grumbling tom-tom of the diesel
> growling rail yards; the calculated crash
> of freight cars; whine and wheel of gears

of semi's pushing through the city;
three kinds of siren in their unique screaming
moving near to far and disappearing;
a mockingbird ecstatically mad
in the drench of moonlight; the bubbling flute
of a screech owl in the midnight dark;
somewhere a baby crying; unintelligible voices;
a jet faint as a buzzing fly overhead;
cars passing on the street, for unknown reasons;
the creak of ties on a railroad bridge
and the horn of the Amtrak; dogs,
always dogs, practicing anger;
cats in their agony of sex;
stairs creaking, adjusting their wooden teeth;
a wind chime like ice clinking;
a fan exhaling, a radio thumping.
Her soft breath on the pillow;
this too a solemn cadence, almost undetectable,
somewhere in the bedding, a heart beating.

A Collection of the First Rank

Including work from Betty Adcock's first two collections, *Walking Out* (1975) and *Nettles* (1983), and from her two subsequent volumes, *Beholdings* (1988) and *The Difficult Wheel* (1995), plus eighteen previously uncollected poems, *Intervale: New and Selected Poems* truly places her in the front rank of living American poets.* Born in San Augustine, Texas, in 1938, Adcock has lived almost her entire adult life in North Carolina, but the most profound source of her writing has remained her memories of people and places in the Redlands area of her East Texas childhood. Above all, it is the intriguing portrait of her father that emerges from *Intervale*, filled in and deepened through this gathering of various poems that touch on his life and his very personal interests in hunting, woodcarving, the Ays Indians, flowers, and colors in artifacts and nature. *Intervale* also adds to our understanding of Adcock's mother and the continuing impact of her early death on the poet, as seen in the volume's opening poem, one of the previously uncollected pieces entitled "Penumbra." Along with the poems associated with her parents, the new and selected poetry demonstrates through a wide range of subjects and voices that Adcock's writing offers some of the most insightful thinking of any American poet active at the beginning of this new millennium.

The poet's father, whose initials are given as R.L.S. in "To My Father, Killed in a Hunting Accident," from *Nettles*, first appeared in Adcock's "Four Short Poems," from *Walking Out*. In that earliest of the poet's books, the father is said to have avoided houses after his wife had died and to have lived "with the running of the hounds and foxes / who made an old fierce grief articulate." The poet declares at the end of the fourth poem of six-lines, subtitled "Gift," that she still learns "from small animals of wood / he carved and put into my hands instead of words." Perhaps the most valuable aspect of *Intervale* is that the reader is able to discover in a small piece like this the origins of the poet's later very pointed and poignant writing, the ampler meaning of

---

* *Texas Books in Review* 21, no. 1 (Spring 2001): 16, 19.

such a limited number of lines and of the word chosen for their simple subtitle. The poet's taciturn father obviously had a "gift" that he passed along to his daughter, but ironically it came down to her in the form of words rather than woodcarvings.

All of this only comes to light through a later poem entitled "Clearing Out, 1974," from *Beholdings*, with its date marking both the father's year of death from the hunting accident, dramatically evoked in the poem with his initials, and the date of the poet's return to Texas to "clear out" the desk drawers of her great-grandfather's, her grandfather's, and her father's "rolltop sturdy as a boat / and ice-locked in a century of deepening afternoon." This emotive poem of three-and-a-half pages itemizes the objects important to the man who was indifferent to all the "leases, royalties, mortgages wadded here like trash" but who, if he did not give them away as gifts, kept like "votive and reliquary" the creatures he could make "walk straight out of wood / into your hand." The entire piece deserves a close reading, but one particular section must be cited, since it, like the "Gift," clearly led to a later poem, entitled "Revenant," just as "Gift" looked forward to "Clearing Out, 1974."

In "clearing out" the desk, Adcock recalls a visit one night by a full-grown buck, who "thumped up the steps . . . onto the porch outside this very window, / slipping and knocking antlers at the rail." Apparently this is the former fawn raised by the grandmother as a girl: "It's the part of every story we remember, / the dream lost track of, changed / and coming back." Just as the spirits of the poet's mother and father often "visit" her in her poetry, another buck pays her a visit in "Revenant," from *The Difficult Wheel*. The title word means, according to Webster, "one who returns after death or long absence." The speaker hears a "crash of leaves" and freezes on seeing

> the heavy-antlered head
> alter its slant.
> He moved in the slow way animals will seem
> to move in children's picture books,
> on each page larger, clearer—
> until he was so close I saw the shine
> on raised black nostrils. . . .

Although this is evidently not the same fawn that had returned full-grown, the speaker still interprets it as something from the past "coming back." Yet she hesitates to offer

> One of those
> dense and symbol-laden moments poets make
> to force and tease, the whole thing false
> with sexual curvature and hidden weight.

Nonetheless, this visitation undeniably

> could be the father coming back
> in the form he killed. Or the father's
> nemesis. Or it could be a sweet communion,
> that old lie.

The autobiographical element in this and the related poems on her father makes these pieces more than invented symbols that tease and falsify. There may be a "lie" here, but it is most likely the one that involves living with the dead and trying to make oneself believe that one can commune with those loved and deeply missed. Adcock's "gift" lies in her ability to bring the dead to life for her reader—or to reveal as she says in "In Another Life" from *The Difficult Wheel*, "the ways the dead stay on."

The father appears in a number of pieces but is depicted most appealingly in two very exceptional poems, "Ays" from *Beholdings* and "In a Trunk Not Looked Into for Twenty Years" from *The Difficult Wheel*. The first poem concerns an extinct Indian tribe from the Redlands area, and once again it was the father's interest in this native people that led the daughter to research their history, what there is of it that remains. She says that she thinks her father,

> with his boyhood's hoard
> of scrapers, handaxes, bowls, and arrowheads,
> must have held the heavy unhearable echo
> of all that was left to know.

Adcock then recounts how the Ays were described, by 18th-century travelers to the Redlands, as

> a ragtag woodland people with a sense of humor.
> Hedonists, by all accounts not violent. . . .
> And surprisingly given to hard argument
> with any priest who spoke to them of the new God.
> An exception is set forth in one report
> by a padre who'd told an unintended truth
> when he announced to the unconverted
> that the God he preached sent pestilence.
> For once, he was not disputed.

The poem on the unlooked-at trunk holds three words written by the father: "*Redbud. Dark red.*" For the poet this key unlocks her memories of his love of flowers and colors. From hunting trips he would bring home "wild orchids we didn't know were rare, / carnivorous sundew, bluebonnets / too blue," or at times "a branch of redbud / wilting beside you in the truck. / You said it kept the winter back."

Like the father, the poet's mother is a figure who passed on to her daughter a sensitive eye and ear. This is most fully revealed in the title poem, "Intervale," which, as the notes to the poem inform us, is an "obsolete form of *interval*" in reference to the hymn music known as Sacred Harp, as well as to "a stretch of low land next to a river." In this piece, the mother's life is recalled through interviews with relatives and one of her students, with the latter's language faithfully reproduced:

> Your mother taught me high school and I never
> was one to love books, but the way she'd read
> poems out loud like it was Bible
> could make me just about hear music.

Books, reading, poems, music—these we know are central to the daughter's life and art. Libraries too are mentioned in one reminiscence of her mother, as well as the way she

> was just hooked on what most people

never notice in their lives because of work,
or not time enough.
She loved a common sunset, stars, ditchflowers,
lightning starting up, anything rare
and lovely like the snow.

One can see that mother and father were made for one another, which seems true as well of the poet and her husband, a musician who is the subject of a moving three-part poem entitled "Pilgrimage," from the section of new work. This piece grew out of Adcock's husband being hospitalized and his "almost-leaving." He is addressed in several other poems, most notably "The Swan Story," from *Nettles*, which had earlier traced the poet's childhood and recalls how her mother went "out spark by spark."

The influence of the poet's husband on her poetry is perhaps most evident in a piece from *The Difficult Wheel*, entitled "Poem for Dizzy." Inspired by the fact that *The Anthology of Jazz Poetry* did not contain a single piece "for, to, or about Dizzy Gillespie, who was co-creator (with Charlie Parker) of bebop, the style that ushered in the modern jazz era," and by virtue of the husband's being an aficionado of jazz and a practicing jazz flutist, this poem renders worthy tribute to the trumpeter, his unique style of appearance and performance, and, most significantly, his way of playing "a soul into the horn." The poet also contrasts Gillespie with other major figures of his generation, who died of dope, demons, and "edgy monologues," while Dizzy, who may have "played clown . . . outlived them all. This too was real jazz."

During the past thirty years, Adcock has continued to grow as a writer, plumbing in the process the emotional and psychological depths of her own experiences and her memories of those dearest to her. The earliest poems from *Walking Out* show her groping for a style and a subject, which she essentially discovered in her own childhood in East Texas. She has mined this personal past in a rich sequence like "The Elizabeth Poems" from *Nettles* and has done the same for the history of her native landscape in such poems as "Big Thicket Settlers, 1840s," "Oil," and "Stories, 1940s," all from *Beholdings*, as well as "East Texas Autumn As a Way to See Time" from *The Difficult Wheel*.

In addition to her many poems on her Texas Redlands, Adcock has written perceptively on Greece, where she and her husband lived for a time, on a modern triptych by the German painter Anselm Kiefer, and on Cambodia and Vietnam, proving that she is in no way a one-theme poet. But ultimately, the greatest strength of *Intervale* is surely that it allows us to know the persons who meant and go on meaning so much to the poet, both personally and artistically. And in doing so, Betty Adcock has enriched every reader by sharing with us such vital lives, making them "revenant" through her own vibrant lines.

The New Formalism in Texas

Austin-born political writer and poet Michael Lind has lately pointed out a fact that is fairly common knowledge: Poetry is little read today, except by academics.* Lind blames this situation on writers who lack a necessary grounding in the traditional forms, including especially rhymed stanza patterns. On the other hand, he praises the work of poet-critic Dana Gioia for being part of a movement known as the New Formalism that Lind believes has rescued American poetry from "a gang of professors [who] hijacked" it and imposed in the place of rhyme their so-called free verse. Dana Gioia, in turn, has written in his introduction to R.S. Gwynn's *No Word of Farewell—Selected Poems: 1970-2000* (Story Line Press) that Gwynn, who teaches at Lamar University in Beaumont, "is surely one of the three or four finest poets associated with New Formalism" but that he is "unique among his contemporaries" in having forged "a distinctive combination of traditional form and post-modern observation."

Whether or not one agrees with Michael Lind that the New Formalism has saved American poetry from the clutches of free verse, there is no doubt that Sam Gwynn is an accomplished writer in such forms as the heroic couplet, the sonnet, the ballad, the villanelle, and a number of other forms of his own invention. Yet to fill these forms does not ipso facto guarantee that a writer will create popular or moving or intellectually stimulating poetry. There must be more than mere rhyming, more than a repetition of standard meters, more than a use of literary wit and allusion, and more than a dependence on biblical and classical analogues if a writer is to engage a reader at the level of deep emotions and enduring delight. Sam Gwynn can in fact appeal to a reader through more than sheer formal ingenuity.

Some of the pieces in "If My Song: New Poems," the first section of Gwynn's *Selected Poems*, will definitely impress the reader through the poet's deft handling of rhyme schemes that combine, as Gioia suggests, traditional elements with the contemporary scene. However,

---

* *The Texas Observer* (August 8, 2001): 28-29.

Gwynn's formal pieces that "cover" such works as the biblical tale of Samson and Delilah (in "Among Philistines") and the drama of Hamlet (in "Horatio's Philosophy") do not plumb the depths of his subjects so remarkably as do his treatments of more personal themes. In one of his translations from perhaps the book's weakest section, "More Light: Translations, Parodies, Verse," Gwynn renders lines in François Villon's "The Debate of Body and Heart" that relate in their way to Gwynn's own situation: "*What gave you all these troubles? A bad start. /* When Saturn packed my bag for years ahead / He added them. *Then learn to use some art.*" Facing surgery for prostate cancer, the poet did in fact muster all his art to control not only the sonnet form in which he wrote "At the Center," among his New Poems, but also to evoke a response in his readers by making them feel viscerally the treatment center's atmosphere, the attempt not to think about "where you are / or *how* you are," and the unspoken thoughts of those who do not ask "how long you plan to stay."

While literary allusion in Gwynn's "Among Philistines" is a valid method of conveying ideas and emotions, it can be overused. Much of Gwynn's poetry relies so heavily on literary references or "updated" renditions of classic tales that it fails to move beyond the forms he follows or the story lines he borrows. His mock-epic, "The Narcissiad," travesties such modern American poets as Daniel Halpern, James Merrill, John Ashbery, Richard Howard (referred to as Howhard), Daryl Hines, Stanley Kunitz (orientalized as Ku-Nitzu), Frank O'Hara, Anne Sexton, and Sylvia Plath. In order to parody the pretensions of one strain of post-World War Two American poetry, the poem invokes Aeneas and Turnus, Greek gods and goddesses, and Alexander Pope and Dante, and the clever writing reveals that Gwynn has certainly done his homework. Even so, the mockery is mostly an insider's view that comes to very little. The post-modern slant is slightly present in this particular passage:

> Pallas Athena, hands clasped to her head,
> Escapes the roar by taking to her bed,
> While pale, forlorn and sulky, Aphrodite
> Slouches about in curlers and torn nightie.

Similarly, Gwynn's "Versions for the Millennium" includes this especially witty example of his writing in the stanza entitled "Upon Demi's Breasts" (a remake, like most of his epigrams, of 17th-century classical verse):

> Display thy breasts, my Demi, like a bough
> Hung with such fruits as only gods enDow,
> Upon which I would lie, my lips implanted
> Against what looks as succulent as granite.

Gwynn can rhyme with the best of them and his wit is sharper than most. But he is better when he takes aim at himself, as in "Before Prostate Surgery," where he writes that not only is his member "too downcast to raise a fuss / Or much of anything," but his "Epic intentions [have] shrunk to epigram."

The final section of the book is devoted to early poems which appeared in his previous full-sized collection, *The Drive-In*, published by the University of Missouri Press in 1986 as number 50 in its "breakthrough" series. I reviewed that volume at the time and still find some of its poems quite appealing. A poem like "Mimosa," which I praised, does not seem to hold up so well as I remembered it, but this may be owing to the fact that the first section of the *Selected Poems* offers work of greater affectivity and maturity.

It is not clear to me when, in relation to Gwynn's illness, he wrote the poems in the first section of his new book, but it is certain that a number of the most impressive pieces date from that period. The experience, as would be expected, changed the writer, causing him to look at the world more empathetically, less sardonically. He can still be cynical about the promised cures offered in "1-800," a poem in six-line stanzas with such clever rhymes as lewd/food/screwed, money/gun he/sunny, or "Discover how today! Write this address!" chiming with Success and UPS. Only occasionally do Gwynn's poems exhibit local settings, but "Coastal Freeze" is one of a number of pieces in the New Poems section that refer to the area where he lives and teaches, the Gulf Coast of Texas. The false hope in "Laying bets on gulf-born breezes harboring . . . spring" is dashed by the cold "front's relentless lashing" that

drains each bud-
Full of blood,
Laying low without distinction as it kills
Daffodils,
Calla lilies, bougainvillea, mustard greens.

The rhymed form of this work is a combination of a line of five tro-
chees followed by a line of three syllables or beats. The setting can be
compared with surely the most convincing poem in the book, entitled
"Cléante to Elmire," in which the coastal hurricane known as Cara
brings memories of a girl of the same name with whom the speaker
acted in a school version of Moliére's play, *Tartuffe*. In heroic couplets,
the poem recalls that time "Heady with epigram and foiled seduc-
tion. / It was The Coastal Players' great production." Remembrance
of the Cara who acted the part of the faithful spouse is mixed with
the reality of a marriage that brought about her murder at the hands
of her ex-husband. Ironically, Cara—both the storm and the dead
friend—serves the speaker during his time of sickness to pass through
the shadow of the valley of death as his "rod and staff." All the allusions
here work toward "a curious *dénouement*" that is truly touching in a way
that most of Gwynn's writing is generally not.

Doubt, fear, frustration, and failure are constant themes in
Gwynn's New Poems, and one piece that represents these dramatically
is a three-sonnet sequence, "Body Bags," on schoolmates, two of whom
died in Vietnam or afterwards by suicide. The poet recalls, in one telling image, how

A scaled-down wild man, . . .
Like Dennis 'Wampus' Peterson, could haul
His ass around right end for me to slip
Behind his block. Played college ball a year—
Red-shirted when they yanked his scholarship
Because he majored, so he claimed, in Beer.

Another similar piece is entitled "Randolph Field, 1938," and this essentially unrhymed poem, set in the San Antonio airbase named in
the title, is more direct, less allusive, and very humanly sympathetic.

It concerns a father who is unable to complete his flight training and "has missed the chance . . . / To burn above Berlin" like his "buddies," who "Saunter in after class with Cokes and Luckies."

The range of Sam Gwynn's writing is perhaps unmatched today on the levels both of technique and wit. But what remains more vivid for me are not the parodic epigrams, the very competent translations from the French and German, or the darkness of poems such as "Black Helicopters," "At Rose's Range," and "Audenesque: For the Late Returns," with their depiction of an American siege mentality, but the poems where he delves into personal encounters with those who have suffered some setback in life. Gwynn's own coming face to face with the possibility of death seems to have caused him to draw upon his past for a more profound poetry. Evidence for this appears in lines from "Cléante to Elmire," where this poem attempts "To salve my wreckage and restore your face," to bless the memory of one who failed in love or one who, like the father in flight training, "Washed out a week before he gets his wings."

The first section of Gwynn's book ends with a subdued, prayerful poem, entitled "Release," which contrasts with many of the rather bitter pieces that precede and follow it. This poem lends not only this section but the entire book a sense of acceptance and empathic understanding that offsets the work's somewhat oppressively biting wit, revealing another side to the writer that renders the overall volume more fully and richly humane:

> For all that lags and eases, all that shows
>   The winding-downward and diminished scale
>   Of days declining to a twilit chill,
> Breathe quietly, release into repose:
>   Be still.

A Pair of Poetesses

Over the years, a number of poets—both from here in Texas and from abroad in Latin America, Spain, and England—have sent me their books of poetry to review.* For the most part I have tried to do so, feeling that otherwise their work would probably not receive much attention. It is not only difficult to find an outlet for publishing poetry, but having it reviewed is in many cases even more problematic. Unless published by major trade presses or successful university presses, poetry does not sell and therefore does not generate receipts for publishers nor advertising for newspapers or magazines. Many poets must publish themselves if they are to have their poetry read and critiqued, but even then self-publishing is no guarantee that libraries will acquire a book, that periodicals will review it, or that local stores will stock it, much less a national chain like Barnes & Noble. Mainly, I much prefer to review the work of writers that I know and admire, in order to keep up with and promote their careers, but I am also eager to review the work of unknown writers whose books immediately interest me for one reason or another.

In the case of Del Marie Rogers and Beverly Caldwell, I already knew and admired their writings, having included Rogers' poetry in my 1973 anthology, *The New Breed*, and having reviewed and praised her earlier collection, *Close to Ground*, from 1990, just as I had read with pleasure Caldwell's poems in *Borderlands: Texas Poetry Review* for 1994. The title of Rogers' latest book could perhaps, facetiously, be applied to being reviewed: *She'll Never Want More Than This* (from Firewheel Press, her own invented imprint), but this title line comes from "We Bring Life to the Angel," one of many poems in this new collection that speaks urgently of the desire for and the need for love. Like other such volumes from long-suffering regional poets, Rogers' collection is not only a beautifully produced book, with four-color artwork on the cover by Native American painter Fritz Scholder, but the poems require and reward multiple readings.

---

* *Texas Books in Review* 22, nos. 1 & 2 (Spring/Summer 2002): 22-23

Rogers' poetry has consistently been marked over the years by elemental images that offer a special haunting effect. In the phrase that served as the title of her first full-length collection, her writing has remained "close to ground." Her descriptions of earth, rivers, trees, grass, sand, and mountains have always served as the sources for evocations of human alienation, loss, and longing. They are also attempts to make connections and to achieve self-sufficiency, as well as to maintain a search for answers to fundamental questions of existence, even when they seem despairingly elusive.

One particular theme in Rogers' second full-length collection is specifically survival of loss, with the first section of the book designated "Survivors." The need for restoring a sense of connection with life comes in a number of poems as a result of the end of a love relationship, movingly described in "Sleeping on the Floor of an Empty House": "I want to go back to our life together . . . . / Strange world we built, so easily / blown from its hinges." The poem is populated with Rogers' customary imagery of leaves, branches, stars, waves, sand, and especially the moon—the latter a symbol of the inward-looking eye, the dark side of life, and the need to learn to live with uncertainty and fear. While Rogers' imagery has been largely limited to the natural world, her descriptive writing has always managed to draw from her images insights into what she characterizes in another poem as "Survival Skills." Throughout this collection, Rogers not only creates what she refers to as "lifelines" between nature and humankind that provide essential links to a type of saving grace, but she also unites the reader with a sense of the glory of living on earth despite the disappointments and difficulties that go along with it. This new book testifies to the fact that, as a poet, Rogers is a survivor, one who "will never stop looking" and who finds comfort in the thought that she knows "what no one else believes," that the simplest element of nature, a "frost-flattened torn weed / battered earthward," or a man-made object, like a clay shard, can serve as seeds underground to let us "stay alive" and keep us "from old defeat."

Often Rogers' poems are filled with matter-of-fact statements, one- or two-line sentences. There is little musical flow to the writing but rather a piling up of image after image, building toward a conclusion that can verge on the mystical or, as suggested at the end of the poem entitled "On Stone," a sort of triumph:

> Wheel-spokes of sun. Mist bandages.
> I can see the bones of my hand through a cloud.
> Blood pulses to my fingertips.
> The earth has lived many times.
> I wake from sleep, no longer afraid.

In 1973 in *The New Breed*, Rogers commented that she rejected "the temptation to make a polished poem that falsifies experience, to write poems about what we already know." While her poems are replete with common images from the natural world, they tend ever to lead her to a new understanding, to a meaning that she had missed or a state of mind that she had not known or had lost. Her poems often speak of the act of writing, or of speech, which in "Talking to the Moon" she says is "vital for us."

"Commitments" is one of the most effective poems in the collection in terms of delivering a clear, direct statement that is filled with a deep understanding that

> Some words are too important to take back.

> . . . [Y]ou don't know what you feel until you've said it.
> Life and the words to tell it are a knot
> you can't undo and wouldn't want to.

First published in *The Texas Observer*, where I originally read it, this poem immediately struck me by its unusual penetration into the question of whether attachments in love are ever lost, whether or not by not discussing a past love it will disappear, or whether once there is love it can ever be wholly obliterated. The language here is different from much of Rogers' writing, less dependent on nature imagery, more given to a recalling of conversational comments that relate to a love that is limited to sexual needs: "*I don't give a hoot in hell if you love me or not, / I've got to have it.*" But the real issue here is the unwillingness to live with love, to remain true to its vows, never to "stop seeing / the infinite in each other's eyes," to recognize that "[t]he spell of love is something you make together," and that love cannot be denied or cannot, like history rewritten by the "new regime," be purged or reinterpreted. As Rogers observes so poignantly,

> Whatever lived is permanently real.
> It's as simple as that, as hard to live with.
> In some fine limbo where the words can breathe,
> somehow we love each other still.

Shortly after I received a copy of Del Marie Rogers' book, I was sent another thin volume by Beverly Caldwell, entitled *Life Sentences*, published in 2001 by Trilobite Press. Rogers too has been published in the Trilobite chapbook series edited by former *Texas Books in Review* editor Richard Sale. In 1982 Trilobite issued Rogers' *To the Earth*, whose title poem is included in her *She'll Never Want More Than This*. Sale's small press has been doing important work for over 25 years, counting back to its 1976 hardcover edition of J.M. Linebarger's *Five Faces*. It has also published outstanding chapbooks by Leon Stokesbury (*The Drifting Away of All We Once Held Essential*, 1979), Walt McDonald (*Splitting Wood for Winter*, 1988), and Charles Behlen (*Texas Weather*, 1999), among others, and now has come Caldwell's *Life Sentences*, which belongs in the fine Trilobite tradition.

All six of the titles mentioned above are distinctive, one from the other, even though all but the Rogers and McDonald share more of an ironic, at times witty, take on life. Caldwell's "In Jefferson, Texas," plays with the idea that railroad tycoon Jay Gould bypassed the Texas town because it denied his trains a right-of-way and his curse on the town came to fruition as it grew stunted, partly as a result of the dried-up waterway that terminated riverboat trade. The speaker in the poem, however, finds that the town's people (including herself) "choose our history, / cook it up sweet like Mayhaw jelly." Not only this, but she and her lover,

> [u]nder the East Texas moon . . .
> in an old house,
> . . . discover fresh ways to love. . . .
> Later, we're eased toward sleep

by the drum and moan of another train
skirting Jefferson,
leaving tracks
we can follow
dreaming.

Caldwell's poems contain no self-pity or resentment; rather, they seem to thrive on recognizing the ironies in others' lives and in her own life. This is illustrated by her portrait in "Brother Beau" of a minister whose own family departs from his sermon's admonitions against sin, while he himself commits perhaps the worst sin: suicide, as the poem paints a bleak picture of life's unexpected contradictions. The same type of ironic view is made humorous in the chapbook's title poem, "Life Sentences." Here, the speaker reveals that a young boy summed up his life in seven very simple (though loaded) sentences:

I have bronchitis. I've missed
a whole week of school already,
but the doctor says I can go back soon.
My stepfather owns this restaurant.
My real dad never comes to see me.
That's my mom over there.
She's a waitress.
I like school a lot.

The speaker had only listened to the boy with something of a superior attitude, but later she heard herself during a party summing up her own life in a few simple sentences:

I live alone. I have a small apartment.
I like Mexican art, Henry Miller and poetry.
I prefer making love in the afternoon.
Some nights the moon is the only face I see.

Caldwell's "Confessions of a Lapsed Baptist," not included in *Life Sentences* but published with her book's title poem in *Borderlands*, also summarizes something of her life:

I've taken the name of the Lord in vain
three thousand sixty-two times
since losing my virginity,
I swapped Thunderbird for Welch's
during the Lord's Supper,
I coveted my neighbor's hairdo, . . .
wore shorts to the Easter cantata
and yes
I'm afraid I danced.

In "Why I Invented Loneliness," Caldwell offers surreal answers or justifications for choosing this state over happiness, or as a change from what the speaker considers in herself less desirable or admirable traits, or even those she may think too goody-goody. Happiness she sees as having been put on a pedestal, and loneliness will bring it down where it belongs. She suggests that a "certain perversity in [her] nature" made her want to "flash its derriere" so that her "solitude could have its evil twin." Loneliness also gives her tongue "a vacation," implying that it has tended to run on for too long and needs a rest, or its listeners do. Caldwell is a clever writer, but she can sound some very uncomedic chords, as she does in the two poems entitled "Dust" and "Dust Story." In the latter she describes how what has not been touched can feel unloved, like a book or a piano:

Wrapped in stillness, the pages of a book lament:
when did she read us last?
The piano keys concur: *We are not as loved*
as we once were.

Although Del Marie Rogers' probing, analytical lines and Beverly Caldwell's serio-comic confessions are clearly worlds apart, both poets have in common, as we all do, histories of love, loneliness, and loss that they may have chosen for themselves. In writing about such histories and sharing them, both poets have entertained and instructed us and have at the same time demonstrated the wonderful range of poetry that has been developing in Texas for much longer than most readers may realize. Thanks to small presses like Trilobite and small magazines like *Borderlands*, poets in Texas have been showcased for decades as they truly ought to be. Of course, many poets like Rogers have had to resort to self-publication, but this has been a time-honored practice, dating back at least to Walt Whitman in the 19th century and to William Carlos Williams at the beginning of the 20th. And thanks to a publication like *Texas Books in Review*, small press and self-published chapbooks have been noticed and paid attention to for now approaching thirty years, helping keep the spirit of poetry alive even here in the Lone Star State.

Briny, Sharp, Clear-Eyed Poems

2001 was a banner year for books by Texas poets.* Reportedly, the three titles in the final running for the Texas Institute of Letters award for poetry—Betty Adcock's *Intervale*, R.S. Gwynn's *No Word of Farewell*, and Susan Wood's *Asunder*—were considered so close in quality that hardly even a knife blade could separate one from the others. It surely must have been a difficult decision for the judges, perhaps even a heart-rending one, since but a single prize could be given (even though in the past two poets had shared the award, as was the case with books by Thomas Whitbread and Naomi Shihab Nye). This, of course, is the unfortunate thing about such prizes—they celebrate only one book when others deserve to be recognized and read just as much.

The 2002 Pulitzer Prize for poetry was awarded to *Practical Gods* by Carl Dennis, whose book was published by Penguin, as was Susan Wood's *Asunder*. After reading the Dennis collection along with the volumes by the three finalists for the T.I.L. award, I feel certain that any of the three Texas contenders could have been picked for the Pulitzer, and in fact I prefer the three Texas books to Dennis's. This may seem chauvinistic on my part, but I assert my preference on the grounds that the Texas books are more engaging as poetry, more penetrating in their thoughts and emotions, and more intimate on meaningful levels than Dennis's rather exercise-like treatment of the mythological gods. If nothing else, the bumper crop of Texas books from 2001 demonstrates once again that Texas writers can compete nationally with the best, as attested by the fact that Susan Wood's book won a national prize—selection for The National Poetry Series. Likewise, Betty Adcock's *Intervale* was named the "Outstanding Book of Poems Published in 2001" by the *Dictionary of Literary Biography Yearbook*.

Having already reviewed Adcock's *Intervale* for *Texas Books in Review* (Spring 2001) and R.S. Gwynn's *No Word of Farewell* for *The Texas Observer* (August 8, 2001), I was surprised to learn before the T.I.L. award winner had actually been announced that neither

---

* *The Texas Observer* (August 2, 2002): 26-27.

the Adcock nor the Gwynn book had won. Although I knew Susan Wood's work and had reviewed her previous collection, *Campo Santo*, for the *Observer* (March 27, 1992), I was not aware that she had a new book out, even though I had seen a note in *Poetry* magazine identifying her as a winner in the National Poetry Series. I was in no way disappointed that this English professor at Rice University had beaten out Adcock and Gwynn, although I can fully appreciate the qualities in the other two poets' books that are not to be found in the Wood collection. Adcock's nature imagery is evocative and moving in ways that neither of the other two poets can quite manage, while Gwynn's handling of poetic form is magisterial. Yet Susan Wood has her own strengths that make her work as appealing as anything being published today. In the only rhymed poem that I have detected in her collection (entitled "Photograph, Circa 1870"), Wood has, like Gwynn, created an ingenious stanza form and handles it subtly and superbly. With regard to "Laundry," the first poem in Wood's new collection, I will admit to a certain bias in that this piece first appeared in my own 1999 anthology, *Roundup*. I should add that Adcock and Gwynn also are represented in that gathering of poetry by Texas poets from my quondam imprint, Prickly Pear Press.

Re-reading "Laundry" after a couple of years of not having looked at the poem, I was struck once more by the linguistic power of the poet's diction. Wood plays with such words and phrases as "soiled," "scale" (for weighing the sacks of clothes), "fondle," "rinsed," and "everything white" to work her way through motifs of guilt, "appraisal," troubling memories, and a present sense of the precarious nature of relationships, arriving ultimately at a new respect for "the god of cleanliness." This is not a mythological allusion, but just a realization that every washday is a type of offering to "the god of fresh starts." As Wood frequently does in this new collection, she implies that everyone needs a chance to start over, to cleanse him- or herself of past mistakes, erroneous judgments, and deadening fears.

Much of Wood's book is taken up with a facing of her own fears (in "de Kooning's Women," "Tenderness," and "Balloons"), of a tendency to indulge in self-pity and suffering (in "The Venice Ghetto" and "Chekhov"), of being aware that she is perhaps morbidly drawn to sadness, loneliness, and loss (in "Loss," "Quattrocento," and "Last

Resort"), and of lacking the courage to endure so much grief and the consciousness that those one trusts and believes in most can disappoint (in "The Trick"). But ultimately Wood's poems consistently register the fact that she, and others she admires, "still desire / to go on living," which is "the human, / the remarkable thing" (in "Analysis of the Rose as Sentimental Despair").

Some of Wood's general claims may not ring true for all readers, as when she repeatedly uses such phrases as "we're all, aren't we, tricked in the end," "lost the way / everyone is, or will be," "Each of us wants what everyone wants." But there is no denying that much of the power and appeal of her poetry derives from her ability to speak to the disillusionments and longings that probably every reader can to some extent share with her. Often she is talking about other writers and artists and their own sufferings, struggles, and shortcomings (her depiction of Billie Holiday in "Strange Fruit" is a personal favorite), though she often begins with herself and always comes back to herself at some point in the poem, as when in the Holiday poem she says

> It's hard to say
> whether she was brave or just foolish, a girl who liked
> to get high and have a good time, an ignorant girl, really,
> who left school when she was ten, the same age I was
> when I saw her on TV, a girl who once swept floors
> in a whorehouse, even turned a few tricks. I didn't know
> anything when I sat, a child, in that warm living room
> and saw her stand stock-still and sing every pain
> she ever felt, and I don't know why I'm remembering that
> tonight, more than forty years later, almost as many years
> as she was alive.

Speaking of her friend and fellow poet William Matthews ("In Cortona, Thinking of Bill"), who died at age 55 in 1997, Wood observes that, like herself, he was afflicted by "a strain of terminal sadness. It could kill us all / in the end," and that also like herself, he "had a nose for self-pity, especially your own," just as she says of herself (in "Chekhov") that she "sounded childish and self-pitying—laughable really."

In "Last Resort," Wood speaks mostly of a stranded whale washed up apparently on the beach at Provincetown where she had been staying for a time. But in this poem she also evokes the spirit of Anne Bradford, wife of the Puritan leader William Bradford, and her drowning herself from despair when the *Mayflower* was anchored offshore. The poet says bluntly that she knows "it's courage I'm trying to find here." She finds it primarily in the right whale, which she compares to "that vast ocean of loneliness, his own kind / dying out." Her purpose in the poem, she writes, is "to understand / such sorrow, a great beached whale of sorrow / stranded in air." Parts of the conclusion have to be quoted entire:

> This is my grief. Not his.
> I know that. But what made him
>
> trust them, those other mammals, made him
> swallow his need and his fear as if faith
> were his last resort? Made him open that secret cave of a mouth
> to her, one of his rescuers, and lie still
> as a passive lover while she reached deep
> inside the darkness to untangle
> the lines from the baleens.
>
> . . . Maybe she knew then
> the world is lit from within. She saw
>
> that she could never go back
> to the ordinary afternoon, with its mild, patient blue,
> its bland sadnesses and common self-pities,
> now that she had touched such otherness.

One of the remarkable features of Susan Wood's poetry is to be found in the opening lines of each of her poems. She immediately and very naturally leads us into the dilemma or question that she is confronting. For example, "Balloons" begins with these two-line stanzas, the form in which the entire poem is cast:

> It was something I thought I'd never do,
> be cut loose like that from all the ropes
>
> of earth and float into the sky, but then
> you told me not to be afraid and so
>
> I followed you, one that I loved, my heart
> in my throat, into the balloon's small space.

Yet the best part is always still to come, as the poet maneuvers her way through so many associations between the particular object or subject and her discoveries (here) of the meaning of letting go, of trusting, of seeing life from a different, higher perspective. This is true for every poem in this fine book, which, like the volumes by Betty Adcock and R.S. Gwynn, has truly merited an award.

Wood is especially deserving of the prize for her highly accessible style and her fearless delving into her innermost thoughts, including her confession (in "Chekhov") about how she has "always chosen people who couldn't love me, whom I couldn't love. / About how much I'd hurt my children." Wood, also like Adcock and Gwynn, deserves a wider readership than most Texas poets have been accorded, and one hopes that Penguin's publication of *Asunder* will assure that her work will indeed reach all those who need her "navigable sadness. Briny, sharp, but clear-eyed."

Stan Rice's Final Message

In Geoffrey Chaucer's "The Parliament of Fowls," the poet asserts that "out of old books . . . comes all this new knowledge that men teach."* From the epic traditions of Greece and Italy, we have the age-old motif of the hero's descent into the underworld: Odysseus in Homer, Aeneas in Virgil, and Dante in his own *Inferno*. In American literature we have William Carlos Williams' *Kora in Hell* and Hart Crane's "The Tunnel" section of *The Bridge*. Dallas native Stan Rice (1942-2002), before he died at 60 of brain cancer, rang his changes on this infernal theme. Set in the French Quarter of New Orleans, the city where Rice had lived since retiring as head of the Creative Writing Department at San Francisco State University, his 15-page poem entitled "The Underworld" is perhaps the most striking piece in *Red to the Rind* (Knopf, 2002), a collection that finds the poet "singing yet" with alternating poignancy and black humor, in occasionally rhyming lines that achieve viscerally rending and tenderly surreal connections, which are his alone.

The opening stanza of the book's touchstone poem, subtitled in underlined bold type "A messenger from the underworld," harks back to the traditional summons to the nether region for purposes of penance and recovery. The image in this stanza is a telling introduction to Rice's wonderfully probing and enlightening piece: Here, the speaker receives a visit from a hummingbird, described acutely as a

> . . . hypodermic
> Between two blurs,
> Polished and honed
> By use, like a spur, come
> From the underworld.

Just prior to the necessary descent, the speaker in the poem reports from a parking lot, by means of a two-way radio, responding to "Where

---

* *The Austin Chronicle* (December 20, 2002): 33.

are you now, 10-4," and observing that

> What's happening here is definitely not life after death.
> The muscular bouncers in their mirrored sunglasses tell us that.
> Teenage girls behind velvet ropes are screaming
> And holding their heads as if to keep them from breaking in half.
> The living corpses attached to IVs in cancer wards
> Are a Marx Brothers movie compared to this scene.

He describes portable toilets having overflowed, which he compares to the after-effects of a flood:

> I assume you are familiar
> With . . . how
> After the water has receded the grass lies flattened
> And cars stand on their noses in mud
> . . . how eighteen-wheelers
> Have been bent in half by the water's force, how the curled
> Has been straightened and the straight curled,
> Well that's how it looks all the time in the parking lot
> Outside the door to the underworld, Over.

Note the biblical allusion in the curled made straight, an indication of the moral/spiritual undertone to most all the poet's writings.

Rice's shorter poems, usually much less than one page long, have their own special appeal. But his two longer poems—"The Underworld" and "Dismemberments"— represent most fully Rice's amazing range of wit and insight. Despite his awareness of the loss or remorse that never leaves one alone but returns to haunt and plunge one into self-inflicted torment, a kind of Mardi Gras Dis where

> a blue black jackal
> Guards the oval . . . resembling the trunk
> Of a car. Which is the last shape you'll see,

Rice recognized and learned to accept and sing the praises of life's paradoxes, in particular the one found in his short Edenic penal-colony poem, "Garden Doghouse," with its contradiction that lies at the very heart of his poetry: "The love that died is teaching me to love."

The Bible of a Texas Poet

What, after all, *is* a Texas poet?* Must he or she depict a West Texas sandstorm or cattle grazing in a flat, seemingly barren pasture? Or can such a messenger merely dredge up from age sixteen the time when he or she listened to the radio and it revealed to him or her "the dream of the end"? Would the simple fact that such a messenger was born and raised in Dallas qualify him or her for the label of Texas poet? I am describing the case of Stan Rice, who was born in Big D in 1942 and died on December 9th, 2002, leaving his final book, *False Prophet*, to be published posthumously in 2003 by Alfred A. Knopf, which had printed his four previous volumes: *Singing Yet: New and Selected Poems* (1992); *Fear Itself* (1995); *The Radiance of Pigs* (1999); and *Red to the Rind* (2002). Rice died in New Orleans, where he had lived with his wife Anne after they moved from San Francisco. After studying creative writing at the University of North Texas in Denton, he had moved to San Francisco in 1962 and had never returned to live in Texas, and yet references to his native state appear in every one of his Knopf books, mostly to towns and cities: Dallas in the first; Waco and Midland-Odessa in the second; Paris, Palestine, Moscow, and Athens in the third; and Fort Worth in the fourth. In *False Prophet*, which consists of 60 psalms (the same number as his age at death and beginning with "Psalm 151" where King David left off in the Bible), only one overt reference to Texas appears, when he writes in "Psalm 193" that "I was from Texas and as a result / My valuable time was no problem." But even without his naming the state or parts of it that he had known, Rice has long been one of my favorite Texas-born poets, and to me a genuine product of this godforsaken place.

In an essay entitled "The Argentine Writer and Tradition," Jorge Luis Borges notes that he had discovered in his reading of Gibbon's *Decline and Fall of the Roman Empire* "confirmation of the fact that what is truly native can and often does dispense with local color." He goes on to say that Gibbon saw the Koran as "the Arabian book *par*

---

* *Texas Books in Review* 23, nos. 3 & 4 (Fall/Winter 2004-05): 25-27.

excellence" because "there are no camels." Borges explains that since Mohammed was an Arab and knew camels as part of his reality, "he had no reason to emphasize them; on the other hand, the first thing a falsifier, a tourist, an Arab nationalist would do is have a surfeit of camels, caravans of camels, on every page." The title of Rice's book to the contrary, this poet was no falsifier, no "false prophet" who needed to identify in his native state the sources for his moral messages in order for his poetry to be categorized as Texan. Of course, it helps those like myself who are always on the lookout for Texas poets to have a little help in recognizing the origins of their poetry in the Lone Star State. But just because Rice's poems do not rely on a typical imagery of West or East Texas to develop their themes and points of view, this does not mean that his upbringing in Dallas does not account for much of his poetry's Bible-belt morality. It may not be possible to specify what is peculiar to a Texas background that would result in the surreal sermons in Rice's psalms and many of his earlier poems, but it is clear from his various books that the Bible held a central position in his thinking, as echoed in the often Old Testament ring of his prophetic lines. It is also clear that Rice saw himself as a "false prophet" because he was unworthy to judge others or to condemn their wickedness when he knew himself to have "sinned" in the same way as those he calls to task for false pride, for wanting "that promotion," for being "lovers of jobs," for being "scared of love," for being "caught / A day late with a goat head / On our shining table," for thinking "that old sock in the back yard / In a coffee can" or "a Superdome full of screaming women" "worth going to hell for," and for having "forgotten about mercy." Two lines from his poem "Of Heaven" in *Singing Yet* are emblematic: "If only I had acquired the skill of empathy. / What you take for granted will destroy you."

Rice's poem entitled "On the Murder of Martin Luther King"— later changed to "Whiteboy," the title of his second book, from 1976—was published in 1969 in the seminal anthology *Quickly Aging Here*. The third section of this poem concerns "The Texan [who] returns to the Texas State Fair and sees the source of his racism sitting in a glass cage over a tank of water." This was a typical scene at the Dallas fair into the 1960s and is rendered by Rice in terms of his own admitted racism as representative of all "whiteboys" of the day:

You can kill a nigger at last.
You can throw a baseball at the target hooked to his body.
Now you can pay him back for his sensual blackness.
You can drown him and drown him but still
he will laugh like a sleek, stupid ape,
because that's what he is.

This was moral outrage directed at the poet himself, but also at all of us who held the same type of incomprehensible racial resentment.

Rice is one of the few poets of his generation to delve deeply into the psyche of his times, and in doing so he often had in mind his growing up in Texas. In a piece entitled "The Underworld" from *Red to the Rind*, he describes the nightclub host of this poem set in the French Quarter, who looks

like a televangelist.
He looks like a rockstar at 60.
He wears a pin-striped black
Double-breasted sportcoat over
A grey athletic t-shirt with
The orange word TEXAS across
The chest and black denim pants. . . .

In exiting this underworld, the poet goes hatless (because he couldn't find one "in a pork plant in Fort Worth") to ask "the lord of mattresses . . . for a vision of experience / Befitting my ambition." As he states in a poem from *The Radiance of Pigs*, whose first line is its title, "I am only looking for things / I cannot fathom," which means that he "is cursed with ten thousand angers / And the small vision / Of what's wrong with things." Though "small," Rice's "vision" is reminiscent of the great cloud and the four-winged creatures seen by such a biblical prophet as Ezekiel. Rice says in "Psalm 195" that

. . . the saints made like you most of the time
Rise from the pillows of hell
Out of shame for their burning birthplace.

> ... The exalted see urine as it is.
> I had a good ear for wings.

In a poem like "Doing Being" from *The Radiance of Pigs* (which is divided into three sections: "Childhood," "Hades," and "Resurrection"), he cites lines from Job, giving in parentheses chapter and verse (4:15), and later in this twelve-page poem, after observing that "Jesus / Cracketh no jokes," he provides a "vision" of his staring

> ... down into the empty
> Washing machine, so clean,
> Its paddles as smooth as a photo.
> This, also, sits at the right hand of God.

Having read such earlier "moralistic" poems, I found it only somewhat of a surprise to discover that Rice's final book was a collection of psalms.

Not that the Bible is Rice's only source—far from it. His work reveals that his reading was wide-ranging, including in particular Greek tragedy, which figures significantly in a poem like "The Proud One" that parallels his own life with that of "the proud boy" Pentheus in Euripides' *The Bacchae*. A similar situation is described in "The Punishment" from *The Radiance of Pigs*, where the poet asks "Will I be punished for having written 'Ignore Thyself' / In a reversal of the Socratic dictum" and

> Will my vanity and lack of empathy haunt
> My old age as my obsession with sensual pleasure
> Haunted my youth; will I be punished
> For my constant presumption of innocence
> Even though I can see my guilt clearly
> In the way I walk ... past the hidden
> Video camera ... in Sears?

But it is in *False Prophet* that Rice shows his truest colors, for ironically—though Rice's "Psalm 208" asserts that "In prophecy nothing is irony"—the book recalls the admonition of Jesus that "false prophets will appear and produce signs and omens, to lead astray, if possible, the elect. But be alert; I have already told you everything" (Mark 13:21-23). And once again, Rice's moral indignation is directed first at himself ("I can only / Speak for myself") but also at all of us who will recognize in his lines that

> . . . we can nail one hand
> To the altar
> Then go forth in the willingness
> To be comfortable
> And liked.

This Texas poet is a type of Ezekiel who realizes that he will be held accountable if he does not give warning to the wicked man, "to save his life," for if "the same wicked man shall die in his iniquity . . . his blood will I require at thine hand" (3:18). Ezekiel goes on to quote the Lord as saying that if he, Ezekiel, warns the wicked man but he does not turn from his wickedness, "he shall die in his iniquity; but thou hast delivered thy soul." Rice offers something similar in his "Psalm 154" (NB: Rice at times eliminates apostrophes):

> Im burdened for you.
> . . . Day after day
> You must pay the bills, but until you do that
> You have been told.
> Families have perished, have turned
> And burned. Yet you have not heard
> The soft-soap of flesh in the message.
> Hell wont be hot enough to roast the both of us.
> . . . Death wont
> Wear off like aftershave.

The sound of Rice's psalms certainly echoes those of King David, in wording if not exactly in meaning. For example, in "Psalm 191" Rice writes "Surely / Something wants to discourage me / From intimacy," which may remind one of "Surely goodness and mercy" from the famous Psalm 23, at least if it is added to the lines in Rice's

"Psalm 192" that seem even more clearly to paraphrase King David when the Texan writes "Still waters / Submit to abuse." Yet here the meaning is probably the opposite, since Rice finds no "green pastures" to lie down in or "still waters" to be led beside, and certainly he does not seem to delude himself into thinking that he "will dwell in the house of the Lord forever." Instead, as he reports in "Psalm 197":

> Showers call to our house
> To have mercy. . . . If you pray
> Mercy will flower from silver,
> And gold from the glove.
> I have tried other patterns
> And blamed the cheeseburger's blood
> But my wonder came due
> When I was washed of time.
> Deception turned to me
> In my desire and fainted
> In the harvest. The laborers
> Had compassion on me
> And listened carefully
> To my message. After which
> I lost my job. . . .

Rather than repeating, Rice's psalms are an updating of the biblical versions, as perhaps is evident in these lines from his "Psalm 198": "Save me from the wrath of love. / Touch me each day with the sword of / The egg, of the dishwasher, of the authentic. / Selah." Other biblical parallels include such "modern" lines as these: "The invisible man is straining to get through the knot hole"; "Rise and walk through the principles"; "The voice lies down beside you"; "A log falls from my eye, a lion from each ear"; "I remember mercy in my praise of the chain"; "I stared at my darling over the pillow / At morning. The Lord was with me"; "Lord, why do you / Keep me on the phone until / I am deaf";

> I am as anointed as a fish in the waters.
> My yoke is destroyed.
> My burden must slip from the oil.

Here is the parable.
I cant just take this suit off and live in rags and dig ditches.

Rice's impending death obviously moved him to sing his "broken-down songs in the hell of the hour" when "the spiritual side / Prepares for the end of time." Even though he declares that "Suddenly all prophecies are vile," still, in remembering his youth in Texas (as he does in "A Boy's Satan" from *Fear Itself*), Rice recalls listening to radio prophets by short-wave and of repenting as he listened, "embarrassed by war," of being

held over hell and shaken.
. . . After the changing I nonetheless
Rushed into life. I pondered my cursing.
It lasted for about four days. Then I was 16.
I was up in the radio room.
As I am while alive to inform you.

In his final days Stan Rice continued to "inform" us in his witty, contemporary, prophetic voice full of a biblical but straightforward intoning of our shortcomings, or as he phrases in "Psalm 152" one of his/our failings (which include not seeing "the miraculous because we need / Props"): "This is the dollar I am short." Paradoxical as Rice frequently is, he can also say "I / Am better off not having / Lived in the age of / Miracles for I can / Believe in them." As he had always done in his several volumes of memorable, serio-comic poems, Rice combined for the last time his black humor and tragic vision in this moving collection of psalms in which "the prophecies meet and are sealed in the ink."

Prowling the Same Old Haunts

Since the appearance in 1976 of Walt McDonald's *Caliban in Blue*, published by Texas Tech University Press, this publisher has promoted the work of Lubbock's native, nationally-known poet and now retired Tech professor, issuing some half-dozen collections of his writings.* In 2002 the Press published a collection of essays by writers from across the nation in celebration of McDonald's poetry, a volume entitled *The Waltz He Was Born For*, after the title of one of his poems. But the Press has outdone itself with the spectacular color-illustrated *Great Lonely Places of the Texas Plains*, a book of McDonald's poems paired with facing photos by Wyman Meinzer, the official photographer of the State of Texas.

The pairing of poem and photo is not a novel idea. In 1989, Texas Christian University psychology professor and photographer Richard Fenker, Jr., teamed up with East Texas poet Sandra Lynn for their own volume of poems and photos, *Where Rainbows Wait For Rain: The Big Bend Country*. Although Lynn's descriptions of such scenes as a moonrise over Alamo Creek and a morning in Laguna Meadow are matched by Fenker's black-and-white photos of these same Big Bend sites, and the photographer offers as well an almost epic shot of storm clouds over a lone windmill at Chinati Peak, their combination of poems and photos cannot compare with the drama of *Great Lonely Places of the Texas Plains*. This is partly because Meinzer's photographic compositions are so breathtaking in their rendering of the surprisingly rich palette and the naturally-aesthetic contrasts of the Texas Plains, but also because McDonald's poems capture in words the same juxtapositions of the stark and vivid, not only of the landscape but in the mindset of a West Texas life. Some people see the flatness of the Plains and become depressed, but McDonald and Meinzer seem never to have tired of "prowl[ing] the same / old haunts," and in doing so have revealed the depths of beauty and insight in the simplest West Texas scene.

---

* *The Texas Observer* (April 23, 2004): 25-25, 27.

In a poem entitled "Bowing to Skies in a Hat," which involves memories of the Vietnam War and of old vets now in boots and Stetsons who "wait / by the windmill grinding its clatter," McDonald says that they and he are "killing nothing / but time, riding home to our wives after dark." The facing photo of a half-moon yellow against the horizon, next to a solitary windmill, and with a sky full of clouds tinted an autumn orange, reflects perfectly the poem's evening setting when such men have grown "calm" and "mellow / after steaks and biscuits, ready to patch barbed wires // and brand, to break strange colts with words, / *easy, easy.*" Contrary to what the poet says, he has certainly not been killing time, for poems like this piece of penetrating sound and sight have been flowing from his pen or through his computer keyboard for decades, until today he has amassed a publication record of twenty books of poetry, many the winners of prestigious prizes in and outside the state.

At first it may not be clear how the photos in *Great Lonely Places of the Texas Plains* relate to the writing, but there is always some parallel between the two. In "The Waltz He Was Born For," McDonald says that

> What matters
> is timeless, dazzling devotion—not rain,
> not Eden gardenias, but cactus in drought,
> not just moons of deep sleep, not sunlight or stars,
> not the blue, but the darkness beyond.

The photo illustrates such thoughts through its depiction of a stone monument "of unknown origin" in Foard County and through the bluish, violet, pinkish evening sky and the suggestion both of something "timeless" and of "the darkness beyond." The source of each photo is supplied at the back of the book, which allows the reader to try to discover the connections between poem and photo before searching out the exact location of a Meinzer image.

Perhaps my favorite complementary pairing of poem and photo comes with the opening selection of the third section, subtitled "Prairie Was a Tableland of Praise." Here McDonald's poem concerns, as the title declares, "Finding My Father's Hands in Midlife." The facing photo does not picture the hands of the poet's own father, but rather the father of the photographer wearing his Stetson hat and orange-yellow cowboy shirt with pearl buttons, his creased, sunny skin and slightly watering, piercing eyes, and a rope hanging on the wall behind him. This is a classic photo, and although not a one-for-one illustration of the poem's portrait, it mirrors it somehwat in its western motifs:

> I see his blood in veins here
> and here, like dry Texas streams
> that flow and disappear in limestone.
>
> When I make a fist, I see his
> half-moon thumb fold over four
> tight fingers, a picture of family,
>
> that big thigh-muscle shank
> of his thumb something we closed on,
> muscle we loved.

The title of this entire volume derives from a line—"great lonely placcs of the Plains"—in a poem whose own title is taken from a traditional cowboy song, "Home on the Range." Just as McDonald has "prowled" the same old Plains landscape, he also has revisited in a number of poems the lines of this famous song, with one of his books entitled after the line "Where skies are not cloudy." One poem of his that I have long admired is entitled after part of another line in this song, "Where seldom is heard," which concerns not "a discouraging word" but the idea that on the Plains sounds are "seldom heard" because they are so soft or subtle, as suggested in *Great Lonely Places* by the "deep bumps" of a horse's heart and rattlesnakes that can "hear the skin of cactus stretch / and squeak like leather."

In "Home on the Range," we find the poet and his wife in the front porch swing (a frequent scene in the book), rocking as he watches

> the moonlight in her eyes, the haze
> of silver in her hair. Windmills whir the same

old songs, roar of tires on the highway,
headlights of neighbors coming home.

McDonald repeatedly discovers connections between the local and other worlds, as here with the sound of the windmill and the allusion to an "old song" like "Home on the Range." Meanwhile, the haunting sunset photo on the facing page contains an empty highway reflecting the moonlight, with cloud formations once again a natural work of art captured by Meinzer's camera.

Oftentimes the photographer's cloudscapes remind me of abstract paintings, especially the one that accompanies "Let Thunder Rattle the Glass." Here again is a characteristic sound to be heard on the Plains, and a welcome one too, since, as the poem says, "Call the bank, / even that cautious banker's awake, / enough rain to plant sorghum." This poem also paints a typical scene in which "Lightning gashes the night / like lake ice shattered," just as the facing photo displays a lightning crack straight down from the top of the frame to the black horizon, with above it layers of orange-yellow sky and dark, threatening clouds whose thunder, as the poem has it, "bashes" husband and wife "both to silence / beside the blinds raised high." Meinzer's compositional artistry can especially be seen at work in the image paired with "Under Blue Skies"—a foreground of green and yellow wildflowers with cactus in between, and the layers of reddish sandstone of a triangular rise against a pure blue sky. Another magnificent composition faces the poem entitled "Two Years After World War II," with Meinzer's image of green and white wildflowers, shocks of dead straw-like shoots, and angular sandstone buttes jutting into a brewing storm. The eye of the photographer has once again revealed the natural art of the Plains, just as in the poem on a wedding of two veterans "Uncle Carl / lifted her veil with his only hand // and saw how beautiful a marine could be."

The variety of settings and scenery in this book is greater than a short review can hope to suggest, but it should be noted that even though the poetry focuses on a limited number of situations and scenes, it still manages to convey a wide range of images and emotions, as does Meinzer's photography. Taken together, the two media broaden the book's theme of the ironic vastness of a "lonely," seemingly desolate place, causing the reader/viewer to discover unsuspected significance in the work of poet and photographer. In the poetry, religious motifs abound, in the title "Windmills Like Cathedral Windows," in references to prayer, Quakers, faith, and God, and in such lines as these on

> Windmills
> spinning on massive posts,
> foursquare gospel of water power
>
> bolted to hold the blades
> and rudders, to aim the ranch
> toward God's almighty gales,
> to face whatever blows.

There are also repeated allusions to time and its effects (imagery of rusting machinery, paintless houses falling down, granite turning to sand); an emphasis on the importance of home and family ("Prairie never lets us / forget we live on a hill called here"); and perhaps above all the revelation of the endless reward of looking closely at the Plains landscape. Each poem contributes, in conjunction with the photographic imagery, to the making of this volume more than a coffee-table book—though it can serve that end as well, since it is so deliciously gorgeous to look at. But in reading the poetry alongside the photography, one comes to an awareness of the spiritual in West Texas life, as seen through the eyes of these two master artists, to a profundity that is far from a mere luxurious publication meant to impress.

The poetry in *Great Lonely Places* most often presents a realistic view of the red-in-tooth-and-claw existence of a habitat where buzzards' "whirling funnel of wings" wheels "a slow blessing / of flesh" and a mouse squeals "when an owl grabs it and flaps away." But there is humor as well, as in "The Perks of Being a Greenhorn," which describes high school girls enamored of horses and a neophyte cowboy. The poems also lovingly portray the habits of Plains people, as they drink coffee, smoke (or not: "I kicked the habit / four years ago after the last grassfire / some trucker started"), rock in the porch swing, or care for their animals ("the oldest mare on the Plains, / drools when I rub her ear . . . slobbering oats from my glove"). Always both McDonald and Meinzer clearly revel in the close observation of the little (or much) the environment has to offer. As the poet says and the photographer illustrates, they are never "alone, here with dry wind to amaze," watching as the "bluebonnets / and Indian blankets dazzle the roadside" and "windmills . . . spin their rapture."

Houston's Panamanian Poet

Lorenzo Thomas was born in Panama in 1944, grew up in New York City where he was active in what became the Black Arts Movement, and served in Vietnam before moving to Houston in 1973.* His first collection of poetry, *Chances Are Few*, appeared in 1980, and his fourth, *Dancing on Main Street*, was published by Coffee House Press in 2004. Thomas is a thinking-man's writer. His critical studies of folklore, Modernism, and music are substantial works, and in both prose and poetry he always addresses the difficult issues. In "God Sends Love Disguised as Ordinary People," he asserts that

> We never quite could tell
> strength from stupidity
> Pride in perseverance
> The point where stubbornness
> Purchased a harvest of futility

In a prose passage, he is as concise, cutting, and full of telling sound as in his poetry: "For a population addicted to entertainment, demented leaders have invented real war presented as games." Laced with unusual metaphors ("Mocking as sunrise / To insomniacs"), jazzy language ("It's tough being enough"), and with witty love talk ("Still / If we have nothing left / But carnal beauty // Well, I can live with that"), Thomas's book is more than the sum of its varied parts, since certain poems rise above even the best of his jivey, swinging pieces. "Dirge for Amadou Diallo" is a masterful elegy developed from a simple but poignant opening: "It is hard to have your son die / In a distant land." Here Thomas asks questions with no satisfactory or justifiable answers, but along the way offers his unabashed moral philosophy:

> We'd understand
> If someone said he was,

---

* *The Austin Chronicle* (December 31, 2004): 33.

This son, a prodigal:

> The kind of man who desperately
> Needs the vise of suffering
> And hurt and desolation
> Some eccentricity to hold him firm
> To help him shape his heart
> Into an instrument of praise

Repeatedly Thomas calls into question our so-called values, as in "Dangerous Doubts," where he declares

> That maybe exercise shows on TV
> Are really harmful
> That sound bodies just
> Amplify our empty minds

Thomas's poetry brims with "dangerous" thoughts, expressed in phrases and images that are his alone. His latest book will satisfy discriminating readers long after the run-of-the-mill type has been quickly and rightly forgotten.

A Galaxy of Luminous Lines

In *Walter Benjamin at the Dairy Queen*, novelist Larry McMurtry has written that early in his career as a "book scout" he judged seriousness in all things, especially authors and their books, by comparing them to his father's "attitude toward cattle."* McMurtry found that Ezra Pound's *ABC of Reading* impressed him when he first came across it because the poet clearly took his subject as seriously as his father did his cows. Walt McDonald has for over thirty years been dead serious about his poetry, producing by the latest count twenty-one books. Many of his poems are about cattle, including "Hammering Ice to Slush," with its line from which his new collection, *A Thousand Miles of Stars* (Texas Tech University Press, 2004), takes its title. This poem revisits a view of cattle as being unperturbed by drought or harsh weather, a theme that the Lubbock poet has often crafted into vivid, rhythmic lines:

> Cattle wait out the storm in windbreaks
> far from barns. They know when it's over
> we'll drive out on tractors, hauling hay
> and hard alfalfa pellets. They fear no evil,
> since every dawn we come and hammer ice to slush.

In addition to alluding at times to the Bible, McDonald knows both how to start a poem and how to end it. In this new collection, one of many examples of a felicitous McDonald beginning and ending is found in the poem entitled "In Arnold Schwend's Saloon," which opens with a line that concisely and musically sets the scene: "Plant me down by long-armed soda taps." The ending of the poem is absolutely right-on, its subtle off-rhyme combining with the final description of the Colorado bar's pin-up girl to complete the picture with a perfect, voluptuous touch:

---

* *Texas Books in Review* 24, no. 4 (Winter 2004-05): 20-21.

moose heads and mirror,
spittoons, the Rockies' maja with ribboned wrists
behind her neck, those pink and naughty lips.

The range of McDonald's subjects may be somewhat narrow (the most common topics being the Llano Estacado landscape of West Texas, memories of the Vietnam War, and flying), but even within these perhaps seemingly limited spheres his imagination has managed to encompass a wide variety of scenes and situations. In this new book, the poet devotes most of one section to the North Carolina coast, wherein he describes "a mollusk / carved like scrimshaw," but also alludes to the state's historic connections to flight:

Grandfather fished for flounder, croaker, drum,
his beachfront house no bigger than the shack
the Wright boys hung their hammocks in at Kitty Hawk.
Grandmother heard a clatter of pistons, but guessed
it was only their glider crashing again and didn't watch.

There are also many poems depicting the aging process and the enduring love between a speaker and his wife (named Ursula in poems that trace their life together from their first date up to their holding hands at seventy). Related to the aging-love theme in this collection and in most of the poet's other books is family, with references here to a pilot son stationed in Bosnia, cousins, uncles, aunts, in-laws, father, mother, grandfather and grandmother (as in the poem on Kitty Hawk), and grandchildren. A disclaimer in the book declares that "every poem" in the book is fiction, "freely invented . . . from Walt's imagination," and that "any similarities between the real lives of any persons living or dead are unintended and coincidental."

Whether fictional or autobiographical, every McDonald poem is significantly unified by a thematic thread or an analogical image pattern, as in the case of "A Little Night Music," which concerns Mozart and the flight of birds. Here musical analogies abound, as the composer is imagined to have

detected melodies heard from bats,

heard wings in that dimension,
harmonies odd but clear as bird songs
in his ears.

McDonald's poetry exhibits an uncanny ability to take any subject and weave a spellbinding narrative around it, building up each stanza with the same number of lines (most often three, four, five, or six), through which his voice works its metaphorical way relentlessly to a very natural, convincing, satisfying conclusion. A fine instance of this is another poem related to music and flying, "Jukebox Nights in Georgia," where the young pilots-in-training practice with their hands: "the left, the bad guy; us, the right hand / banking to shoot him down." After having danced at night to Johnny Mathis who "swore / we'd love until the twelfth of never" and to "country-and-western words" full of "rhymed honey for the heart," the speaker recalls those who died in war, contrasting this later fact with that time in Georgia when "war seemed distant as the twelfth / of never, our wings only weeks away." Note the natural but strongly rhythmic alliteration—another of the poet's literary devices that helps make his lines both musical and illuminating.

Frequently in this latest collection, McDonald connects an immediate subject, like composting, with his constant awareness of growing older. The aural and descriptive power of "October Compost" appears especially in lines like these:

Now let the dark pot boil, autumn sun

turned down, continual simmer
into December, nights chilly enough
for fire,

with that last image serving as a transition to the poem's concluding image of the aging couple:

On the sofa,
we lean and hold each other's hands

and watch flames leap and flicker.

Logs in the hearth break apart by midnight,
orange embers holding heat like fists.

In "Leaving the Middle Years," the speaker and his wife had been recalling the death of Franklin Roosevelt in 1945 and suddenly realized
that they were now "*exactly*" that President's age when he died: "That
night, we held hands a little longer, / in the dark, with the TV off."
Once again, the poet achieves just the right combination of image and
sound to finish the poem, even as he unites past and present in making
his momentous comparison.

Within McDonald's theme of flying, which he has mined ever
since *Caliban in Blue*, his first collection from 1976, and continuing up
to this volume of 2004, there are several poems that bring together the
quite different, dramatically contrastive worlds of games and wars. In
"Too Far from Town to Play Baseball," the speaker remembers softball
games that pilots played in Vietnam against the Air Police, who "hated
wimps . . . who flew" and "packed no weapons / but ordnance other
enlisted loaded." A reference to the Ho Chi Minh Trail, "no wider
than a baseball diamond, cargo / always moving down from Hanoi
docks," ties the game to the war in an ironic juxtaposition that involves
the observation that both sides in the game (and by extension the war)
"hated to lose." Prior to the Vietnam War, the speaker in the poem
entitled "Practice During the Cuban Missile Crisis" reports on having
observed from an Air Force jet as the Green Bay Packers practiced in
Wisconsin snow:

We were boys who'd never been to war,
but dots below us were men, x's and o's on a gridiron
like a battlefield.

The speaker goes on to link once again the two different times, past
and future:

That month, we didn't know there'd be Super Bowls
someday, didn't know if there'd be another game,
if today was our last flight before missiles.

Here game and war are paired in a relationship that enables the poet to illustrate so tellingly his poignant point that for those participating in war it can end all games, that the loss can mean more than just defeat. Along with such an ironic linkage in this new book there are numerous allusions to the Vietnam Veterans Memorial Wall in Washington, D.C. (depicted on the dust jacket of the poet's 1995 *Counting Survivors*), which in touching with his own hand evokes for the speaker his fallen comrades in arms. In poem after poem McDonald returns to the lasting effect on one's life that a wartime experience can have. The title of one poem concisely states the case: "War Never Stops Even When All Vets Are Dead." This realization surely makes McDonald a major poet of the Vietnam era.

Along with the topics and themes of McDonald's writing, it is the longevity of his career as a prodigious poet that continues to amaze. But it is not just the more than 2,300 poems that he has published that impress by their sheer number but the fact that each poem begins with a gripping first line that instills in the reader a need to know where it is going and then closes with a line that leaves him or her feeling that everything in the poem has come to a head, to a fulfillment of the initial claim or declaration. That this poet has been able to start hundreds of poems so inspiringly and to follow them to their closures so convincingly is truly a marvel. His use of language carries one along irresistibly, naturally, happily to revelation after revelation. In many ways, the title of this latest collection sums up the now overall achievement of Walt McDonald's observant work as "a thousand miles of stars."

A Religious Texas Poet

It has now been thirty years since the appearance of Walt McDonald's first collection of poetry, *Caliban in Blue*, issued by Texas Tech Press in 1976.* Since that time he has, by my count, seen the publication of twenty-one more volumes of his poems, including the most recent, *Faith Is a Radical Master*, published in 2005 by Abilene Christian University Press; the other twenty titles are: *One Thing Leads to Another* (1978); *Anything, Anything* (1980); *Burning the Fence* (1981); *Working Against Time* (1981); *Witching on Hard Scrabble* (1985); *The Flying Dutchman* (1987); *Rafting the Brazos* (1988); *After the Noise of Saigon* (1988); *Splitting Wood For Winter* (1988); *Night Landings* (1989); *The Digs in Escondido Canyon* (1991); *All That Matters: The Texas Plains in Photographs and Poems* (1992); *Where Skies Are Not Cloudy* (1993); *Counting Survivors* (1995); *Blessings the Body Gave* (1998); *Whatever the Wind Delivers* (1999); *All Occasions* (2000); *Great Lonely Places of the Texas Plains* (2003); *Climbing the Divide* (2003); and *A Thousand Miles of Stars* (2004). The titles themselves reveal three of McDonald's pervasive themes: the Texas Plains, the Vietnam War, and flying; yet his latest title, *Faith Is a Radical Master*, is the first to call attention to the fact that the poet has spoken at times of his religious convictions, even though *All Occasions* can reveal this as well, once the reader recognizes that this two-word title derives from a sermon by John Donne. While McDonald's various volumes frequently contain lines that allude to the Bible, not until this latest collection has the central focus been placed on his Christian faith. However, this is not a shift in emphasis, since this New and Selected Poems presents many pieces already familiar to his readers; nevertheless, the book has gathered the poems into sections that make one more fully aware of their religious implications. In addition, commentaries by the poet at the back of this new collection underscore the spiritual aspect of a number of the poems reprinted from his earlier books.

---

* *Texas Books in Review* 25, nos. 3 & 4 (Fall/Winter 2005-06): 17-18.

In McDonald's poetry, retellings of biblical stories abound; titles of poems refer oftentimes to biblical characters or events; and in *Faith Is a Radical Master*, epigraphs that introduce the book's five sections are drawn from a hymn, Psalms, the book of Acts, and religious poems by Catholic poet Gerard Manley Hopkins. On rereading "Sleeping With the Enemy," from section two, subtitled "For God in My Sorrows" (a poem title as well), I did not remember having read this war poem previously, but the last two lines with their "holy bush / still burning" reminded me of McDonald's "The Food Pickers of Saigon" from his *After the Noise of Saigon*, which also evokes the image of the unconsumed burning bush in Exodus 3:2. I noticed that "Sleeping With the Enemy," unlike most of the poet's work, is in rhymed stanzas, and out of curiosity I looked at the credits to see in which magazine it had originally appeared. (McDonald's books have from the first listed magazine credits, which must number hundreds of different periodicals, from *Poetry*, *The Atlantic*, *New York Review of Books*, and *Kenyon Review* to *Christian Century*, *Presbyterian Record* [Canada], and *JAMA: The Journal of the American Medical Association*.) To my surprise, "Sleeping With the Enemy" was not printed in a magazine, but in looking back through his books I found that it had been included in his *Blessings the Body Gave*. Locating the poem in that collection, I discovered that in reviewing the volume in 1999 for *The Texas Observer* I had made marginal notes to myself, observing the poem's rhyme scheme and comparing it to "The Food Pickers of Saigon." The point is that McDonald's output has been so voluminous that only with *Faith Is a Radical Master* does a reader of the poet's work begin to notice the larger pattern of religious thought present in his many books.

With some 2500 poems published over McDonald's career, it is difficult to recall every poem and every allusion, even though on any given day I will find myself remembering a particular favorite. It is easy enough to forget in which collection a specific line appeared, since he has reworked certain images and themes, though without his ever quite repeating himself. This is true of "Sleeping With the Enemy," which concerns the poet's recurring middle-of-the-night memories of his tour in Vietnam that become confused in his mind with sights, sounds, and biblical scenes he experiences once back home in Texas. In this poem, he relates the hard epoxy used for termite holes in his house with the body armor he wore; and he associates the burning bush passage from Exodus with "the fire I took" during combat. In another poem on this same theme, "What If I Didn't Die Outside Saigon," he imagines himself a wounded soldier appealing to a medic for his life. Again the poet awakes in his bed at home to find that he has been dreaming and that everything the soldier on a stretcher with a *"Killed-in-Action* tag" on his chest had asked for in the dream has come to pass: the room is filled with pictures of the children he hoped to have and "a woman a little like my wife / but twice her age, still sleeping in my bed." Another poem that reworks a frequent theme is "Wishing For More Than Thunder," which echoes his "Wind and Hard Scrabble," included in *All That Matters*. Both poems find that cattle do not wonder if "God's in his heaven," but are satisfied so long as the grass grows or the fodder supply lasts; for them alfalfa is paradise. But in the last section of McDonald's new collection, he himself is thinking more of life after death, which gives rise to a poem like "The Dark, Hollow Halo of Space." Here there is not so much a metaphorical allusion to a biblical passage as a more direct address to God, the speaker's

> Rock of all, my marble, stone
> of my tomb and my stairs. More firm
> than granite in mountains, you are older
> than immortal diamond and gold.

This poem reminded me of Puritan poet Edward Taylor, who ends each of his more than two hundred Meditations by appealing to God to save him, in return for which he will sing his praises, as he does in each of his poems based on a passage from Holy Scripture.

"Praise" is a word that often appears in McDonald's poetry, as in his poem of that title. This particular piece is a kind of doxology, in which the poet entreats himself (and the reader) to "Praise God who made . . . water tumbling down from snow, / the tap I'll turn today," to "Praise God / for sleep, for grizzlies / wild in the mountains, massive," for "breath / that puffs away," and "for my wife's eyes / I need to open once more, soon." Words like praise, blessing, grace, and mercy pepper many of McDonald's poems and/or poem titles. Two poems that share the same title, "All the Old Songs," differ greatly, partly because the one collected in this new volume retells an episode that appears in his poem entitled "Rembrandt and the Art of Mercy." The poet also refers to popular songs, like the one that declares "I'll be loving you, always," which points up his theme of loss, "everyone's theme / after Eden." The desire for "always" is developed by the poet by recalling once again the tale of Rembrandt's wife Saskia, whom he "caught / on canvas, but couldn't save." The phrase "After Eden" also serves as the title of another poem, but this time in reference to a cow enjoying its "last meal / before the slaughterhouse." The speaker in the poem, "a death angel," has come to drive the cow to the truck backed up to a loading ramp, and like the prairie dog that a rattlesnake slithers after down its hole, there is nothing he "can do to save" it. McDonald does not preach salvation in his religious poems but rather gives thanks, "praising," as he says in "Sunday Morning Roundup," "each crumbling step of shale – oil rich / if I could afford to drill it." In this poem, the "virtue" involves killing on Sunday–while "godly men" are in church–a cougar that believes "spring calves / are born to feed" her. McDonald is not unrealistic in his religious poetry, and yet always he finds it possible to be grateful for everything in life, even the fact that man at times may serve as an angel of death.

On a lighter note, McDonald is capable of wry humor, as in two of his poems on dogs. In his commentary at the back of the book, he furnishes a bit of background information on his poem entitled "Baptizing the Dog at Nine." Here he summons up the "neighborhood bully who scoffed" when someone buried his pet and asserted that dogs don't have souls, that once "Rover dies, he's dead all over." The desire to keep a dog forever is, as the poet says, the dumb wish of any kid, and the desire to save his own dog by almost drowning him in the act of baptism captures the comedy of such youthful religiosity. In "Boys with Chihuahua Dogs," the poet offers up the same theme of dogs without souls, but here the situation concerns the trouble soulless dogs cause when they are sneaked into Sunday church:

> Once
> they scampered like devils down aisles

while the preacher convinced us all
we were starving for mercy, choking back laughter,
dying for benediction.

More often, McDonald combines "Living on Open Plains," as one of his typical titles has it, with a religious point of view. He ends this short piece with an image of spring "storms without clouds" and sand like "our own souls // harrowed and seedless, / waiting to be given wings." As in so many of his poems, the Vietnam War returns to lend spiritual insight; in "Billions of Stars to Wish On," the war helps develop his theme of the difficulty of, but need for, belief. Referring to the constellations observed while zipped up in "twin sleeping bags // before Saigon," the speaker recalls how

We counted myths made up by others
like us, needing to believe in something,
projecting filaments like spiders

spinning tales to turn stark fear to faith.
Somehow we survived that war
and raised our share of children

who've moved away.

At this point in the poem, his wife turns to him in bed and asks him to hold her, "although I have no answers." McDonald's poems do not attempt to provide any answer to "the one unanswered question, millions / of light years back toward beginnings, // before myth." Instead, he speaks for his wife and himself when he announces simply that "We say whatever is, / we'll accept."

One of the most touching poems in this new collection is entitled "Bargaining With God," which was written, as an epigraph indicates, on the death of a granddaughter. Comparing himself to Cain in his rage, Job in his loss, and "Jeremiah in tears," he asks God to "Take me / instead of my darlings," "Take the ranch / and bank account, the mountain cabin, / but save our granddaughter now," "heal this little child now." The poem concludes: "if not today, tomorrow, / good God, soon." Even without the response to his prayer that he wished for, McDonald does not grumble. Relatedly, with regard to children, the epigraph taken from Acts 17:28 for section three of *Faith Is a Radical Master* demonstrates not only McDonald's thorough knowledge of the Bible but its meaning to him as writer and man of religion: "As some of your poets have said, 'We are his children'." In his prose commentary on "Sunday Morning Roundup," the poet speaks of his pleasure in writing as both discovery and play, and justifies his fooling around with words by finding biblical approval: "Accepting whatever comes has been the best thing for me, as a writer. I go back to the book for assurance that writing is all right. . . . 'Whatever your hand finds to do,' Solomon wrote, 'do it with all your might' (Eccl. 9:10)." Walt McDonald's many volumes of moving and artfully crafted poems stand as a remarkable witness to his having abided by that Old Testament injunction, for which we can all render him our endless thanks and praise.

Clowning Around With Junk Mail

In Richard Sale's new collection of poems, *Freeze & Thaw*, he refers to himself as having gotten, "with the stretching of the years," the reputation "if not of wit, at least of clown."* As a Texas poet, Sale has certainly played the fool for quite a while, and his uncommon humor (especially unusual among the state's poets) has grown ever more impressive and salutary. Although as an English professor he retired from the University of North Texas a number of years ago, he has kept active instructing us through his creative wit, turning out poems that address rather wide-ranging subjects and concepts, mostly satirical in tone and intent. He often takes aim at our over-inflated egos and ambitions, but as Sale himself says in this new volume, he is the "self-aware narrator" in his own story and has now become the one satirized, the one who is "outside the narrative loop, outside / the corral of criticism, out into the meta- / range we used to call the psychological." But despite his seemingly critical self-image as a clown and writer who all his life has "drawn blanks on the simplest of words" and makes "jokes" out of a "frigid" language, Sale employs his poetry as an "unguent" for curing serious wounds suffered in war and the loss of a son to AIDS, and also to keep those of us born north of Mexico from having our "Soul . . . siphoned off before we even know it's there. . . . / Sucking the absence of [our] thumbs" while we go on being "out of joint with the lay of the land."

Like most light verse, Richard Sale's witty poems present a comic view of life, frequently of his own career as a college prof. This is true, for example, of "The Day I Was Bucked Off the Horse and Broke My Hand." After being thrown, he is asked by a farrier what he really does for a living, since the blacksmith does not believe the speaker's claims that, first, he is a farmer and then a horse breaker. Finally, the thrown one "almost" comes "clean" when he says that he teaches "philosophy," to which the farrier responds: "That figures. Casey Tibbs couldn't a-stayed / up on that horse with stirrups that high."

---

* *The Texas Observer* (May 19, 2006): 26-27.

Sale's book also includes poems that reveal his erudite reading of medieval philosopher William of Ockham, while others are based on the Sumerian epic of *Gilgamesh* and the Chinese *Book of Songs*. From the latter we find in Sale's rhymed version this universal expression of the struggle to understand a state of overwhelming sorrow:

> In my grief what can I do?
> What is my crime against heaven?
> I am sad as if beset with a sickness.
> The road to Chou is level and even,
>
> But overgrown with brush and weeds.

A humorous treatment of Oriental literature appears in his "Generic Haiku," which refers to the classical form of 17 syllables and its traditional content: "5 / 7 / 5 / (But always mention the seasons!)." The poet also provides an example of a "straight" haiku: "Four moths on a twig, / Maybe late fall hatchlings? No, / Four pairs of brown leaves." As the title of one poem has it, the poet is "In Training," getting a

> notion of the universe
> . . . learning to leave that anxious
> mirror-man out of the game,
> an apprenticeship in reality,
> and vision, and illusion,
> all three good words to me these days.

As a professor, Sale learned the hard lesson that comes from seeing one's students do well–even worse, better than their teacher:

> those who apprenticed
> to you . . . turn out to be journeymen and more,
> taking braver steps than you had balls
> and brains to take. It produces
> pride with a dash of humility. Pride
> with a dash of envy.

One question that occurs throughout *Freeze & Thaw* is what and how much one should wish for, which is not a "lite" consideration. In "Redundancy," Sale speaks of things he does and does not want:

> I don't want Reason, don't want
> even one reason, not even ten
> good reasons. Want a heap
> of hypotheses and then some.
> . . . Don't want it all made clear to me
> when I have (Hoo, Lord!)
> crossed the bar.

If here and elsewhere allusions to medieval philosophy and Victorian literature crop up from time to time, along with a bucking horse or "the tail end of a Texas August," the poem entitled "Vibrating Crystal" evokes a more "postmodern" image as it pokes fun at a typical can't-do-without offer that comes in the mail uninvited and highly presumptuous. In this "found poem" that reports the terms of the offer, Sale explodes the notion that we need more than we already have. Not only does the offer include the speaker's own "one-hundred-dollar / Four-Million-Year-Old / Vibrating Crystal," which has been "gemologically classified and / is a power stone treasure" and is being held for him in the Company's "Security and Safekeeping Div. / in Safe Deposit Vault #565 / under [his] personal registration file 37A," but he will receive in addition, just for the $19 he's to send for covering "shipping, jewelry handling, / insurance, and certification processing," a free "special edition of / *Crystal Power News* which tells [him] how . . . / to gain money, love, and happiness." After finishing with his account of the contents of the offer, the speaker concludes with this comment:

> They don't know I already have
> all the money and love I want
> and how close their Crystal letter
> comes to making me perfectly happy.

The love reference at the end of "Vibrating Crystal" is obviously to the poet's wife Teel, an artist who designed the attractive cover of Sale's new book. A delightful tribute to Mrs. Sale counts "The Ways," a la Elizabeth Barrett Browning, of the poet's better half and why he adores her so. Among the list of 66 of her qualities that serve as his birthday gift to her, as it were in place of 66 candles on the cake, are the following:

> Puts stray objects together in ways they become united.
> Is a democrat and a republican, distrusts Democrats,
>   hates Republicans.
> Lets compassion win over practicality.
> Cleans house with love and attention.
> Designs and develops (over thirty years) beautiful bathrooms.
> Gives her art away joyfully.
> Stays cool toward the faddish ways of the computer.
> Can never get reconciled with unfairness, earthly or cosmic.
> Suffers one fool gladly.

One can easily see why the poet does not need a "power stone treasure" to bring him love and happiness. As for money, he has this to say in "Play Money, Counterfeits, and Reales": "Look, I don't need a whole chest / full of coins: I'd take just one for now, for ever."

Other poems look closely at animals and discover misconceptions regarding their true nature. This is the case with "Snake," which, alluding to Genesis, the poet says is a creature that has

> no gravity-
> defying impulse to uprightness
> just one straight shot
> that then kinked along
> the ground in sequential esses,
> that could grab bank and circle boughs,
> swallow a full-grown pigeon
> in unhinged spasms whole,
> the polished berry eyes that could see

back before good and bad,
before A & E, even before G . . .
[and yet she was] demoted by storytellers
as symbol in the book to mere tempter,
tester, tease, corrupter (says the book)
of her own progeny! and since,
as living symbol who issued
from deeper down than language,
she will not speak, it falls on me
to speak for her this emblem and lament:
      paradise is always after or before.

Another "animal" poem is entitled "Pigs, Mules, Homing Pigeons," but this is really about a man named Victor who died in 1996. Like the poet himself, "Nobody had a better bullshit detector than Victor," and like several poems in *Freeze & Thaw*, this is a touching elegy to a man the poet knew and compares to Thoreau, in that both men once owned animals that they lost but never stopped looking for. The poem ends: "You can make something of that if you want to." Another poem, entitled "Ambsace," is about a friend with whom the poet rowed on a lake, whom he also compares to Thoreau (Sale being a member of the Thoreau Society) since he is:

      no scientist
but something of a seer, a seer-through-foliage.
A country-man, lover of solitary places,
the kind of man to build a cabin on a pond,
dig in the earth and think elevated thoughts.

The best way to close this review of educator Richard Sale's "light verse" lectures is to quote entire his "Whale Song," the final poem in his witty, rewarding, and certainly welcome new collection:

Sitting at the desk in front of the window
watching the gulls bob in the bay,
I had just finished typing these words:
"If a whale doesn't show up in this cove

in ten days, I'm out of here" when
a whale rolled over slowly fifty yards
from the shore. Must have been
the Great Ear out there listening.
After I had focused my attention
the whale rolled a second time.
I called Teel to the window and
the whale did it a third time for her.
There are those, I hear, who check
each item off their list: Whale, saw a,
or Wall, of China, Great. Not me.
Imagine, never seeing another whale,
never again climbing Macchu Picchu—
probable, but why plan on it?
I want to walk, on foot or crutches,
the streets of the Marais, forever.
If a whale doesn't show up in this cove
shortly, truth to tell, I'll be back.

A Painter Speaks in Poetry

Having known James Hoggard's work for many years, I was curious as to why he would base a series of poems on the work of American artist Edward Hopper.* After reading his revealing and thought-provoking introduction to *Triangles of Light*, from Wings Press, I learned much about the inspirations that led him to write, in his latest book, his poems in the voice of the painter, beginning with the Texas poet's discovery of Hopper and other American artists through his elementary-school art teacher. Comparing Hopper's work to that of American modernists like Eugene O'Neill, Sherwood Anderson, Hemingway, Faulkner, T.S. Eliot, and William Carlos Williams, the latter a favorite of the painter's, Hoggard conceived the idea that such writers and contemporaneous artists like Hopper had found meaning in their age's fragmentary, "intense but godless and pointless world" through their own artworks produced as extensions of their selves. But having only seen a few of Hopper's paintings and etchings I could still not quite understand why Hoggard and a number of other poets had taken a special interest in Hopper's art and wondered what it was that drew them to the New York painter's stark, flat, even drab canvases, despite their blocks of color and their trapezoids and triangles of light.

Once I had read Hoggard's introduction and several of his poems in Hopper's voice, I set the book aside with the intention of coming back to it after I had looked into, and at, more of the artist's work. Only then did I remember that Chilean poet Enrique Lihn had written a poem entitled "Edward Hopper," in which Lihn reports (in my own translation) that the artist painted "the place in which actions occurred and/or are about to happen . . . a world of cold things / and rigid meetings between living mannequins" or he painted "the gleam of twilight rails / . . . a road without beginning or end / a Manhattan street between this world and the other." I also recalled that Houston-born B.H. Fairchild had written a poem

---

* *Texas Books in Review* 29, no. 2 (Summer 2009): 17, 20.

entitled "All the People in Hopper's Paintings," and on rereading his piece in *The Art of the Lathe* from 1998, I found that he related to Hopper's paintings because their people "were touched by the light of the real," but more personally "were lonely / as I was and lived in brown rooms whose / long, sad windows looked out on the roofs / of brown buildings in the towns that made / them lonely." In an interview, Fairchild referred to a book on Hopper written in 1994 by poet Mark Strand, in which I found that Strand had questioned "why vastly different people should be so similarly moved when confronted with [Hopper's] work." Strand asserts that "Hopper's paintings are not social documents, nor are they allegories of unhappiness or of other conditions that can be applied with equal imprecision to the psychological make-up of Americans." Essentially Strand is captivated by the fact that Hopper's works are "saturated with suggestion," and he declares that "invitation to construct a narrative for each painting is . . . part of the experience of looking at Hopper," that "the shadow of dark hangs over [the paintings], making whatever narratives we construct around them seem sentimental and beside the point," and that his *Pennsylvania Coal Town* is actually transcendent.

In returning to Hoggard's book, I could see that he was quite aware of all the possible, even contradictory narratives in Hopper's work, and that he had brought them to life through his invention of the painter's voice, aided apparently by the biography of the artist by Gail Levin. And in keeping with Strand's declaration, Hoggard makes the narratives that he has constructed around Hopper's works both unsentimental and to the point. Like Strand, Hoggard observes the artist's structural use of the triangle, what Strand calls at times "pictorial geometry" and "geometric calm" and Fairchild refers to as "a pyramid of light." Yet Hoggard goes further and interprets such "geometry" as "both crutch and guide. . . . No shape was more stable than the triangle. Nothing matched it for preventing collapse." Just as Strand notes that Hopper "did not idealize his figures," Hoggard has the artist declare "my world / forbids you to drift / to places where sweetness sits." One of the poems closer to home is Hoggard's piece on Hopper's 1925 watercolor, *Locomotive, D. & R. G.*, in which the painter begins by stating frankly that

Santa Fe was too damn pretty . . .
and I didn't like the stuff
the natives had for sale –
turquoise and silver and corn beads –
though I did like the way the indios
seemed inclined to be distant,
sweetly laconic, like stone

That world, though, wasn't my world –
New Mexico a damn fool dream . . .
I don't give a damn
about piñon pine and aspen stands
or a bunch of goddamn mountains
reputed to hemorrhage like the Lord

Hopper's no-nonsense utterance represents but one voice in which Hoggard has the painter speak his mind. Other Hopper voices range from philosophical about "absentness" and the nature of time to being analytical of his work, as when he says of the woman in his *Cape Cod Evening*, "Hell yes she's unhappy: / alone out here near the woods / with her troglodytic mate spending too much time / tossing trinkets for a dog," or he can be revelatory of his attitudes toward both life and art, as when in "Rooms by the Sea" he contrasts his paintings with those of Magritte:

I don't need people
floating goofball through my skies
or breasting through my walls

Inanimate things,
like planes of light, door and sea,
speak well enough for me

Nothing's inviting me out
into oblivion of sky or sea,
and nothing says stay put

Nothing, in fact, addresses me

Hopper's voice is, in many ways, Hoggard's own characteristic speech, his own recognizably tough, uncompromising approach to the art of poetry. I can hear the Texan in person, in his many books of poetry, and in both his non-fiction and fictional prose. It is now quite obvious to me that Hoggard has seen in Hopper's work a reflection of his own values and his own practice as a poet. In "Mass of Trees at Eastham," he clearly places lines on his own poetics in the painter's mouth: "what I've done here / is what I've always done: / chuck anything that's crap."

Facing the Reality of Anywhere Else

In 1991, Jerry Bradley's first collection of poetry, *Simple Versions of Disaster*, appeared from the University of North Texas Press to great acclaim.* Excerpts from a number of the commentaries on that earlier volume are included at the back of Bradley's new collection, *The Importance of Elsewhere*, published by Ink Brush Press. For example, Clay Reynolds wrote that *Simple Versions of Disaster* contains "a remarkable wisdom that emerges from experiencing the disasters of everyday life" and Richard Sale observed that for Bradley's clearly expressed vision of "life's emotional explosions and the psychic craters they leave behind," he "should be recognized as one of the charter members of the New Clarity School of Poetry." For those like David Vancil, who had been eagerly awaiting Bradley's second collection, *The Importance of Elsewhere* has proven worth the wait and has brought not only more of the poet's "insight and humor" but poems "closer to him personally than in his previous book. . . ." All of these observations are borne out as accurate characterizations of Bradley's new volume of poetry, in particular the view that his writing continues to concern itself with "the disasters of everyday life," and primarily, it would seem, of his own life.

In the new collection, several poems recall the poet's boyhood when his mother told him that he would "never amount to much" and his father scolded him throughout his youth for opening his mouth and wore him out with a belt when he "came home with C's." Bradley's poems are the vividly rendered craters of his "disastrous" life, as he "squeeze[s] the bruise / of childhood into words"; they are also a tribute to the poet's survival and his skill in recreating for the reader the pain and sorrow that, as Betsy Colquitt wrote of the poetry in *Simple Versions of Disaster*, have been "redemptive for the artist . . . and an inspiration for us all."

The title of Bradley's new collection does not, unless I am mistaken, appear in any of the poems in *The Importance of Elsewhere*,

---

* *Southwestern American Literature* 35, no. 1 (Fall 2009): 98-101.

and consequently I have wondered about its meaning in relation to the contents of the book. Does it imply a form of escapism? If so, the poems tend to deny that it is possible to avoid ourselves and our "disasters" by leaving one physical place for another, since, as Bradley declares in "One for the Road":

> home
> is so strange; tired of it, we leave
> only to find ourselves reflected in chips
> and cubes at every destination
> and in return bringing part of what
> was already us back to itself.

Typically, the speaker in many of the poems says that "now all you can do is listen to the anguish / as it tries to howl away the past." Whether in a plane, at home in bed, or in dreams, the settings of the poems are almost always pervaded by a sense of possible calamity. In "Buying a Vowel," the speaker describes a flight attendant giving instructions that he can't make out, his looking out the window at "the sprawling interstates you would use to flee earthly disaster," and his wondering if "This flight . . . like all blanks is numbered" and "forty-eight is really headed down." In "The Sad Mistress," the speaker finds that "even when I hold her melting / marshmallow breasts / she thinks about crying // her heart is a wound / she says that will not heal," and in "Simple Division," a poem on residents of a new subdivision, the speaker concludes that

> things that are are
>
> and derive little benefit
> from being explained
> one looks for clarity
>
> in simple promises
> but every heart that opens
> leaves a wound that never closes.

Awakened by a dream of being strangled and drowned in kelp-clotted surf, the speaker in "Counting" still risks "dreaming you into bed / where, knees to stomach, you round / like a conch in my embrace." But, as so often happens in Bradley's poetry, this piece ends darkly, with the thought that "time is always on the ocean's side."

Even when the poet or his persona sees the highway signs "warning of danger in the unseen breeze" and tries to pay attention to whatever confers "shape / to life, to confirm the right road, / our way of behaving, to square adversity / and keep us from slaloming through the curves / at unsafe speed," he is reminded that "most roads / remain dark. The physics of our safety / is always understood too late." Here the poet works out effectively his road and geometry analogy in order to conclude with these telling lines: "Our fears / circle in traffic until they collide / like two strangers at an intersection." The "too late" theme is especially well-developed in "Earshot," where hiking in a canyon with a supposedly female companion, the speaker states "We want ... a warning shot, thunder beating light / down the arroyo in time for us to hear what comes." But the speaker recognizes that we fail to pay heed to or express what it was that should have been heard:

> Dumb instrument, the tongue's
> too subtle a thing; it means to report
> what someone needs to hear but always arrives too late,
> just as something lovely has gone out of sight,
> leaving it to stammer in the rinsing rain,
> *you were the most wonderful person in the world.*

When we do escape the everyday with its "natural disasters" and take a "Vacation," as in the sonnet that bears this title, we find nothing but disappointment. We expect to find a fascinating "elsewhere" in the famous sites and scenery cataloged in the octave, but the guidebook's promise or come-on proves in the sestet quite different from the expectation:

> What the desert saw was this: a trail
> cold as one of the mountain's many stones,

ghost towns, a bullet from a narrow gauge
shell speeding as if along a greased rail,
graveyards with flush toilets at the trailhead
teeming with the silent, historic dead.

In a similar poem, "A Field Guide to Dreams," the speaker in sleep sees himself swimming "the long shadow upstream to her" and becomes "something orchestral," until

day comes
and you resort to common life again

this morning when I opened my dream box,
all there was was the moon[.]

One of the most powerful descriptive poems in the book is entitled "Snowdeaf." Here Bradley depicts an angus calf separated from the "drove," "his mother dead," and he fearful he has "fallen in the snow somewhere // shy of the warm lot and the hay-filled barn." As in so many of the poems, there is a sense of hopelessness, an imagery of darkness, and of "plaintive / protests ignored by the idling motor," the last of these a type of Hardyesque indifference of the universe and of God who, as in "Moon above Palo Duro," "struck his tarnished coin / before he beat the daylights out of the land." At times there is wit and humor, with "Cat as in Catastrophe" offering the assertion that "Even the wheels tire of it all," or in "Burning Love," which is about a boy who had seared into his flesh the three-letter name of his girlfriend Sue, before he saw her kiss a schoolmate and came to the realization that he should be thankful at least that he had not fallen in love with Elizabeth. For the most part *The Importance of Elsewhere* is a book short on joy and celebration but long on lament. Even "Hark, Harold!," a poem on Christmas display windows, strikes chords of regret and remorse as the notions, cologne, shampoos, and depilatories evoke "absent friends, / The unexpected gifts that fell upon us / Once like love." And in "Diving into Love," there is only the speaker's fear of "what your heart has to say" and his

hoping to be lucky
if only for tonight
when you open the motel door

but already knowing
the tequila bites
just like a South Valley girl.

Bradley's book is marked throughout by fear, anguish, disappointment, disillusion, mental cases, disease, cadavers, and, in "Cleaving a Valentine," a heart severed by separation from a loved one who, apparently, has left the speaker. These and other human emotions and experiences are for certain "disasters" of everyday life; but in Bradley's poems they are also emblems of endurance, of an acceptance that "things that are are," even though, as in "Procrastination," the poet was determined early in his life to "'be someone someday, Mama' I said, renouncing my fate. / 'I will. You'll see. Just you wait. Just you wait.'" And thus, as Betsy Colquitt noted of Bradley's first collection, his poetry can be "an inspiration for us all," as can his academic career, which has included the earning of the Ph.D., receiving the CCTE Frances Hernandez Teacher-Scholar of the Year award for 2005, and serving at present as a Professor of English at Beaumont's Lamar University.

Eulogizing the Simple Life

Texas has produced only a few poets who have achieved national renown and, so far as I know, none who has attracted an international readership.* Certainly Texas cannot claim a single poet who readers outside the state would compare with such master wordsmiths as Frost, Eliot, Stevens, Williams, and any number of other perennially-anthologized poets. But this does not mean that some of the poetry that the state has inspired hasn't been worthy of the land and its people. Poets like William Barney and Walt McDonald have certainly paid tribute to the state's flora, fauna, and folk in highly artistic form, and this is true as well of Robert Burlingame, whose New and Selected Poems offer up some of the most moving and artful poetry based on the region that I have ever read. Indeed, Burlingame's book contains work that merits the widest audience, but it should especially be welcomed by anyone in Texas who seeks an authentic and penetrating appreciation for the state's natural features and its historical figures.

Divided into four sections that deal with Personal Histories, Others, The Desert Southwest, and A Poet's Journey, *Some Recognition of the Joshua Lizard*, published by Houston's Mutabilis Press, is most impressive for its third section, in which the poet celebrates the life that he has found surviving in the harsh West Texas landscape near his home in the Guadalupe Mountains. But this is not to say that the other three sections of the book are lacking in poems of great interest and artistry. Personal Histories, the first section, is important in establishing the poet's early awareness of the peculiar beauty of the arid Southwest, as in his poem entitled "The Yellowwood," where he declares that "Others said / it was ugly. It was, I suppose, but not when / it blazed in the Panhandle fall—yellow, / like an Indian fire rooted down, or a low star." Even though this first section focuses on the poet's early memories of growing up in Kansas, where he was born in 1925, its personal family poems prepare the reader for the poet's later

---

* *Texas Books in Review* 29, nos. 3 & 4 (Summer/Fall 2010): 19-20.

writings once he moved to Texas in 1954 to teach at the University of Texas in El Paso. Also, in "Thinking of Fairy Tales," the poet reveals that his own early reading of such stories would lead him in years to come "to stoop down to the littleness of the polliwog," thus laying the groundwork for the concern in his poetry for the small and often overlooked within his adopted Desert Southwest.

The book's first section focuses, then, on the poet's early appreciation of the value of "ordinary things," a phrase crucial to the poem entitled "Tuesday." Burlingame's "recognition" of such a creature as the Joshua lizard, "this sleek saurian, this less than finger shape" of the book's title, is fundamental to his West Texas poetry, which time and again eulogizes the simpler forms of life. The book's first section also pays homage to his mother's knowledge of the names of plants and insects, of which "to spare" and which to "spray . . . stiff." In turn, the poet himself would learn the names of local West Texas flora and fauna, understanding in "Desert Ironwood" that such a tree "demands / fixed attention" and in "No Song Here" that a thoughtless boy's shooting of a cougar had deprived us of the lessons of that "Old teacher," a "creature at one with the world, she'd / walked in beauty, always in beauty," "her once heroic tail now bones / rattling in the wind."

Burlingame's poems can at times allude to other writers, as he does in "No Song Here" through his use of Lord Byron's famous phrase, "She walked in beauty." In the second section of his New and Selected, his readings in world literature reveal his devotion to some of the writers obviously vital to the poet, among them Frost, Yeats, Joyce, Melville, Dickinson, Poe, Chekhov, D.H. Lawrence, Thoreau, Ovid, Saint-Exupéry, Cabeza de Vaca, Li Po, Lu Yu, and Basho. Here the poet touches on central images and themes in each writer's work, such as Frost's "neither out far nor in deep" and of a life ended by either fire or ice; Yeats's gyres and Crazy Jane; Lawrence's coal miners, his "old song of passion," and his "man who will incorporate beast"; Thoreau as a "half-Indian Yankee" who "praised our radiant earth"; Saint-Exupéry who "calibrated man's essence / with an engineer's precision"; and Cabeza de Vaca, who knew "this immense Southwest" as "a tender-minded / conquistador, doubting healer / daring yet to dip / into the bloody meat of an Indian's breast" to extract the embedded arrow point.

Throughout the book, the poet's erudition is fully evident but in no way intrusive. One example appears in the very fine poem entitled "Felix McKittrick / Lifelines," in which Burlingame describes the sheriff-soldier-explorer's death by means of an allusion to Euripides: "tangled like a grizzled Hippolytus in your horse's reins." The poet can also allude to the work of painters like Utrillo, Monet, and Marsden Hartley, the latter's poetry and paintings the subject of Burlingame's doctoral dissertation. Of Hartley the poet says that he "never trashed the park of the imagination," and in recalling Monet's "seas of mist, mists of meadows" he contrasts these with the "chemical sores" of Chernobyl and other modern catastrophes. Another literary allusion appears in the aforementioned poem on the dead cougar, in which the speaker says that "He imagines Gawain, green, / full of juice, / libidinous and polite," contrasting the scene of the heroic animal's "winter / heart missing beats" to the Middle English hero's temptations and harmless wound.

A Poet's Journey, the fourth section of the New and Selected, takes up a favorite theme of poets: the poet's own life and his/her making of poetry. One key piece in this section is entitled "small poems," which may recall for many Texas readers the work of Naomi Shihab Nye, to whom Burlingame has in fact dedicated another, related poem in this same section, one entitled "The Immensity of Not Much." With its intentionally lowercased title, "small poems" involves several especially apt similes:

> in their lostness
> they drift down like the floating
> seeds of dandelions
> tenacious, hopeful
>
> so they catch in the high grass
> or in the purely private
> crevice of a city
> gutter
>
>   they're like snowflakes
> new yellow leaves

or the wind-divided notes of meadowlarks
they drift bravely
to lodge in some forsaken place

there they change
they rot, melt, or sing
because it is all they can do
they are like everything

In another key poem, entitled "The Red Herd," the poet comes to one of his frequent confessional conclusions, addressing himself as he ends the piece with the assertion that "You know you have not made sense of anything," a statement that his poetry would seem to contradict. Earlier, in section three's "A Dream of Time," a lovely poem addressed to the poet's artist wife Linda (whose beautiful painting graces the cover of the poet's attractive book), he declares that "we realize no way can be truly learned." Even so, it is clear that the poet has learned the way to create affective poems, such as "A Dream of Time," and another love poem entitled "A Clean, White Handkerchief," also for his wife, who "washed / and ironed it / for me." On seeing the sweet, quiet morning that "shows itself at [his] window," the poet praises both it and his wife's "clean, white / handkerchief." Through such a "small," everyday object, the poet reveals the life of a man and woman together and still in love after sixty years of marriage.

Despite the many telling poems in the other three sections, for me the third section, Desert Southwest, contains the most power-ful poetry in Burlingame's high-quality selection. Among the finest offerings in Desert Southwest are the poems that treat of the natural world of the poet's immediate surroundings: "Blue Milkwort," "Words for Wild Cherries," "Netleaf Hackberry," "The Woodrat," "Obit for Pebble," "A Death in West Texas," "No Song Here," "After Bird Watching near the Mexican Border," "Sandhill Cranes," "Words of a Sort on the Mountain Laurel," "Sycamore," and "At Nickel Creek" (the last of these dedicated to Burlingame's former student, Joseph Rice, who contributed the book's Introduction and shepherded the selection into print but who sadly did not live to see its publication). Other poems in the third section, such as "Elizabeth Garrett" and

"West," are marvelous portraits of Southwesterners the poet knew from books or encountered in person. Each desert poem discovers for the reader insights that arise naturally from the subject on which the poet has focused his "fixed attention."

The philosophy behind Burlingame's creation of his outstanding poems in the Southwest section is encapsulated in the poem entitled "Desert, not Wasteland," in which the poet infers that his poetics derive from his region's own "hard, curt, unpretentious poetry," its "half-claw, half-flower." For this reason, poem after poem in the Desert Southwest section has as its object one phrase that appears in "Words on the Tree Named Madrone": "I extend my esteem." Likewise, in "Blue Milkwort," the poet informs us that because Pliny recommended the plant of the poem's title, he will through "this simple Texas flower" always praise the "Old / Taoist of Rome, scholar of love / and snowy sex." A particularly central poem in the third section is "Netleaf Hackberry," and this is apparent from the fact that Burlingame has included at the back of the book an explication of his thinking and writing about this "committed desert tree." Although the poet acknowledges that the netleaf is "vague" and "unimpressive / doomed to be infested," he yet calls it "noble" and testifies to its being "loved by desert birds / and small animals." To the poet this "simple tree" deserves respect, and belongs among the great trees of literature, for "stung by parasites" and like a "crucifixion" it yet shares its "berries that float / into the next life of a common glory."

Another Burlingame poem that refers to a small life is "The Woodrat," which presents the creature's "small death." Obviously for the poet, however, the woodrat's death is a moving event that he describes with deep feeling, even as he reveals a "minor" drama whose outcome involves more than meets the eye. This rather short poem deserves to be quoted entire:

> What he can't forget
> is the drowned woodrat he fished
> from the cattle trough a morning ago.
> She had gone to drink
> but found death instead,
> harmless rodent, white-throated, moon-driven.

A small death,
hardly even casual news,
in truth, an invisible event, yet
    a wild struggle must have taken
        place inside the metal lip,
a repeated, frantic circling.

Had she gotten out,
she'd have run up the desert slope nearby,
she'd have returned to her burrow and slept,
new life around her.

Like William Barney's "The Cranes at Muleshoe," Burlingame's "Sandhill Cranes" is a magnificent poem, though in almost no way similar in style, conception, or meaning to Barney's equally wonderful celebration of "these noble creatures," as Burlingame calls the cranes, which "For millions of years, / before the Platte was the Platte even, / have lived near the stars . . . their wingbeats toward love." Again, in poem after poem, Burlingame renders obeisance to the flora and fauna of his landscape, saying of the mountain laurel, "Let us kneel to it and praise its lunar / blossoms," and of the sycamore, let us "give thanks to this / tree on the narrow shelf of this cataract world." Of the birds that cross from Texas to Mexico, the poet notes that they are "elegant trespassers of man's ignorance" as they "irreverently" fly "across the uniformed border." Looking closely about him, the poet has observed not only the beauty, endurance, and "common glory" of simple sights and sounds but has comprehended the lessons inherent in the natural and human worlds that he inhabits, as did the writers he has admired and emulated, from Cabeza de Vaca to Henry David Thoreau. The result of Robert Burlingame's attentive life as a poet is a book of which Texans can be ardently proud and to which readers in other places will surely respond with gratitude.

The High Art of Noticing

There's a new poet on the block and she's street smart when it comes to starting and finishing a poem.* Ezra Pound himself asserted that anyone can begin a poem but only the true poet can end it. For this and other reasons, Carrie Fountain is the real thing and *Burn Lake* (Penguin Books), her debut collection of poems and a winner in the National Poetry Series, demonstrates her ability not only to pull readers in from her opening lines but to carry them along to captivating conclusions. In following her narratives, readers will find that the poet is testing out a number of what she considers "prevailing" theories about human behavior, perfection, and fate, which she examines closely and measures against her own "Experience," the title of her book's first section and of its first poem, where she sounds a note heard throughout the volume, one that recalls the indifferent universe of Thomas Hardy and Stephen Crane. If Fountain may at times seem fashionably negative, she reveals after a hard-nosed manner that she is determined to see life steadily and to see it whole, in almost Matthew Arnold's words, and to remain, as in "Want," faithful to "the heart's constant / project: this simple / learning; learning / how to hold / hopelessness / and hope together . . . to recognize / both and to make / something of both. . . ."

A native of southern New Mexico and a graduate of the Michener Center for Writers program at the University of Texas at Austin, Fountain introduces readers to her birthplace of Mesilla through a number of poems, including "Late Spring in the Mesilla Valley." In this piece the poet thinks to herself, "What if I stop saying / the little no I'm always saying?" Part of Fountain's "no" is to life itself, and in several poems she recalls her desire to die, as in "Burn Lake 3" where she remembers the time she tried holding her breath until she was dead, but only "fell face-first // into the closet" and "came to in a panic, / thinking for a moment / that I'd done it, and that death // was just my little blue room / at the back of the house. . . ." She compares

---

* *Texas Books in Review* 30, nos. 2 & 3 (Summer/Fall 2010): 19-20.

her state of mind to a mallard with its head split, apparently dead on the shore, which when touched shudders, stands up, and then really dies. In her own case, she is shocked to discover her body's "plain intention to continue / with or without me." Like the mallard, she can be "that animal scrambling // to its feet, desperate // to be living." This, however, is not the ending of the poem, which goes on to say of her life: "Because it's mine, I wait for it to die. / Then I bury it." Rather than a positive conclusion Fountain has chosen here a negative, which may be the mark of Pound's true poet, but I must confess that I would have preferred that she had stopped before those last two lines, which probably just proves that I'm a sentimental old fool. More to my taste is the ending of "Embarrassment," in which, after having locked her best friend and herself in the trunk of the family car, the two are found and saved by her parents. While she wanted to explain, she "could do nothing / but breathe. My lungs / took all they could. My life was a bird / on a branch. . . . Oh it wasn't beautiful. / But I knew better than to hate it."

In "Burn Lake 2," the poet had already presented a life-death scenario, in which from wanting "to feel dead and alive / at the same time," she swims to the deepest part of the lake, but once more the "lights go on inside my body / and my legs pump" until she reaches "the living world again." Likewise, in "Late Spring in the Mesilla Valley," the poet finds that although one half of her says *Don't breathe,* this is only a half of her self. The situation of a divided personality, or a divided allegiance to being and not being, either in a place or relationship, is most fully developed in the poem entitled "The Continental Divide." Just as in a number of the poems that borrow from texts by Juan de Oñate, the leader of the first Spanish expedition into New Mexico, so in "The Continental Divide" Fountain alludes to the voyage of Columbus by way of relating her disappointment in love to the claims made by early conquistadors: "We were simply an example. 'Love,' / we said, and planted our flag, and took stock / of our natural resources. // Then the bottom fell out / of the economy, and I was left // carrying fistfuls of bills that meant nothing, could buy me / nothing." She had wished that like Columbus she could leave love's "large // and violent country . . . But there was no more ocean. There was / no going back." And as she says in another piece, entitled "Restaurant

Fire, Truth or Consequences," "the precise heartbreak / of the past [is] that it doesn't return, not even when you don't want it to." In all these poems, Fountain probes deeply the images and issues of wishes and desires, of past vs. present, present vs. future, offering insights into wanting "everything / and nothing / at once and . . . / all the time" (from "Want"). "Want," it turns out, is a key word in Fountain's book, since as her epigraph from Henri Michaux has it, "You are now on the / continent of the insatiate."

It seems clear from *Burn Lake* that Fountain must have experienced a difficult childhood and adolescence, but just as the "wet, / white hearts" of Mesilla onions would go on "still dumbly growing" (from "I-10"), she obviously shed her "dead, outer skins" and broke through to a mature understanding of what she wanted in life, and that in order to achieve it, she would, as in "Burn Lake 5," "grab [hope] quick and tight behind its fanged head." In "Burn Lake 4" she had learned that childhood was "an ongoing lesson / in physics and disappointment," but this hardly held her back from investigating her "interests" and exploiting her "potential," as she suggests in this same poem. In a piece like "Father and Son at the Mesilla Valley Drive-In Bank" Fountain showcases not her "high art of not noticing," as she says in "The Change," but both her high art of noticing and her capacity for rendering with absolute accuracy the typical transaction that all have observed on engaging in drive-through banking:

> The car in front of them pulls forward,
> and the boy's father feeds the zipped bag of money
> to the open mouth of the building.
>
> From behind the glass, the woman speaks
> into a long, thin microphone. She's so close,
> if it weren't for the glass, she could lean over
>
> and touch the roof of the car.
> "This will only take a moment," she says,
> smiling broadly.

These are not the last lines of the poem, which are not affirmative but unflinchingly "telling"—an unavoidable pun. Another poem, "Rio Grande," employs the noun form of the word "zipped" in "the zipped bag of money" and for a most effective metaphorical conclusion. Two boys had drowned in the river and were commemorated by a plaque, given to their mother, "into the dark argument of [whose] face" onlookers stare, while now with spring the river rises as usual, "filling with water from far away, / cold water from the Rockies, the snows / melting, falling, simple, pulled / down the continent like a zipper."

In taking a wide-screened view of her subjects, Carrie Fountain does not blink on noting the indifference of nature to man's hopes and dreams. And even though she may often feel, as in "Rio Grande 2," that much of life and, in this poem's particular case, much of religious symbolism seems to end up "meaning almost nothing," yet she like Juan de Oñate can still be thankful after passing through the desert of the Jornada del Muerto to find the river again and be "back . . . at the lip of wanting."

A Bonding of Opposites

Winner of the 2013 Texas Institute of Letters poetry award, Ken Fontenot's *In a Kingdom of Birds* is a book full of thoughts that flow easily from one to another, almost always encouraging the reader to join the poet in paying attention to the wonder of the simple things in life.* Born in New Orleans in 1948, Fontenot has been a highly-esteemed fixture on the Austin poetry scene since the 1970s. In 1988 his second collection of poems, entitled *All My Animals and Stars*, won the Austin Book Award, and his poetry has appeared in such publications as *American Poetry Review, New Orleans Review, Southern Review, Georgia Review, Kenyon Review*, and *The Texas Observer*, and has been collected in the anthologies *Is This Forever, or What?* and *What Have You Lost?* Many of Fontenot's poems concern his memories of his Cajun relatives in Louisiana, especially his father and mother. One of the poems in *All My Animals and Stars*, entitled "Ambivalence: To Darken Like a Fig and Still Not Know What the Fig Feels Inside," contains a touching vignette from the poet's family history, one which is also a fine example of his facility for characterizing the meaningfulness of things that all too often we take for granted: in this case, our memory. Here are the lines from "Ambivalence" that in general epitomize for me Fontenot's artistry, with the final line personifying and celebrating our capacity to recall past events and people:

> What good is it to smell the salt air and not be moved,
> not be borne back to your childhood?
> . . .
> Each day my boyhood returns to me.
> Each day my mother picks me up
> from the wreckage that is my bicycle,
> and combs my hair with her fingers.
> Each day my father helps me reel in a fish.
> Memory, what gift can we give for your joyous presence?

---

* *Southwestern American Literature* 39, no. 1 (Fall 2013): 93-97.

In the first poem of *In a Kingdom of Birds*, Fontenot announces that in his "later years . . . of gray hair / and pleated pants" he is "going / to try to discover whatever / bond there is between thinking / and feeling. It will be / a limpid enterprise: pure, / sincere, and without beauty." Like other Fontenot poems, this one does not end on a sentimental note but surprises by the speaker's remembering as a boy that he killed a neighbor's dog with his B-B gun and denied that he had done so. The speaker in Fontenot's poems is often ambivalent about his past, his present, and his future, and yet it seems that he can accept things for what they are and appears comfortable living with contraries, without taking sides, as he may be suggesting in "A Dream Welcomes Everyone," where he says:

> In a dream patience comforts its opposite.
> Desire enters. So does ambivalence. Both
> have lead roles in our play: a country play.
> The stage: earth. A dream welcomes everyone.

In another poem, entitled "We Are Here Because the Clouds Believe in Us," the speaker is trying to get to the other side of courage, even while he is content to believe that we are here "because the stars knew us / in another life." Once again his thinking from one thing to another brings him back to the issue of antitheses, here feeling and thought, or heart and mind:

> Everywhere
> and for most of the day we are busy putting
> the heart aside for the mind. Is that what
> you want? Not me. I want to be able
> to feel my heart when I have to. And when,
> as time allows, I don't want to feel my heart,
> I want to give myself over completely to my mind.
> I've been wading in the shallow waters
> of courage for a long time. Now it is time to get
> to the other side. Will you join me? Oh will you?

The poems in *In a Kingdom of Birds* often invite us to consider possibilities and yet to be content with what we have, even though many times the poet, or speaker, wants something other than what he has. For instance, in "From a Son Who Only Knows Books," he asks "What is it like to have / a son like me? I don't know. Will I ever know?" and implies by this that he would like to but probably never will. In "A Study of Two Girls," he reports that, from having surreptitiously witnessed two girls at summer camp kissing one another, his "heart thrilled for those girls," and after they were dismissed from the camp by the director, he knew deep down that he "could have loved both of them / although they could have never loved me." When he imagines the girls later in life, he sees them "walk surely, / confident now in just the simple clothes they wear," whereas he "cannot even bleed when it counts." But the speaker in the poems never really complains so much as he reveals both his and our fluctuating thoughts about what we want out of life. In one poem he says that "people are asking for something different," suggesting that we are never satisfied, while in another he admits that he would like to have a sky all to himself. Mostly he offers contradictory statements that make it clear that he probably would not change things as they are for anything else, as in "One for Rita," where he states that "The world is bleak. The world is / glorious." Like Whitman, the speaker in Fontenot's poems could ask "Do I contradict myself? / Very well then I contradict myself, / (I am large, I contain multitudes.)" In a poem from *All My Animals and Stars*, entitled "Poem Ending With Resolutions, Half-Baked," he even declares that "I'm going to steal everything I can / from my beloved Whitman, too, / believe you me."

Fontenot's poems are sure to remind readers of Whitman's great empathy for others, human and animal alike. His poems clearly owe something as well to Whitman's free-flowing lines, with thoughts moving by sometimes seemingly unrelated associations but always ending with everything contributing to the making of a particular point. Even though his lines range loosely and widely, there is a unity to each poem as it returns to an idea hinted at in the title or developed from one central image or incident. Like Whitman, Fontenot is ultimately on the side of a positive view of life, finding, as he does in "Looking Out My Small Window in Summer I See the Oak Prematurely Yellow," that, even though God has not sought out man as a friend, "This is what He / has left us. Trees to admire. Animals / to eat. A window to the world, small and dim." It is not really typical in Fontenot's poems for creatures to serve as merely a food source, as they do here, although on occasion they can elsewhere as well, as in a poem about eating fish; more often animals and especially birds teach us lessons about human relations, as in the title poem where

> . . . bigger birds, want the nest.
> They come with a lot of squawking
> and puffing of feathers. They come with
> a lot of elegant, but pretentious twittering.
> You can guess what happens, my friends.
> In a kingdom of birds no one is safe.

In some poems the speaker refers to what seem to be his health problems, his dependence on medications, his boss who has it in for him. With "Internal Revenue Service," the speaker says of his work that he "came here looking for a way out of / another life," recalling that "They say great men started at desk jobs, / and I, too, mean to make my beginnings / a sure thing, a thing of beauty and respect," but in the end he can only say "Oh Momma, I gots dem paper-pushin' blues!" In "Reverie" the speaker contrasts his two feet with a centipede's many joyous feet, saying of his own that they "have both/ limited joys and even some pain / after I stand on them all day like a waiter," concluding that we "Can't kiss the sun, can't hold it / in our hands—as much as we'd like to." Overall, Fontenot's poetry is filled with the small windows that reveal to us his insights into the benefits of patience, being content with little, searching for more in life than money, the heart "pumping hard for merely the sake of living at all," wearing the wind, since "a strong wind can change / anybody's mind," and seeing that "The sea is full of nouns. / The sky is full of verbs. But no syntax could / quite replace what the stars send down / in their wisdom." In "Remembering the Wind," such words as "content," "simplicity," and "welcomes" seem key terms for the poet, as he surely intimates, yet doesn't openly preach, that they should be for us:

It seems the intellectual dwarves have
taken over. And who would want it
otherwise? We are content with those
who claim simplicity is better than
knowledge. Give us the gentle embrace of
the wind and we will be happy.
Give us the cool nights of November,
and we'll trust the earth once more.
Which is not so unusual considering how
November, like a dream, welcomes everyone.

Of course, I may be misreading this and other poems, since in "For a Young Boy Who Asks Me Why He Should Study," the speaker answers the boy's question as to what he should learn, his "knowledge far / from over," by saying "learn everything you can." But then, earlier in this poem, the speaker also asks a series of questions that would seem to support my interpretation of "Remembering the Wind" as a championing of simplicity over knowledge:

What will it take for us to see that spring
is really a messenger? That winter is aware
of much more than we give it credit for?
That nights are real because the stars are real?
It's nice to know the sky doesn't think less
of rain because the rain is sad. It's nice
to know that clouds are older than the heart.

It could be that Fontenot is just contradictory, but if so, "who would want it / otherwise?" Indeed, a contemporary poet—or any for that matter—appeals most when he or she is not straitlaced and predictable, but understands that both thinking and feeling have their good points and can at times bond with one another, as do other opposites, such as male and female. Whatever may be the "correct" reading of any one Fontenot poem, all the poetry in his award-winning volume challenges our petty dissatisfactions, our lack of imagination and empathy, and our "ignorance that falls through the cracks," as the poet puts it in his humorous but telling "'Robbing the Cradle'." And certainly any reader's way of looking at and comprehending the world will be vastly expanded and improved by Ken Fontenot's fresh, thought-provoking, and positive poems.

About the Author

Dave Oliphant, a native Texas poet, was for 18 years the editor of *The Library Chronicle* at the University of Texas at Austin; in 2006 he retired from the University as a senior lecturer in Writing and Rhetoric. For 25 years he was the editor/publisher of Prickly Pear Press, and is a noted writer on the history of Texan jazz. His recent books include a collection of essays, *Jazz Mavericks of the Lone Star State* (2007); two translations of collections of Chilean poetry: *Love Hound* by Oliver Welden (winner of the poetry prize at the 2007 New York Book Festival) and *After-Dinner Declarations* by Nicanor Parra (winner of the Soeurette Diehl Fraser Award for best book translation from the Texas Institute of Letters, 2011); and a collection of his own poetry, *The Cowtown Circle* (2014). His volume, *The Pilgrimage: Selected Poems, 1962-2012*, was published in 2013 by Lamar University Press. Dave Oliphant's 548-page memoir, *Harbingers of Books to Come: A Texan's Literary Life* (2009), and his book-length poem on Texas trumpeter Kenny Dorham, *KD: a Jazz Biography* (2012), were both published by Wings Press.

Oliphant was born in Fort Worth in 1939. He graduated from Lamar University with a B.A. and the University of Texas at Austin with an M.A., and took his Ph.D. at Northern Illinois University. Dave and his wife María, a native of Chile, have been married for 49 years and have a son and a daughter and four grandchildren.

*W*ings Press was founded in 1975 by Joanie Whitebird and Joseph F. Lomax, both deceased, as "an informal association of artists and cultural mythologists dedicated to the preservation of the literature of the nation of Texas." Publisher, editor and designer since 1995, Bryce Milligan is honored to carry on and expand that mission to include the finest in American writing—meaning *all* of the Americas, without commercial considerations clouding the decision to publish or not to publish.

Wings Press intends to produce multi-cultural books, chapbooks, ebooks, recordings and broadsides that enlighten the human spirit and enliven the mind. Everyone ever associated with Wings has been or is a writer, and we know well that writing is a transformational art form capable of changing the world, primarily by allowing us to glimpse something of each other's souls. We believe that good writing is innovative, insightful, and interesting. But most of all it is honest. As Bob Dylan put it, "To live outside the law, you must be honest."

Likewise, Wings Press is committed to treating the planet itself as a partner. Thus the press uses as much recycled material as possible, from the paper on which the books are printed to the boxes in which they are shipped.

As Robert Dana wrote in *Against the Grain,* "Small press publishing is personal publishing. In essence, it's a matter of personal vision, personal taste and courage, and personal friendships." Welcome to our world.

Colophon

This first edition of *Generations of Texas Poets*, by Dave Oliphant, has been printed on 60-pound Accent Opaque paper containing a percentage of recycled fiber. Titles have been set in Rosewood and Cochin type, the text in Adobe Caslon type. This book was designed by Bryce Milligan.

On-line catalogue and ordering:
www.wingspress.com
Wings Press titles are distributed to the
trade by the Independent Publishers
Group
www.ipgbook.com
and in Europe by Gazelle
www.gazellebookservices.co.uk

Also available as an ebook.